REAL POLITICS

JEAN BETHKE ELSHTAIN

REAL POLITICS

At the Center of Everyday Life

THE JOHNS HOPKINS UNIVERSITY PRESS / BALTIMORE AND LONDON

To the memory of my father, Paul G. Bethke,
who taught me how to make peace, and of my mother,
Helen Lind Bethke, who taught me how to fight.

© 1997 The Johns Hopkins University Press
All rights reserved. Published 1997
Printed in the United States of America on acid-free paper
06 05 04 03 02 01 00 99 98 97   5 4 3 2 1

The Johns Hopkins University Press
2715 North Charles Street
Baltimore, Maryland 21218-4319
The Johns Hopkins Press Ltd., London

Library of Congress Cataloging-in-Publication Data will be found
at the end of this book.
A catalog record for this book is available from the British Library.

ISBN 0-8018-5599-3

Contents

Preface & Acknowledgments

Those of us who write a lot create problems for ourselves. They are interesting problems but problems nonetheless. Then a few of us compound these problems by republishing in book form essays and articles, many of them *livres de circonstance,* many of them written in the heat of battle, that no doubt only serve to deepen the trouble by reminding people of just how roily the waters have been. But if you live in the heart of your own time, and if you are of the view that human life is always smudgy, always a mixture of limit and possibility, hope and despair, it is worth taking stock in this way; it serves some purpose beyond adding yet another text between hard covers to one's shelf.

What is that purpose? Reminding oneself and others that the vocation of the political and social theorist is, or can be, a rough-and-tumble series of engagements with hotly contested and deeply divisive issues. There are some (and I do not fault them this; indeed, I envy them from time to time) who find that they can best live the *vita contemplativa,* and contribute to our storehouse of knowledge and insight and even wisdom, by staying above the battle. They prefer not to smell the grapeshot wafting over the hill at first light, knowing the foe is ready to hand and they just might be ambushed. They prefer not to think about the messy stuff of everyday life—of babies born and schedules juggled and feeling torn between good and worthy purposes. It is enough to have to live it: why concentrate on it or write about it? Shouldn't scholarship take one out of the quotidian rather than place one at its pulpy center?

There is no one right way to do it, clearly. Plato wouldn't be Plato if he had busied himself with the antique equivalent of house-husbandry. We rightly honor him for his timeless work. But there is other timeless work that must be done—hard work of the sort that makes life a bit better, perhaps, or at least helps to stop the worst from happening. Work that takes as its task undermining certain pretensions and calling into question calls to action that would lead us, if not over the abyss, at least deeper into the morass. Looking back over the past several decades, I recognize that much of my work has about it the quality, Block That Kick! It is counterpunching; responding to the proclamations of others, to promises that seemed to me false or feckless, to ideologies that seemed to me cruel and reckless, to policies that spoke more to our resentments than to our self-respect, to visions of the future that left too many outside the circle of concern. Why is it, I wondered over the years and continue to wonder, that we so readily reproduce in our protest many of the worst features of the order of things we would change? Why is it that, in coming to a recognition that all is not well, we decide that all is ill, that everything is dust and ashes in our mouths? Why is it that we so readily take leave of terra firma and live in worlds of fantastic projection that have very little to do with the tough realities of our world as it is?

For I am one of those who believes there is a world; there is dense, thick stuff. We are creatures as well as creators. We are beings for whom much is simply given. We can carve out some possibilities; we can stake out some new territory. But we cannot remake the world. When we try we do more damage than would otherwise be done if our intentions were more humble; our actions more modest; our aim, therefore, more true. When we theorize grandly, we often theorize *in extremis*. That is, we represent the situation we hope to transform as dire, pitiless, a scandal. And yet somehow, out of this debris, we erect a shiny new world, a world that must itself embody a stark alternative to the present because we have represented that present so darkly.

Tending to the quotidian, to the politics of everyday life, helps us to keep our feet on the ground, our head out of the clouds. We understand that we need the saving presence of our fellow human beings. We appreciate fellowship and friendship as well as antagonism. We understand that theory is not a realm apart from life but, rather, a part of life, one of the activities that some of us are called to; if we are called well, we play our parts to the hilt and hold nothing back except, hopefully, what Albert Camus over forty years ago called "our places of exile, our crimes and our ravages." He reminded us that "our task is not to unleash them on the world; it is to fight them in ourselves and others." That is the spirit in which I try to write. The reader must judge whether I have, in large part, succeeded.

My biggest debt is to Henry Y. K. Tom, who first suggested this volume and prodded me to make selections from a mass of material. Much is left out and must go into another volume or simply be left to rest where it appeared originally—not the worst of all possible fates, after all. I also want to acknowledge the contributions that my critics, whether friendly or otherwise, make to my work. None of us labors alone. To see oneself as an active participant in the arena is a great thing, and this would not happen without the response of many known and unknown to me. I am, at base, a counterpuncher. This means I am never without work to do. It is a great blessing.

Chapters 3 and 23 appear for the first time in this volume. All previously published material appears substantially as it did in the original versions.

Real Politics

At first glance, the three essays gathered in this opening section appear not to have much to do with one another. The "civic sermon" that takes up an essay by Václav Havel talks of narrative and moral acts but concludes with politics as a realm of conflict without end. To segue from the eloquent and elegant Havel to "mainstream political science" circa 1980 jars. But hold. This essay was a determined effort on my part to undermine the epistemological underpinnings of the behaviorism (or behavioralism) then in its prime in American political science and had, as its underlying *raison d'être*, creating space for a politics that refuses to quash or to negate what Havel calls "the moral act." For to do that is to lose what I call the "authentic heart and soul of politics and political contexts as couched in our resonant conceptual language—the language of justice, freedom, liberty, peace, order, equality, liberation, community, the polity" itself. "Arendt's 'Truth and Politics,'" a piece delivered in Prague on the occasion of the second meeting of the Prague Colloquium on Political Philosophy, a circle for political theorists restored after fifty years of dark times, reiterates the stubborn quality of truth, especially the sturdiness of our descriptions of events if we refuse to avert our eyes from terror, yet, at the same time, open our hearts to joy and illumination.

1

Politics without Cliché

This will be a brief civic sermon. I take as my text moments from essays by Václav Havel. The first is drawn from a speech Havel delivered in 1965 at a Union of Czechoslovak Writers meeting, "On Evasive Thinking." Havel attacks "pseudoideological thinking," thinking of the sort that separates the words we use from the realities they purport to describe; as a consequence, evasive thinking has, "without our noticing it, separated thought from its immediate contact with reality and crippled its capacity to intervene in that reality effectively." Words lose their meaning. They become the occasion for drawing attention to an ideological nostrum rather than to a genuine human dilemma, fear, or hope. Language, rather than signifying something real and "enabling us to come to an understanding of it," becomes, instead, "an end in itself."

The second Havelian moment to which I want to draw attention appears in a speech delivered in his stead (he was not permitted to travel) on the occasion of his receipt of the Peace Prize of the German Booksellers Association in 1989. Words are mysterious and ambiguous, yes, and all too often humble words get translated into arrogant ones, Havel notes. The upshot can be fatal to our understanding of our human place in a wider scheme of things human beings did not create and over which we assume control at our peril. For, "arrogantly, he [mankind] began to think that as the possessor of reason, he could completely understand his own history and could therefore plan a life of happiness for all, and that this even gave him the right, in the name of an ostensibly better future for all—to which he had found the one and only key—to sweep from his path all those who did not fall for his plan." Once again, words lose their meaning as they become arrogant. Havel urges his listeners to "keep a weather eye out for any insidious germs of arrogance in words that are seemingly humble," noting that "this is not just a linguistic task. Responsibility for and toward words is a task which is intrinsically ethical."

Platitudes Deflect

Now I know, of course, that these brief texts for the day will have aroused many readers and prompted a flurry of linguistic and epistemological consternation. Words cannot be taken neat! Surely Havel overshoots the mark here in his eagerness to unmask the abusers of words! How can Havel possibly endorse such a simple notion of reference! Does he not realize that language and the world enjoy no transparent relation to one another! And so on. Once this sputtering has died down—at least for those who can get past these preoccupations in order to consider Havel's meaning—perhaps the import of what he here warns us against can be revealed. For what Havel insists upon is that whether something is "right" or "left" is the last thing that should interest any alert and concerned citizen. Rather, what we should be about is eschewing political labels that fail to capture the complexity of social life, fail to come close to the content of our actual beliefs and actions. The old categories of ideological contestation have become hopelessly clichéd: they refer only to themselves in tendentious circles of self-referentiality.

Havel offers up a wonderful example of this tendency, indeed this rush toward the tendentious, in "On Evasive Thinking." A stone window ledge has come loose, fallen from a building, and killed a woman. The response of the communist regime is, first, to assure everyone that window ledges "ought not to fall" but look, after all, at what wonderful progress we have made in so many areas and, what is more, we must always think about mankind itself and "our prospects for the future." A second window ledge falls and kills someone else. There is another flurry of reports about the overall prospects for mankind—rosy, as it turns out, as socialism spreads and workers' states proliferate! In the meantime, ledges fall and particular people in real local places are killed. The prospects of mankind are, Havel warns, "nothing but an empty platitude if they distract us from our particular worry about who might be killed by a third window ledge, and what will happen should it fall on a group of nursery-school children out for a walk." Language and not only language is degraded if hollow platitudes deflect our attention from concrete worries and dangers.

But has it not always been the case with ideological thinking? Is not the whole purpose of such thinking one sustained act of systematic deflection— away from the local (how petty!), the particular (how insignificant!), the concrete (how uninspiring!) in favor of a glorious surge toward the universal, the abstract, the marvels of a future perfect or nearly so world. Havel is right: if we can't see "individual, specific things, we can't see anything at all," and ideological thinking has functioned to stop us seeing individual, specific things. Politics as a realm of concrete responsibility gives way to politics as a sphere of magical dialectical maneuvers aimed at curing the universe of all its woes. And does it not look great on paper! Where the ideologist mystifies and tries to unify, the thinker and actor devoted to politics without cliché tries to demystify and diversify, to look at the messy, complex realities of *this* situation, here and now, rather than some simulacrum constructed as the artifact of an overarching system or schema.

Utopianism, the search for a *Weltanschauung* (among the fondest wishes of humankind, Freud notes), yields inevitably to an impersonal "juggernaut of power," in Havel's view. The vision of a radiant tomorrow masks a sordid present. To move beyond clichéd left-right categories is to disown utopianism, once and for all. Havel scores utopianism as a "typically intellectual phenomenon. . . . It is an arrogant attempt by human reason to plan life. But it is not possible to force life to conform to some abstract blueprint. Life is something unfathomable, ever-changing, mysterious, and every attempt to confine it within an artificial, abstract structure inevitably ends up homogenizing, regimenting, standardizing and destroying life, as well as curtailing everything that projects beyond, overflows or falls outside the abstract project. What is a concentration camp, after all, but an attempt by utopians to dispose of those elements which do not fit in?"

In response to those who parry by suggesting that a life without utopias would be horrible and unthinkable, would reduce life to hopelessness and resignation, Havel replies by contrasting "openness towards mysteriously changing and always rather elusive and never quite attainable ideals such as truth and morality" by contrast to an unequivocal identification with "a detailed plan for implementing those ideals which in the end becomes self-justifying." To be sure, the theme of *trahison des clercs* is nothing new. What adds freshness and piquancy to Havel's project is that he has personally paid the price for his resistance to the seduction of ideology and that he does so, not in the name of a restorationist ideal, but in the name of an elemental, forward-pressing, yet limited ideal of free responsibility. Havel's "higher horizon" opens up rather than forecloses genuine political possibility.

In Havel's world, individual responsibility deepens and expands to the extent that utopianism—giving oneself over to a *Weltanschauung*—is eschewed. Politics beyond cliché means one must always look to the human dimension of things, a dimension that cannot be derived from a flatness of being, a world cut and dried to our own measure. Havel here brings to mind a lecture by Flannery O'Connor about the vocation of the novelist. She told her audience of eager young students, who would be writers, that unless they were interested in dirt and dust and bones and musty things, they had better find another vocation: writing was far too humble a trade for them. Similarly, Havel suggests that the aggrandizing, arrogant world-changer aims not to fulfill but to destroy politics, for politics is obviously far too humble a trade for him.

Concrete Responsibility

For politics is a sphere of concrete responsibility. Its antithesis—its clichéd opposite—is a blurred, all-purpose, grandiose, and limitless leap into universal dogma that promotes a vapid because unbounded pseudoresponsibility for everything elsewhere. How odd it is, then, that so many of our contemporary antifoundationalists in the academy remain wedded to a teleology of progress, a nearly unbounded faith in the possibility of enlightenment in that glorious epiphany once the debris and clutter of metaphysical thought is swept away once and for all. Havel is utterly resistant to this sort of thing: the here and now, a concrete moment carved out against a wider horizon not given or defined by man, is shimmering in vitality and importance.

One way to imagine all of this is to think of a children's coloring book, with scenes outlined but not "colored in"—that is the child's job. One page outlines a cluttered room, perhaps; a second, a bustling city street. There is, in each instance, a wealth of detail awaiting its coloration in order that many moments might stand out. These moments are complex—in the first scene, the mother appears to be angry at the mess in the child's room, the child may be trying to hide something behind his back, clothes spill out of a dresser drawer. In the street scene, the fellow on the corner may represent a menace to a passer-by, a cluster of folks appear to be having a debate or discussion of some sort in front of a newsstand, some shoppers look harried, a child tugs on her mother's skirt, pointing to something in a window. Now imagine a third page in the coloring book. The scene outlined is of a pristine, uncluttered room, or city, or countryside: everything is in its proper place, there is no untidiness anywhere, and each human being represented has a big satisfied look on his or her face. There are no messy details.

Now those drawn to the pristine scene, if given a box of crayons, will highlight all in roseate hues, and they will disdain the scenes of clutter and bustle precisely because that is what they want to flee, to eliminate, to "cure." If forced to color things in on the messy pages, they will try to blur all the edges, to deflect from all the moments of tension and to disguise the clutter. It is those lovers of the pristine Havel challenges, for they are the ideologists who disdain the messiness of the human condition and want to clean things up, the sooner the better. In doing so, however, they must falsify what they see, color it out, blur it over, somehow do it in: everyday life in all its ambiguity is not grand enough for them. The humanly possible work is tawdry and unworthy by contrast to creating some earthly paradise—if only we can get the clutter cleaned up.

Don't get me wrong: Havel is not in love with messiness; rather, he recognizes that society is a "very mysterious animal with many hidden faces and potentialities." For this very reason one must turn away from "abstract political visions of the future and toward concrete human beings and ways of defending them effectively in the here and now." Responsibility to and for the here and now—easing the suffering of "a single insignificant citizen"—is far more important to the antiutopian than "some abstract 'fundamental solution' in an uncertain future." For "without keeping one's eyes open to the real dimensions of life's beauty and misery, and without a moral relationship to life, this struggle will sooner or later come to grief on the rocks of some self-justifying system of scholastics."

A politics beyond cliché is one in which the political actor refuses what Havel calls a "messianic role," an avant-garde arrogance that knows better and must run around ceaselessly with furrowed brow "raising the consciousness" of all those "unconscious" bumpkins out there—one's fellow citizens. Authentic political hope, by contrast, laughs at the notion that somehow glorious heroes or vanguard parties or grasping "the totality" will save the day and, instead, endorses Havel's hope that human beings, in taking responsibility for a concrete state of affairs, might "see it as their own project and their own home, as something they need not fear, as something they can—without shame—love, because they have built it for themselves." My hunch is that some folks, when they read such words, are a bit embarrassed and tempted to see Havel as a nice guy but, surely, a bit naive! As if projecting a classless society or perpetual peace were not naive—and dangerously so at that. For promoters of these latter projects grow impatient fast with the human beings who appear to stand in the way of attaining one's fondest ends. There is a further temptation to eliminate opponents who rather quickly turn into "enemies." But that is not the way of democratic politics, of a politics stripped of cliché where everything has a neat label on it telling us whether it is "left" or "right" and hence whether we are enjoined to cheer or to hiss.

The Purely Moral Act

Havel's response to those who claim his own thought is murky and unrealistic and cannot survive practical politics is complex. Suffice it to say that Havel insists that society is a very "mysterious animal with many hidden faces and potentialities." No one knows the full potentiality of any given moment, for good or for ill. Here lies the importance of "the purely moral act that has no hope of any immediate and visible political effect," for such acts can "gradually and indirectly, over time, gain in political significance." One must be patient and neither so excessively result-oriented nor grandiose that the humanly possible work begins to look tawdry and unworthy. Havel tells one interlocutor that he tries to "live in the spirit of Christian morality," not as a doctrinalist but as a practitioner of hope who attempts to see things "from below" in a tough-minded, not a sentimental, way. His unabashed embrace of life is precisely an embrace of a post-Babelian world in which there are wondrous varieties of human homes, identities, languages, particular possibilities, but there is as well a transparticular world framing our fragile globe, united perhaps only in its travail.

Havel's own work is deeply indebted, in a rough and ready way, both to the phenomenological tradition of Husserl and Heidegger as "translated" by the great Czech philosopher Jan Patôcka, who died under police interrogation, and to Masarykian humanism. Shaped by the overlapping of many movements and traditions, Havel places himself under no obligation to systematize or, for that matter, to synthesize. He is not only temperamentally unsuited to the logic-chopper's or Hegelian "over-comer's" task, he is opposed on principle to both sorts of efforts—the former because it issues into a penury and niggardliness of thought; the latter because it promotes ideology whose dead hand soon closes over "life itself." Havel notes the "intellectual and spiritual" dimensions of his own cultural identity as a complex but very specific amalgam of many currents, many forces.

Departing from Masaryk's "positivist belief in progress," Havel found a philosophical home inside the general themes offered up by Patôcka, a philosopher nearly unknown outside Czechoslovakia who, with Havel, was one of the original signatories of Charter 77. For Patôcka, philosophy begins once life is no longer something that can be taken for granted. The alternative to a world of sure and certain meaning is not subjectivism but another sort of engagement with the world, specifically with the life-world rooted in a distinctly premodern sensibility which the modern sensibility must knowingly affirm and grant as "that which is"—something objective and tangible—in order to get out of a perverse preoccupation with self-absorbed wishes, preferences, and feelings: the Oprah Winfreyization of culture, one might call it.

A central preoccupation in a world which ceases to respect any so-called higher metaphysical values—the Absolute, something higher than themselves, something mysterious—necessarily becomes the self—human identity—and, with it, a concentration on human burdens and responsibilities appropriate to this self. But the self is tempted to become godlike and to forget the quotidian. There are philosophers who hold the everyday in contempt as womanish stuff, a potion that dilutes the bracing tonic quaffed by real thinkers. Patôcka and Havel do not. Both begin with philosophy "from the bottom," and from a "humbly respected boundary of the natural world." Both view the self as one who, while passing away, has an identity and his or her own unique and independent purposes. We become acquainted with others through acts of responsible surrender to that which is required of us rather than acts of supererogation or arrogation. One begins by taking the natural world as the horizon of doing and knowing—a horizon that is always there and against which we define our own being.

Freedom in this scheme of things is not the working out of a foreordained teleology of self-realization; rather, freedom comes from embracing that which it is given one to do. The "secret of man," writes Havel, "is the secret of his responsibility." This responsibility consists, in part, in knowing rejection of God-likeness and mastery. For when man takes on this hubristic role he becomes the sole source of meaning in a world rendered dead and meaningless. Man exceeds his strength and he becomes a destructive Titan ruining himself and others. We are not perched on top of the earth as sovereigns; rather, we are invited into companionship with the earth as the torn and paradoxical creatures that we are.

Tracking the question of responsibility in Havel's most famous political essays as well as his *Letters to Olga,* the casual or careless reader might be tempted to jettison the philosophical frame within which Havel nests his own understanding of responsibility as unnecessarily cumbersome, a clumsy and even redundant accessory to an otherwise very straightforward insistence upon accountability. But this would be a mistake. On this score Havel is quite insistent. Humans confront nothing less than a general crisis that manifests itself in many ways, and this crisis is, at base, spiritual. Something is "profoundly wrong," for the horizon of thought itself is increasingly beclouded, even despoiled; the order of nature is ruptured and the result is demoralization and indifference. We face a crisis of human identity, and this crisis *must* be understood—can only be understood—when projected against a shrinking screen emblematic of declining human awareness of both "the absolute" and the tragic. Human reason has wrenched itself free from this awareness, and the results often are both tawdry and harsh.

Post-totalitarian Politics

When I was in graduate school in the late 1960s, it was in vogue to mock the warnings of Sir Isaiah Berlin about the dangers inherent in many visions of "positive liberty," turning as they did on naive views of a perfectible human nature and sentimental views on the perfectibility of politics. Berlin was accused of being a liberal sellout, a faint-hearted compromiser. But compromise, not as a mediocre way to do politics but as the *only* way to do democratic politics, is itself an adventure. It lacks the panache of revolutionary violence. It might not stir the blood in the way a "nonnegotiable demand" does, but it presages a livable future. In any democratic politics there are choices to be made that involve both gains and losses. Conflicts about moral claims are part of what it means to be human, and a political ideal stripped of sentimentality and the utopian temptation is one committed to the notion that political life is a permanent agon between clashing, even incompatible goods. As the political philosopher John Gray recently observed:

> Berlin uttered a truth, much against the current of the age, that remains thoroughly unfashionable and fundamentally important—[he] cuts the ground from under those doctrinal or fundamentalist liberalisms—the liberalism of Nozick or Hayek no less than of Rawls or Ackerman—which suppose that the incommensurabilities of moral and political life, and of liberty itself, can be smoothed away by the application of some theory, or tamed by some talismanic formula. . . . It is in taking its stand on incommensurability and radical choice as constitutive features of the human condition that Berlin's liberalism most differs from the Panglossian liberalisms that have in recent times enjoyed an anachronistic revival. Unlike these, Berlin's is an agnostic liberalism, a stoic liberalism of loss and tragedy. For that reason alone, if there is any liberalism that is now defensible, it is Berlin's.

These words might have been written about Havel. For we live in an era in which we are not well served by the old political categories as we witness, to our astonishment, the political realities of a half-century crumple and give way. The drama of democracy, of conflict and compromise, turns on our capacity for making distinctions and offering judgments not clotted and besotted with clichéd categorizations. Havel insists that between the aims of what he calls the "post-totalitarian system" and life in all its "plurality, diversity, independent self-constitution and self-organization" there lies a "yawning abyss." The post-totalitarian system, whatever its political self-definition, pushes to "bind everything in a single order." Havel calls this "social auto-totality," a system that depends on demoralization and cannot survive without it, a system that ignores falling ledges in favor of glorious proclamations concerning progress. By contrast, politics beyond cliché is ironic and skeptical but no less committed—simply insistent that one's own commitments, too, are not exempt from skeptical evaluation. A politics beyond cliché is a politics that refuses to deploy cynically base methods in order to complete an agenda. The political agent always asks, "What is to come?"—not, "Is this a left- or a right-wing argument?" One recognizes that one is never playing chess alone; the board always includes other agents as independent loci of thought and action. Recognition of the stubborn reality of the "other before me" makes contact with a political vision that acknowledges the vulnerability of, and the need to nurture, all new beginnings, including those of a political sort. This may seem a weak and problematic reed, but it is, I believe, the point from which we should begin, from which alone we enter the world of politics without cliché, hence of political conflict and debate without end.

Originally published in *Social Research,* vol. 60, no. 3 (fall 1993). Reprinted by permission.

2

Methodological Sophistication
and Conceptual Confusion

American political analysts work within a polity which has been denuded systematically of shared public moral values; a polity in which inequality of class, sex, and race are constituent features of the status quo; a polity in which the private sphere is seen as a haven from the competitive realities of the world of work and as the single arena within which the expression of sentiment and values as idiosyncratic private preferences is acceptable. I shall argue that this cluster of often unstated assumptions is imbedded within the framework of analysis adopted by political scientists who represent the mainstream of their discipline. The tacit categorizations of women as apolitical creatures and of politics as the pursuit and exercise of that public power whose chief purpose is to meet "legitimate" group interests and demands are imperatives that restrict the scope and subject matter of political discourse and thus have an effect upon the practice of politics itself.

Any final definition of or limitation on the scope of what constitutes politics may (and does) hide the fact that interests are served by these very limitations. The analyst who begins a discussion with the assumption that politics has to do with tough bargaining processes for which men, for a variety of reasons, are most suited, and that moral values are part of the "softer" virtues relegated to churches, women, and private lives, will be blinded to certain features of the social and political world which an observer who is critical of the status quo will see as problems to be explained rather than givens needing no explanation.

To examine the relationship of women to politics and of both to values one must, first, ascertain the ground upon which contemporary political inquiry and methodology rests. If one probes beneath the surface of facts labeled "objective" and hypotheses termed "scientific," one discovers interlocked images of human nature and politics which form the foundation for the "facts" and hypotheses on the surface. The responsible political analyst should open up to public scrutiny and review all the dimensions which cohere within his or her explanatory theory of politics, a perspective. A perspective, according to William E. Connolly, includes a set of fundamental (if tacit) assumptions about the "normal" operations of politics and an integrated set of concepts through which the analyst interprets the political and social world.[1] The analyst's initial expectations shape the conceptual system he or she adopts. These concepts, in turn, enable analysts to absorb or to ignore (if, indeed, they even see) "deviations" from their original presumptions.[2] "A perspective," Connolly writes,

> is a set of presumptions about social and political life derived from selective social experience; the conceptual system it sustains focuses on those aspects of the environment most congruent with those presumptions and tends to divert attention away from other possible dimensions. Since the investigator is seldom sharply aware of his own perspective and its role in inquiry, he is likely to ignore or underplay its tendency to push his interpretations in a particular direction.[3]

Practitioners of contemporary political science tend to presume and to celebrate their own commitment to neutral, scientific objectivity. To this end they have expunged values as a central feature of political study. Women, as the traditional bearers of morality and virtue within the Western culture, are identified with a private sphere that is seen as apolitical and infused with affect. The conceptual association of women with values understood as privatized, subjective preferences which are neither rationally defensible nor amenable to coherent adjudication is not a contingent but a necessary feature within mainstream political explanation. A framework of explanation that factors out women and values includes among its devotees behaviorists who assume political science is a value-free enterprise and those empirical political theorists who admit values, shrunken to "opinions, attitudes, and preferences," into their calculations. (These empirical theorists accept the designation "behavioralist" for their enterprise in order to distinguish themselves from the behaviorists, who do not concern themselves with values at all.)

I shall begin my examination of mainstream political inquiry with David Easton, a leading exponent of the behavioralist persuasion. Easton holds that most students of politics would probably agree about the general nature of the assumptions and objectives of behavioralism. These assumptions and objectives include the presumption that there are "discoverable uniformities in political behavior"; that these regularities are akin to the laws of physics; and that they provide the grounding for explanatory theories in political science which are verifiable (or falsifiable) empirically and have predictive value. The behavioralist effort, Easton declares, shares the scientific rigor of its counterparts in the physical and natural sciences; moreover, the facts of political life and the values one appends to those facts are "two different kinds of propositions that, for the sake of clarity, should be kept analytically distinct."[4] Easton's assertions are correct in this sense: students of politics, including many who claim they do not share behavioralist assumptions, can be seen, under scrutiny, to have adopted its key propositions. The separation between ethical evaluation and empirical explanation, between descriptive and evaluative statements, is widely, if implicitly, accepted and infuses political explanations with what Charles Taylor terms a particular "value slope."[5] Because the practitioners of an ostensibly value-free social science deny that their work is infused with values, they cannot recognize, and thus cannot articulate, the implications of their conclusions for human wants, needs, and purposes within political and social life. In this manner much contemporary political science is both a priori and presumptuous.

I shall expose several of the unexamined assumptions of mainstream political inquiry with specific attention to their implications for women and politics. First, what are the assumptions about human nature and human action which underlie contemporary political inquiry? No theory of human nature, as Ellen Wood points out, is empirically verifiable.[6] Yet theories of human nature, of what it *is* or means to be human, are central to social and political thought. Aristotle, Hobbes, Locke, and Rousseau, for example, formulated and defended theories of persons and related these persons to politics; indeed, without the articulation of what persons are, or can become, a theory of politics remains, at best, incomplete. The important question for our purposes is whether or not it is possible to discern a *particular* notion of human nature and mind within contemporary accounts of politics.

Perhaps the best way to begin is to ask, On *what* set of assumptions concerning human nature and action *must* contemporary inquiry be based if its conclusions are to be logical and internally consistent? For example: suppose I were to declare in an obdurate and uncompromising manner that people are by nature amicable, sociable creatures who cooperate voluntarily without any external coercion, who spontaneously engage in meaningful group action within social contexts (that is, the action has a common meaning for the purposive, intentional agents who undertake it); that these beings recognize that their way of life is constituted, in part, by their beliefs; and that these beings, finally, celebrate a life of thought and reason as an important activity. Suppose, further, that at the request of a community of such beings I am commissioned to write up plans for a governing system for these peace-loving social beings. I devote myself to the task of determining how beings like themselves would order their life in common. The plan I come up with is called *The Leviathan* (my name, you see, is Thomas Hobbes).

I begin my tract with the argument that, in the absence of authoritarian control by a single ruler, political life would dissolve into a war of all against all.

The response from the community of peace-loving beings who commissioned me to create a form of government in their behalf would no doubt be one of confusion and extreme consternation, as these cooperative beings had never engaged in a war of all against all. If I were to continue to insist that although I saw human beings as cooperative and peace-loving, as they did, I nevertheless found it necessary to create a polity ruled by a sovereign with absolute, unchecked power to make all judgments, determine all laws, and set forth the "truth" to his subjects, I would either be sent away for a prolonged visit to some tranquil spot in the country until such time as I regained the power of coherent thought, or I would be tolerated as someone engaged in a not-terribly-funny ruse. The more mistrustful members of the community might suspect that I was some sort of enemy agent hired by another society to undermine the morale of this community's naturally cooperative way of life.

The point of this tale is to indicate that there is a direct, if implicit, link between a theorist's views on what human beings are, how these beings come to learn and to reason and to act in common, and his or her logic of inquiry and political explanation. The conclusions about politics will flow in large measure from some prior commitment to a theory about the nature of persons. That political analysts refuse to lay all their prior commitments on the table does not mean they have none up their sleeves. At this point I can only suggest briefly certain connections between particular theories of human nature and the prevailing mode in political science. Modern political inquiry occurs within a particular context. That context includes a society characterized by sexual, as well as by class and racial, inequality. The view of human nature and the human mind which informs and helps to legitimate such inequities can be traced from certain dimensions within classical liberal political theory which emerged in conjunction with empiricist accounts of the operations of the human mind. Contemporary political scientists, for the most part, are unaware of the philosophical foundations of their enterprise and thus cannot even consider the contestable assumptions concerning human nature imbedded within their frameworks of analysis. Indeed, the problem "What kind of being does your analysis presuppose?" is neither a question to be asked nor an issue to be explored for modern political scientists, whose images of persons remain a series of unreflective prior commitments.

The human being who is the subject of political inquiry and the object of mainstream pluralist political science is best characterized in paradigmatic form as an *abstract individual* who is said to be *sovereign*. For classical liberal thinkers, a human being is real to the extent that she or he is posited as ontologically prior to society and alone.[7] He or she is a social atom whose relevant features "are assumed as given, independently of a social context. This givenness of fixed and invariant human psychological features leads to an abstract conception of the individual who is seen merely as the bearer of those features, which determine his [or her] behavior, and specify his interests, needs and rights."[8] The relationship between one abstract atom and the next, and between an aggregate (not a community!) of such atoms and their society, is external and instrumental. Society is an artificial aggregate which exists to serve specific instrumental purposes—called "group interests."

Abstract Man's involvement with others in society is measured by a calculus James Glass has termed "the phenomenology of liberal externality," a mode of perception tied to what Hobbes called "reckoning consequences."[9] Abstract Man behaves or acts from a calculated, prudent self-interest which, in the liberal view, redounds ultimately to the good of all. Neither Hobbes nor Locke nor contemporary political scientists believe that persons are changed in any *fundamental* way by living among one another in a society rather than singly, say, on hundreds of desert islands, each populated by a single Abstract Man. The life of Abstract Man is characterized by a rigid split not only between the public and the private but between the economic and political spheres; indeed, the presumption of such splits is parasitical upon the atomistic self the theory presupposes. A theory of Abstract Man cannot take social contexts of meaning into account systematically. The social world is given and is featured variously as an entity which may threaten to destroy the sovereign individual's liberties and must be watched carefully, or as a powerful conglomerate of means which can be deployed on behalf of private interests. Classical liberal theory cannot provide the grounding for a shared political life in common. As Robert Paul Wolff points out, the liberal theory of the Abstract Man assumes that all values are simple private values or aggregates of private values.[10] In contemporary political science, Abstract Man is further reduced to a being with roles and functions as even more of his or her social attributes are stripped away.

The human mind featured in classical liberal and contemporary mainstream accounts is also construed as asocial. According to defenders of "autonomous rationality," persons are free beings who constitute their own "universe of meaning."[11] There is an ineradicable solipsism—an ontology of atomistic individuals who alone are basic and real, who are the only true and "ultimate constituents of the social world."[12] The minds of such atomized beings, according to the empiricist epistemology that has predominated in Western discourse since Locke, Berkeley, and Hume, can apprehend self-evident facts (which, apparently, are sprinkled generously about in un-adorned fashion) and reach conclusions on the basis of this evidence. The empiricist version holds that the mind works in much the way a Xerox machine replicates a sheet of printed matter: it makes copies or images of the impressions it receives, and these are "ideas." This particular theory of mind (part and parcel, remember, of the liberal theory of the individual) concludes that once the mind has an image or a copy of an impression given to the senses, it, too, can produce copies. New sets of ideas may be derived from solipsistic introspection, which involves a private definition of external reality.[13]

Abstract Man's mind, like his world, is bifurcated neatly: on the one hand, it contains an aspect associated with dispositions or desires; on the other hand, it is capable of cognition based on a passive capacity to "copy" the outside world. He reacts to forces and pressures from the outside. One aspect of reaction may be a piece of behavior which other passive humans who happen to be studying him observe and note down as data. But the behavior in which this subject engages also includes a subjective aspect, that is, the individual reacts to situations in one way or another depending upon biases, subjective preferences, attitudes, likes, dislikes, and so on. The com-bined behaviors of a number of passive, abstract human subjects will mean something different to each one, depending upon the idiosyncratic and private preferences of each. There is and can be no shared world of common meaning within this perspective.

Mainstream political inquiry cannot be understood apart from these links to the empiricist theory of mind and the classical liberal theory of Abstract Man. These views on human nature, thought, and action remain imbedded within contemporary accounts. The ideal subject of so-called sci-entific observation in political science is not (and cannot be) a self-reflexive, purposeful agent who engages the world actively and helps to shape it with thought and action, but is a narrowly calculating being who adapts, con-forms, and engages in self-interested behavior, rather than in action with a social as well as a private meaning. The behavioralist enterprise rests on a set of tacit assumptions shared by those who labor within its framework of explanation. These include the conviction that human behavior is a rela-tively reliable variable within a scientific hypothesis. The idea, a simplistic one, is that an aggregate of human beings, exposed to a particular external force, will react and behave in ways that are predictable in advance; thus behavioralist "hypotheses" conform to the requirements of a method which assumes the possibility of prediction in the first place, given its narrow understanding of human reason and its mechanistic account of human emotion and action.[14]

The goal of behavioralist explanation is neither the *understanding* of human beings and their social and political world, nor the *interpretation* of that world of self and others, but the construction of verifiable hypotheses with the power to predict. In order to predict, one needs behavioral regularity which follows an inexorable logic; behavior, in other words, must be *caused*. The test of lawlike generalizations within political and social life is implicit within a logic of explanation that assumes the possibility of prediction and regularity. The aim is to strip away the apparent complexities of political life and human action, to get rid of anything untidy, so that one might engage in a search for lawlikeness in political life. The political and social context itself is accepted as a given rather than questioned or criticized. Issues of political justice; legitimacy; sexual, racial, and class inequality; and political reform or revolt cannot arise as problems, for these issues call the context into question and make the behavior of social participants less amenable to lawlike predictability. All resonant themes and issues must either be expunged from view before the analyst beings work (the context-as-a-given), or, for the more scrupulous who are somewhat aware of these matters, contested issues may be incorporated in a way which fits within the boundaries of their logic of explanation.[15] Within a pluralist society such as our own, for example, a mainstream analyst might accept the possibility that a few running repairs are needed here and there. This, in turn, will lead to demands and activities on the part of certain groups. But these groups and movements (dubbed "interest groups," thus narrowing all group efforts to the level of self-interestedness) are treated differently depending on whether they play by the "rules of the game"—that is, are rational and reasonable on the pluralist model—or whether they refuse to play by the rules and behave in ways which provide evidence of immaturity and rabid ideological commitments. (Once ideologues have matured and rid themselves of *parti pris,* they, too, may be admitted into the game on good behavior.) The analyst who grasps the particulars of the political system under the description proffered above excludes grasping them under a divergent description.

How do mainstream political scientists characterize their enterprise? What are the implications of this enterprise? What are the implications of this enterprise for women and politics? First, the analyst starts from what Steven Lukes terms rock bottom and Charles Taylor calls brute-data identifiable behavior. For example, Heinz Eulau, a leading figure in the behavioralist revolution in political science, declares that any science of politics "which deserves its name" must be built "from the bottom up by asking simple questions that can, in principle, be answered; it cannot be built from the top down by asking questions that, one has reason to suspect, cannot be answered at all, at least not by the methods of science. An empirical discipline is built by the slow, modest, and piecemeal cumulation of relevant theories and data."[16]

Scientific inquiry in politics starts from the bottom with simple questions presumed to be objective and neutral. T. D. Weldon discusses what this demand for objectivity entails: "In fact the demand for 'objective' standards in politics and in morals is simply a demand for a criterion which enables us to grade people and institutions with the same sort of certainty and confidence as that with which, with very minor qualifications, we can grade physical bodies in terms of size and weight."[17]

Within the epistemological presumptions of behavioralist political thinking, to describe and to evaluate, to state what is and to state what ought to be, are *two entirely separable activities*. Those who mix the two are considered fuzzy-minded, impressionistic, and incapable of rigorous analysis—a description not unlike stereotypic characterizations of female thinking processes. A bifurcation between descriptive and evaluative statements is essential to behavioralist inquiry. The hypotheses formulated and the tests constructed to verify (or falsify) these same hypotheses are all contingent upon a prior separation of statements.[18] The goal of behavioralism, its *raison d'être*, lies in "coming as close as possible" to a description of the political world as it *really* is, stripped to the bare bones of objectivity. "Values, biases, attitudes, and emotional preferences"—subjective dimensions—may be appended later if the analyst chooses.

Laborers in the mainstream vineyard assume that in statements other than those which cannot be falsified (or analytic statements which entail a nonfalsifiable correspondence between subject and predicate by definition—for example, "All married women are wives"), the political analyst is presented with a problem of linking, or establishing a relationship between, subject and predicate which can be explored and adjudicated only through empirical investigation. This investigation will demonstrate (the assumption goes) a correlation between the subject of the statement and its predicate. Two statements requiring investigation might be "All married women purchase Crunchy Creatures for breakfast," or, more troubling but not so problematic as to give pause to the intrepid, "All married women are happy." The relationship between "married women" and the predicates in each sentence is called a "synthetic" one and is stated in quantitative terms. The nearer the investigator comes to a correlation of 1.0 the closer he or she is presumed to be to the truth and the greater the power of the statement, couched as a hypothesis, to predict. The researcher must strive to reduce or to bracket ambiguity, imprecision, complexity, and ambivalence in order to come as close as possible to symmetry between naming (the subject) and meaning (the predicate which expresses the truth of the statement). In the sample sentence "All married women are happy," for example, a researcher set on precision (and a high correlation) must first arrive at final cloture on a definition of *happy*, a notoriously rich, open-ended, and imprecise term of ordinary discourse. Despite the open-endedness of usage of a term within a way of life, the logic of this method forces the behavioralist to adopt a series of arbitrary and fixed definitions so as to construct the hypotheses. The result is a particularly crude verificationist theory of meaning.[19]

The theory of meaning imbedded in mainstream political inquiry claims as a central presumption that the *meaning* of synthetic statements ("All married women are happy") is *exhausted* once a relationship between the subject and predicate has been established via correlations. Yet even before such tests begin, the hypothesis has been impoverished by the arbitrary reduction of rich, reactive terms central to human social relationships (*happy*) to one among a number of possible definitions. Thus the definition of *happy* in my example constitutes an a priori. In Taylor's words, "The profound option of mainstream social scientists for the empiricist conception of knowledge and science makes it inevitable that they should accept the verification model of political science and the categorical principles that this entails. This means in turn that a study of our civilization in terms of its intersubjective and common meanings is ruled out. Rather this whole level of study is made invisible."[20] Should the critics of mainstream inquiry cavil at the "results" which emerge from such research, they are often confronted with the self-serving insistence that the tests are neutral and prove something whether others like it or not.

"Liking" or "not liking" the results of someone's research is not the point at all. What is the point is that test procedures, and what counts as evidence, are inseparable from a framework of analysis which provides for such tests in the first place. But this framework goes unexamined and thus unchallenged within mainstream literature.[21] Methodology can never be free-floating; it grows out of epistemological commitments. Those obvious facts which dot the pages of contemporary political science emerge within a perspective which holds that facts can stand naked and alone—that there is an unbridgeable gulf between descriptions and evaluation.

Yet, as Julius Kovesi argues in a compelling critique of the presumptions undergirding behavioralist political inquiry, these presumptions have normative implications for persons and politics, for there is no such thing as mere description.[22] Description is always from a point of view and hence is evaluative.[23] We describe situations on the basis of those aspects of that

situation we deem relevant or important. In this way, we "always evaluate
under a certain description."[24] Contrary to behavioralism, the most important contrast is not between description and evaluation but between "description from the moral point of view as opposed to other points of view."[25]
Description is always to a purpose. This purpose may, and often does, remain
hidden from view—imbedded in a series of tacit prior commitments the
analyst or researcher does not acknowledge and therefore need not defend.

Three contrasting descriptions of the process of modern industrial wage
labor will serve to demonstrate the evaluations for persons and social life
which flow from the language of description itself (emphasis mine).

1. What dominates the labor process and all work processes which are performed in the mode of laboring is neither man's purposeful effort nor
   the product he may desire, but the motion of the process itself and the
   rhythm it imposes upon the laborers. Labor implements are drawn into
   this rhythm until body and tool swing in the same repetitive movement,
   that is, until the use of machines, which of all implements are best suited
   to the performance of the *animal laborans,* it is no longer the body's
   movement that determines the implement's movement but the machine's movement which enforces the movements of the body. *The point
   is that nothing can be mechanized more easily and less artificially than the
   rhythm of the labor process, which, in turn corresponds to the equally automatic repetitive rhythm of the life process and its metabolism with nature. . . .
   complaints about the "artificial" rhythm which the machines impose upon the
   laborer . . . characteristically, are relatively rare among the laborers themselves,
   who, on the contrary, seem to find the same amount of pleasure in repetitive
   machine work as in other repetitive labor. . . . They prefer [it] because it is
   mechanical and does not demand attention, so that while performing it they
   can think of something else.*[26]

2. When a workman is increasingly and exclusively engaged in the fabrica-
   tion of one thing, he ultimately does his work with singular dexterity;
   but at the same time, he loses the general faculty of applying his mind to
   the direction of his work. He everyday becomes more adroit and less
   industrious. *In proportion as the principle of the division of labor is more
   extensively applied the workman becomes more weak, more narrow minded,
   and more dependent. The art advances, the artisan recedes.*[27]

3. The capitalist mode of production (essentially the production of surplus-
   value, the absorption of surplus-labour) produces thus, with the exten-
   tion of the working day, not only the deterioration of human labour-
   power, by robbing it of its normal, moral and physical, conditions of

development and function, it produces also the premature exhaustion and death of this labour-power itself. *It extends the labourer's time of production during a given period by shortening his actual life-time.*[28]

The first description of the division of labor in assembly-line production conveys, through the language chosen for description, the assurance that such wage labor is natural and pleasurable to those who engage in it. The analyst whose description provides this uncritical reassurance, Hannah Arendt in *The Human Condition,* does not preface her description of the work process with a caveat to the reader that she accepts and celebrates a stratified system of inequality which relegates a portion of its population, male and female, to daily repetitive labor and denies to that portion the social goods which routinely set the contours of life for the more privileged. Yet her description of the process as natural and pleasurable constitutes an evaluation of assembly-line work as good—as no imposition whatever on *animal laborans.* If one accepts Arendt's description of the work process and its benign and soothing correspondence with the body's rhythms, the effects of that process upon persons will not be called into question, and the social placement of such persons will remain hidden from critical scrutiny.*

The second description, proffered by Alexis de Tocqueville, uses language which implicates him in an evaluation of the work process as one often harmful and ultimately demeaning to those who must engage in it. De Tocqueville's depiction has imbedded within it an evaluative dimension that allows the reader to question the beneficence of a highly specialized division of labor. With the third characterization of wage-labor production, drawn from Karl Marx's *Capital,* volume 1, the reader is confronted with a descriptive vocabulary consisting of a number of powerful critical terms. These terms allow the reader to probe beneath the appearance of things in order to explore, from a critical and skeptical stance, what may be deeper meanings and realities. Marx speaks of human deterioration under the circumstances of wage labor, of robbing the worker of "normal, moral and physical" development and functions. Thus, de Tocqueville's and Marx's descriptions implicate them in criticism of, or dissent from, a process which is an integral feature of the capitalist socioeconomic and political status quo. Because the second and third descriptions make reference to human beings as purposive and intentional agents with wants, needs, and the capacity to feel pain, they can be said to be formed from a moral point of view. De Tocqueville and Marx are disturbed or outraged by a process which undermines human dignity and self-respect and vitiates the capacity for creative or independent

---

*This is too rough on Arendt. I had only just begun to read her in the late 70s and I really didn't understand her categories very well. But the general point holds.

work. Arendt's description, however, is formed without regard to a moral point of view. Those who remain within the language of Arendt's description cannot make reference to questions of respect for persons, or human beings as intentional and purposeful agents.

Despite the nexus between description and evaluation demonstrated by the examples above, the behavioralist imperative remains that of bifurcating statements of fact from statements of value, of exempting description from evaluation. The assumption is that the analyst describes objectively a problem or situation or issue in political life or thought, verifies the truth or meaning of hypotheses grounded in this objective characterization, and then, if he or she chooses, layers a patina of value judgments on top of neutral descriptions and the objective facts. Opinions, biases, and values (all are presumed to be rationally indefensible within the rigors of this logic) are related to facts and descriptions in much the way that clothing and accouterments are related to a department store mannequin. A window decorator begins with an unadorned mannequin and dresses or undresses it as he or she (and the store manager) sees fit. In much the same way, the political analyst may add values to the objective facts which constitute his or her description of political life and social reality. These facts, like so many immobile, silent mannequins, remain unaltered through such external operations.

Ramifications of the behavioralist presumptions flow into moral theory as well. A link between political inquiry and moral imperatives was presumed explicitly by classical theorists in the history of political thought; however, contemporary political science tends to divide politics from moral considerations. This is yet another base from which a critique of the perspective can be mounted. Focusing on a moral dilemma should serve to illustrate further the inadequacy of the bifurcation between description and evaluation. Imagine that a group of persons are gathered around listening to a description of a brutal event in which young children were tortured systematically by sadistic adults. The account is replete with details of the desperate implorings of the children and the impervious cruelty of their torturers. One of those who hears this tale of terror and tragedy is a social scientist who accepts the dichotomy between description and evaluation. The social scientist insists, once the speaker has recounted the tale in all its graphic horror, that the group now be told whether the actions of the torturers are approved!

Would such a demand make sense? Remember, the situation is characterized by the speaker on the basis of those aspects considered relevant. These included the details of the suffering of the children at the hands of torturers depicted as brutal and sadistic. The *description* of events constituted an evaluation from a moral point of view. A person devoid of moral perspective would have described these events in different language—in language not designed to arouse compassion, sorrow, moral indignation, and outrage from the listener.

If we place these considerations within the context of contemporary political inquiry, we find that those analysts who adopt a moral point of view from which to describe, and thereby evaluate, political reality—including inequality, the plight of the poor, indignities suffered by the elderly, and the indifference suffered by the mentally handicapped—characterize social reality in very different language from that deployed by those analysts who presume they have at their disposal a "neutral" language of description. Precisely the obverse pertains: we evaluate the world through our descriptive notions. In Kovesi's language, "Moral notions describe the world of evaluation."[29] Behavioralist "neutral" language is simply language not formed from a moral, or critical, point of view.

The response of mainstream scholars to the criticisms proffered above would be that researchers do have their own values, often termed biases. "We know," they would argue, "that biases and our own values are a problem. We have developed test procedures to cope with this problem, to correct for our values—to neutralize them for purposes of research." Values are left in a shadowy realm from which they may inform or push the analyst toward "constructive research." Easton goes so far as to admit values as a component, or variable, within his model. The "major kinds of propositions," for Easton, are factual, moral, applied, and theoretical. Although moral propositions help analysts to build "constructive theoretical research," ultimately the validity and utility of empirical political theory rests upon its correspondence with political reality.[30] Analysts, in this view, must isolate and bracket values as they go about their work. Values remain on a par with preferences, expressions of taste or distaste, or emotions and feelings presumed not to be rationally defensible. Moral notions are just one type of opinion among many.[31]

Those committed to the view that moral notions, opinions, biases, and beliefs can be stated apart from description and research methods and findings, that such notions are indefensible rationally, and that they can be bracketed after they have pushed the researcher toward certain questions have adopted tacitly a theory of morality known as *emotivism*. Emotivism is an account of moral notions compatible with and imbedded in behavioralist presumptions. Emotivist accounts hold that such terms of moral evaluation as *good* or *bad* are purely emotive. That is, these terms stand "for nothing whatever" and merely "serve as an emotive sign expressing our attitude . . . and perhaps evoking similar attitudes in other persons."[32]

According to the emotivist account, that which is called good depends upon one's values or biases. Should individuals commend a course of action to us as "good," they are merely recounting their biases or feelings or tastes—none of which comprises an evaluation for which reasons can be adduced and given. Should my own taste happen to concur, I will be likely to accept the commendation as "good." But suppose I am confronted with a moral dilemma. One day I find myself sequestered with a sadist who delights in lighting afire the tails of captured stray dogs. Wishing to draw me into the enterprise of maltreating and abusing animals, this person tells me, "It is *good* to torture helpless creatures and to make them feel pain." Why is it good? Because this individual feels it to be, and "feels good" when engaging in the torture of animals—and thus commends these actions to others so that they, too, might "feel good." How am I to respond to these claims? I could try to get out of the problem by declaring the puppy-torturer a psychopath whose views must perforce be ignored. But perhaps the torturer's behavior betrays no signs of irrationality; indeed, the person is calm and cool throughout. All that is left me, if I am a consistent emotivist, is the reply: "Well, you have your opinion as to what is good and I have mine. Personally, I do not feel it is good to torture animals. My feelings are different from yours. So why don't we agree to disagree, and I'll leave now if it's all the same to you."

The emotivist account of moral notions, imbedded within the behavioralist perspective, requires that all arguments for or against social structures and arrangements formed from a moral point of view (through the language of injustice, oppression, exploitation, discrimination, etc.) be allowed to fall through the sieve of those who claim value-neutrality for their work and of those who insist that they do incorporate or defend values, if by values one means rationally indefensible personal preferences.[33]

My central point is this: problems presented by questions of biases or values cannot be dealt with simply by admitting, as mainstream political scientists long ago began doing, to one's bias and claiming to set these biases to the side for purposes of research.[34] This response does not touch the heart of the matter, namely, an epistemology which requires the severance of fact from value.[35] The problem is more complex and fundamental than any charge of bias! *It is that every explanatory theory of politics supports a particular set of normative conclusions.* To have an explanatory theory, the analyst must adopt a framework linked, implicitly if not explicitly, to notions of human nature and human purposes. This framework sets the boundaries of the phenomena to be investigated. Some factors of social life will be incorporated, and others will be expunged from view before research begins. The framework gears choices, celebrates some interests, excludes others, and precludes seeing the political world under an alternative characterization.

What has all this to do with women, politics, and values? The relationships are on the level of depth connections within a tradition of moral and political discourse which has linked women traditionally to values trivialized as emotive and subjective preferences; which ties political behavior to a narrow view of rationality associated with a belief in predictable behavior (women, as irrational creatures, are shoved to the periphery of rational political behavior as thus understood); which sees the polity as an aggregate set up to serve instrumental purposes or interests which is bifurcated conceptually and objectively from the private world of emotions, feelings, and noninstrumental relations. Women express values reduced to subjective, private, irrational, and emotional beliefs or affects and reign in some natural realm outside politics, power, and the world of rationalistic, calculated decision making.

An alternative explanatory theory must deploy divergent criteria as to what counts as a political activity or issue and what does not. These criteria are imbedded within the concepts and the descriptive terms the analyst utilizes. Despite the smug self-assurance which emanates from the pages of so much contemporary political inquiry, no definition of *politics*, its range and purpose, is given either simply or a priori. Concepts and contests about what politics is slice up the world of thought and action in certain ways. Within mainstream political science, what has been described traditionally as politics tends to factor women out of the activity and has excluded for many years the questions raised by feminists. Such questions are relegated to a sphere outside organized political activity and are dismissed as private "troubles." Women have had to struggle not only against political policies, structures, and arrangements but against definitions of politics and modes of political explanation as well.

The view of politics proffered by several well-known practitioners of contemporary political science will clarify my argument. Harold Lasswell, in his classic book on influence (*Politics: Who Gets What, When, How*) describes politics as the study of the influential. Who are the influential? They are those who get more of what there is to get: deference, income, safety. "The science of politics states conditions; the philosophy of politics justifies preferences. *This book, restricted to political analysis, declares no preferences.* It states conditions."[36] Yet the title Lasswell chose for his book tells us in advance that politics is about who gets what, when, and how. By relegating politics to the study of the influential, Lasswell adopts complacency toward the reality that disproportionate numbers of women, minorities, and working-class persons fall into the category of the uninfluential and are thus defined out of politics (save as those over whom influence is exerted).

Bernard Crick, in his *In Defence of Politics,* published in 1964 when politics-as-usual was under challenge from civil rights activists and student rebels, calls for a reaffirmation of the traditional view that politics "can be simply defined as the activity by which differing interests within a given unit of rule are conciliated by giving them a share in power in proportion to their importance to the welfare and survival of the whole community."[37] Women do not represent a differing interest to be conciliated for Crick because their traditional activities fall outside Crick's political purview. Crick denies explicitly that personal relationships, marriage, and the family have anything to do with politics. Politics is the "master science among men. . . . a preoccupation of free men." But Crick's free men, as they go about their "preoccupation," are compelled to justify wide-ranging social inequality and injustice if they accept his definition of the activity and purpose of politics. If differing interests are conciliated by giving these interests a share in power "in proportion to their importance to the welfare and survival of the whole community," large segments within a given population are defined out of politics by fiat. Those who hold power are placed by Crick in a position to determine who shall or shall not be conciliated, depending upon their relative importance or unimportance to the welfare and survival of the unit of rule. Women, perhaps, might struggle to make their case within Crick's tidy universe, but the severely disadvantaged, the diseased, the infirm, the handicapped, could not. Perhaps Crick would allow them charity if not conciliation. In any case, the range over which he allows politics to operate restricts incorporating the concerns of the socially abused and disadvantaged into the heart of political debates.

Seymour Martin Lipset, a political sociologist whose most important book remains his 1963 volume, *Political Man: The Social Bases of Politics,* seems at first glance to meet criticism of the Lasswell-Crick approach to politics as too restrictive and narrow. He expands politics by defining it as a set of processes which are nothing more than "special cases of more general sociological and psychological relationships."[38] Unfortunately, Lipset's definition is so diffuse that the distinguishable activity one designates as "politics" gets lost in a blur of social undifferentiation. Lipset, too, manages to factor women out of political participation as measured by indices of voter participation. Lipset cites evidence for the relative nonparticipation of women in politics as a sign of female apathy and overweening concern with social values. Absorbed within these traditional family and community activities Lipset clearly accepts as their natural sphere, women are unconcerned with politics save when a "morality" issue like gambling or prohibition is at stake.[39] Lipset construes women's apathy as evidence of the *satisfaction* of women with their lot; thus, women's nonparticipation fails to become a problem to be explained.

For Lipset, only issues that are organized around bargaining groups within a pluralist polity need to be explained and analyzed. He fails to recognize that a *nonissue* may be the outcome of a political process which skews the results of that process toward those who already have access to the system of rewards. He accepts as apolitical or nonpolitical all issues he locates at the level of personal troubles, problems, or values. Suppose, instead, an analyst viewed apathy or nonparticipation (utilizing the same data cited by Lipset) as a political issue or problem rather than a nonissue or an expression of personal values or problems. From some alternative perspective, apathy might indicate erosion of support for a political system rather than serving as proof that people are so (relatively) satisfied they can afford to be apathetic.[40]

Lipset's understanding of politics and of the apathetic underwrites his justification of the exclusion of the lower class from political participation. He assigns to lower-class apathy and political silence an important function as a prop upon which system stability rests. If too many participated too often about too much, it would result in political instability. As it is (one thinks of women, slaves, and under-classes as Aristotle's "necessary conditions" for the existence of the *polis*), lower-class people are "much less committed to democracy," as evidenced by their "lower voter turnout."[41] Lipset does not recognize (or, if he does, he makes a secret of this realization) that his conclusions reflect his attachment to a particular political status quo and serve simultaneously to justify and to legitimate stratified and inegalitarian social structures and arrangements. He rests his case on the facts of apathy and nonparticipation by women and the lower class in politics. Then he utilizes these facts to make the case that the situation is all right because the lower class is less committed to democracy than the middle class, and women are immersed in their apolitical social values and their divergent social roles.

Two observations are necessary. First, politics and the power which flows from holding political responsibilities may be reflected in *limiting* the scope of the political process in the service of a given status quo. This limitation may be couched in the guise of preserving traditional values, or protecting politics from extremists who would pervert it should they gain power. There is often some truth to such charges. But the salient point for our consideration is that certain specific interests are served by these limitations and that this fact is hidden or remains opaque. Peter Bachrach and Morton S. Baratz, in their ground-breaking 1962 critique of pluralism, "Two Faces of Power," observed that although some issues are organized into politics and others are not, *power* is implicated in eliminating certain areas from explicit political consideration, just as it is involved in adjudicating between extant interest groups.[42] Power, they argued, is not limited to public debates and decision-making but is deployed in confining the scope of the political to consideration of issues not threatening to those interests who do not wish to see certain problems and issues opened up for political debate.

The women's movement has thrust issues previously declared private or nonpolitical into the midst of political debates. Together with the other liberation movements which emerged in the 1960s, the women's movement helped to forge a redefinition of political power to include both dimensions of unintentional power and power as productive of unintended consequences.[43] Power as unintentional, or as productive of consequences which may be unintentional, is that possessed by a particular class, group, or sex by virtue of its position within a set of social structures and arrangements—a position from which that group derives benefits and privileges but which it did not intentionally seek to create. For example, a white individual in a racist society may himself be nonracist, but in that society he possesses greater unintentional power than a black individual. Similarly, men *qua* men have greater unintentional power than women in a sexist society. An avid anti-Suffragist, writing in 1889, observed that husbands could not avoid possessing power over their wives: "He has not assumed it: it has existed as a consequence of the natures and constitutions of the two sexes. True, he need not exercise the power, but notwithstanding this, he cannot emancipate his wife therefrom."[44] This concept of unintentional power, in turn, may be tied up with notions of authority and legitimacy, concepts traditionally deployed as characterizations of the state or the highest level of political power. Yet familial relations involve (although they are not defined exclusively by) both power and authority. Men and women alike may exercise power as coercion, manipulation, or persuasion within the boundary of an intimate relationship, but the male is the sole possessor of unintentional power with a public meaning having political consequences. When he exerts power, it is considered legitimate—perhaps neither wise nor beneficent, but legitimate.[45] The women's movement, in this sense, is a legitimation crisis. Certainly not all instances of unintended consequences involve power. The important point is that by narrowing the scope of politics in the ways I have criticized, leading analysts representing mainstream social science have lent their support to those who benefit from inegalitarian social arrangements and who seek to maintain and to defend the politics which helps them to get more of what there is to get.

A political scientist who denies to the majority of women, minorities, and poor a central role in politics because he or she has defined politics in a manner which eliminates those not already ensconced within the system of rewards and benefits is not engaged in some mere reflection or neutral description of political reality: he or she is providing a normative justification for an extant way of life. Women must fight both political reality and purportedly neutral statements about that reality, which, in fact, secrete normative dimensions supportive of the status quo. Mainstream political science, consciously or unconsciously, tacitly or openly, has adopted an interrelated set of presumptions; thus, it must be held responsible for the outcomes which flow from them.

An analyst who accepts the framework I have explicated and criticized in this essay is forced, through the logic of explanation, to accept all or some of the following presumptions: (*a*) a narrow definition of politics which excludes by fiat the cluster of issues, problems, and values focused on the family or private life; (*b*) a concept of political participation which involves a standard of an ideal, active political citizen and judges individuals against that norm without seriously considering factors which mitigate against participation or, having considered such factors, decides that participation is not necessarily desirable for everyone; (*c*) a focus on interest groups and pluralist bargaining, given the liberal dogma of politics as a sphere within which individual self-interest or aggregations of self-interest are articulated and adjudicated; (*d*) a privatization and trivialization of moral concerns or values as these relate to public, social issues; (*e*) a justification or rationalization of a system of stratification by sex, race, class, age, and so on, so long as system stability is maintained.

It would be difficult to find a political scientist who would own up to supporting all of these presumptions; nevertheless, if a perspective leads the analyst to accept any *one* of these dimensions, he or she is committed, in complex, tacit ways, to aspects of all the others. Despite the flurries, debates, and surface changes of the recent past, contemporary political inquiry continues to rest upon a philosophical foundation inhospitable at its core to rigorous, critical exploration of the deeper relations between women, politics, and values. Its practitioners continue, as they must, to toot the horns of scientific rigor and predictability, despite the remarkable fact that their colleagues in the natural sciences long ago junked such unacceptable constraints to creative scientific research. The physicist, for example, faces the astonishing truth that it is impossible to predict the behavior of subatomic particles. Behavioralist inquiry eviscerates our understanding of the complexity of human beings and the astonishing multilayered textures of their social world, for it cannot accommodate a logic of political explanation which incorporates a critical theory of both persons and politics formed from the moral point of view.

That the majority of women in contemporary political science have been trained within and have thus adopted the very presumptions which served and still serve to legitimate sexual inequality so long as it, in turn, serves the status quo indicates the strength and power of the dominant paradigm and the distance we have to go to achieve an equitable pursuit of knowledge. So long as feminist criticism of bias in scholarship takes place within the presumptions of the dominant mode of political inquiry, feminist scholars will fail to create a powerful alternative framework of explanation. Mainstream political science claims it has already dealt with the matter of bias by adopting an impoverished set of values even as it retains the conceptually fatal bifurcation between description and evaluation. Within the mainstream perspective, a feminist scholar can lodge charges of bias, or set forth her own biases, to her heart's content, but she cannot articulate serious moral claims which would serve to describe and to evaluate her society and her discipline.

Feminist scholars must not be fooled by the few victories women have achieved in those minor skirmishes over whether Professor So-and-So's data on female nonparticipation really correlates at the level claimed, or whether some other Professor So-and-So's research model or design fails to control for variables x, y, or z. Such victories are in the nature of family feuds: they occur within what Wittgenstein would call a single language game, an arena, in this instance characterized by refined and sophisticated techniques coupled with conceptual confusion. Perhaps this combination of sophistication and confusion helps to explain why so much contemporary political science is so trivial and leaves us so cold.

To move toward a critical perspective of politics we must begin as I have done in this essay: we must, first, bring the predominant presumptions of the discipline to the surface and, second, subject them to rigorous and unflinching scrutiny. As our tacit commitments are brought out into the open where they can be debated, we uncover internal inconsistencies, incoherence, and confusion in our own position as well as in the positions of others. A critical science of politics, in contradistinction to that which now wraps itself in the cocoon of neutral objectivity, incorporates interpretive self-criticism as a central feature of its logic. It is only through self-aware reinterpretations of thought and action that human beings can replace confused, tedious, and conformist accounts of the political and social world with more coherent, rational, lively, and critical accounts. Until we move to adopt a rich descriptive vocabulary with which to characterize and evaluate critically political life and thought, we must remain, whatever our stated and heartfelt intents and our radical noises, stuck within a framework of inquiry which neither transcends nor understands but simply reflects (and thus justifies) what is.

The equitable pursuit of knowledge will always involve a political struggle. The relationship between persons of critical mind and society and discipline will always be marked by tension. As traditional, unreflective positions are opened to scrutiny and debate, as critical awareness is attained painfully and arduously, the scholar finds it to be neither a passive nor an altogether pleasant experience. But this dynamic process of breaking through and breaking down the encrusted blur of "political science as usual" is a necessary step on the road toward critical interpretation. In our perplexing era, any method of political inquiry which thinks to find peace within itself, or between itself and society, has nothing to do with a restless, searching inquiry which intensifies political struggles and methodological debates as part and parcel of the pursuit of equity in knowledge and in social life.

To adopt the dictum that political science has to do with closed definitions, impoverished meanings, passive human actors, functions and interests, who gets what, when, and how, interest group articulation, inputs, outputs, managerial techniques and game theory scenarios, is to forsake the authentic heart and soul of politics and political contexts as couched in our resonant conceptual language—the language of justice, freedom, liberty, peace, exploitation, equality, liberation, community, the polity. Our long and turbulent history of politics and political discourse is punctuated, as is all history, with ennobling visions of great minds and ignoble machinations of tyrants and petty sycophants, with heroism and cowardice, the grandeur of the high and mighty and the stoic, mute suffering of the oppressed. The vision of politics I here recall predates its taming under the banner of value-free social science: sometimes bogus, always boring. Feminist political scholars can perform no greater service than to move beyond mainstream constrictions by tapping some of the verve, audacity, and pathos of our shared political tradition. One place to begin is with Jean-Jacques Rousseau's resounding declaration: "Those who wish to separate politics from morals will never understand either."

Notes

Originally published in Julia A. Sherman and Evelyn T. Beck, eds., *The Prism of Sex: Essays in the Sociology of Knowledge.* © 1979. (Madison: University of Wisconsin Press). Reprinted by permission.

1. William E. Connolly, "Theoretical Self-Consciousness," *Polity* 6 (fall 1973): 5–25, passim. A perspective in politics is analogous to a paradigm in scientific inquiry—an "ideal of the natural order."

2. Ibid., 13.

3. Ibid., 25.

4. Behavioralists, oversimply but not inaccurately, hold that the only valid data of political analysis is observable behavior. Behavioralism is a variation on the theme of epistemological positivism. For positivists all true knowledge is based on positive, observable facts or data given to the senses. See David Easton, "The Current Meaning

of 'Behavioralism' in Political Science," in *The Limits of Behavioralism in Political Science*, ed. J. C. Charlesworth (Philadelphia: American Academy of Political and Social Science, 1962), 5. After reading Easton's piece, turn to Alasdair MacIntyre's pithy critique of the fallacies involved in the quest for lawlike explanation as part of a general theory of politics, "Is a Science of Comparative Politics Possible?" in his collection *Against the Self-Images of the Age* (New York: Schocken Books, 1967), 222–79. See also Connolly, "Theoretical Self-Consciousness," and two seminal critical essays by Charles Taylor, "Interpretation and the Sciences of Man," *Review of Metaphysics* 26 (1971): 4–51, and "Neutrality in Political Science," in *Philosophy, Politics, and Society*, ed. Peter Laslett and W. G. Runciman, 3d ser. (Oxford: Blackwell, 1967), 25–57. For studies which exemplify the genre I am criticizing, turn to any current issue of the *American Political Science Review*, where examples abound.

5. Taylor, "Neutrality in Political Science," 25–27.

6. Ellen Meiksins Wood, *Mind and Politics* (Berkeley: University of California Press, 1972), 4.

7. Ibid.

8. Steven Lukes, *Individualism* (New York: Harper and Row, 1973), 73.

9. James Glass, "Schizophrenia and Perception: A Critique of the Liberal Theory of Externality," *Inquiry* 5 (1972): 116.

10. Robert Paul Wolff, *The Poverty of Liberalism* (Boston: Beacon Press, 1969), 197.

11. David M. Rasmussen, "Between Autonomy and Sociality," *Cultural Hermeneutics* 1 (1973): 8–10.

12. Lukes, *Individualism*, p. 116. Lukes's exposition of methodological individualism serves as a critique of much contemporary behaviorist and behavioralist political science. Methodological individualists can incorporate only individual predicates, which by definition have "minimal social reference," into their logic of explanation.

13. Norman Malcolm, *Problems of Mind: Descartes to Wittgenstein* (London: Allen and Unwin, 1972), 2–16 passim. In the view of empiricist philosophers of mind we can never be certain that minds other than our own exist, although we can make arguments for their existence from analogy.

14. Cf. Wood, *Mind and Politics*, 182–85. For an articulation and defense of lawlike generalizations in political and social life, see Carl G. Hempel, "The Function of General Laws in History," *Journal of Philosophy* 39 (1942): 37–48. See also the critiques by MacIntyre, Connolly, and Taylor already cited.

15. The reaction of mainstream political scientists to the student activism of the 1960s ran from rather condescending chiding to hysterical condemnation—with such notable exceptions as Sheldon Wolin at Berkeley. The volume by Bernard Crick cited later in this essay contains a reprimand and a warning in the matter of student politics.

16. Quoted in Sheldon Wolin, *Politics and Experience* (Boston: Little, Brown, 1970), 127.

17. T. D. Weldon, *The Vocabulary of Politics* (Baltimore: Penguin Books, 1953), 148. Physicists in our post-Heisenberg age would be bemused at Weldon's outmoded misconceptions concerning the nature of "hard" science.

18. See Connolly, "Theoretical Self-Consciousness," as well as his *Terms of Political Discourse* (Lexington, Mass.: D. C. Heath, 1974), for a full and rigorous articulation of the depth connections between explanatory theories, test procedures, and normative implications.

19. Lukes, *Individualism,* 166ff.

20. Taylor, "Interpretation and Sciences of Man," 33.

21. Connolly, "Theoretical Self-Consciousness," 11.

22. Julius Kovesi, *Moral Notions* (London: Routledge and Kegan Paul, 1967). But see, for example, David Easton's insistence, in *The Political System* (New York: Knopf, 1967), 221, that facts and values "are logically heterogeneous. . . . The moral aspect of a proposition, however, expresses only the emotional responses of an individual to a state of real or presumed facts."

23. Kovesi, *Moral Notions,* 151–52, 156.

24. Ibid., 151.

25. Ibid., 63.

26. Hannah Arendt, *The Human Condition* (Chicago: University of Chicago Press, 1972), 145–46 n. 8.

27. Alexis de Tocqueville, *Democracy in America,* ed. Richard D. Heffner (New York: Vintage Books, 1956), 217–18.

28. Karl Marx, *Capital,* vol. 1, ed. Frederick Engels (New York: International Publishers, 1975), 265.

29. Kovesi, *Moral Notions,* 161.

30. Easton, *The Political System,* 226.

31. See W. H. Hudson, *Modern Moral Philosophy* (Garden City, N.Y.: Doubleday, 1970); especially helpful is sec. 3 of this book, containing "Stevenson's Account of Emotivism," 121–25. Kovesi's *Moral Notions* is a powerful work, which articulates a nonemotivist account of moral notions. Kurt Baier, "The Moral Point of View," in *The Definition of Morality,* ed. G. Wallace and A. D. M. Walker (London: 1970), 188–210, is worth reading, as is Bernard Williams, *Utilitarianism: For and Against* (Cambridge: Cambridge University Press, 1973), esp. 77–150.

32. Quoted in Hudson, *Modern Moral Philosophy,* 125. Wolff, in *The Poverty of Liberalism,* 90, argues that the identification of goals with feelings and means with reason leads to that "much-celebrated value neutrality with which modern liberal social scientists emasculate their research. They are unable, for example, to see that a society which fails even to set itself certain social goals . . . is to that extent an *irrational* society. Naturally, since they cannot see this fact, they cannot undertake as social scientists to explain it. Hence, they remain at the level of predicting variations in public preferences among toothpastes of presidential candidates."

33. See Malcolm's *Problems of Mind,* especially his section on logical behavioralism, 80–103.

34. Read Stuart Hampshire, *Thought and Action* (New York: Vintage Books, 1959), particularly chap. 4, "Criticism and Regret."

35. Taylor, "Interpretation and Sciences of Man," 21.

36. Harold Lasswell, *Politics: Who Gets What, When, How* (New York: Meridian Books, 1958), 13. Emphasis mine.

37. Bernard Crick, *In Defence of Politics* (Baltimore: Penguin Books, 1964), 21. As Christian Bay observes, the view that politics is a system of rules for facilitating peaceful battles between competing private interests is "professedly conservative." Bay, "Politics and Pseudopolitics: A Critical Evaluation of Some Behavioral Literature," *American Political Science Review* 59 (May 1965): 40.

38. Seymour Martin Lipset, *Political Man: The Social Bases of Politics* (Garden City, N.Y.: Doubleday, 1963), 839.

39. Ibid., 216–17.

40. Ibid., 14. Lipset's countermodel to our "healthy" apathy is the highly politicized, dangerously unstable Weimar Germany prior to the Nazi takeover. The Germans had very high levels of political participation, he appears to argue, and what happened? They got Hitler. Lipset provides no consideration of the vagaries of German history, including the fact that the Germans had no tradition of democratic self-rule; nor does he discuss the disastrous nature of the post–World War I period, in which Germany faced runaway inflation coupled with depression, enormous war debts, and the official burden of guilt for the war itself. Yet Lipset's abstract and ahistorical reference to Germany of the 1930s is supposed to convince mid-twentieth-century Americans that the price of high political participation is volatility at best, a Hitler at worst.

41. Ibid., 27.

42. Peter Bachrach and Morton S. Baratz, "Two Faces of Power," *American Political Science Review* 56 (December 1962): 948–49.

43. See William E. Connolly, ed., *The Bias of Pluralism* (New York: Atherton, 1969), for a series of critiques on pluralistic theory.

44. Quoted from Hervert Leonidas Hart, *Women's Suffrage and National Danger: A Plea for the Ascendancy of Man* (London: Alexander and Shepheard, 1889), 118.

45. Alexander Passerin d'Entrèves, *The Notion of the State* (Oxford: Oxford University Press, 1967), 141. D'Entrèves points out that the word *authority* derives from the Latin word meaning "to augment" and posits the notion of possession of a special qualification which authorizes whoever is invested with it to exercise a particular power or right.

3

Arendt's "Truth and Politics"

In order for the truth to be told, it must be recognized. It was Hannah Arendt's contention that politics was a sphere of human activity peculiarly dependent upon truth. This truth she distinguished from the "relentless logic" of a Thomas Hobbes, who was able to drive his argument precisely where he wanted it to go, even to the most absurd conclusion. Hobbes embraced a system that he could put on automatic pilot, so to speak. As well, Arendt insisted, anyone who understands "political action in terms of the means-end category" will too easily come to the "conclusion that lying can very well serve to establish or safeguard the conditions for the search after truth." Arendt herself resisted means-end argument and repudiated the notion that, to achieve a political end or aim, truth may be sacrificed in the name of other values. She knew that an "amazing amount of lies" were used in political controversies. It was this latter recognition that spurred her own rueful commentary.

I will concentrate on two themes. First, how do we come to recognize the truth, and how do we tell this truth once it is recognized? Is the truth whatever we claim it to be, based upon how we have described or redescribed an event? Second, I will question the adage that truth must be told "even should the heavens fall" and ponder how Arendt would respond. Let me here note that Arendt's essay, "Truth and Politics," on which I will rely, was her reaction to the controversy surrounding the publication of her book *Eichmann in Jerusalem*. That book had been the occasion for a firestorm of rebuke and even condemnation. Arendt was accused of insufficient sympathy for the victims of Nazi genocide because she represented Adolf Eichmann as a diminished limited figure—a cog in the machinery that reduced evil to a banality rather than a seductive voluptuary of evil—and because she insisted on "telling the truth" about the role of Jewish councils in facilitating the Nazi policy of rounding up and transporting Jews to death camps.

"Without Jewish help in administrative and police work—the final rounding up of Jews in Berlin was, as I have mentioned, done entirely by Jewish
police—there would have been either complete chaos or an impossibly severe drain on German manpower. . . . this role of the Jewish leaders in the
destruction of their own people is undoubtedly the darkest chapter of the
whole dark story" (117). Arendt was told by her critics that this claim was
either not true, or not true in the way she claimed, or that it was a truth that
should not be told because it would embolden the forces of evil and undermine the forces of good.*

How did she respond? She began by insisting that there are truths that
can and must be recognized and that these truths are not inherently ambiguous. She knew that truths acquire political import by "being placed in an
interpretive context." But the truth itself has the status of "facts and events,"
and these "constitute the very texture of the political realm" (231). These
facts and events are fragile things—far more fragile than "axioms" and "theories"—because they occur in the "field of the ever-changing affairs of men, in
whose flux there is nothing more permanent than the admittedly relative
permanence of the human mind's structure." Facts can be lost, and once
they are lost they cannot be brought back. Facts and their particular truth are
the purview of the citizen. The philosopher, by contrast, has bigger fish to
fry: he or she distinguishes truth of the philosophic sort from a lower order
of utterances or claims, namely, opinion. In this sense, philosophy since
Plato has often constituted a powerful antipolitics, a concern with the one.
But politics has to do with the life of the many, or "life in the plural," as
Arendt calls it, and it is this plurality that must tend to "factual truth." Yet we
find factual truth under incessant assault "if it happens to oppose a given
group's profit or pleasure" (236).

For Arendt there is such a thing as a historical record. We are not permitted to "rearrange the facts" in order that they might better comport with our
own perspectives. She cites Clemenceau who, when asked what future generations would say about responsibility for the outbreak of World War I,
replied that he wasn't sure how the war guilt question would finally be
ironed out. "But I know for certain that they will not say Belgium invaded
Germany." This stubborn fact—"brutally elementary data," Arendt calls it—
will remain; if it is destroyed, much more will have been lost than this one
forlorn fact: a whole political world will be forfeit. For at the sad moment
when a power monopoly can eliminate from the record "the fact that on the

*Note that I am not myself adjudicating whether Arendt situates the role of the Jewish councils in a
manner beyond dispute; rather, I am interested in her response as it bears on truth.

night of August 4, 1914, German troops crossed the frontier of Belgium," at that moment "power interests" will have triumphed over, and utterly shut down, a political sphere of opinion, a public world of freedom.

What, then, would Arendt make of the claim in contemporary discourse that anything can be "redescribed" in order to make it seem "good" or appear to be "true"? The fragility here alluded to is not so much that factual truths can be ignored or suppressed but, rather, the epistemological claim that factual truths are themselves pretty much up for grabs, almost wholly subjectivist. This is a development Arendt would lament. If "simple factual truths are not accepted," she wrote, "the suspicion arises that it may be in the nature of the political realm to deny or pervert truth of every kind, as though men were unable to come to terms with its unyielding, blatant, unpersuasive stubbornness" (237). Factual truth is "always related to other people, it concerns events and circumstances in which many are involved; it is established by witnesses and depends upon testimony; it exists only to the extent that it is spoken about, even if it occurs in the domain of privacy. It is political by nature" (238). Indeed, freedom of opinion itself is a farce unless "the facts themselves are not in dispute."

To those who claim we establish truths through the terms we use to describe or to redescribe, Arendt's insistence on the stubborn autonomy of truths, of a historical record, would seem naive at best. Resolving this dispute requires taking a good, hard look at the issues. My example will be drawn from an exchange I had with Professor Richard Rorty. In an essay called, "Don't Be Cruel: Reflections on Rortyian Liberalism" (reprinted in this book as Chap. 20), I took Rorty to task on a number of fronts, based on one fundamental disagreement. Rorty has a tendency to argue along these lines: Either you are a "liberal ironist" or you are an essentialist or a foundationalist. Debunking foundationalism, Rorty opts for an alternative cast as wholly contingent, utterly historicist, nominalist "through and through" or "all the way down." My riposte is that one can reject the correspondence theory of truth without opting for the view that truth is solely a property of "linguistic entities." For Rorty, the truths we are deeded from the past emerge from the fact that "Europe gradually lost the habit of using certain words and gradually gained the habit of using others." His example of dramatic redescription is the French Revolution, which changed the way people described things "almost overnight." (The "whole vocabulary of social relations" is the way he puts it.) This permits him to ignore what Arendt finds absolutely essential to establishing historic truth: eyewitnesses, testimony, activities of people among people—for truth is not an isolated "fact" but a "fact" that becomes such only in a dialogic realm of plurality.

The truth of the Terror is overwhelmingly established by historic witness.

Some lamented it; some exulted in it. But no one denied it—not, at least, at the time. Isn't Rorty's ability to ignore this reality a way of excising or expunging truth of the Arendtian sort? I am not, of course, claiming that Rorty would endorse the cruelty of the Terror, but that, by ignoring it, he more easily preserves intact his own rather casual and lighthearted perspective. It is precisely when we make things easy for ourselves in this way that Arendt gets mightily perturbed, for we have then signed on with a project that is deadly for politics. Thus Rorty's claim that anything can be made to look good by being redescribed is genuinely troubling.

Rorty's way of describing omits certain stubborn facts—the terrible bloodshed, the Terror, with seventeen thousand guillotined between 1792 and 1794 alone. Rorty believes he needn't bother with this because the French Revolution moved things along pretty much the way they had to go, in a more "progressive" direction of the sort he endorses. Rorty ignores the mounds of bodies on which revolutionary politics rests. Paying attention to the stubborn realm of facts need not result in condemnation of the French Revolution, but it does require paying some attention to the cost in wrecked lives and institutions. Rorty doesn't believe he need acknowledge these realities. But Arendt, of course, would insist that one must attend, for if one does not one buys into the "means-end" way of thinking that all too easily justifies horrendous present deeds in the name of a future good. Rorty takes this one step further: he ignores the horrendous in favor of marveling at the dramatic overturning of old vocabularies of description in favor of new ones. In "Don't Be Cruel," I quoted from a story that Albert Camus narrated in a 1946 speech. The tale exemplified a "crisis of world-dimensions, a crisis in human consciousness."

> In Greece, after an action by underground forces, a German officer is preparing to shoot three brothers he has taken as hostages. The old mother of the three begs for mercy and he consents to spare one of her sons, but on the condition that she herself designate which one. When she is unable to decide, the soldiers get ready to fire. At last she chooses the eldest, because he has a family dependent on him, but by the same token she condemns the two other sons, as the German officer intends.

I criticized Rorty's insistence that the story, which Camus recounted in order to reinforce the necessity for maintaining an ethical stance against evil, could be recast to make the German officer "look good." But, I argued, it is not possible to cleanse this story of its horror. Events of the sort Camus describes meet Arendt's criteria for a stubborn historical truth—they are related to other people, there is testimony and eyewitness.

Rorty, in response to my criticism, argues as follows: He says the German officer in question in the Camus story perhaps saw himself as a fine fellow, striving to become a counter-example to Nietzsche's slave morality. He and others of his sort scorned weakness. "Home on leave, the officer tells his friends the story of how he broke a Greek mother's heart. He tells it as an episode in the saga of German will gradually cleansing Europe, enforcing its distinction between the pure and noble races and the ignoble and despicable ones. His friends, hearing his story, are envious of the robustness of his moral stance; they secretly wonder if they themselves might not, at the last moment, have succumbed to weakness and sentimentality, might not have heard their own mother's sobs when the Greek mother was faced with her choice." Thus, in this way, to his comrades, the German officer redescribes what he has done as good. But does it follow that he has thereby established a truth, or the truth of that event? That is, might we not grant Rorty's point in a limited and circumscribed way—yes, an ardent Nazi might describe to other Nazis an event in a way that makes it seem "good"—but that that description not only does not exhaust the "truth" of the event but actually falsifies or obliterates it. Rorty has perhaps illustrated the fragility of truth by giving us an intimation of what it might have meant had the Nazis actually triumphed and set about destroying all eyewitnesses and testimony to events that did not square with their descriptions. But he has also evaded or excised the stubbornness of truth, as Arendt puts it.

The stubbornness is there in Camus's description, which is remarkable for its simple factuality. Rorty's imagined Nazi could use it himself by appending an additional sentence, perhaps along these lines. "In this way the steely courage of an unsentimental and elemental honor of the triumphal forces of the Third Reich enjoyed yet another victory over womanish sentiment." But the terrible truth embodied in the description remains. There is no way to describe this event without telling a story of how a mother, under compulsion, picks one of her sons for execution. That is, the truth of the story is in that description. My hunch is that if the Nazis had in fact triumphed, their likely move would have been to obliterate all such stories, along with the witnesses to events, rather than to preserve them intact as a catalogue of the glories of the triumph of the Third Reich. Why? Because even Nazis would realize that some stories cannot be satisfactorily and finally redescribed to make them look good. They cannot do this because try as hard as they might they cannot altogether obliterate the "element of coercion" Arendt detects in the truth. "Even God cannot cause two times two not to make four," she avers, citing Grotius.

Facts, then, are hateful to tyrants, "who rightly fear the competition of a coercive force they cannot monopolize. . . . Unwelcome opinion can be argued with, rejected, or compromised upon, but unwelcome facts possess an infuriating stubbornness that nothing can move except plain lies" (241). The redescription of the horrendous event I cited as an example, then, would not alter the horrible fact of coercing a mother to (in effect) execute a child. Would the view of the German officer imagined by Rorty count, then, as an opinion, or the representation of a political perspective, for Arendt? I doubt it. To be sure, Arendt insists that political thought is always "representative" and that the way one comes to form opinions is "by considering a given issue from different viewpoints, by making present to my mind the standpoints of those who are absent. . . . The more people's standpoints I have present in my mind while I am pondering a given issue, and the more I can imagine how I would feel and think if I were in their place, the stronger will be my capacity for representative thinking and the more valid my final conclusions, my opinion" (241). But because the Nazi opinion is one that aims to obliterate a political world, I doubt that Arendt would see its representation as central to the capacity for that "enlarged mentality" that alone enables us to make political judgments. Validity of opinion "depends upon free agreement and consent" and is "arrived at by discursive, representative thinking" and "communicated by means of persuasion and dissuasion." Is an opinion that spurns argument and consent to be taken into account in deciding whether an opinion is valid? Again, I doubt it. But this, however, is not the crux of my concern here, so I will just leave this matter dangling, so to speak, and move on to my second major concern: are we always obliged to tell the truth even should the heavens fall?

Arendt, following Kant, suggests that truth must be told if it is known. But she doesn't tackle directly the question of whether, in the interest of an abiding truth—the truth of a value under siege—one may not be obliged to tell a lie. (She suggests indirectly that, on the whole, she does not find this possibility compelling.) Here is what I have in mind. The concluding section in Dietrich Bonhoeffer's unfinished *Ethics* is an essay called "What Is Meant by 'Telling the Truth.'" The essay was prompted, in part, by Bonhoeffer's anguish over the lying and deception of which he was a part as a member of the anti-Nazi resistance. Bonhoeffer goes after Kant in severe terms, the Kant who insisted one must tell the truth to a murderer who has come to the door looking for one's friend, who is hidden on the premises, and whom the murderer aims to kill. For Bonhoeffer this makes of the truth teller a "fanatical devotee of truth who can make no allowance for human weaknesses; but, in fact, he is destroying the living truth between men." The truth, that is, of friendship and loyalty and courage.

But Bonhoeffer is no situationist. He is not a means-end thinker who believes "the truth" can be cut and trimmed to suit our immediate political purposes; rather, he aims precisely to preserve the preconditions within which factual truth can be recognized—a world in which its coercive force can be felt—and made a part of the clash of opinions central to politics. But if one lives in a world in which those preconditions have been utterly destroyed—and betraying a friend to a murderer aids and abets such destruction—then the most important task is to "discern the real," in Bonhoeffer's phrase, meaning that one must evaluate "what is to come" in an unflinching way, and act accordingly. Bonhoeffer calls for respecting the boundaries of realities of multiple institutions of social life—family, church, school, politics. Bonhoeffer gives an example: a zealous teacher asks "a child in front of the class whether it is true that his father often comes home drunk. It is true, but the child denies it" (367). The child denies it because to admit it is to expose his family to the interference of a zealous do-gooder. "The child's answer can indeed be called a lie; yet this lie contains more truth, that is to say, it is more in accordance with reality than would have been the case if the child had betrayed his father's weakness in front of the class." The fault here is the teacher's and his or her illegitimate prying in a public setting, not the child's: "Since the term lie is quite properly understood as meaning something which is quite simply and utterly wrong, it is perhaps unwise to generalize and extend the use of this term so that it can be applied to every statement which is formally untrue" (368). What Bonhoeffer is doing is alerting us to context and occasion—something quite different from the arbitrariness inherent in the view that anything and everything can be redescribed and that there is no truth to be found.

Arendt would, I think, be sympathetic to Bonhoeffer's case and claim. Truth and falsehood help to give us, in her words, our "bearings in the real world," but each is disturbingly contingent in the sense that things "could just as well have been otherwise." But once things have happened, they cannot be undone. The systematic attempt to falsify the past is what is politically deadly, not the lie of a child seeking to protect himself and his father, to spare them the shame of exposure before a class. The problem with many energetic "redescribers" is that they would treat the past as if it were the future—a realm of potentiality—and, in so doing, deprive the political realm of "one of its main stabilizing force[s]." That which is new emerges out of a ground of the "already happened." If we treat the past as if it were up for grabs, depending upon who had the power to redescribe, we create a cynical world in which either violence or persuasion can destroy truth.

Truths are always bound to be more or less unwelcome to political actors who want to move toward their goals unimpeded. But the truth-teller cannot permit this: he or she must insist that there is a stubborn reality not under our complete control. The "political function of the storyteller—historian or novelist—is to teach acceptance of things as they are." This is not an invitation to passivity but an injunction against ruthlessness. The stubborn truth-teller, outside the swirl of opinion, helps to show us that the sphere of politics is great but limited—it "does not encompass the whole of man's and the world's existence. It is limited by those things which men cannot change at will. And it is only by respecting its own borders that this realm, where we are free to act and to change, can remain intact, preserving its integrity and keeping its promises. Conceptually, we may call truth what we cannot change; metaphorically, it is the ground on which we stand and the sky that stretches above us" (264).

It is my sober assessment that the considerations Arendt here evokes are becoming more difficult to articulate because we (I mean here the industrial-democratic West; I mean particularly the United States) have to a great extent already succumbed to the view that truth and falsehood are meaningless in the political realm and because a "peculiar kind of cynicism" defined by Arendt as "an absolute refusal to believe in the truth of anything, no matter how well this truth may be established" is a widespread if not yet utterly triumphant position. But we are headed down that path. I hope I am wrong in this. I fear I am not.

Prepared for the Prague Colloquium on Political Philosophy, July 4–6, 1994.

T W O

Political Languages,

Political Realities

Many of the most vexing problems political theorists in the last half of the twentieth century have faced are how to sort out the relationship between the thoughts we think, the words we use, and the actions we undertake. Over the years I have been of several (related) minds on this subject, and the six essays here gathered offer a sense of the range of my concerns. I do not think language *creates* the world. There *is* a there there. But language is importantly constitutive of the world as we come to know it. We cannot capture everything we think and everything we think we know in words. We cannot carpet the world with words. But words are our entry point into worlds. The repertoire of words available to us, as persons and as citizens, helps to forge and to shape our possibilities for action and reaction in the world. It's a fascinating business. Hannah Arendt credits Augustine with "discovering" the faculty of "the will." He named it; described its workings; helped us to see its inevitability. Was there no "willing" before Augustine's great works? Surely that would be going too far. But after his works, the will as a philosophical problem and a human faculty was forever before us; it had become part of our linguistic and moral inheritance. Language carries us into worlds and takes us out of them.

My ire with the writer Doris Lessing, in a 1980 essay on the then-state of her fiction (she has, of course, written much since, but I have not written more on her), lay in her departure from our world, including the world she had so determinedly created in fiction, for intergalactic scenarios from which language had simply been eliminated. Lessing's own search for "cosmic harmony" has to eliminate language as a source of division. We must go back behind the back of the Tower of Babel. In "Presidential Voice," I find myself testing the waters of the so-called rhetorical turn, and the way it invited us to see ourselves in a rhetorical world and to see the rhetor and his audience as equally composing a text. This probably goes a bit too far, but there is an insight here worth preserving. That insight also lies at the heart of my discussions of feminist political rhetoric and feminism and politics. A longstanding worry of mine, posed as a question, goes like this: What are the performative requirements and possibilities of *this* way of looking at the world? What are we called upon to do? How are we called upon to act? Would we want to actually live in the world this rhetoric advances? In "Sovereignty, Identity, and Sacrifice," this theme, building on my book *Women and War*, gets played out against the backdrop of war and the ways in which we have (so to speak) sacralized sacrifice. Criticizing the will-to-sacrifice, I nonetheless leave the door open to following a course of suffering. The reader will discern the distinction between these.

4

The Relationship
between Political Language
and Political Reality

Albert Camus's ironic judge-penitent, Jean-Baptiste Clemence, remarks to his compatriot in the seedy bar Mexico City, in a shadowy district of Amsterdam, the mist rising off the canals, the fog rolling in, cheap gin the only source of warmth, "Somebody has to have the last word. Otherwise, every reason can be answered with another one and there would never be an end to it. Power, on the other hand, settles everything. It took time, but we finally realized that. For instance, you must have noticed that our old Europe at last philosophizes in the right way. We no longer say as in simple times: 'This is the way I think. What are your objections?' We have become lucid. For the dialogue we have substituted the communiqué: 'This is the truth,' we say. You can discuss it as much as you want; we aren't interested. But in a few years there'll be the police who will show you we are right."

Now this is still an imperfect method of control—the enforcers are clearly identified and the coercion is too obvious. Not so in Orwell's *1984*. As Syme, the chilling destroyer of language proclaims: "It's a beautiful thing, the destruction of words." Speaking to Orwell's protagonist, Winston Smith, Syme continues: "Don't you see that the whole aim of Newspeak is to narrow the range of thought. In the end we shall make thoughtcrime literally impossible, because there will be no words in which to express it. Every concept that can ever be needed will be expressed by exactly *one* word, with its meaning rigidly defined and all its subsidiary meanings rubbed out and forgotten. . . . Every year fewer and fewer words, and the range of consciousness always a little smaller. Even now, of course, there's no reason or excuse for committing thoughtcrime. It's merely a question of self-discipline, reality control. But in the end there won't be any need even for that. The Revolution will be complete when the language is perfect."

What habits of mind, what epistemological and political commitments, what structural features of our contemporary world promote the ends of Orwell's Syme, working to narrow the range of thought, oversimplifying and making crude our moral sensibilities and our capacities to perceive reality? I shall focus on a range of possible answers identified by Lasswell or Orwell or exemplified, perhaps, unwittingly in the work of each, beginning with the problem of the total state as the pursuit of war by other means.

On the totalitarian potentialities, even tendencies, of the modern state Orwell and Harold Lasswell concur. Both identified forces at work that undermine democracy. In his essay "The Garrison State and Specialists on Violence," Lasswell speaks of a world in which "the specialists on violence are the most powerful group in society" and evokes the image of a highly mobilized state with compulsory labor groups, surveillance, propaganda, manipulation of symbols, a controlled press, plebiscitary voting, the abolition of parties or a one-party system, and incessant pumping up of war scares to help maintain the edifice intact. The contraband text by Emmanuel Goldstein, "Enemy of the People" in "Oceania," argues that war, by becoming continuous, has fundamentally changed its character: that war is the state's most important product and the state must work to shore up and perfect "the mentality appropriate to a state of war. . . . The very word war, therefore, has become misleading. It would probably be accurate to say that by becoming continuous war has ceased to exist": that is the theory and practice of oligarchical collectivism as articulated by Goldstein.

War, of course, has always been one of the state's prime functions and prerogatives. But something has changed—and not for the better. We must look, it seems, not only to the compulsions of international relations and dictated ways of viewing them if we are to understand the phenomenon of "false peace," of a state continuously armed to the teeth and working up abstract hatred against an abstract enemy, but to the ordering of modern, technocratic statist societies themselves. Dulled by the accretion of "truths" and necessities that help us talk ourselves into war, situated inside a world of armed peace, Norman Mailer's claim in 1948 that "the ultimate purpose" of modern society is the continuation of the army by other means seems not all that far-fetched. Michel Foucault, too, argues that "politics" has been "conceived as a continuation, if not exactly and directly of war, at least of the military model as a fundamental means of preventing civil disorder. Politics sought to implement the mechanism of the perfect army, of the disciplined mass, of the docile, useful troop," and so on. And political life—even in democracies—can become a mimesis of warlike struggle, whether, Orwell argues, through talk of class enemies or visions of apocalyptic struggle with promised, or threatened, eschatological endings. Irving Howe, in an essay entitled "1984: Enigmas of Power," seems right—in the decades since Orwell wrote, "we have gone a long way toward domesticating the idea of the total state . . . to the point where it now seems just one among a number of options."

Harold Lasswell, however, and despite his sketch of the garrison state, holds onto a thin strand of hope. The "friend of democracy," he writes, "views the emergence of the garrison state with repugnance and apprehension." However—and it is a fairly booming "however"—should the garrison state become unavoidable, "the friend of democracy will seek to conserve as many values as possible within the general framework of the new society." And what are the democratic values that might be preserved, if fitfully? Lasswell looks to the mobilization of the populace imbedded in the notion of the garrison state. By requiring the participation of all "with the everpresent exception of the lowest strata," the garrison state is compatible with democratic respect for human dignity—understood as the need and desire to make some contribution to the overall good of the order. Because Lasswell views democracy in formalist terms—as the authorization of majority participation—he need not plunge himself into the darkness of Orwell's forebodings. During the course of his recent presidential campaign, Jesse Jackson was fond of saying, "Under slavery everybody had a job"—the point being that work itself, contributing to the maintenance of the order, does not suffice if our concern is either democracy or human dignity in any substantive sense. Here Lasswell's essentially instrumentalist vision of politics undermines his humane concern with individuals and democracy.

Lasswell wants government to be a science and holds up the relation that "medicine has to biology" as a model for the relation political science should enjoy with democracy. Leaving aside the problems with the medical metaphor, what is vexing about Lasswell's triumphalist vision of political science is, in large part, its self-assured search for "the more perfect instrumentation." He calls for a "permanent corps of research assistants" to busy themselves making more useable instruments of democratic "control"—the two terms in tandem constituting an oxymoron from Orwell's standpoint.

The relation of political language to political reality, in Lasswell's view, is that of a to-be-made-more-perfect instrument. On this Lasswell leaves no doubt—no doubt at all. "Language is an instrumental power" just as power itself is instrumentally defined. We must use language to do away with language—with ambiguous language that derails attempts to "postulate definitions" and to articulate "operational rules." Alas, there is nothing in this vision of language to forestall the eventuality Lasswell himself dreads but believes we must one day live with—the garrison state. Indeed, Lasswell—and Orwell, too, must share in this criticism—failed to appreciate the teleology of control built into the very idea of unchecked, or nearly so, technological "progress" itself. Improving capabilities for prognosis, planning, and direction of the civilization of productivity, calling for technological mastery of technological problems, many thinkers and activists who see themselves as good democrats nonetheless endorse forces that assail democracy over the long run by deepening and legitimating the spirit of calculation and exploitation inherent in the scientistic, instrumentally rationalist world-view.

Orwell had some intimations along these lines. For example, he found in state encouragement of science an effort to put science "in the service of ideas appropriate to the Stone Age." But surely this is misconstrued. Science, technology, and the language of technologese are put at the service of imperatives that could arise only within a world that viewed others—human beings, the natural world, all of creation—as potentially exploitable resources: this is a complex of ideas that received fullest expression only in modernity, not some "Stone Age." There are specific structural features at work in any centralized, highly developed, and concentrated economy: as sketched by Johan Strasser in an essay "1984: Decade of the Experts?" these include acceleration of centralization in the political system; opening up more and more segments of life to the market through complex strategies; working more areas of life into the grid of the technological apparatus; promoting, in turn, a political agenda that widens daily the gulf between "experts" who know how to keep the whole thing going—or that is their claim to legitimate authority and to legitimate *their* authority—and "laypersons" who cannot understand and thus have no substantive say over the course of events. When Lasswell defined and reduced *homo politicus* to a *homo psychologicus* whose distinctive mark is the rationalization of private motives and their displacement onto public objects; when he located the demand for power in a kind of insatiable longing; and, more importantly, when he called for his own "reign of experts," he tended to give politics over to specifically antidemocratic forces at work among us.

Orwell is a more complicated case. I will spend the remainder of my allotted time interpreting those complexities, coming round explicitly to the relation of political language to political reality—with war as the reference point. Orwell calls for what one critic has labeled a "doctrine of plain representation" as a compelling way to combat the debasement of language, such debasement being one part of a wider deformation of social and political life. Orwell shares with Lasswell a hankering after linguistic simplicity and designativist clarity. He, too, would do away with "meaningless words"—"romantic, values, sentimental, natural" being among his candidates for the linguistic garbage heap. But a difference between the two—and an important one—is the fact that in Orwell this imperative exists side by side with the expressionist demands of an aesthetic of writing that he defended against any and all of its detractors. Language, for Orwell, must be up to the task of "thick description"; the writer must have at his or her command words powerful and evocative enough to convey often unpleasant truths.

Orwell notes explicitly an epistemological problem with totalitarian-ism—with the world of the absolute state stripped of any autonomous ref-erence groups and points of shared meaning. The "shared" and "groups" essential for control in Oceania require that nothing be available as a mea-suring rod or corrective compass outside the wholly subjectivist prison of the human mind. The individual *must* believe what he or she is told, not simply because the state controls all information, but because language—Ingsoc as presage to Newspeak perfection in this regard—makes impossible "any description of, debate about any kind of difference." Doublethink, as Mark Crispin Miller notes in "The Fate of *1984*," "makes difference abso-lutely inconceivable, by subsuming every contradiction, every possible ex-ception or disproof, into its own incontrovertible logic." Just as party uni-forms make all bodies indistinct, language eliminates distinctions. Michael Walzer speaks of "mental habits proper to the devotees of Ingsoc" that "make all other modes of thought impossible"—not just explicit politically oppositional thought "but irony, sarcasm, parody, doubt." Social control brings about linguistic control, perfects social control, and so on.

Even these comments understate the epistemological problem of the total state and the "carceral" society as Orwell unfolds it in *1984*. He asks us to imagine—for, he suggests, it is not that wild a conjecture—a world in which memories no longer constitute a form of knowledge. "If the Party could thrust its hand into the past and say of this or that event, it never happened—that, surely, was more terrifying than mere torture and death. . . . He, Winston Smith, knew that Oceania had been in alliance with Eurasia as short as four years ago. But where did that knowledge exist? Only in his own consciousness." Reality control, it was called, doublethink. Everything is alterable. Nothing lasts. You can prove nothing. The one unmistakable piece of documentary proof of the falsification of a historic fact Winston Smith had held in his hands had disappeared down the memory hole. "Everything faded away into a shadow-world in which even the date of the year became uncertain."

It is not merely the validity of individual experience that comes under savage and systematic assault but "the very existence of external reality." For if both past and the external world "exist only in the mind," and if the mind itself is controllable—what then? What then indeed. No complex "fact" or event or process or relation is self-evident. We require a "public realm in which evidence can be debated and reproduced," argues Bernard Avishai. Without standards of comparison, cut off from the past, all things mutable, nothing is really real.

Just as particular understandings are dependent upon a contextual and social space, a realm of appearance and revelations where we can get out of ourselves, so particular loyalties and their possibility are dependent upon similar social "space." Knowledge is a threat and hence becomes impossible in *1984,* and the same fate awaits *any* concrete commitment and loyalty— whether to an ideal, an association, a family member, a friend, or a religious belief—and must perforce be destroyed. It is the love of one person that poses the greatest threat to Oceania's order just as the attack upon the family is always an undertaking of the absolute state and totalitarian society. Cut off from bonds that help us to hold our "selves" intact, we are more readily ground down to become the generic mulch of the order. Neither a public realm, with space for debate and appearance and testing of complex truths, nor a private realm of lively, concrete individualities can exist in Oceania.

Undifferentiated loyalty and those indistinct prepackaged shadows that pass for reality—that is the terrifying vision Orwell presents. Worst of all, he suggests not only that we are closer to this world than we like to think but that totalitarian ideas have "taken root in the minds of intellectuals everywhere"—that modern intellectual culture pushes toward oppressive or- thodoxies. Orwell's particular targets were the "friends of totalitarianism," whether of left or right, in his own country who leapt from a wholesale relativization of truth—we don't really know what's happening anyhow so we can't criticize—to the feckless conclusion that "a big lie is no worse than a little lie." Fearful of offending the public opinion within his own group, the intellectual lives in dread of being tagged with a label—reactionary or bour- geois or antiprogressive—and trims his thought and words energetically in order to conform and stay in good graces with the group. Undifferentiated loyalty to Big Brother is a magnification of this dynamic, among other things.

How does Orwell justify these sober reflections? He points to the debase- ment of political speech, the euphemisms, the question begging, much of it put out and promoted by a pseudo-intelligentsia—much of it war-related, entering in full force in time of war and becoming a more generalized habit of mind in peace. For example, "defenseless villages are bombarded from the air, the inhabitants driven out into the countryside, the cattle are machine- gunned, the huts set on fire with incendiary bullets: this is called *pacifica- tion.*" We can proliferate examples. Acid rain becomes "poorly buffered pre- cipitation." Or, during the Three Mile Island incident, the inability of atomic energy commissioners to admit what they were really talking about and what the real possibilities were is striking. As dissected in Wendell Berry's brilliant discussion in *Standing By Words,* we find the commissioners speaking tech- nologese and throwing out all sorts of metaphors about horse races—for example: "Do we lose the horse race or do we win the horse race?"—when what they were talking about was a meltdown and a terrible danger to many people. Committed to the absurdity of emergency planning, of a "controlled catastrophe," a group of intelligent, concerned men could not admit that things were not really under control and that disaster was but a hair's breadth away.

One by now habitual way of thinking and writing and speaking that deepens the forces of control and unfreedom of which Orwell warned might be called "disassociated abstractedness." At present, Hannah Arendt argues in *On Violence,* hundreds of think tanks, universities, and government bureaucracies support the efforts of "scientifically minded brain trusters" who should be criticized not because they are thinking the unthinkable but because "they do not *think* at all." Hyper-rationalism and the fetish of control have been turned upside down—if one can but see what is going on—and have become unreason, guaranteeing in turn a diminished capacity to see and to act realistically.

The danger, Arendt argues, is this: A world of self-confirming theorems with its delimited and evasive language invites fantasies of control over events we do not have. This "scientization" of discourse in international relations, for example, eclipses the strengths classical realists could claim, including awareness of the intractability of events and a recognition that relations between and among states are necessarily alienated—foreign countries. But a corrupted language—corrupt because it can no longer make contact with its supposed object—reduces states and their relations to simulizable games. Consider the following depiction of Western Europe in the language of one strategic analyst—one dangerously removed from its putative discursive object: "Western Europe (like South Korea) amounts geographically to a peninsula projecting out from the Eurasian land mass from which large contingents of military force can emerge on relatively short notice to invade the peninsula." Western Europe having been reduced to an undifferentiated, manageable piece of territory, "it" becomes theoretically expendable, or usable, in the plans that follow.

"If truth is the main casualty in war, ambiguity is another," notes Paul Fussell, and one of the legacies of war is a "habit of simple distinction, simplification, and opposition." Mobilized language, wartime's rhetoric of binary deadlock, may persist and do much of our thinking for us. The absorption of politics by the language and imperatives of war becomes a permanent rhetorical condition. One basic task of a state at war is to portray the enemy in terms as absolute and abstract as possible in order to distinguish as sharply as possible the act of killing from the act of murder. It is always "the enemy," a pseudo-concrete universal. This moral absolutism is constituted through language: there is no other way to do it. We are invited to hate without limit and told, in time of war, that we are good citizens for doing so.

Paradoxically, at one time war fighting served to deconstruct abstracted war rhetoric as soldiers rediscovered the concrete in tragic and terrifying ways. For example: Erich Maria Remarque's protagonist in *All Quiet on the Western Front* bayonets a frightened French soldier who has leapt into the trench beside him in a panic, seeking refuge. Four agonizing hours later the Frenchman dies and when he has died, Remarque's hero, his capacity to perceive and to judge concretely restored, speaks to the man he has killed: "Comrade, I did not want to kill you. . . . But you were only an idea to me before, an abstraction that lived in my mind and called forth its appropriate response. It was that abstraction I stabbed." Because it is now possible for us to destroy "the enemy" without ever seeing him or her, abstract hatreds are less likely to rub up against concrete friction. We can remain on the plane of disassociated language. Orwell's Goldstein notes in *1984* that war was once a peculiar "safeguard of sanity" because particular wars could be won or lost and ruling classes could be held responsible. But this no longer holds as robustly—not in an era of continuous war, not in a twilight zone of covert operations. Certainly this horrific vision seems far from our reality, but Orwell warns us that the habits of mind that might help to bring this vision into sharper focus are already delineated in present reality.

Having warned us of what happens when words no longer have meaning and meaning itself is lost because a shared world is gone, what hope does Orwell offer to keep oppositional habits of mind and language alive? To sustain difference, to nourish individualities, to make possible the coming together of difference, one must use and cherish language that helps to promote democratic values. The writer must resist orthodoxies, of "whatever colour." The writer must point out corruptions in language and the use of morally deadening euphemisms. The writer must rejoice in the complex discriminations the English language makes possible—for the existence of such linguistic choices helps us to discover what we think as we write; helps us to become individualities ourselves. Winston Smith's opening words in his illicit journal, by signaling what *1984* has destroyed, remind us of what is required if freedom is to have any ongoing substantive meaning. "To the future or to the past," Smith writes shakily, "to a time when thought is free, when men are different from one another and do not live alone—to a time when truth exists and what is done cannot be undone: from the age of uniformity, from the age of solitude, from the age of Big Brother, from the age of doublethink—greetings!" Newspeak interdicted—in one word—"ownlife," meaning individualism and eccentricity.

Orwell would keep "ownlife" alive. Yet his own insistence that "good prose is like a window pane," his celebration of "a doctrine of plain representation," which has a "simple, noble, fundamentalist ring to it," in Roy

Harris's words, does not suffice to sustain Orwell's most dearly held imperatives and is an inadequate way to characterize his own greatest essays and reportage. Certainly it is to Orwell's everlasting credit that he raised in dramatic form a much "wider issue for any community . . . the question of our social responsibilities as language users." Yet Orwell himself distrusted words—not only words of "humbug" but words of strong emotion and transcendent possibility. He feared verbal persuasion—not simply or only coercive and manipulative uses of language. Mistrusting words as the means to connect us to meaning and to hold us "in reality," Orwell dwells on the dangers of concealment and misrepresentation.

But in his struggle for lucidity he oversimplifies. One cannot always, as he puts it, "call a spade a spade." Matters are usually not so simple. In fact, received linguistic distinctions may downplay or deny difference. One argument by feminists sensitive to language, for example, is that the presumably clear distinction between male-female, masculine-feminine, and so on, is not really so clear at all. This linguistic distinction may cover up real and important differences that fall through the net of received terms. But this point takes us down another track—to explicit consideration of contrasting theories of language. Oversimply, then, it must suffice to say that words are often murky, ambiguous, concealing—not because some chicanery is afoot, nor because the language user is thinking sloppily, but because reality does not, most of the time, lend itself to common sense representation. In his struggle against the abuse of language and the role of language in abusive politics, Orwell sometimes overstates both the desirability and the possibility of a limpid prose.

But he leaves us with unforgettable images—political portraits in prose that should frighten us—not into inaction but into vigilance. O'Brien says to the tortured and defeated Winston Smith: "If you want a picture of the future, imagine a boot stamping on a human face—forever." To condemn a pessimistic vision for its putative defeatism is, as Camus insisted, puerile. In an era when it is not so easy to distinguish the marvelous from the terrible because everything moves so quickly, having both feet on the ground is a surer guide to the terrain than having one's head in a cloud of linguistically dictated historic triumph. This Orwell understood and conveyed through language honed on the horrors of this century's history.

Presented at a plenary session honoring Harold Lasswell at the annual meeting of the American Political Science Association. Originally published in *PS: Political Science and Politics* 18 (Winter 1985). Reprinted by permission.

5

A Controversy

on Language and Politics:

The Post–*Golden Notebook*

Fiction of Doris Lessing

I think it's a true prophecy. . . . I believe the future is going to
be cataclysmic.

Doris Lessing, The Four-Gated City

Then I saw a new heaven and new earth; for the first heaven
and the first earth had passed away, the sea was no more.
And I saw the Holy City, new Jerusalem, coming down out of
heaven from God, prepared as a bride adorned for her
husband.

Revelations 21:1–2

Margaret Drabble dubs her "our Cassandra," a towering doyen of the Last
Days warning all who have ears to hear that the end is nigh. Drabble's characterization is apt, for with her post–*Golden Notebook* fiction Doris Lessing
has forsaken the ranks of mere writers and become a prophet. Through her
prose she first condemns the world—its politics, history, wars, calamities,
and blind human subjects—and then, with great narrative skill and power,
proceeds to wipe it out as a badly botched job. Lessing's repudiation of
history and the present prompts her to evoke strange new worlds, horrific
and wondrous, but unrecognizable as evolutionary outgrowths of contemporary reality; indeed, much of her appeal surely lies in her ability to fuse
the hideous and the fantastic. Apocalypse and utopia meld in her work: the
former paves the way for the latter. Lessing shares with other writers in the
prophetic genre an approach at once fantastical and acrimonious. Her retreat from politics and the novel of social realism into a realm in which she,
as a cosmic alchemist, transforms contemporary and future horrors into a
cosmic world without end, is a retreat with troubling artistic and political
implications. Lessing is not the first writer to grow thoroughly disenchanted

with her own epoch; nor is she alone in embracing an imperious yearning for totality, wholeness, an order and unity beyond the bustling messiness, confusing diversity, and ordinariness of everyday life. But as her contempt for the present and her eschatological zeal have grown in scope and breadth, her fiction has become increasingly remote and abstract, laced through with bitterness and residues of regret, bespeaking a view of life turned sour, the sourness of one who has tried the world and found it wanting.

One effect of her political and literary transformation is that the persona of Lessing herself has moved to the forefront as compelling characters have faded from her fiction. She and her preachments are ineluctably linked in the public mind. She has become as important as her work: is this not the way with our prophets? To become a Cassandra is to invite a response from one's audience which goes beyond discussions of symbolism, form, narrative, and structure. Because the prophet presumes to speak to us with divine or inspired guidance, prophetic utterances require a view of those being prophesied to different from that presumed by most works of fiction. The aim is not so much to interpret, to understand, or to evoke as to judge and to foretell. Likewise, the demand on the reader is not only that he be engaged and sympathetic but convinced and moved to convert. By altering the terms of the relation of writer to reader Lessing invites an aroused response, particularly from those who cannot share her vision.

Lessing's uneven but steady retreat from an engagement with her own time is most dramatic in her major post-*Notebook* novels: *The Four-Gated City* (1969), *Briefing for a Descent into Hell* (1971), *The Summer Before the Dark* (1973), and *The Memoirs of a Survivor* (1975). Themes and problems posed in these works, and adumbrated in *The Golden Notebook* (1962), include her view on human nature and the human condition, her understanding of human thought and emotion, her stance on language, and her position on questions of individual moral responsibility and historic agency.

But Lessing's millenarianism has seriously eroded her ability to evoke a coherent artistic vision, particularly of the world she rejects. That there is political import in all of this is clear. By embracing a future without politics, Lessing is required in effect to eliminate those passional, cantankerous human beings who engage with and against one another in history, through politics. She fails to distinguish between the unspeakable terror characteristic of times in our century when politics has been replaced by destructive raw force, and that purposive and potentially creative conflict and debate which is the very stuff of political life. Lessing, who yearns for unity, cannot abide the human diversity of purposes. This leads her to suggest that all conflict and dissension lead inevitably to divisive horror. Like the political philosopher who would create a polity without conflict, Lessing loses more than conflict in the process: she must simultaneously expunge from the world human beings as we know them.

Lessing's repudiation of politics is wholesale. Human history is for her an unbroken record of dissolution, terror, war, riots, breakdowns, devastations, "sudden eruptions of violent mass feeling, like red-hot lava, that destroys everything in its path,"[1] plots, conspiracies, disgust, chaos, annihilation, misery, despair, disease, madness. For her there are no transformative possibilities within history; thus no set of partial solutions or less-than-total responses can meet the dimensions of the apocalyptic reality she sees. Her response is to leap into utopian solutions. Those who either cannot or will not enter the realm of the *illuminati,* all those "blind" individuals who carry on as best they can, however modestly, in the face of calamity and breakdown, are treated to an occasionally mean-spirited dose of Lessing's condescension, like the poor fools who laughed as Noah built his ark.

A typical passage will illustrate the point. Lessing's views, here as elsewhere, are expressed primarily through the vehicle of her protagonists, often the novel's central characters. I am not making the facile presumption that Lessing and her fictional personae speak with a single, unified voice. But the weight of the internal textual evidence, together with Lessing's pronouncements in interviews, nonfictional essays, and speeches, lends credence to the view that there is more than a little of Lessing herself in the messages which are represented most powerfully, repeatedly, and preeminently in her fictional works. The passage, then, from *Memoirs of a Survivor:*

> Or what can one say about the innumerable citizens' groups that came into existence right up to the end, for any ethical or social purpose you could think of: to improve old-age pensions, at a time when money was giving way to barter; to supply vitamin tablets to school children; to provide a visiting service for household invalids; to arrange formal legal adoption for abandoned children; . . . *Farce. Spitting into a hurricane;* standing in front of a mirror to touch up one's face or straighten a tie as the house crashes around one; extending the relaxed accommodating hand of the Royal handshake to a barbarian.[2] [emphasis mine]

Lessing reduces the hapless citizens in a society coming apart at the seams to the level of nonthinking drones, creatures who are pitiful and whose attempts to keep up appearances and the regular activities of daily life are pointless. These unreflective human subjects do not realize that there are powerful external forces at work making "things happen" and that their own actions are hopeless. Indeed, they are not human at all but "objects" in the grip of a higher will. The prophet sees that which mere mortals cannot.

Lessing's lack of compassion toward ordinary folk who press ahead seems somewhat less severe if one considers that even those to whom she allows choices find themselves severely limited. Kate Brown, the protagonist of *The Summer Before the Dark,* comes to recognize that her months alone after several decades spent *en famille* lead ultimately to a conclusion that what she does with her hair is her only genuine choice. Earlier, too, Kate had thought that her physical appearance was her one arena of "conscious, deliberate" choice.[3] Later Kate sees even this as a delusion, a mere chimera, for it was "as if the rest of her—body, feet, even face, which was aging but amenable—belonged to everyone else. But her hair—no!" (273). Kate's resigned reaction to the recognition that her only choice is what to do with her tresses is, simply, "Isn't that extraordinary?" (274). The statement *is* extraordinary in how little it allows us to care about Kate and her fate, for it does nothing to make her a fully embodied person. Second, it is extraordinary to reduce what promises to become the painful struggle toward self-awareness to a concern with hair. Were Lessing a different sort of writer, one might see in all of this a kind of ironic commentary which criticizes the constriction of women's choices. But this is clearly not the case. Lessing's turgid humorlessness has often been noted and cannot be missed: we *are* in fact required to take seriously the culmination of Kate Brown's summer odyssey in her discovery that the graying locks are her "freedom." Kate assures us she intends to make other statements, "though I'm not sure what about" (274). But neither her conclusions nor her uncertainties earn our concern. How could a character who scarcely exists at all, by her own admission, engage us as great fictional characters do and must? Kate is a victim of Lessing's prophetic and political purposes, which demand less than robust and self-determining characters. She intends the evocation of a malaise in which nothing makes sense and everyone is in the grip of uncontrollable forces.

Kate shares with other Lessing characters, especially her women, a passive or reactive stance toward the world: they are beings to which, or through whom, things happen. In Kate's case a job falls fortuitously and unexpectedly into her lap with little effort on her part; a relationship with a younger man presents itself through no action of her own; a mysterious illness first lays her low and then mysteriously departs. The narrator-protagonist of *Memoirs of a Survivor* calls "waiting" her occupation. Other Lessing characters are invaded by alien forces or "walk into" ready-made personalities. In the post–nuclear holocaust world of *Four-Gated City,* Lessing depicts the infinite passivity of human mutants whose bodies are machinelike and whose minds are "nothing but a soft dark receptive intelligence,"[4] silent receivers and senders of unspoken messages. Her characters fall victim to ineffable, irrational, and powerful forces; and these forces—not self-reflective, passional persons—have real agency in Lessing's world. Her people wait to be used, for good or ill, and in general are not deluded about their ability to act and think autonomously. In *Four-Gated City,* for example, Mark Coldridge rejects Martha Quest's contention that much of the writing which grew out of World War II contained a genuine note of protest with these words: "I don't see protest. *Things happen*" (130). The exchange between Quest and Coldridge suggests that Lessing was still involved in an inner dialogue or debate and was as yet unwilling to embrace a thoroughgoing, deterministic, quasi-religious view of reality which required human passivity and wiped out individual agency. But "events" prove Coldridge correct, and the nihilism of "things happen" ultimately prevails.

The views of human nature voiced by several of Lessing's protagonists provide a good index to her political retreat and parallel novelistic transformation. These views are not noteworthy in themselves—indeed, they are quite ordinary and unexceptional—but significant in that they indicate the manner in which naive belief in unlimited human possibility can pave the way for later cynicism and despair. Lessing suggests that man is born good and with boundless potentialities. "Babies are born into this, what there is," one character laments. "A baby is born with infinite possibilities for being good. But there's no escaping it, it's like having to go down into a pit, a terrible dark blind pit, and you fight your way up and out."[5] The "pit" is life itself as lived among others in history. Lessing's "natural man" enjoys a fleeting moment in the sun but is soon tainted by the constraints of civilization, limitations indictable before the court of transcendence denied.

If children are born without guile and are potentially perfectable, with no inborn constraints or limiting conditions, what forces sully their ontological purity and undermine their infinite possibilities? Lessing first indicts language, as words divide and distinguish among phenomena, objects, and qualities: they split the idyllic oneness of the womb. We are all, she suggests, born twins with the dissimulation and destruction made necessary by the fact that in this vale of tears we all come to use words. Recall briefly Anna's terror in *Notebook:* "words lose their meaning suddenly. I find myself listening to a sentence, a phrase, a group of words, as if they are in a foreign language—the gap between what they are supposed to mean and what in fact they mean seems unbridgeable."[6] This refrain recurs fifty pages later: "words lose their meaning. I hear Jack and I talking—it seems the words come out from inside me, from some anonymous place—but they don't mean anything" (352). Anna's fearful obsession is voiced a third time: "I am increasingly afflicted by vertigo where words lose meaning. Words mean nothing. They have become, *when I think,* not the form into which experience is shaped, but a series of meaningless sounds, like nursery talk, and away to one side of experience" (476).

In *Briefing for a Descent into Hell,* the hero, Watkins, indicts education as a co-conspirator with language in the destruction of infantile innocence and "oneness" with the universe. Watkins condemns schools not so much because they are all too often places of barren, pompous solemnity and brittle conformism, of social *control,* but because in schools children are taught to use language, to put "labels" on feelings, states of mind, objects and things, "in short, to describe." Through this process, Watkins continues, children are deluded into believing that they have in fact "understood and experienced a feeling, state of mind, or accurately depicted an object." Foolish kids! Clearly, through the development of their human capacity for conceptualization through words, children are prepared for their roles as unseeing and ineffectual adults. In their adult lives they will believe that words and deeds have meaning, when in fact they only constrain recognition of the general unity of things and prevent awareness of those forces Lessing calls "it," which alone have causative influence on human history and events.

The novelist's repudiation of language, the medium through which she must convince us of her vision, is strange and requires an explanation. Lessing is not among those modernists whose rejection of old usage or traditional linguistic forms is coupled with an imperative to create new and innovative modes of expression. (Beckett, Artaud, Joyce come to mind as such linguistic revolutionaries.) Her prose, if somewhat turgid, is quite conventional. Watkins's stream of consciousness report of his voyages into "inner reality" is as close as Lessing comes to linguistic innovation. But even here the author is not searching for new modes of expression so much as rejecting verbal expression in general.

What arouses Lessing's ire is that very function which *is* language's purpose, namely, to differentiate and to divide reality in order that human beings might apprehend their world and communicate with others. Through learning and using a language we distinguish one thing from another, "we . . . have the means of referring to elements in reality which have a history."[7] To participate in what Wittgenstein called "a language game" is to share a way of life. Wittgenstein underlines the fact that speaking and using a language is not some abstracted formal exercise but an activity constitutive of a way of life, one expressing the needs of a society's participants none of which can ever "return to a state of nature and to an innocent eye."[8] Through ordinary discourse we praise or condemn the actions of others, characterize our states of mind, express our feelings and emotions, and delimit the meaning of our world. Language is not a tool in some crude sense but an ineradicable feature in the emergence of self-identity, enabling "us to put ourselves into somebody else's place."[9]

Lessing will have none of this. Positing a primordial, speechless, ontological unity as her beginning point, language becomes the Great Divider which rends asunder a mythic state of original harmony and undifferentiatedness one might see, from a divergent vantage point, as a primeval pulp. In order to make her case against language, Lessing must first reduce it to the blunt instrument of linguistic nominalists for whom language is the application of external labels and the deployment of ostensive definitions. Paradoxically, the presumption that language is an instrument designed to constrict rather than enrich reality, to limit rather than expand understanding, is congenial to the person of mystic and utopian proclivities. To aim to enlarge our conceptual resources would seem to be more in order. Mystics and positivists alike trivialize language before seeking its elimination.

Lessing yearns for a language, or some means of "communicating," which behaves differently from that of all past and present human languages, which have all had as their *raison d'être* the division of the world into subjects and objects of reference in order that we might think, act, and work within it. Lessing's protagonists are uncompelling as they go about assaulting words. The reader tires of characters, themselves adroit in the use of words, condemning and berating words as so many external and arbitrarily imposed labels we would be better off without. Lessing's impoverished view of language allows her to avoid facing the question of whether human beings could have any life in common without language, or whether a languageless person would be reduced to a hapless creature condemned to wander the earth, fearful and alone, trapped in a blur of undifferentiated terrors. She evades these considerations in part by populating her futuristic cosmic utopia in *Briefing* with beings who are not persons as we know them at all, creatures who have no history, no social relations, and no embodied existence. If Lessing's view were that language is often inadequate to our purposes, particularly as we attempt to depict powerful emotions and awesome happenings, a more measured response would be possible. But her purpose is not to enrich our linguistic resources in order that we might more closely approximate the task she sets forth. Rather she is opposed to language itself, since it serves only to keep us trapped inside our own skulls.[10] To depersonalize one's fictional characters one must first deny them language, history, and a role in the present. Lessing's migration from social realism to a remote utopian abstractness cannot be understood apart from her assault on language and her disparagement of human reason en route.

Again, as in her treatment of language, Lessing stacks the deck in her favor by offering, as if it were uncontested, a definition of reason as nothing but a shallow and instrumental "know-somethingness." She goes on to indict this thin view of reason and finds it guilty as charged of subverting human potentialities for transformed and transcendent consciousness. Lessing's mechanistic view of reason, like her crudely nominalist perspective on language, serves her chiliastic imperatives and utopian impulses well, for it allows her to repudiate "reason" in favor of an alternative, ineffable form of "knowing" without any consideration of substantive and noninstrumentalist understandings of reason.

The eclipse of reason in Lessing's later work is clear. As Martha Quest delivers an obituary over the corpse of reason in *Four-Gated City,* she refers to a "rationalism which once had been useful" but has become, in sociological parlance, "dysfunctional." The protagonist of *Memoirs* holds "reason" responsible, in part, for the imminent destruction of the world, even as she rates it "over-valued." In a passage bristling with an arch bitterness, Lessing's protagonist declares:

> As for our thoughts, our intellectual apparatus, our rationalisms and our logics and our deductions, and so on, it can be said with absolute certainty that dogs and cats and monkeys cannot make a rocket to fly to the moon or weave artificial dress materials out of the by-products of petroleum, but as we witness the ruins of this variety of intelligence, it is hard to give it much value: I suppose we are undervaluing it now as we over-valued it then. It will have to find its place: I believe a pretty low place, at that.[11]

The caveat, "I suppose," suggests condescending charitableness rather than ambivalence toward those still locked into "our rationalisms." Surely there are few sensitive persons who would take up the cudgels on behalf of a technocratic intelligence that specializes only in sending monkeys to the moon. One might, however, defend the notion that reason is a critical passion which treats important, not trivial, issues and questions the answers that emerge. To repudiate reason is to pave the way for the excesses of unreason, including those forces of the irrational which threaten to take over public life. If we consign reason and politics to the historic dustbin, we give politics, in Paul Ricoeur's chilling phrase, "over to the devil."

Human emotions fare little better than reason under the sway of Lessing's prophetic imperatives. Her characters frequently regard their own emotions as alien, inappropriate, and destructive adversaries. Martha Quest, in *Four-Gated City,* dissects those human emotions she distrusts and treats them as unwelcome visitors, atavisms of some other time and place not unlike the body's vestigial organs. She concludes that her emotions are "irrelevant." To allow Quest to declare them so and to view them as dangerous, misleading forces is to reduce not only her emotional capacities but to lessen the possibility that she might, with grace, subtlety, and power, understand her emotions; nor can Lessing readily find a way to make them each accessible and relevant to readers.[12] The inner life of many Lessing characters becomes what Freud called "foreign territory"; some even come to see themselves as mere repositories or reflections of "it" forces outside themselves. They are individuated only insofar as they see themselves as a "reflection of that great archetypal dream."[13] Lessing's embrace of ontic thinking requires that her individuals exist in a fuguelike state, more objects than subjects, who can attain an authentic state of mind only if they shed, or declare their indifference to, the personal, the individual, and a social existence. Moral agency evaporates in the wake of "it."

Lessing's individuals can be invaded from the outside either alone or en masse. Her answer to the query "why can't people—I mean people in the mass—be invaded by alien personalities?"[14] is that they can. In *Four-Gated City,* Martha refers to whole nations "going mad." The human race itself has "driven itself mad, and these sudden outbreaks of senseless violence in individuals and communities were early symptoms" (613). Stalin's Russia, Hitler's Germany, England during World War I, and the United States during the McCarthyite period are cited as examples of the phenomenon of mass, sudden, collective madness (210).

Whenever a writer, whether political thinker or novelist, accounts for complex social and historic phenomena through the appropriation of terms designed originally to explain and to understand the psychological states and actions of individuals, the inevitable result is a reductionism which is curiously abstract. Talk of nations "going mad" mystifies rather than enhances our capacity to penetrate the intricate dynamics of complicatedly socio-historic, political-economic, and individual-social events.

I am not claiming that for a writer of fiction there is no valid approach to group psychology; rather, I am insisting that Lessing's evocation of group phenomena through the mass convergence of individual psychic states, brought about through the workings of certain ontic entities postulated a priori and to which real agency in the world is assigned, not only treats these phenomena inadequately but represents a capitulation to moral and conceptual nihilism. Her "group psychology" requires that individual beings be drained of any normative significance in favor of a collective "psyche" that is itself indifferent to individual beings. Persons, groups, whole nations become the playthings of "it" and are not responsible for what they do. Like Jung's "pantheon of psychologized god-terms," the archetypes, Lessing's "it," to whom they are indebted, operate within, upon, and outside of human history "with no regard for human needs or morality."[15] Mankind's puniness in the face of an "it-storm," man's faltering attempts to keep his balance before the onslaught, are things of little moment to those who would ride the whirlwind, and the hero of *Briefing* denigrates "humanity's ethics or codes" as nothing but "the pack's morality."[16] He would junk it, for the attempt to create ethics and codes for human conduct is, like the presumption of individual responsibility, autonomy, and choice upon which it is dependent, but a "vestigial organ in humanity."[17]

Lessing's negation of human subjects as self-reflective agents who think and act responsibly has coordinates other than her repudiation of reason and language. One is a view best characterized as moralistic hubris, the stated conviction that each individual is responsible for *everything* that goes on in the universe. Anna's "whole person" in *Notebook* is one which is "striving to become as conscious and responsible as *possible about everything in the universe.*"[18] What appears at first glance to be an attempt by Anna to grant human beings choices and to assign them shared responsibilities turns out upon reflection to involve the imposition of a burden impossible to attain and doomed to failure, thus justifying in part Lessing's move toward that moral chaos in which the *force majeure* of "it" is created or blamed with responsibility for everything from pestilence, wars, and famine to alterations of the climate and boils. The narrator of *Memoirs* evokes "it":

> For "it" is a force, a power, taking the form of an earthquake, a visiting comet whose balefulness hangs closer night by night, distorting all thought by fear—"it" can be, has been, pestilence, a war, the alteration of climate, a tyranny that twists men's minds, the savagery of a religion . . . that was "it," *there was never any good reason for things . . . something happened. . . .* [emphasis mine][19]
>
> Perhaps, after all, one has to end by characterising "it" as a sort of cloud or emanation, but invisible, like the water vapour you know is present in the air of the room you sit in. . . . *"It" was everywhere, in everything, moved in our blood, our minds.* "It" was nothing that could be described once and for all, or pinned down, or kept stationary: "it" was an illness, a tiredness, boils . . . (155) [emphasis mine]

"It" shares with other images of divine force and occult magic at work in the world an inescapable yet ephemeral pervasiveness which eludes all attempts to describe, localize, and situate and, like these forces, can be drawn in to explain everything from the most trivial phenomenon ("a boil") to the most monumental ("a tyranny that twists men's minds"). Lessing's godlike, malevolent "it" is a kind of amoral religion, or the fundaments of one, a religion which allows neither redemption, forgiveness, nor human salvation through personal choice. She offers instead a world run amuck in which things happen for no reason and human beings cannot truly choose, but submit unwittingly to the will of "it" as it moves in their "blood" and "minds." Like Jung's archetypes, "it" forces "operate of their own accord, using groups and individuals as their instruments."[20] If a Lessing character does choose, the choice is based on the false premise of individual thought, reason, and moral agency, and is therefore not serious.

Lessing's pre-scientific *Weltanschauung* and her conviction that life and the world are beyond human reason result in a particular view of the individual which has much in common with certain schools of contemporary social and political theory to which one might at first presume her work to be antithetical, theories which require, in the interest of an unimpressionistic, hard, predictive "science of human society," the eradication of complex human beings. Whether behaviorists or structuralists, these social "scientists" who would uncover society and history's ineluctable "laws of motion," or predict human behavior after they have controlled for the relevant "variables," assume that individual members of a society are unaware of the deep structural, or externally manipulative, forces at work within it, and upon them, and that they must in principle remain so. A "genuinely scientific" understanding of what is going on, one which adduces the "laws of motion" and predictable responses at work, is sometimes available to a minority of elite "knowers" just as the knowledge of the forces of "it" can be attained by a select society in Lessing's fiction. Prophets, like the "scientific" thinkers who populate social inquiry, see themselves as a vanguard of unmaskers who both prophesy and theorize. The "hard" and the "soft" meet on mutually shared turf: the graveyard of the human subject.

For the scientific theorists of society, the way out of the tentacles of ideological distortion, history, and the present is either for an elite to point the way by riding the crest of history or for the forces at work in and within history to coalesce of their own accord in some spontaneous *unité de rupture* whose fusion and explosion make way for the new world. In either case individuals play little or no role. Lessing's option is the dream of a golden age to follow after the destruction of a world grown tawdry and horrible. Total despair requires a total solution and the terrible solace of a happy ending: this has always been the stuff of terror as it is translated into a political imperative. One can readily discern the seductiveness of the vision: through some mysterious cosmic alchemical process, the present hideousness is transformed into the new Jerusalem, a world of unity and peace, where human needs no longer exist as man himself has cast off his mortal coil and become like unto the angels. Before the lure of utopian endings, the advocate of a human responsibility who requires that we undertake the long haul of political struggle and unceasing efforts to transform the present, who urges us to accept our mere humanness, often seems ordinary and hopelessly compromised. Indeed, a refusal to embrace Thanatos and to call forth the Four Horsemen of the Apocalypse as the fleet-footed harbingers of good tidings and peace on earth may even brand one as a fool who engages in futile efforts to preserve and restore even as he would change and reconstruct.

Utopian thinking and literary expression appear in two predominant modes: the contemplative and the active. Characteristically, the utopian prophet of the contemplative mode sees the decay of the old and coming of the new as a foreordained certainty. Human beings are consigned to waiting and, if need be, suffering in the interim. The activist mode, however, places demands upon an individual or a select group to perform sufficient social surgery in order to guarantee that a new world is dragged from the entrails of the old. Perhaps the greatest expression of the activist-utopian genre is Plato's *Republic,* in which the Guardians and philosopher-king do not shrink from treating human society and character as an artist's palette to be "scraped clean"[21] before creating a righteous community. Plato takes steps to create a world in which competing passions, beliefs, purposes, and loyalties are eliminated in order that harmony, equilibrium, and unity might prevail. Lessing's utopianism inclines toward the contemplative mode. Her characters tend to be visionaries or passive observers, not activists and social engineers, and one of the recurrent contemplative images she evokes through her characters is that of "the City," a theme with a long history in Western utopian and political thought.[22]

Lessing's treatment of "the City," as the core of her utopian vision, is anticipated by reflections in *Notebook.* Ella, in a discussion with Paul, conjures up a bleak description of the ugliness and horrors of contemporary England, London in particular. She would raze the whole sordid mess. "So you'd like to put a giant bulldozer over it all, over all England?" Paul queries. Ella's terse reply is "Yes."[23] Paul's rejoinder to this chilling abruptness is couched in terms which bespeak historic awareness and a sensitivity to the reverberations of too rapid social change and its effect upon persons. "If you had your way, building the new Jerusalem, it would be like killing a plant by suddenly moving it into the wrong soil. There's a continuity, some kind of invisible logic to what happens. You'd kill the spirit of the people if you had your way" (190). In her subsequent works, Lessing either forgets or chooses to ignore this moving dialogue. Paul's forebodings are suppressed as the problems of the relationships between "old" and "new" are treated apocalyptically and abstractly rather than historically and personally. The process of destruction through which history is passing, prior to the birth of some new world, like all stages of history, lacks any meaning or integrity. Lessing bypasses these issues as she goes on to develop her vision of "the City."

In *Four-Gated City,* Martha Quest takes up the theme of "the city" by recounting Mark Coldridge's depiction of a mythical city for his novel, *A City in the Desert*. Mark's fictional city is archetypal and hierarchical. "Every house in it had been planned, and who would live in each house. Every person in the city had a function and a place."[24] Inside this city harmony, order, and joy reign. This order was not totally static, as people "could move out and up and into other functions, if they wished to" (140). But the idyllic city is soon threatened by an outer city of "hungry and dirty and short-lived people" who mirror the good city in their own hierarchical arrangements but who fight ceaselessly "for power and money and recognition" rather than exchanging functions amicably (141). Eventually these nasty, brutish members of the outer city overrun and destroy the inner city; it is through this loss of innocence that the city, sullied and tainted with the stains of its bloody origin, enters history.

The theme of the city and its imagery will be familiar to anyone who has studied utopian religious and political thought in the West. Although the concept of the city has a broadly shared reference point, that bizarre new world depicted in *Briefing for a Descent into Hell* has nothing recognizably human, historical, or political—thus nothing shared—about it. Giving her utopian impulses their widest berth, Lessing's "schizophrenic," drugged, and hospitalized voyager, Watkins, takes a series of "trips" into inner space where he finds a world of harmony and unity. His vision, as portrayed by Lessing, is one of pure, passive utopian contemplation sundered altogether from material and historic considerations. During one of his voyages to the core of his being, Watkins loses his ego-identity and comes to recognize that his own self is not "his" at all, in a historically specific, developmentally shaped, and individual sense, but instead is part of an undifferentiated, ahistorical, impersonal and collective "self" within a world he beholds and goes on to recount, a world which existed before the destruction of the Good City.

Lessing's imagery is more akin to that "oceanic feeling" Freud used to characterize the perception of mystics than it is to the defined and structured societies of utopian polities like Plato's *Republic,* or Thomas More's *Utopia*. Her utopian entity is a grotesque, living organism of cosmic scale which links all nations, countries, groups, individuals, and creatures through a system of pulses, organs, and wavelengths. All individuals who perform similar functions within this throbbing cosmic whole comprise a single organ in the overall body no matter what their country or nationality. Thus judges, farmers, civil servants, soldiers, money men, and writers are one "insofar as the atoms of each of the categories were one."[25] Held together by a "nourishing web" of fluid pulses and wavelengths of sound and sight, this vast conglomerate eliminates individuals and collective categories prevail (101). One is who one is only as part of an organ within the total system, "merely parts of a whole" which includes all humanity, animal species, Nature. (Lessing mentions "plants, animals, birds, insects, reptiles.") Watkins can recognize himself as an I "who am not I, but part of a whole composed of other human beings as they are part of me" (109). All that which we characteristically associate as "human"—joy, love, conscience, trust, the need for purposive action, justice, and reflective thought—disappears as persons do. Lessing's utopian message is that Cosmic Harmony is attainable only when individuals are "merely parts of a whole" within a total system which includes all humanity, animal life, and nature. Lessing appears to regard her throbbing Cosmic Totality as the just reward of a human race which has stubbornly refused to respect the mysterious, transcendent Laws of Harmony and insisted upon differentiating and dividing life through words and deeds. This has brought down the wrath of "it" upon us.

Hence her alternative: an enormous, pulsating unit of organs and functions where anything and everything which might serve to distinguish between persons and objects has disappeared, including language. With the sloughing off of language, like an old, threadbare coat no longer needed nor worn, human beings lose that which sets them apart from other creatures. The distinction between nature (*physis*) and the sphere of human creation (*nomos*) first made by the Greeks in order to distinguish persons from things, and human action from mere happenings, disappears. Human beings blend indistinguishably back into Nature and retain an identity only insofar as they are functioning units within the Cosmic Whole.

Some might object that Lessing does not intend her vision of "Cosmic Harmony" to be taken seriously, or literally, as the evocation of an ideal state of affairs. Whatever her intentions, Lessing's vision is a representation of a Truth, higher and deeper than any available to ordinary human beings within history: The result of an aesthetic utopian vision which is too abstract and impersonal to serve as the cogent indictment of any ongoing society's social and economic arrangements, yet which carries certain ominous possibilities if it is translated, however roughly, into a set of political desiderata. Lessing makes her image of Cosmic Harmony an object of contemplation which affords aesthetic pleasure and a world without end once history has run its sordid course. The response demanded from her reader cannot be specific action within a political context; instead, we are to make a contemplative leap into an ontic realm of ahistoric truth, to silence that doubting, skeptical, rational voice within us. The invitation to be swept away in the infinite passivity of Cosmic Harmony, as evoked by Lessing, is not unlike the coerced silence of utopian activists whose demonic vision of peace is the silence of a graveyard of their own creation.

What is most disturbing about Lessing's generalized utopian vision is not simply that paeans to eternal peace and never-ending harmony lack "zest and energy"[26] and fail to engage us as do the struggles of real men and women who are content to "find themselves" through thought and action within a less than perfect world. More significant is the ominous fact that *all* calls for total unity, harmony, and freedom as part of some overarching whole enter the political arena through the agency of terror. For the activist, utopian action without limitation is justified and may be required to bring about a new world: the cosmic passivity of Thanatos triumphant. Lessing's is not some dark vision of a demonic community of the damned, but her obsession with undifferentiation, with the fusion, ultimately, of nature and culture where human life ceases to exist in a distinguishable form, calls to mind both earlier and later dreams of unity and cosmic harmony. J. P. Stern, for example, cites—as a harbinger of later fascist ideology—the work of nineteenth-century German Romantics whose dreams of an "organic national community" that would be "non-political in the sense of freeing . . . its citizens from the need for democratic choices . . . promised . . . integration with a traditional, anti-urban, rustic, 'natural' community."[27] The German Romantics stressed the "oneness of all things"[28] and used a "nature vocabulary" which presumed a pre-existent ontological unity of man and nature which was spoilt by modern civilization, particularly the Enlightenment with its "unnatural" emphasis upon reason, the individual, equality, democracy, the rights of man, and a politics not of unanimity but of debate, compromise, and limitation. These debates were often viewed as "anti-Nature";[29] ontic thinking dominated the Romantic *Weltanschauung,* both as the foundation of the entire edifice of harmony through conceptual fiat, and as an ideal to be attained once the forces of anti-Nature were routed. History suggests that the ideological blending of aesthetic and political imperatives is ultimately fatal to political life itself, for politics is an irritant in the harmonious cosmos and must be eradicated if order is to be achieved.

Aesthetic imperatives become political demands: Lessing, like the German Romantics and fascist ideologues, invites the intervention of a ruler-as-artist who, following Plato's Guardian, would paint his picture of the new world only after he had wiped clean the slate of the old. This requires a "license to kill," to eliminate human beings individually or en masse should they stand in one's way or fail to fall silently within the structure of the transcendent realm in which the constraints of the human body, mind, nature, and civilization have all fallen away. Lessing does not call for a Master Painter to bring her aesthetic vision into being, but chilling implications remain nonetheless. Her utopia, as recounted by Watkins, requires the elimination of human diversity in order to attain harmony and order. Lessing would free us from the burdens of our inadequate judgments, our physical and mental limitations, our individual responsibilities; our personal and historic self-identities are stripped away after having first been drained of their normative significance.

Lessing's response to the malaise which has eroded and undermined those traditional shared meanings she values is also, paradoxically, a contribution to that very erosion. Having concluded that we are all doomed, Lessing as prophet and seer gives the inevitable a boost through her wholesale condemnations of the present. She finds nothing hopeful nor potentially redeemable in politics or the struggles of everyday life. To those who persist in struggling to maintain their identities and to preserve some individual and historical meaning even as their world is crumbling, who work to prevent the worst from happening, Lessing offers only cynicism, scorn, and occasional derision. She thereby feeds the most reactionary forces at work within the culture. Those who will step in to replace the "boulder pushers" (as Lessing herself once characterized those who persist, knowing they can but stem the tide) will not be the prophets, visionaries, devotees of altered or transformed consciousness, but the unscrupulous, manipulative, rageful, and vain: all the ruthless necromancers who create deserts in the name of peace or harmony.

In 1969 a group of Canadian poets then in a "flower power" phase were treated to a bit of Doris Lessing's ire after they told her that "flowers were mightier than tanks." This, Lessing said, was "sentimental rubbish"; it was "too late" in the day for "romanticism."[30] Is it not, ten years later, too late in the day for romantic, effulgent evocations of Cosmic Harmony? The prophet requires of other persons not so much rational interpretation and understanding but a credulous faith, a conviction of religious intensity and childlike acceptance of authority. This is to compound romanticism with an overarching spiritual order, a kind of pseudo-religion, but one without God and without solace, one which negates human choice and moral responsibility, one which must wipe out human existence as we know it in order to achieve its ends. Lessing's characterization of that which she sees happening, or about to happen, is powerful and at times moving. But because it is couched in terms which distort, mystify, abstract us from our thoughts and words, making us puppets controlled by forces unknown, her fiction taps irrational fears and legitimates moral nihilism. The image of human life, and her alternative to it, developed in her major fictional works over the past ten years, leaves little doubt that Lessing has taken on herself the role of prophet. But she is increasingly a voice crying in a wilderness of her own devising, a desert of the spirit within which Lessing has given up on human beings. She has repudiated the fundamental wager of our time, that human beings must be allowed the choices of free persons and that politics, therefore, cannot be settled once and for all.

Notes

Originally published in *Salmagundi* (winter–spring 1980).

1. Doris Lessing, *The Four-Gated City* (New York: Bantam Books, 1970), 480. For an anthology of essays treating Lessing's work from a variety of perspectives, see Annis Pratt and L. S. Dembo, eds., *Doris Lessing: Critical Studies* (Madison: University of Wisconsin Press, 1974).

2. Doris Lessing, *The Memoirs of a Survivor* (New York: Knopf, 1975), 219–20.

3. Doris Lessing, *The Summer before the Dark* (New York: Knopf, 1973), 8.

4. Lessing, *Four-Gated City,* 36.

5. Ibid., 72.

6. Doris Lessing, *The Golden Notebook* (New York: Ballantine Books, 1968), 300–301.

7. Stuart Hampshire, *Thought and Action* (New York: Viking Press, 1959), 17–18.

8. Ibid., 31.

9. Lynn Sukenick, "Feeling and Reason in Doris Lessing's Fiction," in Pratt and Dembo, *Doris Lessing,* 98–118, passim.

10. Doris Lessing, *Briefing for a Descent into Hell* (New York: Bantam Books, 1972), 128–29.

11. Lessing, *Memoirs,* 81.

12. See, for example, in addition to Hampshire's *Thought and Action,* several of the essays by Wollheim in Richard Wollheim, *On Art and the Mind* (Cambridge, Mass.: Harvard University Press, 1974), especially "The Mind and the Mind's Image of Itself" and "Identification and the Imagination."

13. Lessing, *Golden Notebook,* 471.

14. Lessing, *Four-Gated City,* 623.

15. Thus Jung saw Nazism as "illustration and further evidence for the existence and power of the archetypes," with Nazism depicted as "near to being a religious movement as any movement since A.D. 622." Hitler was characterized by Jung as a "true mystic and prophet of the Third Reich" who, seized by the pagan god Wotan, was forced to "communicate his ecstasy to the people." The implications of any retreat from reason and moral agency are potentially pernicious, and Jung is a perfect case in point. Citations from Jung's own essays are drawn from J. P. Stern, *Hitler: The Führer and the People* (Berkeley: University of California Press, 1975). See also Clarence J. Karier, "The Ethics of a Therapeutic Man: C. G. Jung," *Psychoanalytic Review* (spring 1976): 115–46, for another treatment of the political implications of Jung's amoral psychologisms.

16. Lessing, *Briefing,* 101.

17. Lessing, *Memoirs,* 105.

18. Lessing, *Golden Notebook,* 360.

19. Lessing, *Memoirs,* 151–52. One critical reader of an earlier version of this essay

reminded me that Joseph Heller's title (*Something Happened*) occurs here in Lessing and that I seem to have misread the thrust of a particular species of modern satire to which, he argued, Lessing owes a debt. I cannot speak to Lessing's indebtedness to a particular mode of satiric fiction, whether Celine's or others'; moreover, I do not find this the most salient point to be made about her capitulation to moral nihilism. Heller's *Something Happened* is the ironic, somewhat weary lament of a man who has come of age and entered adulthood in a transpositional epoch and who has, as we all must, grown older and not necessarily wiser. But Lessing's "something happened" does not refer to the inevitability of growing older and being unprepared for it all; rather, it is the evocation of dark, capricious forces which operate with no regard to justice, fairness, decency—any known human *or* divine virtues of the sort attributable to the Judaeo-Christian God-head.

20. Cited in Volodymyr Walter Odajnyk, *Jung and Politics: The Political and Social Ideas of C. G. Jung* (New York: Harper and Row, Colophon Books, 1976), 63. See also my critical review of this volume in *Political Theory* (August 1977): 425–30, passim.

21. Plato, *The Republic,* trans. Francis MacDonald (New York: Oxford University Press, 1962), passim.

22. The theme of the city is evoked in the works of Plato, Augustine, Rousseau, and Hegel, among others. For a recent treatment of the cluster of issues intertwined with our concept of "the city," see Raymond Williams's provocative treatise, *The Country and the City* (New York: Oxford University Press, 1972).

23. Lessing, *Golden Notebook,* 189.

24. Lessing, *Four-Gated City,* 139–40.

25. Lessing, *Briefing,* 99–100. See also Douglass Bolling, "Structure and Theme in *Briefing for a Descent into Hell,*" in Pratt and Dembo, *Lessing,* 133–47, passim, and Roberta Robenstein, "Briefing on Inner Space: Doris Lessing and R. D. Laing," *Psychoanalytic Review* (spring 1976): 83–94.

26. Elaine Showalter, *A Literature of Their Own: British Women Novelists from Brontë to Lessing* (Princeton: Princeton University Press, 1977), 263.

27. Stern, *Hitler,* 53. See also Stephen Eric Bronner, "Martin Heidegger: The Consequences of Political Mystification," *Salmagundi* (summer–fall 1977): 153–74, at 170. Bronner writes: "All the leitmotifs of Heidegger's thought involve a reaction against the bourgeois world: the emphasis upon language, provincialism and anti-intellectualism became tools of the right. Each, in its own way, contributes to the attack upon Enlightenment rationalism and reason which assumed a terrible clarity during Heidegger's association with the Nazis."

28. Stern, *Hitler,* 49.

29. Ibid., 51. Nazi ideology was heavily indebted to the nature vocabulary of the nineteenth-century Romantics. To be "antinature" was to be labeled a "bacterium" or a "parasite," some alien substance in the body politic. To label a group of persons "parasites" is to invite through politics the deployment of one of several powerful "cures," including surgical excision, the administration of potent antitoxins, or, should the "parasites" prove to be intractable, some total "final solution." This vocabulary has resurfaced recently in the rhetoric and arguments of those radical feminist

separatists who characterize men as "unnatural" biological phenomena, as literal "mutants" who will one day be unnecessary for the purpose of reproduction. Women will reclaim their "natural" ability to reproduce parthenogenically—only female children will be reproduced, of course—and the male "mutant" will wither away and eventually die out altogether.

30. Doris Lessing, *A Small Personal Voice* (New York: Vintage Books, 1975), 71.

6

Presidential Voice

Epideictic Moments

January 28, 1986. Having postponed the State of the Union speech, the Great Communicator addressed the nation on the space shuttle tragedy in words of eloquent simplicity and homey directness. He and Nancy, Ronald Reagan said, were "pained to the core," and they knew their pain was shared "with all of the people of our country. This is truly a national loss." For "we mourn seven heroes," and, in Reagan's by now familiar (and familiarizing) style, he listed their names, spoke of their families, reminded us that we have become inured to the "wonders" of this century, leading us to forget that "we've only just begun. We're still pioneers. They, the members of the *Challenger* crew, were pioneers."

He had us with him in a few moments, drawing us into the tragedy by acknowledging the tremor the shuttle explosion had sent rippling through the body politic. (As indeed it had: television monitors set up in the lobbies of the campus center at the university where I teach were mobbed, students elbowing and jockeying for position in order to see the horrendous and fascinating replay of the doomed shuttle's lift-off over and over.) Reagan's next move was a stroke of genius, an example of epideictic oratory in the television age at its most effective. "I want," he continued, "to say something to the schoolchildren of America who were watching the live coverage of the shuttle's takeoff. I know it's hard to understand that sometimes painful things like this happen. It's all part of the process of exploration and discovery. . . . The future doesn't belong to the fainthearted. It belongs to the brave." Part the understanding ministrations of the father/therapist, part Periclean reaffirmation of the *polis,* these words from the Great Communicator held out succor and held up the pioneer ethos in a language similar to that with which Thucydides constructed Pericles' funeral speech honoring civic virtue: "the way of life whose practice led to these achievements and the form of state and character which made them great."

Reagan on the space shuttle, Pericles on the public funeral of Athenians killed in battle—two epideictic orations, speeches made for public occasions imbued with an explicit political content, separated by thousands of years, yet marked by signs that link them together. Hence Reagan: "The crew of the space shuttle *Challenger* honored us by the manner in which they lived their lives. We will never forget them nor the last time we saw them this morning as they prepared for their journey and waved goodbye and 'slipped the surly bonds of earth to touch the face of God.'" Thus Pericles: "In reality the dead have received their first distinction in this burial. The second is that their children will receive their sustenance from the city till they are grown men, and this is the city's crown of aid to them and to all who are left alive after such struggles. For where the greatest prizes of valor are set, there the best citizens are to be found. Now, therefore, weep your last for your own, and so depart."

Pericles, as orator, was by definition a speaker distinguished for his skill and power, trained in the art of speaking in public eloquently and effectively. Reagan, the actor-president, is called a communicator, one who imparts, transmits, informs, gives, and "shares in common" with those to whom he speaks. Each used his funeral and space shuttle tragedy speeches for very similar purposes. We who study history honor Pericles' speech as one of the most celebrated exemplars of Attic oratory—an oration that has met the test of time. Few of us would be inclined to grant a similar status to Reagan's space shuttle address to the nation. In its artfulness we skeptics see artifice; in its evocation of shared emotion we detect manipulations of the sort Jean-Jacques Rousseau insisted were the stuff of modern pseudo-eloquence, particularly the eloquence of the theater which draws us into tragedy and "feigned misfortune." Swept up in a mimetic tide, we find ourselves bombarded with imagery that produces desired effects—but the effects are phony, dissimulations. "In ancient times," writes Jean-Jacques, "when persuasion played the role of public force, eloquence was necessary. Of what use would it be today, when public force has replaced persuasion. One needs neither art nor metaphor to say *such is my pleasure.*"[1]

In this Rousseau would concur with the later observation of Camus's ironic judge-penitent, Jean-Baptiste Clemence, as he remarks to his compatriot in the bar called Mexico City, in a shabby district of Amsterdam, "Somebody has to have the last word. Otherwise, every reason can be answered with another one and there would never be an end to it. Power, on the other hand, settles everything. It took time, but we finally realized that. For instance, you must have noticed that our old Europe at last philosophizes in the right way. We no longer say as in simple times: 'This is the way I think. What are your objections?' We have become lucid. For the dialogue we have substituted the communiqué: 'This is the truth,' we say. You can discuss it as much as you want; we aren't interested. But in a few years there'll be the police who will show you we are right."

If the Great Communicator merely issued communiqués of stipulative simplicity, if force had indeed wholly replaced Rousseau's vision of eloquent classical oratory aimed at persuasion rather than manipulation, we would inhabit the worlds both Rousseau and Camus either foresaw or found ready to hand. But our communicator president *does* communicate, and the ancient oratory Rousseau extols was by no means so exemplary as he claims. Jean-Baptiste endorses dialogue; Jean-Jacques rehearses one of his many assaults against artifice and the loss of authenticity, civic and oratorial, he finds in the modern world. Both intimate a loss—of dialogue, hence genuine communication, and of persuasion toward which eloquence was a means—and a substitution, that of edicts and force. To reflect on this perceived loss as a felt cultural deformation requires a brief genealogical construction of our present-past and its reception of rhetoric.

Rhetoric Re-collected

Putting one's mind to the task of thinking about presidential rhetoric, or several recent presidents as orators/rhetors/communicators, is vexing *if* one does not share our culture's automatic denigration of "mere rhetoric." To call a speech-act "rhetorical" or to proclaim, "After all, it's just a matter of semantics," is to give voice to a widely held piece of folk wisdom as knowing cynicism. One is additionally vexed *if* one finds the usual academic approaches to the topic (word analysis, evaluation of "propaganda techniques," endless disputes about form versus content) less than robust, so much frenzied dancing about on the head of a pin by those who do "communications studies" or some subdiscipline of the genre as an academic specialty.

Modern American culture is of at least two minds on the question of political rhetoric: either (*a*) it's "mere rhetoric" and doesn't matter anyhow because nobody really believes what those guys (and, increasingly, gals) are saying, or (*b*) we are all being manipulated by smooth-talking politicians who are capable of getting just the "results" they want from us by pulling the right rhetorical strings. In scenario (*a*) we are knowing listeners who take everything with a grain of salt. In scenario (*b*) we are a passive mass seduced by the clever whose eloquence is a trap for the vast unwary many.[2]

That we hold these views simultaneously and feel no apparent need to jettison one in favor of the other in the interest of conceptual coherence says something important. It signifies that we "double up" when we listen: one part of the self is drawn in, but not altogether, for there is another part of the self that not only remains aloof but blocks full inducement into the world of the rhetorician. We hold an inner dialogue, if not a public one: we are free to withhold full assent to what is being communicated *to* us in situations in which communication *with* the other (the president, for example) is impossible. Ronald Reagan's genius, and a partial explanation for his success, has been his ability to mute the cynic in his listeners, to disarm the voice that shouts "Keep your distance!" He has done this not through a series of tricks and manipulations but because, on some deep level, he understands and can practice a rhetoric that bursts with *surplus* meaning. Not only is there an immediacy of understanding when one listens to a Reagan speech, there is a plenitude of meaning, some no doubt intended, but some no doubt unaware—on Reagan's part and ours. This all sounds rather mysterious and it is a point to which I will return after several circumlocutions.

The "mere rhetoric" school of denigration finds it most eloquent champion in Plato and subsequent interpreters who accept Plato's sharp divide between rhetoric and dialectic, between opinion and knowledge. Greek oratory, *pace* contemporary fantasies of philosophers holding forth in the agora, was preeminently forensic in nature and intent, speeches delivered in courts of law and aimed at securing the acquittal or condemnation of the accused. We would call such an actor a lawyer—and our suspicions of courtroom skullduggery would come into play immediately, reinforcing Platonic censure of the forensic and the fustian. What lowered rhetoric irredeemably in Socrates' eyes was its instrumentalism. Rhetoric had a functional purpose: to persuade in the interest of winning or losing a case. The high-minded search for truth should not look anything like that, he insisted; hence the emergence of a dialectic of knowledge *in opposition to* a rhetoric of persuasion.

Some of the Sophists, those who formed schools and composed a *technē*, or rhetorical handbook larded with tricks of the trade, played directly into Socrates' hands. They pandered; he opened a quest for truth or, better, Truth. If the Sophists were spellbinders, Socrates was a truth-teller or discoverer. Between spellbinders and truth-discoverers lay a great, incommensurable divide. Socrates proves his point by stretching poor Gorgias to the end of his rhetorical tether in the Platonic dialogue that bears the name of Socrates' hapless interlocutor.

Socrates maneuvers Gorgias into declaiming that oratory is not concerned with helping the sick learn how to live in order to become well; it is not, in other words, concerned with *the* good but with making men "good at" speaking. Gorgias rebuts that "the art of oratory is the art of speech par excellence" and that this involves not only "freedom for" oneself but "the power of ruling" one's countrymen by convincing them to concur with one's argument "in a court of justice . . . and any other gathering of citizens whatever it may be." With this definition, Gorgias plays into Socrates' dialectical hands and the master administers the *coup de grace* with mock innocence: "If I understand you aright, you are saying that oratory is productive of conviction, and that this is the be-all and end-all of its whole activity." Gorgias repeats that this is indeed the case. Socrates has all he needs to put Gorgias away by noting that Gorgias by his own admission has shown that oratory does not teach "about right and wrong"; instead the orator "merely persuades," making of oratory a subdivision of "pandering . . . a spurious counterfeit of a branch of the art of government."[3]

"Mere rhetoric merely persuades": the Platonic view decocts to this locution and is picked up by Aristotle, who, less convinced of the possibility of Truth than Plato, is more certain of, and comfortable with, the influencing of opinion. Taking a leaf from the Sophist notebook, Aristotle (in his *Rhetoric*, book 3), gives a few lessons himself on delivery ("a matter of voice . . . when it should be loud, when low, when intermediate"), acknowledging as he does so that the whole business has been "thought vulgar." Locating rhetoric contextually in the law courts and public assembly, Aristotle plays the trimmer: we must pay attention to "the whole business of Rhetoric" because it is "necessary" and because "we" (the we here is the collective civic being) should aim for a rhetoric that fights "the case with the facts alone, so that everything else that is beside demonstration is superfluous." "We" have a stake in avoiding speech that overexcites pain or pleasure.

Indeed—and this is Aristotle's final word on the subject, appropriately enough given his quest for an economy of style—"speech, if it does not make the meaning clear, will not perform its proper function." The implication for style is that "perspicuity" becomes "one of its chief merits." Through this early doctrine of plain representation, Aristotle presages later commentators (most notably Orwell) who hanker after linguistic simplicity and voice suspicion of the obscure or the ambiguous. *If* rhetoric is not to come under indictment, in the Aristotelian construction of its necessary role, the meanings of words used must be clear; speech must be neither below nor above "the dignity of the subject" but wholly "appropriate to it." No more and no less. Rhetoric is not on trial for its life, as in Plato's dialogue, but is constantly in danger of indeterminate sentencing if it falls into impropriety.

The Roman reinscription of rhetoric as a gentlemanly pursuit, with the orator serving as exemplar of cultivated individuality, further severed the orator from the philosopher and politics from a disinterested quest for knowledge. Cicero presupposes political life as the highest expression of human achievement. He is quite willing to yield to others in philosophy, but "I reserve for myself that which is essential to an orator: speaking to the point, with clarity and with style." Writing to his son, Cicero urges him to study his father's public speeches but not to neglect "the philosophical way of speaking, sustained and calm": this too "must be cultivated." Going on to observe that "not a single Greek ever succeeded in working and trying to achieve something in both areas; that is to say in forensic oratory and in the category of private discussion," Cicero puts a hypothetical question geared at closing the gap between public speech (oratory, rhetoric) and private discussion (philosophy) by insisting that if Plato "had wished," he could have been "an extremely impressive and eloquent speaker."[4]

To the camp devoted to the great divide, Cicero's "if he had wished" only serves to deepen a shared conviction that Plato did not thus wish because he disdained to engage in such a flawed enterprise as rhetorical persuasion. But that isn't all Plato eschewed. He also repudiated *politics* as the unseemly cacophony of opinionated voices. Plato despised the politics of his day and made several abortive attempts to create alternative orders. We also know that Plato was coldly wrathful toward the political system that had put to death the man he revered above all others as the most just, most righteous: Socrates. Disheartened with the treatment accorded just men on this earth, Plato would create a world in which the just man is not only secure from the hounds baying at his heels but in which that man, and others of his kind, immune to the seductions of "false and boasting speeches and opinions," hold absolute power. Plato would preclude all debate and controversy leading (inevitably, he believed) to social chaos and discord. It is only when Truth triumphs that the din created by disparate voices being heard in the land ceases. Rhetoric is the medium through which politics is conducted and politics must be transcended.

Ancient and modern suspicion of "mere rhetoric," I am here suggesting, goes hand in hand with ancient and modern disparagement of the vulgar unseemliness of politics. A contemporary comedian gets laughs when he proclaims, "Comedy isn't pretty." Neither is politics, especially democratic politics. And democratic politics without rhetoric, without attempts to persuade, is impossible. Plato's contrast between rhetoric, which he attacks, and dialectic, which he defends, is, in James Boyd White's view, a way of highlighting the difference between ways of speaking and being and "of establishing community with others."[5] True. But White errs in going with the flow of Socrates' representations in his brief against rhetoric, accepting the stipulation that the power to "persuade others" is synonymous with reducing them "to one's will."[6] This reduction of the other follows only if one endorses the Socratic insistence that dialectic and persuasion are opposites, the former treating people as "ends in themselves," the latter constituting others as means to one's end.

In White's reconstruction of Plato's argument, the dialectician opens debate by setting himself up as an interlocutor to be refuted and corrected. The rhetor, on the other hand, persuades "not by refuting but by flattering" his counterpart, "appealing to what pleases rather than to what is *best for him*" (emphasis mine). With the locution "best for him," White signals the underlying teleology of the Socratic dialectic. Socrates really does *know* in advance what is "best for" his interlocutors. The sparring of the Platonic dialogues has a predetermined end point: to gain the concurrence of participants with what is best *for* them and, by indirection, for the *polis,* thereby bringing the just man and the just city into closer proximity. This enterprise is less one of truly open persuasion than a teleologically driven manipulation of knowledge/power. Upon closer examination, dialectic is far less pure than Socrates, or White following Socrates, claims. For the end of dialectic is Truth in the singular.

The end of rhetoric, on the other hand, is neither monological nor definitive. Rhetorical persuasion is on *this* occasion, to *these* persons, for *this* possible end. What is mastered is not an object of knowledge (say, the Platonic forms), but a complex dialogical situation in which any sharp line between the performative uses of language and other sorts of deeds disappears. By incorporating the performative dimension of language, rhetoric elides the distance between words, speeches, actions.[7]

In our post-structuralist era, the prevailing idea of discourse also narrows the distance between "truth" and "rhetoric," between "knowledge" and "persuasion." We are instead invited to ask, with White, "What kind of action with words is this? What kind of cultural action is this writing?" (or speaking?) For the modern rhetor, no less than his or her classical progenitors, "must speak a language that has its existence outside himself, in the world he inhabits. . . . This language gives him his terms of social and natural description . . . it establishes the moves by which he can persuade another, or threaten or placate or inform or tease him, or establish terms of cooperation or intimacy."[8] We enter a world of meanings shared but not shared perfectly; a world that simultaneously constrains and imposes limits to rhetoric, persuasion, and mutual understanding, even as it makes possible all three.

The Bad Rhetoric of Rhetorical Analysis: Several Wrong Turns

A bit of debris cleaning before presidential voices are heard.

When I was in high school we were taught how to spot Those Who Try to Trick Us with Rhetoric, or Six (or five or ten) Propaganda Devices. The idea behind such civic lessons was that the forewarned citizen was a forearmed early warning system, quick to spot the would-be Hitlers, the Silver-Tongued

Devils in our midst. There were those out to manipulate us. What we could do was to open their bag of tricks and empty it of its nefarious contents: question-begging, scapegoating, euphemistic phoniness, repetitive truisms, mind-boggling metaphors, carrot-and-stick formulations, and all the rest. Pander, trickery, technique: all Socrates' warnings about the nature of rhetoric were featured in standardized textbook discussions that shared Socrates' collapse of rhetorical persuasion into pandering manipulation.

The problem with these excursions into rigid formalism is easily enough stated: by tending *only* to technique, and ferreting out instances from a shopping list of rhetorical sins, we neophyte students of rhetoric lost sight (or sound) of the content of what was being conveyed. If any propagandistic trick could be found, the rhetor clearly aimed to fool we the people and the speech should be tossed out. I remember feeling quite smug as I trashed great speeches in this way. Even Lincoln resorted to rhetorical knavery! Bristling with skepticism, I recall going through a period when I disbelieved nearly everything I heard or read because I could spot the techniques of chicanery everywhere.

But, of course, none of us can speak without metaphor and multiple meaning and shaping discourse to ends we hope others may come to share. Rhetoric turns on a distinction between literal and proper meaning, sentences that play off literal referents and figurative and proper senses of words. Without such distinction, complex representation is impossible.

That arid exercises in rhetoric bashing—which would, if taken to heart, eliminate the distinctions necessary for complex representation because they may not say precisely *this,* no more and no less—continue unabated at the present moment is explicable at least in part because what is promised is an unmasking and unveiling in order to reveal the nasty truth that there is no truth to be found. A recent example of the genre is an analysis of Franklin Roosevelt's first inaugural (subtitled "A Study of Technique"), whose author, one Halford Ross Ryan, presents "Roosevelt and Hitler Compared" in the penultimate section of his essay. Noting that both leaders shared a zeitgeist, Ryan determines that they used "similar language." The difference is that Hitler "blamed the Jews" for the Depression and Roosevelt blamed Wall Street, the financial establishment, and the plutocrats. Yet Hitler turned out to be a tyrant and Roosevelt did not, though "the possibility certainly existed for FDR to become a dictator."[9] We were, it seems, saved by the skin of our teeth given the overwhelming similarity of rhetorical techniques deployed by Hitler and Roosevelt respectively, only because the United States "had a long history of constitutional democracy" and "Hitler and Roosevelt had critical differences in their conceptions of leadership and the framework in which it should be exercised."[10] This is the sort of flat-footedness focusing on "similar rhetoric techniques" inspires, yet it is precisely this sort of flat-footedness our culture continually doles out, given our suspicion of rhetoric and our disdain for politics.

A more sophisticated wrong turn is a form of ironic discourse that seeks to explain the receptivity of "many normal people" to the cunningly deceptive words of our current president, "the old charmer, the actor with his practiced rhetoric, his histrionics, his emotional appeal" by turning to the *abnormal* few who are not taken in. Oliver Sacks, in a curious piece, "The President's Speech," turns to aphasiacs for reproof: when the president speaks, the aphasia ward roars with laughter. Why? Because "these patients, who though intelligent had the severest receptive aphasia, rendering them incapable of understanding words as such," understood "most of what was said to them." They perceived more astutely than the rest of us, it seems, for the following reason: although words might convey nothing, aphasiacs are unerringly capable of deciphering "all the extraverbal cues—tone of voice, intonation, suggestive emphasis or inflection, as well as all visual cues. . . . It is precisely this expressiveness, so deep, so various, so complex, so subtle, that is perfectly preserved in aphasia, though understanding of words be destroyed." Grasping with "infallible precision . . . the *expression* that goes with words . . . which can never be simulated or faked, as words alone can, all too easily," the aphasiac cannot be fooled as can we "normals" who, understanding words, fail all too often to sift the authentic from the inauthentic.[11]

At first a curious argument, upon rereading Sacks' insistence that "a good many normal people, aided, doubtless, by their wish to be fooled, were indeed well and truly fooled," folds back into our inherited suspicion of the seductive charm of words. Thus those who have no grasp of words but can *hear* more deeply are drawn in for instruction and reproof to demonstrate to the rest of us how gullible we truly are.

The deeper implication is that we can sever "feeling-tone" from spoken sentences and chop sentences into words. On an intuitive level, we "get" Sacks' point: expressivity in itself (the smirk, the grimace, the shrug, the smile, the leer) "says" a lot. But when what is being said is bound up in a complex rhetorical performance—a president's speech, not a street corner exchange—gesture in itself cannot "say" it all. For the president's words are caught in sentences which are themselves woven into a complex web of meaning. Wendell Berry reminds us that the word "sentence" (from the Latin *sentire*) means "a way of thinking," the implication being that the concept of the sentence and sentence structure cannot be parsed into their purely formal or merely expressive elements without losing the sense of the whole.[12]

"The president's speech"—any president's speech—is co-authored by "we the people," by the terms of its reception as a communicative act taking place within a social world whose members receive it and "read it back," reinscribing it with their own sense of the relationship the speech has established with them. The speech takes place within and helps to constitute a complex rhetorical universe. We (the listeners) are not imposed upon by a singular authorial voice so much as called upon to co-author a performative action with and through speech, a form of social action that defines and redefines us, sharpening up some edges of our self and social understandings and muting others. The speech is circumscribed by conventions of argument and action. But these conventions are porous, relatively open, capable of being stretched, even strained.

That is why attempts to perform surgery on presidential utterances by analyzing technique, or by severing style or expressivity from words spoken and meaning intended (or unintended), may provide comfort by assuring us that at least some among us need not be fooled, but fail finally to apprehend the question put by White, "What kind of action with words is this?"

Presidential Rhetoric Re-presented

Evading, or avoiding, rounding up the usual rhetorical suspects via the usual sorts of analyses of presidential speeches means one is thrown into a world of presentations and representations that are heard before they are read. A presidential speech begins life as a written text but takes on its civic life as an aural and, most often, visual event. We "hear" and "see" before we "read"— if, indeed, we ever do (and most certainly do not). That the founders never envisaged any such thing—I mean a president speaking directly to "the people" rather than speaking only to Congress and then rarely (on the State of the Union)—is unsurprising. Presidents have become more and more (potential) tribunes of the people, familiar to us and enshrined through us.

Franklin Roosevelt is the initiator of the process of "more direct contact with the nation" via his fireside chats, homey talks aimed at arousing and reassuring a battered people that although all was not well, it could get better. According to Arthur Schlesinger, Roosevelt prepared for the fireside chats by looking at a "blank wall, trying to visualize the individuals he was seeking to help: a mason at work on a new building, a girl behind a counter, a man repairing an automobile, a farmer in his field."[13] He tried to "take a complicated subject and make everybody understand it" and he did this cannily, sometimes being conciliatory, sometimes denunciatory, always, however, as the end result of a long preparatory process in which "the President himself mused about the general tone, topic, and purpose" of the speech, or the "chat."[14] And "the people" responded, finding Roosevelt "a friend, deeply and personally responsive to their troubles."[15]

A rehearsed informality also characterizes the presidential television news conference, now twenty-five years old, inaugurated by John F. Kennedy. Preparing for rhetorical combat, presidents from Kennedy to Reagan are grilled by aides, provided with possible answers to likely questions, instructed on how to finesse this or strong-arm that, even (in the case of Reagan) primed with seating charts and arrangements so that some reporters rather than others can be called upon to co-author the event. None of the advance planning detracts from the potential unpredictability of such affairs. Kennedy's decision to go for live cameras is one no president can now retract: it would be seen as an act of cowardice, an attempt to "hide in the Oval Office." Presidential news conferences have helped to enshrine a leader as charming, confident, quick-witted, a relisher of controversy (Kennedy) and as surly, defensive, adversarial (Nixon).

Beyond the particular evaluations of presidents as informal combatants lurks a murkier but perhaps more important possibility. Studies of oral cultures, ways of life revolving around the spoken word, signal the vitality of the "word" in a "voice-and-ear world." Writes James Axtell: "To oral man, a word is a real happening, an event of power and personal force. Sound is evanescent and irreversible, and words cease to exist as soon as they are spoken; they are rooted only briefly in the passing present. Therefore, while they are being spoken they are precious, mysterious, and physically efficacious." Oral cultures register the speaker as an "immanent, personal presence" in an "intensely communal" setting, one in which knowledge and truth are a "corporate possession." The setting is "intensely communal" because "speech requires an audience." Accordingly, Axtell continues, "oral man psychologically faces outward, toward the community from which he derives the meaning and veracity of his thoughts."[16]

I may as well throw down the salvo now: to figure out "why Reagan," we (who traffic in the written word) must wrench ourselves out of the text/book into the oral/aural/visual event. Reagan is an exemplar of the outwardly facing "oral man" who can speak with such confidence to a receptive audience, because the "meaning and veracity of his thoughts" cannot be disarticulated from that communal surround. Kennedy was (perhaps, here I am less sure) such a man as well. Though bookish, at least according to his hagiographers, and the literary allusions in his speeches seem to indicate immersion in history and some novels and some poems—those that could be drawn upon to paint a Kennedy sort of picture—Kennedy, too, was an outward-facing man and we were his mirror. How, or why, did this work for Kennedy and Reagan and fail so palpably for Jimmy Carter? If one can wrap one's mind around the successes and failures in an age of presidential rhetoric as the signifier of a past revivified oral culture with roots deep in the *texts* of the American past, perhaps one will come a bit closer to apprehending the dialogic nature of that rhetoric.

The argument I intend to rehearse goes something like this: Kennedy and Reagan offered and offer us (we Americans) a language of universality and immediacy characterized by a kind of civic surplus. There is *more* in what they say, or said, than initially hits the hearer. Or, better, what one hears is deeply irreducible: this is why Reagan's space shuttle tragedy speech and Pericles's funeral oration both work. They are cast in language that entangles the rhetor and the listener in a mesh of contexts as each single word deployed signifies others, said and unsaid: courage, family, tragedy, daring, grace, pioneer, fainthearted, discovery, hopes, journeys, dedication.

Amalgamated tropes, decocted figurations: Reagan rarely fails to touch the chord he himself resonates to. For example: Governor Mario Cuomo, in his keynote address to the Democratic National Convention, July 17, 1984, evoked the family as a metaphor for the country—the "family of America," adjuring us to feel "bound to one another" in a familial sort of way. It was a powerful address, but the metaphor stood out—*as* metaphor. Reagan, however, evokes the family metonymically, tapping the surplus reservoir of meaning of the word without calling attention to its figurative use. Reagan can perform the alchemy that unites universality and immediacy. He speaks not in analogies, in "as if it weres"; instead, he is *inside* the sign, fusing for his listeners signifier and signified. There is no trick here; rather, there is a sensibility so attuned to at least part of what makes us tick as a collective entity that he need not dress his talks up and send them out of the house parading their figurations.

Several examples: Reagan's State of the Union Address, January 26, 1982, proclaimed itself to be about "A New Federalism." We don't remember much about that new federalism four years later: either we agreed or disagreed that many federal activities and programs should be transferred back to states and localities. But we probably do recall "Lenny Skutnik," Reagan's exemplar of "the spirit of American heroism at its finest," a passerby who risked his life by diving into the "icy waters" of the Potomac to rescue a woman victim of an airline crash just as she was about to lose her grip and sink beneath the frigid surface. From "Lenny Skutnik," Reagan segued into a paean to the "countless, quiet, everyday heroes of American life—parents who sacrifice long and hard so their children will know a better life than they've known," church and civic volunteers, "millions who've made our nation . . . so very special." The "unsung heroes" are all of us, at one time or another, anyone who ever dreamt a dream of a better life and made a small stab at achieving it. The civic "we" was drawn in and enlarged, to the extent that that "we"— and by all accounts it is the vast majority among us—assented to the heroic self-definition and simultaneous civic characterization the president offered and evoked. Tapping the same vein as Bob Dylan in his protest song, "Chimes of Freedom," a song for all the "unsung" ordinary people in the "whole wide universe," Reagan bridged the gap between private and public, fusing the two in a homey reinscription of our sense of ourselves as basically decent folks, living our lives, and capable, if the situation demands, of acts of supererogation.

He can call up our mean streak as well, chiding those who wish us ill or mean to do us harm by reminding them that America's patience is not in-finite and that we will hunt down "these monsters" (terrorists who slaughter the innocent) and ensure that they have "no sanctuary." What is recalled here is America's insular capacity for moral self-righteousness, our sense that when we act it is on principle and not from crudely calculated or narrowly defined self-interest. But Reagan's heart is really elsewhere. He will chide the wicked but he would rather be "at home" with us, as his weekly radio ad-dress, July 21, 1985, following his cancer surgery, indicates: he reminds us that he was shot and bounced back. Why should cancer lay him low? He thanks all the "special people"—doctors, nurses, friends, and citizens—who tended to him and wish him well. And then he becomes, in his own words, "Dr. Reagan," telling us that we should pay attention to physical signs and get to the doctor if we detect something has gone amiss. Becoming deeply personal without giving us the sense that we are voyeurs invading his pri-vacy in a potentially embarrassing way, Reagan honors the First Lady, one of those "private persons forced to live public lives," locating Nancy in a list that includes Abigail Adams, Dolly Madison, and Eleanor Roosevelt. "Nancy Reagan is my everything," he tells us, ending "Thank you, partner."

In a transition that defies all the rules of rhetoric, he shifts from a joke to his romance-partner ("By the way, are you doing anything this evening?") to a quasi-mythical celebration of American unity in diversity, "230 million very different souls . . . liberals and conservatives, fundamentalists and ag-nostics, Southerners and Northerners, recent immigrants and Mayflower descendants . . . held together, always held together by a tie that can't be seen, yet can't be broken."

That is it: we are thanked and God-blessed and the president signs off. But we continue to "hear" long past that moment as surplus meaning wells up in us along multiple vectors: illness or wellness, courage in the face of personal disaster, romance and partnership, concern *for* and *with*, diversity in unity. The speech lingers in the air, resonating to the invisible terms of our public and private identities and purposes. Those who "see through" this and don't hear Reagan in the way I am suggesting he is most often heard have not so much penetrated his rhetoric as indicated, by their alienation, that they are also at odds with, that they have marginalized themselves with reference to, the culture that sustains Reagan and that he, in turn, encircles and rhetorically completes.

Kennedy, too, had a knack for evoking "more," though the nature of the surplus meaning that he mined and that Reagan uncannily excavates is very different, suggesting not just the distinction between two different leaders but etching the boundaries of diverse American civic and social self-definitions. America is no singular shared world of meaning but a world of imperfectly shared, multiple meanings. What Kennedy aimed for was not the ordinary, unsung heroes of everyday life of a Reagan portrait but a rather more extraordinary possibility: the citizen, the being who devotes himself or herself to the *civitas,* the individual who gets out of the house and into the *polis.*

"Ask not . . .": we can finish the sentence. These are the words of a civic republican tradition still alive in our Tocquevillian spaces, reverberating in our Deweyite capabilities, however attenuated these have become through disuse. Kennedy's inaugural address concluded with a sentence beginning, "Finally, whether you are citizens of America, or citizens of the world . . ." His "Ich Bin Ein Berliner" speech opens with, "Two thousand years ago the proudest boast was 'civitas Romanus sum.'" His "Speech to the Greater Houston Ministerial Association" put squarely the possibility of a conflict between religious belief and civic responsibility, insisting that should "the time ever come" (and he did not for one moment concede its likelihood) that "my office would require me to either violate my conscience, or violate the national interest, then I would resign the office, and I hope any other conscientious public servant would do likewise."

Finally, on "The Moral Issue of Equal Rights for All Colors," delivered on June 11, 1963, Kennedy evoked citizenship again and again, uniting the tradition of Scripture with the clarity of the American Constitution. The issue of segregation is at once moral and civic and the end is freedom for "all citizens," for until all are free, none truly are. Kennedy invited his listeners to share the despair and poignancy of those who, because of the "color of their skin," found themselves "second-class citizens." Unlike Reagan, Kennedy never traded personalisms and homilies with us, preferring ironic distance and a self-mockingness that fit, and helped to define, the temper of his era.

Above all, he constituted us as citizens. We were summoned from our private pursuits to the *res publica,* the public good, the public "thing." Again, for all our appropriate skepticism concerning what we were being summoned to or for, the point is that Kennedy held up the mirror of specifically *civic* virtues. We were not private beings, in Kennedy's world, but American citizens. That no president since Kennedy has celebrated the *civitas* suggests either that no one has tried or, more soberly, that we are no longer open to the call to civic identity. Perhaps, given the desuetude of civic spirit in the years since 1963, the civic parts of ourselves have become so submerged we would not hear were someone to speak the language of civic republicanism. We can, and do, respond as self-interested claimants to our piece of the public pie or as constituted members of subgroups (environmentalists, feminists, Third Worldists, moral majoritarians). But perhaps with Kennedy's death we have, in Cicero's words, lost one dream of the *res publica*. Perhaps that mirror is shattered. We will not know until a president once again speaks that language and we either turn a deaf ear or hear and put on our civic robes to take on the public's business.

If Reagan and Kennedy are two sides of a dense civic coin whose rhetoric invited and invites us to inscribe, with them, a particular American identity and constellation of meanings and purposes, Jimmy Carter falls haplessly outside such mutually constitutive speech acts. In trying to figure out why, especially in light of the fact that Carter most openly cried out to us for a personal relationship and was least successful in achieving it, it becomes clear that in Carter's rhetoric nothing was left over, no surplus meaning was evoked. There was a penury about the man and his style, a minimalism that added up to less than the sum of its parts. Although mysterious at first, the Carter failure seems to me explicable on several grounds. In his first inaugural, Carter proclaimed the "great responsibility" of the president, one of staying "close to you," being "worthy of you," and exemplifying "what you are." This was his first of many mistakes—not strategic errors but rhetorical illiteracy, an inability to see who he was in relation to us and what we might then hear when he spoke to us.

A penury of meaning, an impoverishment of purpose was conveyed even when Carter aimed to call us to national sacrifice and determination. In his address on "Energy and National Goals," July 15, 1979, Carter told us we were losing faith, on the wane, suffering from a diminution of national will. We weren't facing up to stark realities. We "the people" had become "the problem." In two short years "we" had gone from being honest, decent, open, fair, and compassionate people (the inaugural) to wastrels who overspent, victims of a malaise and loss of faith, individuals in the grip of a crisis of spirit who needed, if not discipline and punishment, then therapy. A peculiar mental health residue clung to Carter's words.[17] The mirror Jimmy Carter held up to us in 1979 was one we did not mirror back, for to do so meant we had to acquiesce in his definition of us as people of little faith, lacking in confidence, alienated—and here was the crux—*from* him. This pained him because he was "not isolated" from us; our malaise was his own. He pleaded with us to come back into the fold, into the relationship of unity with him. But he, the chiding father, held us at arm's length: we were bad, misbehaving children. We had not lived "within our means." We had gone too heavily into debt. We had stopped saving. He used the word *discipline* no fewer than nine times, and *sacrifice* was another favorite term; *discourage, pain, strong medicine, bitter tasting,* and *stern measures* were others. It was clear Jimmy Carter didn't love us anymore, and we responded in kind with a petulance that was no doubt unfair (given his record) but that he himself had created (given his rhetoric).

What All This Adds Up to, or Subtracts from . . .

Our presidents are our foremost rhetors, primus inter pares among civic interlocutors. That they can speak and we listen does not mean, *pace* the traffickers in tales of seduction, manipulation, and false consciousness, that we are inert and they active. It does mean that we are engaged *with* and *in* a wonderfully and frustratingly complex series of speech-acts that not only implicate us, or require us, but of which we are in an important if elusive way co-authors. We respond immediately but we react as well over time, offering up surplus meaning or withholding it, determining whether and how we shall respond as we hear our own words of civic and individual potency activated by a pervasive presence whom we invite among us, or consign to silence, by a click of the on/off switch. If we don't like what we see or hear, blaming presidential rhetorical trickery is the easy, indeed the feckless, response. We must look into the mirror ourselves and ask who we are that such a relationship with us is invited, or required, by he who is most preeminent among us as a rhetorical actor.

Notes

Originally published in Norman F. Cantor and Nathalia King, eds., *Notebooks in Cultural Analysis* 3 (1986). © 1986, Duke University Press. Reprinted by permission.

1. Jean-Jacques Rousseau, *On the Origin of Language,* trans. John H. Moran and Alexander Gode (New York: Frederick Ungar, 1966), 72.

2. An interesting footnote to the seduction thesis, hence the placement of this thought, is the frequency with which the collective "we" to be persuaded is a "she": Athens and America are civic we/shes most often "talked to" or "on behalf of" by powerful male voices.

3. Plato, *Gorgias,* trans. Walter Hamilton (New York: Penguin Books, 1971), quoted from 23, 28, 30, 32, 44.

4. Cicero, *De Officiis,* trans. Harry G. Edinger (Indianapolis: Bobbs-Merrill, 1974), 4.

5. James Boyd White, *When Words Lose Their Meaning* (Chicago: University of Chicago Press, 1984), 93–94.

6. Ibid., 109.

7. See White, *When Words Lose Their Meaning*, 59, and Dominick LaCapra, *History and Criticism* (Ithaca: Cornell University Press, 1985), 368–87.

8. White, *When Words Lose Their Meaning*, 6.

9. Halford Ross Ryan, "Roosevelt's First Inaugural: A Study of Technique," in his *American Rhetoric from Roosevelt to Reagan* (Prospect Heights, Ill.: Waveland Press, 1983).

10. Ibid., 20.

11. Oliver Sacks, "The President's Speech," *New York Review of Books*, August 15, 1985, 29.

12. Wendell Berry, *Standing By Words* (San Francisco: North Point Press, 1983), 53.

13. Arthur Schlesinger, Jr., *The Coming of the New Deal* (Boston: Houghton Mifflin, 1959), 12.

14. Ibid., 559.

15. Not everybody was charmed by the fireside chat, Schlesinger notes, quoting John Dos Passos, who objected to the artifice of a carefully prepared event *seeming* to be an informal, off-the-cuff affair. See ibid., 572.

16. James Axtell, *The Invasion Within: The Contest of Cultures in Colonial North America* (New York: Oxford University Press, 1985), 14.

17. Not surprising considering that he and his wife were both great devotees of more and better mental health treatment, institutions, etc.

7

Feminist Political Rhetoric
and Women's Studies

Women's studies is a highly charged activity, a field of inquiry with explicit connections to a political movement and to the rhetoric of that movement. The nexus between women's studies as an academic enterprise and feminist political rhetoric is clear in a way that most links between academic disciplines and a broader social field are not. At present, women's studies is a rather large magnet drawing scholars from diverse disciplines into an effort characterized, and celebrated, as interdisciplinary. Under the broad umbrella of women's studies one finds a lively, at times contentious, world of competing epistemologies, ideologies, narrative styles, and ethical and political commitments. Women's studies, at this point, crosses the spectrum of academic disciplines and methodologies.[1] Encompassing a diversity of perspectives is the ideal (however imperfectly realized) of the enterprise.

The rhetoric of feminist politics, however, shares with ideologies in general a "will to truth" that quashes ambiguity and squeezes out diversity. The central focus of this paper is the complex and wary relationship between women's studies scholarship and criticism and grand feminist rhetorical strategies. Women's studies seeks to legitimize concern with women within established disciplines and as a field of inquiry in its own right. Feminist political rhetoric aims to provide the ideological glue for sustained political identity and action. This sets the stage for the unfolding of a complex scenario in which feminist political rhetoric and aims, on the one hand, and the scholarly claims and accomplishments of women's studies, on the other, give rise to another politics: politics among writers to determine which rhetorics, forms of discourse, and narratives will take precedence over the long haul.

"Any cultural description," writes James Clifford, "is an ensemble of anecdotes, narratives, interpretations, typical events and characters, allegories, partial arguments—in short, a complex rhetorical performance."[2] The critic who interjects herself into this complex performance—who becomes one rhetor among others—by that act confirms the importance of the narrative voice, of what is communicated and how.

I shall focus on feminist political rhetoric by taking the measure of two strongly teleological accounts that invite closure. The narratives in question create taut frameworks—lockstep sexual scripts. If one works within these frameworks, one poses questions in ways that compel too easy and too universal conclusions. I share Iris Marion Young's conviction that relentless repetition of a short menu of metaphors stifles energetic and diverse discourse. Locutions that may at first enable us to see the world in new and startling ways (for example, "the personal is political"), as "they become worn, too familiar to be visible," go on to "assume a constraining power."[3]

Feminist political rhetoricians have seen as problematic received categories and understandings. This essay aims at a similar defamiliarization with reference to their own, by now familiar, constructions. The critical portions of the essay set the stage for my defense of a more open narrative form. This latter alternative acknowledges uncertainties and ambiguities. I will, in short, be pointing to two narratives that close out space for ongoing, lively scholarship and criticism in order to distinguish these from an open-textured discursive universe that enables women's studies scholars to live with and within fructifying, desimplifying complexities. Confronted by the necessity of embracing vast quantities of work in a single short essay, I shall take up one general theme—the question of *difference*—zeroing in on the way difference is treated in grand political rhetorics and my preferred heterodox alternative. The problem of difference has long bedeviled feminism and currently provides women's studies with an inexhaustible terrain for research and analysis. I shall sketch the alternatives briefly as ideal types before going on to take up each approach in depth, showing as I do overlap and complexity within types.

First, there is the narrative of *sex neutrality*. This form of feminist political rhetoric begins with the presumption that real or presumed sex differences are imposed upon generic human material from birth. Neonates are ungendered, and the social imposition of gender literally engenders maleness, femaleness, and what counts as masculinity and femininity in any and all cultures. The contemporary political vision of sex equality that flows from the presumption of sex neutrality is one in which equality is, or requires, some form of homogeneity, with men and women becoming interchangeable social actors playing out identical *roles*. In other words, the fact that one is a biological male or biological female can and should cease to be a central and defining feature of personal or social identity and need no longer form the basis for either individual narrative or collective political and social history.

Second, there is the narrative of *sex polarity*. This narrative starts with the presumption that the sexes are radically divided and that they must and should remain so. If this separatism is given an ontological base, the sexes are construed as separate species; the world is viewed in potently dualist terms; and politically separatist strategies follow. A softer version of the sex polarity argument subsumes bipolarity into a series of strong epistemological claims.

Third, there is *sex complementarity*. This narrative is less prominently featured in feminist political rhetoric but more visible in women's studies scholarship, particularly feminist social history and cultural anthropology. The starting presumption is that gender differences and embodiment matter—though how much and to what ends is culturally diverse and philosophically contestable. In addition, relations between the sexes present a complex mosaic, tell a story of contextualized complementarities. "Complementarity" is perhaps not the most felicitous term to characterize this more fluid narrative possibility—a position that flourishes, remember, only to the extent that the sex neutrality and polarity postures are exposed and critiqued in their uncompromising form. The term may conjure up, at least initially, images of happy male and female peas in some harmonious cultural pod. It may suggest an unwarranted consensus, and this is not what I have in mind. Complementarities can be antagonistic and conflicted and do not preclude dominance by one sex over the other. On the other hand, complementarity neither presumes nor requires, as the other positions seem to do, a terribly abstract vision of male and female social actors that ignores the body altogether, on the one hand, or constrains women within pregiven ontological forms having a biological base, on the other.[4]

Both the sex neutrality and the sex polarity positions push strongly toward, or are derived from, the foundational presumption of an "original position."[5] Each privileges Archimedean points from which the analyst may survey culture and history, past and present. Each gives "gender" *preeminent* force on all levels of social reality, from individual identity up to and including the structures of modern nation-states, frequently forgetting that human beings are not reducible to gendered categories. The sex complementarity alternative promises and achieves greater complexity by deflating the teleological and rhetorical certainties that follow from such presumptions. It offers, instead, a discourse within which theory can paint its gray in gray, creating a backdrop for unexpected splotches of color and unanticipated ruptures of form. Having (perhaps prematurely) indicated where I wind up, I propose in what follows to unpack how I got there.

Sex Neutrality: The Androgynous Claim

The sex neutrality story, in its prototypical form, begins thus: In the beginning man made oppression. Oppression requires an object, a subject to subjugate, and she was there. The narrative requires a pregiven female "self" that is then denied self-status by pregiven males driven by a collective *intention* to tyrannize. Thus women became the first oppressed class. All subsequent oppression—that of class, race, the "third world"—is modeled on this original fall. But woman's oppression alone is pan-cultural and universal, coterminous with history itself.[6] Women are variously constituted through this discourse as a "sex-class," a "sex-caste," or a permanent "fourth world" that antedates "third world" oppression. "We find it self-evident," begins one early tract, "that women are a colonized group who have never—*anywhere*—been allowed self-determination."[7]

The male sex-class imposes a damaging and defective *role* on women. Although male motivation for women's oppression is variously construed, the male was able to defeat women handily because women's "unfortunate sexual anatomy" (a Sartrianism repeated by Simone de Beauvoir) set them up as the "victim of the species," relegated to *nature*, which the men "transcended," thus beginning the story of *culture*. Culture is and has always been *patriarchal*. Culture, therefore, is the grand target of reproof and ultimate regeneration in this narrative.

The story continues: women to this day are prisoners of gender, caught in the snare of a systemic *sex-gender system*. This system dictates social roles, purposes, and norms. It inhibits, punishes, and devalues women, while enabling, rewarding, and valorizing men. Generic human, the "biological raw material," goes in, and gendered "social products" come out.[8] This system is operative in all societies, for "all sex-gender systems have been male dominated," and hence driven to assign social gender at birth "on the basis of genitalia."[9] Women are consigned to the sphere of *reproduction,* or unfree nature; men are assigned to the world of *production,* or are free to seize their freedom. The dominant male is constituted variously as a true agent, a layer down of the Law (of the Father), and a transcendent being-for-himself who occupies the productive sphere of history making, the superordinate arena of social existence.

Now, this is a powerful story indeed. It features an archetypal account of origins as an initial point of departure and a constant point of reference; it sets up a readily identifiable political target—culture itself—as a focus for attack; it affords a broad historicizing sweep that gathers all differences of culture, past and present, into a single bin; it claims to account for the "rock bottom" to which all societies conform; it revolves around potent dualisms, including nature/culture, oppressor/oppressed, free/bound, powerful/powerless, reason/emotion, that serve doubly as universal categories for analysis and as political rhetoric. Whether in this paradigmatic form or in softer versions, the narrative inspires political and discursive challenges to received social arrangements by problematizing all aspects of human existence around questions of male and female relations and by reopening in new ways some old debates: nature versus nurture, cultural determinism versus free will, and so on. Several acknowledged classics of modern feminism—from J. S. Mill's nineteenth-century essay *The Subjection of Women* to Simone de Beauvoir's seminal *The Second Sex*—belong within this genre.

 But the explanations that flow from, and reinforce, the deep structure of the narrative grant to the feminist rhetor a too smooth sailing from starting premise to inexorable conclusion. A supple narrative clears a space for the introduction of subplots, new characters, story revisions, perhaps even rewrites. A narrative of closure *begins* from a culmination couched in the form of a query. The point of the narration structured by the query can only be to reaffirm the conclusion imbedded in the query in the first place. Thus: How, or why, did the universal story of women's oppression begin? What holds this oppression in place in all cultures? What can be done to undo it? The truth of women's universal subordination is self-evident, and it is the *truth* of that truth which requires a feminist original position, offers the promise of an Archimedean point, and, in practice, tends to affirm a picture of human life that yields devaluations of women in history and in traditional (non-Western, peasant) cultures in the present.

Some important questions do not get asked, for they cannot be posed *inside* the larger picture of the human condition to which sex neutrality commits its interlocutors. These include: why ask why in a certain way? That is, what does one search for when one searches for origins, embracing a discourse that promises the answer or the key to the riddle? How and why are we justified in claiming that we understand a past age and that this past can be conveyed in and through the rhetorical usage of a later time—our own? How and why are we justified in overriding the self-understandings of prior epochs, and other cultures or individuals and groups within our own culture, if these self-understandings do not mesh with our rhetorical requirements? By now, hundreds of books, essays, and tracts are available that subscribe, implicitly if not self-consciously, to the teleological narrative of sex neutrality in one or another of its variants. The variations draw on important features of the discourse in its ideal typical form. For example: an analyst may choose not to commit herself to the radical feminist analysis that the first oppression was man over woman in a direct, unmediated sense but then go on to embrace other central tenets of the sex neutrality myth. I shall sketch the way various narratives unfold by drawing on several of the strongest and most influential texts only.

If the genre in its modern form has an ur-narrative, it is Beauvoir's *The Second Sex*.[10] Her argument begins from a Sartrian ontology that cleaves the world into twains: nature/culture, in-itself/for-itself, determined/free, bad faith/good faith. Civilization is a male project, and men are its essential actors; women (though free in the noumenal sense) lie outside civilization, in nature, stuck in the Sartrian practico-inert. By now we all know this story. Beauvoir and the many who follow her lead begin with a universalistic set of premises that add up to an overdetermined yet simple model of oppression. These premises offer an unambiguous linkage between dualistic pairs: nature is to culture as woman is to man as oppressed is to oppressor, the latter being powerful by definition, the former powerless. Further, commitment to the narrative invites the conviction that all societies can be modeled along dualistic lines, with women everywhere devalued, men everywhere in ascendance.[11]

For example: inserting her anthropological arguments explicitly inside Beauvoir's narrative, Sherry B. Ortner begins her seminal piece, "Is Female to Male as Nature Is to Culture?" with a conclusion: cultural differences are reducible in the first and last instance to the "universal fact" of women's subordination.[12] More troubled by how to explain cultural diversity than Beauvoir, but committed at the outset to the thesis of universal female oppression, Ortner adopts a stratigraphic metaphor. All societies have layers, and once the analyst reaches the bottom, or basis layer, she excavates the foundation of reality. The presumption is that Culture (and cultures) have a rock-bottom level from which all else emerges. This first or primary level is "the universal devaluation of women." With women's devaluation given, all that remains is to puzzle further over how this came about and what can be done to undo it. All the other features of a society—its economic arrangements, its language, its history, its political and social institutions—are reduced to "local variables" of the culture. If one adopts such a presumption as the basis of one's research, one's scholarly mission will be to seek out evidence of that primary level, affirming thereby the deep structure of one's meta-narrative and reinforcing the political strategies it secretes.

Hardening of the categories is unavoidable. For example: Juliet Mitchell, in her bold *Psychoanalysis and Feminism,* declared the Law of the Father (patriarchy) to be "culture itself," with women universally subject to, and subjugated by, this law even into the interstices of "the Unconscious." Mitchell not only presumes that she can advance lawlike claims about *every* culture without describing in detail *any* culture; she is compelled by the force of her narrative to *interpret* all points of contact between women and men, no matter what they may appear to be and no matter how the subjects themselves may understand these matters, as instances of the working out of "the universal culture" of female subordination.[13] Within the rationalism to which the sex neutrality narrative commits its advocates, women will be "free" only when "nature" is *aufgehoben*—both her own "nature" (the species victimization of which de Beauvoir writes) and Nature, those features of human existence, those aspects of the natural surround, not yet brought under rational will or shaped to its specifications. This is the direction in which analysts who are daughters of Beauvoir must move; she closes off other paths. The key—the narrative promises a key—is to transcend the bodily, the unfree, the unthought, the lower (and female) level. Women, too, Beauvoir insists, can enter the world of transcendence—they can remake themselves through an act of will, the possibility for controlling nature being at hand.

In addition to the versions of the sex neutrality tale indebted to de Beauvoir or to the structuralist forms noted above, there is a variant of the narrative that shares its teleological impetus and general picture of human possibility. I refer to analyses that begin from behavioral psychology or from those modes of psychoanalysis most compatible with a conditioning model. The rhetorical picture of human life to which such analysts—currently exerting strong influence inside American academic feminism—commit themselves is one of relentless and total (or nearly so) conditioning under the sway of a sex-gender system. The implicit theory of human nature is familiar: *tabula rasa*. We are raw materials that become social products. That we come out "gendered" means that a system of controls and reinforcements can consistently produce conventional results. In a piece that helped to set the framework for narratives in this mode, Gayle Rubin writes that "a systematic social apparatus . . . takes up females as raw materials and fashions domesticated women as products."[14] We perforce require a new sex-gender system to create "androgynous" or "symmetrical" human beings.

Going in as generic human, no longer assigned more or less arbitrarily to a gender category, we will come out stamped with the imprint of sex neutrality and infused with a combination of "the positive capacities" of each gender "but without the destructive extremes" gendered identity now requires.[15] By resocializing away from sexed identities, we can erase "men" and "women," eliminate any biological need for sex to be associated with procreation at any time or for anyone, eradicate all sex-based role differentiation, and, at last, "transcend sexual gender."[16]

The urge to assimilate is powerfully clear in these formulations: we must rub all the rough edges off human material. The aim is a world in which the sexes can play infinitely interchangeable *roles.* Interestingly, the idea of a social role is of relatively recent vintage, entering sociological discourse in the 1930s. Nobody talked about "sex roles" before World War II. Yet the applicability of this concept is presumed by sex neutralists to be universal and transhistorical. The language of "role" serves this narrative well because of its externalized and instrumental features—deploying sex-role rhetoric means that the analyst can veer away from sharper and deeper questions of human identity.

What does the narrative promise, and what does it require? We are once again promised transcendence—from what is regarded as the prison of gendered identities—and in thus transcending we will also overthrow the systematic denial of our authentic selves by the oppression of the sex-gender system. Despite its deterministic model of the conditioned human, the deeper ontology of the narrative portrays the self as a robust unity, now fractured by faulty and exploitative social forms. Ultimately, patriarchal culture having been deconstructed, human beings will no longer be reared in ways that guarantee a psychology of sex oppression, and hence will no longer "need" to coerce or manipulate others. This is the way the story ends; indeed, this is how it *must* end, given the motor of teleological necessity that drives it. Finally, the sex neutrality narrative is too thin to sustain *over time* a rich rhetoric and to prompt complex inquiries. The profusion of recent and important works in social history, anthropology, epistemology, literary criticism, and myth outstrips the constraints of the perspective, an important development that I note in my discussion of sex complementarity below.

Sex Polarity: Manichean Moments

The original Manichees severed the world in dualistic fashion between a Kingdom of Light, from which sprang the soul, and a Kingdom of Darkness, the realm of the body. I use the term here as shorthand for an essentially dualistic feminist political rhetoric dominated by an ontology that, in the strong statement of this position, divides the sexes into something akin to separate species. What is the attraction and strength of this narrative? Through what rhetorical usages and narrative strategies does sex polarity discourse invite closure? The "manichean moment," with its suggested metaphysic of spirit versus matter and good versus evil, offers clues to the deep structure of the discourse. The critical interpreter is driven by the rhetoric of strong sex polarists to what they take to be the root of the matter—sexuality. Specifically, they are driven to male sexuality, to which authentic female sexuality offers a contrast model. The central concerns of narratives in this mode are sex and violence.

There are antecedents for today's politics and rhetoric of sex polarity in nineteenth- and early twentieth-century feminism. Though it is by no means the whole story, one important feature of this discourse was a vision of sexual hygiene, for male lust was seen as a destructive force requiring taming and domestication. Important feminist thinkers and publicists extolled the broader virtues of healthy and rational sexuality as an essential part of a wider platform of social planning and equilibrium. Male "indulgences, appetites, and vices," in the words of Elizabeth Cady Stanton, at the midpoint in a long and various career that saw her embracing a variety of not always harmonizable rhetorics, subverted, if unchecked and unrationalized, any hope for progress, harmony, and scientific reconstruction of social life.[17]

Suffragist political rhetoric of the sort that Aileen Kraditor has called "arguments from expediency" resounds with claims that women—at least white and native-born women—formed the "large proportion of patriotism, temperance, morality, religion" and as such would, once enfranchised, transform and purify politics itself.[18] Women are "more exalted than the men" because "their moral feelings and political instincts" are "not so much affected by selfishness, or business, or party consideration."[19] Rather than denying or deflecting the insistence on the part of male antisuffragists that women were too "pure" for political life, many leading feminists accepted the appellation and turned it to their own purposes. Thus sexuality entered political discourse and rhetoric within the literary and ideological constraints of the sex polarity narrative.[20]

Although discourses never precisely repeat themselves, there is a mythic, archetypal quality to the sex polarity narrative that helps to give it its compelling power. In common with the sex neutrality narrative, sex polarists tell a tale of the historic subjugation of the female, though she is located more as history's universal victim than as its prototypical oppressed class. This subjugation, in some versions, represents the male defeat of an age of matriarchy: all of "patriarchal history," therefore, is stained with the shame of its origins. The narrative presumes powerful universals. The key is *patriarchy*—a category deployed variously to describe and to explain history and every culture known to or within it.

The remorselessness of male victimization of the female—her enthrallment to his will and design—in turn enthralls the reader, tapping the deeply rooted Western narrative form of goodness enchained. Thus the rhetoric of radical feminist separatism on the matter of destructive versus positive forms of sexual expression has at its disposal the deep structure of the strong narrative. An unmediated conduit is presupposed between the "patriarchal, repressive family" and the heterosexual male's "normal" violence—up to and including militarism, wars, nuclear technology, despoliation of nature, advertising, pornography: all are construed as the predictable, inevitable outgrowths of unchained masculinism.[21] The politics of pornography and antiwar protest are two current concerns that afford evidence of the impossibly heavy burden placed on "female virtues" in challenging military masculinism, on the one hand, or in eradicating the breeding ground of masculinist culture in what is construed as one of its prototypical bastions, on the other. The latter choice of battlefields fills out the story, for pornography is taken to be the graphic public representation of private relations between men and women: it mirrors reality, and the mirror must be shattered. What Catharine Stimpson has called a "vulgar theory of mimesis" comes into play as feminist antipornographers argue for an identity between the "representational" and the "real."[22]

I cannot present in detail the massive literature of the current sexual manicheanism.[23] Essential for the purpose of this essay is the centrality of universal dichotomies of victim/victimizer, innocent/guilty, pure/tainted, in the sex polarity narrative, doubling as metaphor and metonymy and helping to set an agenda both for feminist politics and—certainly this is one aim—for women's studies. There is little room for ambiguity in this highly charged discourse. Those certain of hard and fast truths and the politically correct actions they inspire correctly see theories and rhetorics of complexity, contradiction, irony, and paradox as corrosive of totalized ideological commitment. They recognize that more open narrative possibilities are thorns in the sides of would-be actors, for they complicate the political as well as the discursive universe.

A rhetoric that requires as its original position a picture of woman as ur-victim is additionally troubling, particularly as a basis for women's studies scholarship. This is a question I have addressed before, but it is worth one more pass. In an important 1973 essay in the *Monist*, Abigail Rosenthal wrote of the "masks" through which discourse speaks and how such masks may enable the interlocutor to raise important questions but, finally, send her into a self-defeating rhetorical roundelay because her chosen mask signifies a narration of closure. One mask identified by Rosenthal is the "mask of purity," the presumption that the victim speaks in a pure voice.[24] In order to sustain the mask of purity, and feelings of victimization, rhetoric must bear a heavier and heavier burden of rage. In addition, the mask offers a license to evade the ways in which definitions of "victimization" are also means to coerce or control—but these cannot be acknowledged.[25]

Patricia Meyer Spacks, for example, in an essay on the contributions of feminist criticism, warns that "the discovery of victimization can have disastrous intellectual consequences. It produces . . . one note criticism. Readers newly aware of the injustices perpetrated on one sex find evidence of such injustice everywhere—and, sometimes, *only* evidence of this sort. They discover over and over, in language, structure, and theme, testimony to women's victimization." The upshot, Spacks concludes, is almost invariably a shrill, monotonous rhetoric caught in the self-confirming cycle of its own story. Similarly, Stimpson warns that genderizing too zealously, whether in language or in stories of human culture, casting all into binary oppositions of male and female forms, "is another reconstitution of an older pattern: a dualistic model of human activity that denies the dazzle, the dappledness of life."[26] It is to exemplary, even dazzling alternatives to such rigidified rhetoric and ideology that I next turn.

Sex Complementarity: Staying Alive

As I indicated above, I wish that there were a more apt tag than *sex complementarity* for this alternative narrative form, for I do not mean to paint a picture of harmony between the sexes. Complementarities can be, and often are, antagonistic and conflicted. The point is to put men and women into the same story, but in a supple way at odds with the static oppositions featured in closed narratives. The markers of a narration of closure, remember, are: (1) a search for some "original position" from which history has proceeded, with its beginning determining its forward movement; (2) a clearly identified, universally construed object of critique (for example: patriarchal culture) that gives the political agenda supported by the narrative its form and meaning; (3) an explicit or implied universal subject; (4) a dehistoricizing sweep that deflects from cultural particularities in a search for the root of all ways of life; (5) a defined end-point, whether in the overthrow of patriarchy or the creation of a benign sex-gender system that will resocialize human beings in some wholly new way; (6) finally, an Archimedean point that offers the feminist analyst claims of epistemological privilege. Having discussed the first five of these criteria above, I shall turn to the final point—the question of "speaker's privilege."

All scholars find the prospect of a privileged epistemic ground seductive. Those laboring in the vineyard of women's studies are no exception. The problem of point of view is central to debates within and between feminist thinkers. I shall take up this debate through the work of two anthropologists, both critics of claims to epistemological privilege inside their own discipline. (Of course, this example by no means exhausts the issue, which is being fought out in all disciplines.) Assessing the contention of a group of feminist anthropologists that, as members of a "universal category," they are "somehow . . . free from bias," Marilyn Strathern notes the self-confirming nature of their claims. The argument is that one validates one's anthropology by taking up, and speaking from, the "women's point of view," under the presumption that a woman has a "specific, non-replicable insight" into any given culture that is unavailable to a male researcher.

The self-consciously female (feminist) point of view, the argument goes, is not subject to the charges of bias that can be justly leveled against a male point of view. Moreover, an identity is said to exist between "the author and subject of study," a "naturally grounded" congruity. The result is a position of privilege that enables the feminist anthropologist to dismiss male knowledge claims or interpretations. It also lets her derail challenges from female anthropologists who disagree on the ground that some women who have experienced western patriarchy but fail to see through the double-consciousness that their femaleness/feminism affords them are instead double-blinded. Similarly, Judith Shapiro questions the claim that a double standard in anthropology is legitimate for assessing "male bias" on the one hand and a privileged female "double consciousness" on the other.[27]

Sex complementarity narratives offer no privileged standpoint, presuming instead that all points of view are partial and incomplete. Hermeneutical dilemmas cannot be evaded. Though knowledge and understanding may, in some interesting ways, be embodied—and this might help to explain why men and women, at least some of the time and to culturally specific ends and purposes, experience the world in different ways—no embodied being, male or female, has access to "the whole" or anything like "the totality." One is free, therefore, to explore differences without presuming the superiority of a gendered narrative that closes out alternate or contesting interpretations. Not being hobbled in advance by the conceptual chains of gender as prison, the critic is open to the intimations and possibilities of gender as prism.

Encumbered with culture and history, the analyst not only acknowledges but creates narrative space through her choice of metaphor and her understanding of ontology or being. Unlike the abstract, overdetermined subjects of sex neutralists and polarists, the subjects who populate her world of complex complementarities are engaged in social relations in diverse settings. Although gender may be determinative to some ends and purposes, it also matters whether one is American or Russian, an urban Catholic or a rural Baptist. But one cannot explore these other markers of identity, or describe them thickly, if one begins by presuming that one's ethnic heritage, one's religion, one's community ties, the books one reads, the movies one goes to, the candidate one votes for, the dreams one has, are a more or less trivial icing on the real cake of gender. Notes Stimpson: "Because of the legitimate pressure of such groups as black feminists, feminist critics are now more apt to remember that every woman is more than a woman. She belongs, as well, to a class, a race, a nation, a family, a tribe, a time, a place."[28]

Because the sex complementarity narrative does not invite the analyst to claim either universality or exclusivity, she is free to draw upon particular features of the closed narratives whose overall structure and rhetoric she has rejected. For example, the sex neutrality position reminds her to be vigilant concerning the ways in which social life constructs sexuality, intimacy, education, leisure, and so on: things do not just happen. And she is especially on the lookout for those pervasive images and expectations that push and pummel women this way or that to ends and in interests they have no hand in formulating. From the sex polarity narrative, she takes a concern with the violent face that intimacy may present and with the aggressive forms that the social construction of masculine identity makes more available to all men—though she acknowledges that some men are more immersed in that identity or susceptible to its claims than others. A social narrative, if it is to open up vistas rather than pull down the blinds, must afford supple, not mechanistic, ways of looking at power, authority, equality, freedom, the public, the private, family, meaning, intentionality, decency, and so on.

For example: we have learned from anthropologists that the world is untidy, yet narratives of sex neutrality and sex polarity require neatness, order, and clear lines of power and control. Peggy Reeves Sanday, author of *Male Dominance, Female Power,* offers a particularly interesting example of growth. Sanday began her work from the closed presumption that women were universally subordinate, men dominant. She expected that her analysis of over 150 ethnographies would offer proof along such lines. To her initial consternation, her evidence challenged her theory. Not only was it not the case that men were the universal, culture-creating, dominant sex; there were many societies in which women wielded or had wielded great authority and power. "This realization," she writes, "meant I had to switch my theoretical stance midstream and become at least semiliterate in symbolic anthropology."[29] Her salient point is that the abstractness of global approaches and presumptions blinds the observer to potent symbolic markers of male and female identity, power, and authority. Sanday, Karen Sacks, and others suggest that a pronounced inability on the part of Western anthropologists, including feminists, to see patterns of authority and power in traditional societies may derive from our persistent statist bias, from our tendency to conflate difference with inequality, and, more recently, from an ideological compulsion to read into cultures not our own rhetorical convictions about some universal male/female relation.[30] These writers deconstruct the constitutive criteria of the sex neutrality and polarity positions and open up space for consideration of more complex possibilities.

A second example—and the best way to take the measure of the sex complementarity narrative is through exemplary texts—is to be found in the fluid variety now evident in the field of social history. Social historians offer one rich account after another demonstrating transformations in family life that are incompatible with the presumption of a universal, patriarchal form and showing that preindustrial family life was laced through and through with complex sex complementarity in home and community. A fascinating addition to this growing list is Martine Segalen, *Love and Power in the Peasant Family*. Segalen notes in her introduction that to explore the texture of peasant life, one must first confront the reigning dogma on the rural family. In her words, the notion that the rural family "was 'patriarchal,' that the authority of the husband over the wife was absolute, and the wife's subordination universally accepted, that old cliché is alive and well. Whether they are seen as the good old days, a model for resolving the crisis of contemporary society, or whether such an attitude is rejected—as in feminist pronouncements—there remains a persistent belief in the absolute authority of the husband over the wife, and, more generally, in the domination of the female group by the male group."[31] By asking why such rigidified attitudes persist, Segalen clears the space for exploring the meaning of the "wealth of symbol" in rural discourse (folklore, proverbs, architecture) and dealing with the "content of matrimonial life; relationships of labour and authority; the relationship between the couple, and between the couple and the village community."[32] The world that emerges from her pages is one of complementarities, which differ from region to region and decade to decade.[33]

The sex complementarity narrative acknowledges the forcefulness of this burgeoning scholarship and affords a loose-fitting discursive frame that helps to focus and interpret diverse material. This narrative presumes a world of dynamic sociality rather than static Hobbesianism or structural-functionalism. If we think of male and female relations exclusively along the lines of the oppression model—on individual or social levels—we promote a hollow picture of social life and possibility. No long-term relationship stays the same. What are the patterns of ebb and flow in the forms of complementarity and the shifting patterns of authority, control, and so on? Although the narrative has room for clashes and challenges—these, too, often have a dynamic complementarity—it does turn the perspectival lens toward complex reciprocities and shifting balances of power. The narrative has no predetermined end, no prewritten script, leaving room for social participants to engage in at least some improvisation, for individual and social narratives are not presumed to be precisely homologous.

Take, for example, Marina Warner's *Joan of Arc*. Her Joan is "an individual in history and real time" but simultaneously "the protagonist of a famous story in the timeless dimension of myth, and the way that story has come to be told tells yet another story, one about our concept of the heroic, the good and the pure."[34] In a work that is more a genealogy than a history, Warner constructs Joan's history and the competing histories of that history (Joan's "afterlife") in a provocative way because she is uninterested in playing out a predetermined line (e.g., Joan as the female victim of masculinist power, or Joan as a feminist precursor determined to break gender roles). Alert to the danger of prefabrication, Warner notes in her prologue that in writing female biography, "it is easy to revert unconsciously to known stereotypes."[35] Instead, Warner offers textual space for Joan and her accusers in Joan's time, and those who have used her legend subsequently, to speak to us.

We are reminded of the distance that separates her time from ours because Warner alerts us to transformations in understandings of "the self" by delineating the terms of Joan's self-identity, showing the ways in which she embraced or shook off the markers of both maleness and femaleness. Those markers did not constitute, as the sex polarists and neutralists would have it, some hard cleavage along gendered lines but were more densely located—in competing understandings of embodiment, of the equality of souls despite differences in physical form, in lists of the virtues. Warner writes: "In European languages, the use of the feminine to embody different aspects of goodness is . . . remarkable, and the phenomenon was seized on, in most cases probably unconsciously, by numerous women in Christian history."[36] But it was seized on in such a way that reversals were possible—for example, the association of a queen like Elizabeth with glorious martial virtues. The complexity of it all is the point, highlighting the many questions the sex complementarity narrative enables the interlocutor to ask, since all the answers have not been provided in advance by the trajectory of a closed story.[37]

Similarly, Natalie Zemon Davis, in an essay on men, women, and the problem of collective violence, argues that the opposition presumed by sex polarists between "life-givers" and "life-takers" is not so clear-cut if one looks carefully at "the historical record of the late Middle Ages and the early modern period."[38] She sketches the numerous competing and compelling notions of manhood available in early modern Europe, from warrior to absolute pacifist, and notes the "nuanced" reflections about male violence available in contrast to the "simplistic terms" that tended to dominate discourse on women and violence—though there were "multiple ideals for sexual behavior" for both sexes.[39] The distinguishing characteristic of Davis's discussion is its desimplifying quality, whereas the overriding feature of narrations of closure is the radically oversimplified story they tell.

As a final example, Kristin Luker's *Abortion and the Politics of Motherhood* offers desimplifying discourse and open-textured analysis as an ideal for women's studies.[40] Feminist positions on the abortion debate hardened long ago. Within the sex polarity and neutrality narratives, abortion becomes both a woman's absolute (or nearly so) right and a weapon in the sex war. The presumption is that men have used women's "reproductive capacity" to keep women in their place. It follows that abortion is necessary for liberation or freedom as defined in these accounts. The writer who raises questions about the moral dimensions of abortion in a complex way, or veers from the orthodox position, is located as a reactionary or worse.[41] But Luker's study, involving in-depth interviews with pro-choice and pro-life activists, shows that matters are not so simple. She lets both sides—primarily women—develop their world-views and self-understandings. We come to appreciate—as we cannot if there is a simple contrast of right and wrong or pro and anti—the deeper philosophic presumptions that animate activists on both sides of this highly charged debate. We see dimensions of the abortion controversy that are glossed over or denied in feminist rhetoric, particularly its class features and the question of the cultural hegemony of the upper middle and knowledge classes to which most feminists belong. Luker exemplifies scholarship that is engaged, truly aroused by and involved in its subject, but not blinded by the determination to rank ideological conviction over scholarly curiosity or what Hannah Arendt called the life of the mind.

Feisty Kent, King Lear's combative man, proclaims to a fellow with whom he is engaged in a fracas, "I shall teach you differences." But lessons learned at the end of a Kent's clenched fist, or at the end of a narrative that in answering everything may spark nothing, are valuable largely in a negative sense. If we would learn and teach differences, we must have a discourse and a rhetoric, a language of description and interpretation, sinewy and playful enough to take us into the heart of that which we would understand. We require narrations that help us to tell the story of the embodied, the concrete, the spheres of practical reason, the cross-purposes, overlappings, confusions, paradoxes, inconsistencies, intentions, fears, and hopes of everyday life in diverse settings.[42] This means that we cannot hope to bring all of life under one overarching narration; we cannot pin reality down with a few premises and put it on display as part of a still life.

This means, as well, that we must be circumspect about importing narratives and rhetorics from one arena, in which they help to constitute and shape the reality of a particular activity in a delimited sphere, and make them do double duty in a sphere animated by very different concerns, populated by a different cast of characters whose ends may diverge dramatically from those who actions the narrative described originally. For example: the by now commonplace deployment of the rhetoric of reproduction as the chosen characterization for human procreation in feminist ideology distorts what it purports to describe by presuming that human birth from the body of a woman and the care of a vulnerable infant are essentially functional activities that mimic the instrumentalism of production. But this courts absurdity, albeit of the functionalist sort: it requires that we construe an activity that is embodied, emotional, particular, singular, and irreplaceable with an activity that is (in modern labor) mechanical, detached, shorn of deep meaning, generic, and infinitely replaceable. One could multiply the examples of distortion that result when econometric discourse, game theory, or some other abstract analytic device is brought into the kitchen, boudoir, shopping center, or playing field.

Even as we are alert, in Wittgenstein's wry phrase, to language "gone on holiday," we must also steer clear of language gone wild, of narratives that turn rhetoric loose upon past and present to rampage at will. The sex neutrality and sex polarity narratives begin with the presumption that those in possession of the story line, who know the basic plot and characters, have unlimited access to past and present. They presume, and their discourse constitutes, an omniscient subject: a self or *the* Self, who looks uncannily like ourselves. In this narrative, the Self is wound up, given its marching orders, and sent stalking backward in time, forward into the future, or sideways into all other societies. When the Self reports back, it speaks in our categories, reaffirms our narrative, and legitimates our judgments. The desimplifying discourse I have sketched through example offers no such handy entity, for we understand that the self itself is a contested concept, fabricated variously in and through history.

I began this essay by pointing to the complex connection between women's studies and feminist politics. I suggested that the claims and aims of the two were not identical and might, at times, be at odds. Others share the same concern, and I shall conclude on a note of ambiguity, with reflections from Judith Shapiro and Catharine Stimpson that take up the matter from two distinct, yet not antagonistic, points of view. Acknowledging the energy that feminist political concerns generated for women's studies, Shapiro now believes that the time has come for women's studies to loosen the tie between its endeavors and the political rhetoric and ideological claims of feminism. "The danger," she writes, "in too close an association between scholarship and social reformism is not only in the limits it places on intellectual inquiry, but also in the implication that our activities as social, moral, and political beings are dependent on what we are able to discover in our scientific research. Loosening the tie would have liberating consequences . . . for anthropological investigation and for feminism as a social movement."[43] Stimpson, however, does not want the wedge between feminism and feminist criticism driven so far. She writes that feminist critics "must hold fast to the feminist principles" underlying their criticism. "Feminist criticism began, in part, as an anatomy of the pain that the pressures of history had imprinted on women, as a passion to erase that pain, and as a hope, often inadequately expressed, to ally that passion with other progressive political energies. At their shrewdest, feminist critics also know that such activities must not mask a fantastic desire to regain a human paradise. To long for perpetual bliss is to behave like a consumer whose Visa accounts are never rendered, whose masters never charge."[44] Between Shapiro's voice of caution and Stimpson's voice of passionate, yet disillusioned insistence, lies the narrative ground occupied by women's studies at its best.

Notes

Originally published in John S. Nelson, Allan M. Megill, and Donald N. McCloskey, eds., *The Rhetoric of the Human Sciences.* © 1987. (Madison: University of Wisconsin Press). Reprinted by permission.

1. Elizabeth Langland and Walter Gove, eds., *A Feminist Perspective in the Academy: The Difference It Makes* (Chicago: University of Chicago Press, 1981), covers literature, criticism, theater and related arts, religious studies, American history, political science, economics, anthropology, psychology, and sociology.

2. James Clifford, "The Other Side of Paradise," *Times Literary Supplement,* May 13, 1983, 476.

3. Iris Marion Young, "Is There a Women's World? Some Reflections on the Struggle for Our Bodies," in *The Second Sex—Thirty Years Later: A Commemorative Conference on Feminist Theory* (New York: Institute for the Humanities, 1979), 44.

4. My argument does not turn on the claim that all feminist writers are aware of the underlying ontological presumptions and epistemological commitments that animate their discourse.

5. Neither the sex neutrality nor the sex polarity position corresponds in a tidy way to political divisions between radical, liberal, Marxist, and socialist feminisms; members of each of these political identifications may share some or all of these potent rhetorics.

6. Women's oppression is given as a starting point but is often not unpacked conceptually. A situation of oppression requires that one group of agents enslave, dominate, or pacify some other group. Lurking in the model of oppression is a strong presumption of malicious intent, for oppression is purposive, not simply the effluence of inchoate flailings or haphazard accidents.

7. Barbara Burris, "The Fourth World Manifesto," *Notes from the Third Year: Women's Liberation* (New York: n.p., 1971), 1.

8. The quoted material is drawn from Gayle Rubin, "The Traffic in Women: Notes on the 'Political Economy' of Sex," in Rayna R. Reiter, ed., *Toward an Anthropology of Women* (New York: Monthly Review Press, 1975), 165, and Nancy Chodorow, *The Reproduction of Mothering* (Berkeley: University of California Press, 1978), 9.

9. Kathleen E. Grady, "Androgyny Reconsidered," in Juanita H. Williams, ed., *Psychology of Women: Selected Readings* (New York: Norton, 1979), 174.

10. Simone de Beauvoir, *The Second Sex,* trans. H. M. Parshley (New York: Bantam Books, 1978).

11. A lucid critique of "the promiscuous overuse of nature-culture rhetoric," tracing its emergence in modern form to the Enlightenment, where one first finds sustained arguments that women embody the antinomy to Reason, may be found in L. J. Jordanova's essay, "Natural Facts: A Historical Perspective on Science and Sexuality," in Carol P. MacCormack and Marilyn Strathern, eds., *Nature, Culture, and Gender* (Cambridge: Cambridge University Press, 1980), 42–69.

12. Ortner's essay helped to inaugurate a flood of discourse on the nature/culture theme. Found in Michelle Rosaldo and Louise Lamphere, eds., *Woman, Culture and Society* (Stanford, Calif.: Stanford University Press, 1974), 67–87. Shulamith Firestone, *The Dialectic of Sex* (New York: Bantam Books, 1972), expresses her clear indebtedness to Beauvoir as she takes the argument to its *reductio ad absurdum.* I critique Firestone at length in *Public Man, Private Woman: Women in Social and Political Thought* (Princeton: Princeton University Press, 1981), 204–28.

13. Juliet Mitchell, *Psychoanalysis and Feminism* (New York: Pantheon Books, 1971). This is a bold book because Mitchell offers a sustained defense of Freud, identified as a central villain by many feminist writers. Eleanor Burke Leacock, "The Changing Family and Lévi-Strauss, or Whatever Happened to Fathers?" *Social Research* 44 (1977): 235–59, offers a critique of the urge to universalize abstractly about cultures.

14. Rubin, "The Traffic in Women," 158.

15. Chodorow, *The Reproduction of Mothering,* 218.

16. See, for example, Ann Ferguson, "Androgyny as an Ideal for Human Development," in Mary Vetterling-Braggin, Frederick A. Elliston, and Jane English, eds., *Feminism and Philosophy* (Totowa, N.J.: Littlefield, Adam, 1977), 62–63. The androgyny literature is enormous at this point, having been inaugurated in its current form by essays that date from the early 1970s.

17. Elizabeth Cady Stanton, "Speech to the American Equal Rights Association," *Revolution,* May 13, 1869. The liveliest critical treatment of the link between feminism, moral reform movements like temperance, and "scientific" social and biological engineering is William Leach, *True Love and Perfect Union: The Feminist Reform of Sex and Society* (New York: Basic Books, 1980).

18. Cited from Ida Husted Harper, ed., *History of Woman Suffrage,* vol. 5 (New York: J. J. Little and Ives, 1922), 77. See also Aileen Kraditor, *The Ideas of the Woman Suffrage Movement, 1890–1920* (Garden City, N.Y.: Doubleday, Anchor Books, 1971).

19. From Elizabeth Cady Stanton, Susan B. Anthony, and Matilda Joslyn Gage, eds., *History of Woman Suffrage,* vol. 2 (Rochester: Charles Mann, 1891), 17.

20. For a critique of the narrative, see Emma Goldman, *The Traffic in Women and Other Essays in Feminism* (New York: Times Change Press, 1970). Goldman acerbically condemned the suffragist as "essentially a purist . . . naturally bigoted and relentless in her effort to make others as good as she thinks they ought to be." Although Goldman's

indictment of suffragist discourse in general is too harsh, she shows great insight in zeroing in on this feature.

21. For one of the liveliest recent examples of the genre by one of its most prolific and best-known spokeswomen, see Mary Daly, *Pure Lust* (Boston: Beacon Press, 1984).

22. Catharine Stimpson, "Feminism and Feminist Criticism," *Massachusetts Review* 24 (1983): 282. For a political discussion of this issue, see Jean Bethke Elshtain, "The New Porn Wars," *New Republic,* June 25, 1984, 15–20.

23. For a more complete critical analysis, with bibliographical references, see my discussion in chapter 5 of *Public Man, Private Woman*, esp. 204–28.

24. Abigail Rosenthal, "Feminism without Contradictions," *Monist* 51 (1973): 29.

25. See, for example, Helen Moglen's discussion of this theme in *Charlotte Brontë: The Self Conceived* (New York: Norton, 1976), and Anne Douglas's *The Feminization of American Culture* (New York: Avon Books, 1977). Douglas is critiqued by Mary Kelley, *Private Woman, Public Stage: Literary Domesticity in Nineteenth-Century America* (New York: Oxford University Press, 1984).

26. Spacks, "The Difference It Makes," in Langland and Gove, *A Feminist Perspective in the Academy,* 7–24; quoted material is from Stimpson, "Feminism and Feminist Criticism," 287.

27. Marilyn Strathern, "Culture in a Netbag: The Manufacture of a Subdiscipline in Anthropology," *Man* 16 (1981): 665–88, and Judith Shapiro, "Anthropology and the Study of Gender," in Langland and Gove, *A Feminist Perspective in the Academy,* 110–29.

28. Stimpson, "Feminism and Feminist Criticism," 276.

29. Peggy Reeves Sanday, *Male Dominance, Female Power* (Cambridge: Cambridge University Press, 1981), xvi.

30. Karen Sacks, "State Bias and Women's Status," *American Anthropologist* 78 (1976): 565–69.

31. Martine Segalen, *Love and Power in the Peasant Family,* trans. Sarah Matthews (Chicago: University of Chicago Press, 1983), 1–2.

32. Ibid., 7.

33. Forerunners whose work in social history countered theses of universal female subordination include Mary Beard's classic *Woman as Force in History* (New York: Collier Books, 1972 [orig. 1948]), and Eileen Power's pioneering *Medieval Women* (New York: Collier Books, 1972). See also Power, "The Position of Women," in C. G. Crump and E. F. Jacob, eds., *The Legacy of the Middle Ages* (Oxford: Clarendon Press, 1926), 401–33.

34. Marina Warner, *Joan of Arc: The Image of Female Heroism* (New York: Vintage Books, 1982), 7.

35. Ibid., 9.

36. Ibid., 229.

37. Warner explicitly positions herself against "feminists who wish to abolish the grammatical differences" of gender classification in language, arguing that this would result in a "primitive and monolithic language with lesser flexibility, less accuracy and less capacity to express distinctions." Ibid., 228.

38. Natalie Zemon Davis, "Men, Women, and Violence: Some Reflections on Equality," *Smith Alumnae Quarterly,* April 1972, 12–15.

39. Ibid., 15.

40. Kristin Luker, *Abortion and the Politics of Motherhood* (Berkeley: University of California Press, 1984).

41. See, for example, the ideological rigidifications in Judith Stacey, "The New Conservative Feminism," *Feminist Studies* 9 (1983): 560–83.

42. See, for example, Clifford Geertz, *The Interpretation of Cultures* (New York: Basic Books, 1973). Another example: Carlo Ginzburg, *The Cheese and the Worms: The Cosmos of a Sixteenth-Century Miller* (New York: Penguin Books, 1982).

43. Shapiro, "Anthropology and the Study of Gender," 126.

44. Stimpson, "Feminism and Feminist Criticism," 287–88.

8

Feminism and Politics

Understood historically, feminism is a concern with the social role and identity of women in relation to men in societies past and present, animated by a conviction that women suffer and have suffered injustices because of their sex. The political language and aims of modern feminism emerged from the French Revolution and the Enlightenment. Associated historically with forces combating orthodoxy and autocracy, feminism defined itself as a struggle for recognition of the rights of women, for equality between the sexes, and for redefinitions of womanhood. Drawing upon liberal and rationalist as well as utopian and romantic ideas in Western Europe and America, feminism has long resisted easy definition, and its implications for moral life are ongoingly contested and contestable.

Modern feminism is most often traced to the publication of Mary Wollstonecraft's *Vindication of the Rights of Women* in 1792. Wollstonecraft adumbrated what were to become inescapable feminist preoccupations including, but not limited to, the defense of political and natural rights. She challenged received notions of the distinctive virtues of the two sexes; argued for a transformed education for male and female; attacked martial images of citizenship; and celebrated an androgynous notion of the rational self.

Reason became a weapon for women's emancipation, deployed against the exclusive identification of women with "nature" and their sexual function and capacity. Faith in reason was then coupled with a strong belief in progress. These convictions, refined in and through an already deeply rooted tradition of liberal contractarianism and commitment to formal legalistic equality, are most manifest in John Stuart Mill's classic nineteenth-century tract, *The Subjection of Women* (1869). Counterposing "Reason" and "Instinct," Mill looks forward to a society based on rational principles. Reason, he contends, requires nullifying differences of treatment based on considerations of sex, among other "accidents of birth." Granting women equality of citizenship and civil liberty in the public realm will help to bring about a deeper transformation in the social relations of the sexes.

Liberalism has been attractive to feminist thinkers. The language of rights is a potent weapon against traditional obligations, particularly those of family duty or any social status declared "natural" on the basis of ascriptive characteristics. To be "free" and "equal" to men became a central aim of feminist reform. The political strategy that follows from this dominant feminism is one of inclusion: women, as well as men, are rational beings. It follows that women as well as men are bearers of inalienable rights. Leading proponents of women's suffrage in Britain and the United States undermined arguments which justified formal legalistic inequality on the basis of sex differences. Such feminists claimed that denying a group of person basic rights on the grounds of some presumed difference could not be justified unless it could be shown that the difference was relevant to the distinction being made. Whatever differences might exist between the sexes, none, based on this view, justified legal inequality and denial of the rights and privileges of citizenship.

Few early feminists pushed liberal universalism to its most radical conclusion by arguing that there were *no* justifiable bases for exclusion of adult human beings from legal equality and citizenship. Proponents of women's suffrage were also heirs to a tradition that stressed the need for social order and shared values, emphasized civic education, and pressed the importance of having a propertied stake in society. Demands for the inclusion of women did not often extend to *all* women. Some women, and men, would be excluded by criteria of literacy, property ownership, disability, or, in the United States, race.

At times, feminist discourse turned liberal egalitarianism on its head by arguing *for* women's civic equality on grounds that served historically to guarantee women's exclusion from politics. One finds the case for greater female political participation argued in terms of women's moral supremacy or characteristic forms of virtue. These appeals, strategic though they have been, were never *merely* strategic. They spoke to and from women's social identity. At various times, radical, liberal, democratic, and socialist feminists have paid homage to women as exemplars of particular forms of social virtue.

From the vantage point of rights-based feminism, the emphasis on civic-based motherhood was a trap. But the historic discourse that evoked images of maternal virtue was one feminist response to a complex, rapidly changing political culture. That political culture, in the Western democracies, was committed to liberalism but included as well civic republican themes of social solidarity and national identity. Women made their case within a male-dominated political order from *their* own sphere, a world of female-structured sensibility and imperatives that signified doubly their exclusion from political life and their cultural strength and importance. Less able than men to embrace the identity of a wholly autonomous social atom, often rejecting explicitly the individualist ideal, many feminists endorsed expanded familial values, stripped of patriarchal privilege, as the basis for a new social world.

Feminists also turned variously to socialism, in its utopian and "scientific" aspects, and to romanticism. Finding in notions of class oppression an analogue to women's social position vis-à-vis men, socialist feminists promoted notions of sex-class struggle and revolt. Feminists indebted to romanticism embraced a robust notion of a passionate, feeling self breaking the encrustations of social custom. Pressing a notion that women suffered as much from *repression,* or internalized notions of their own incapacities, as from *oppression,* or systematically imposed rules and customs that guaranteed sex inequality, feminist romantics stressed women's "especial genius" (in the words of the American transcendentalist Margaret Fuller) and hoped to see a social transformation that would free women's "difference" and allow it to flourish, even to dominate.

The diverse history of feminisms in the plural forms the basis of current feminist discourse and debate. These debates secrete ethical imperatives and trail in their wake moral implications whether or not the thinkers involved articulate fully such imperatives or implications. Varieties of liberal, socialist, Marxist, and utopian feminism abound. Sexuality and sexual identity have become highly charged arenas of political redefinition. Some feminists see women as universal victims; others as a transhistorical sex-class; others as oppressed "nature." A minority urge women to separate entirely from male-dominated society. Some want full integration into that society, hence its transformation toward liberal equality. Others insist that the feminist project will not be complete until "women's values," correctly understood, triumph. There are feminists who embrace a strong notion of women's difference, ontologically grounded, and others who reject any such idea as itself sexist. It's hard to wend one's way through the thicket of contemporary feminist discourse without some sort of map. But even with various categorical markers at hand, it is tricky at times to figure out what game is being played.

Is feminist scholarship primarily or exclusively the ideological arm of "the feminist movement"? There are feminist analysts who make this argument and insist that unless a text helps feminist doctrine, as they understand it, to triumph, it does not deserve the name "feminism" and must, instead, be condemned as suspect if not downright heretical. There are other feminists who make a distinction between feminism as politics and feminism as the inspiration and occasion for scholarly endeavor. Anthropologist Judith Shapiro, for example, insists that the time has come for scholars to loosen the tie between their endeavors and the political rhetoric and ideological claims of feminism. "The danger," she wrote in an essay, "Anthropology and the Study of Gender," "in too close an association between scholarship and social reformism is not only in the limits it places on intellectual inquiry, but also in the implication that our lives as social, moral, and political beings are dependent on what we are able to discover in our scientific research. Loosening the tie would have liberating consequences . . . for anthropological investigation and for feminism as a social movement." But the hard-liners counter that a feminist text must exemplify and elaborate a "shared commitment to certain political aims and objectives" (in Rosalind Cloward's words) and that books are properly read and measured against a clear set of ideological criteria.

A will to power and truth as anathematizing the heretical and embracing the politically correct is painfully evident in a number of the texts under review. The *primary* aim of several of these works is to round up and to isolate the usual suspects and to form the friends into one of Milan Kundera's circle dances. Thus Janice Doane and Devon Hodges, in *Nostalgia and Sexual Difference,* attribute a terrible anxiety to those they deem foes, a deep fear of the feminist project as they understand it. The suspect roster includes Thomas Berger, George Stade, Dan Greenburg, Ishmael Reed, John Irving, Christopher Lasch, and Brigitte and Peter Berger. Several "political reactionary" feminists are also indicted as co-conspirators, including Betty Friedan, Germaine Greer, and Jean Elshtain, because they have "expressed concern about feminism's effect on founding structures, life forces, and of course, the family as the home of natural truths about men and women." The circle dance is enfolded by repeated use of the encomium "fine," to endorse articles and arguments the authors embrace. The text is peppered with "in a fine article" or "in her fine article," a locution that makes its way even into the footnotes in a fervor of approval.

What is peculiar about the authors' rogues' gallery is how little its members share with one another. Lasch and the Bergers, for example, are at odds in their assessment of the baneful or beneficial effects of capitalism. Because their views about feminism are integrally related to their general analyses of liberal capitalist society, they vary dramatically. Never mind; in drawing up a hit list, fine distinctions simply get in the way. Appeals from a national abortion rights organization go out under John Irving's name and with a letter "signed" by him. This would seem to make him p. c. (politically correct), but evidently his "anxiety" about female sexuality disqualifies him.

Reed, on the other hand, can scarcely be called anxious. He is just plain angered by what he considers unfair assaults on black men by black feminist writers that serve, in his view, to deepen racist fears of the black man among whites.

Similarly, the trio Friedan, Greer, Elshtain is very odd, as each of our understandings of feminism and its politics differs in important, not trivial ways. None, to my knowledge, have ever fretted about "life forces." Indeed, I have no idea what Doane and Hodges are talking about, and I doubt Friedan and Greer do either. And in light of the fact that each of us, in her own way, has denied explicitly that the family is a home for *natural* truths *simpliciter,* it becomes clear that Doane and Hodges are practicing the dogmatizing, not the expansive and exploratory, sort of feminist scholarship. One telltale sign is this: at least one of the three "reactionary feminists" condemned was not even read by the authors, or at least there is no evidence of this; rather, a debunking essay by a socialist feminist entitled, "The New Conservative Feminism," which indicts the same crew, is used as the sole source for Doane's and Hodges's matter-of-fact, unexplored repudiations. This is not the way scholarship works, but it is the way ideology functions and re-produces itself.

In a like way, Catharine A. MacKinnon, best known for her efforts (to-gether with Andrea Dworkin) to ban pornography as a form of discrimina-tion on the basis of sex (hence a violation of the civil rights of women lodged in the conviction that civil liberties, most of the time, are "bourgeois hypoc-risy," to be overridden when, in Dworkin's words, "We're talking about the oppression of a class of people"), does not shy away in the least from con-demnations of political opponents as enemies. In *Feminism Unmodified: Dis-courses on Life and Law,* MacKinnon sees the First Amendment as the self-interested expression of "white men from the point of view of their own social position. Some of them owned slaves; most of them owned women." The First Amendment was written to guarantee their freedom to perpetuate such ownership. Dubious as legal scholarship, this is impossible as political history. It cannot explain why there should have been any debate about the passage of the First Amendment at all, unless MacKinnon further assumes that some of the writers and amenders of the Constitution didn't know their own true interests and hence failed to push unambiguously for a measure that was to their "sex-class" advantage.

MacKinnon's approach to feminist discourse is relentlessly exclusionary. There is "the feminist theory of power" and "the feminist theory of knowl-edge"—no room for debate; one need only separate the correct from the incorrect. Her work aims at closure, not conversation, and its political im-plications are deeply troubling. By spreading oppression, victimization, and patriarchal horror around so universally and uniformly, women emerge as abject victims, not historic agents. Finally, MacKinnon's totalizing rhetoric blurs the distinction between being raped at gunpoint in a dark alley and confronting, for example, ambiguous evidentiary rules or habitual patterns of academic departmental behavior that have unintentional sexist outcomes. All women are raped: the women in the alley, the corporate female manager, the homemaker, the superstar. "Women are raped by guns, age, white supremacy, the state—only derivatively by the penis," she writes in an earlier text, and that view is further elaborated in *Feminism Unmodified.* When she isn't separating the sheep from the goats, MacKinnon's prose is turgid, sinking under the weight of its own ponderousness. Thus: "Objectivity is the epistemological stance of which objectification is the social process, of which male dominance is the politics, the acted-out social practice. That is, to look at the world objectively is to objectify it." You figure it out. On one point, MacKinnon and I do agree: ideas matter, and that is why hers are so troubling.

Another writer is Cynthia Fuchs Epstein, whose latest work is *Deceptive Distinctions.* As in her earlier work, *Woman's Place,* published in 1971, Epstein laments the fact that women were a resource not being properly exploited to the wider benefit of society as a whole. Epstein criticizes claims that differences between males and females other than utterly trivial ones exist or, if they do exist, that they matter. For Epstein the body, that extraordinary container for identity and being, is seen as "raw physiology."

Her treatment of embodiment positions Epstein squarely on the so-called equality side of the current "difference versus equality" debate, as it has been unfortunately cast. Epstein, however, does not consider the class dimension to this debate historically. Middle-class women have been more likely to push formal-legalistic equality and to challenge exclusion from public life, by which they mean the positions of official power wielded by men. Working-class women, on the other hand, have been less concerned with abstract rights than with concrete socio-economic matters, many of them lodged in recognition of biological difference, primarily the fact that it is women who get pregnant and give birth. Using the findings of science (which is, however, divided on this score, with recent scholarship, much of it carried out by women, emphasizing differences), Epstein insists that in an ideal world gender distinctions would be a matter of complete indifference. Epstein makes judgments about the works of a whole crew of feminist analysts based, not upon their own work, but upon polemical secondary sources. Here are a few examples. I get yet another walk-on role, this time as a "self-identified feminist," in fact a "conservative" who "regards the family in universal terms." As proof, from my book *Public Man, Private Woman,* she cites a few words *as quoted by* the author of "The New Conservative Feminism," the same source Doane and Hodges accept as Holy Writ. In fact, my treatment of the family in *Public Man, Private Woman* is framed with these words: "I recognize that there is no such thing as 'the family' but that there are multiple variations on this theme." Similarly, three feminist writers on motherhood—Alice Rossi, Dorothy Dinnerstein, and "June Flax" (whose name Epstein has wrong as it is Jane, not June)—are excoriated based upon the blasts of others rather than upon a direct engagement with their work. Alice Rossi's "biosocial perspective" is debunked, but none of Rossi's own work appears in the bibliography. Such lapses are disappointing coming, as they do, from a serious sociologist.

Moving from Epstein's report to Claire Duchen's very helpful collection, *French Connections,* a slice of life from the recent past that introduces the French MLF (*mouvement de liberation des femmes*) through "certain key debates," is a dizzying experience. Duchen's selections detail the contentiousness, the internecine ideological warfare, and the remarkable fact that what emerged as the most "telling questions" included: "Can you be feminist and heterosexual? Can men be political allies or are all men always the enemy?" Clearly there is real sectarian battiness at work if those are *the* questions. There are a number of dissenting voices. François Picq, for example, characterizes what the MLF became as a "Parisian, intellectual, narcissistic group." Anne Leclerc also distances herself from the most egregious examples of rhetorical overkill, but she goes on to issue a remarkable utopian plaint: "We have to invent everything anew." This is a recipe for both arrogance and defeat.

More troubling by far, however, are those radical separatists who label heterosexual women "collabos," drawing upon the language of complicity with German occupiers in World War II. Lesbians who believe they can work with the "collabos" are smeared as "kapos," prisoners in Nazi concentration camps who helped the guards. Thus: "A 'Feminist' who loves her oppressor is a collaborator." Or: "Hetero-'Feminist'-kapos for patriarchy." This is repugnant. Not only does it "turn feminism against the vast majority of women," as one of Duchen's interlocutors notes, it banalizes the Shoah, cheapening and trivializing its horrors and the mass slaughter of World War II in general by comparing it to ordinary, everyday heterosexual relations. This is not political thinking, as Hannah Arendt has so brilliantly argued: it is violence; it is a terroristic alternative to civic discourse. To respond to it by pointing out that, after all, we are talking about just a few extremists will not suffice. Those prepared to ravage the world in order to change it must be exposed and criticized, no matter what stalking horse they are riding or how few or many their numbers.

The contrast between the narrowly ideologizing and the more expansive instances of feminist and women's studies scholarship grows more and more apparent with each passing day. Even works under review here that are neither particularly expansive nor gripping, for example, Demaris Wehr's *Jung and Feminism* and Donald Meyer's *Sex and Power,* which is less than the sum of its 721 pages, offer *something* to the reader beyond categorical rigidities or rhetorical overkill. Wehr's effort is marred by overgeneralizations about androcentrism, sexism, and misogyny—they are not one and the same—and underlaboring in her attempt to convince the reader that Jung's psychology of types, with its essentializing categories, has something to offer modern feminism. I doubt it, and merely intoning the virtues of holism doesn't do the trick. Jung's Manicheanism, which identifies "the feminine principle" with matter and the "masculine principle" with spirit, has in the past and will in the future work great mischief; moreover, Wehr's definition of "internalized oppression" as something that "feels a certain way inside a woman, it speaks with a certain voice, and it has a certain effect on her" evaporates as soon as one focuses on it for more than a fleeting moment.

Meyer's troubles, on the other hand, are reminiscent of the story Abraham Lincoln once told a group of interlocutors who were pushing a particular author upon him, and he replied that no one had ever delved deeper into the well of knowledge or come up drier. Meyer tells four stories of the rise of women in the United States, Russia, Sweden, and Italy from the mid-nineteenth century to 1987. He makes the solid and welcome point that women are not to be construed as history's victims but as active persons confronting concrete dilemmas in particular times and places, and he notes that many formidable early historians of women, Mary Beard among them, mocked "relapses into the pathos of victimonology, when their own data showed strong effective women." He assumes a 5,000-year-old conflict between men and women that takes particular forms in diverse societies. But his work is too atheoretical, missing an animating vision, and by its conclusion one is caught muttering, as political scientist Jane Jaquette has pointed out, "A woman's work is never done."

By contrast, the texts by Thurston, Banta, Scott, and Loraux, and those edited by Haus and Higgonet and associates, offer solid food for thought, many pleasures to the reader, a plethora of challenges to received wisdom, and as they do so display feminist scholarship at its most engaged yet thoughtful best. Their subjects range from the popular romance novel to classic Greek tragedy; from the construction of bodily imagery to war as a "gendering activity"; from Foucaultian insights to culture-constituting imagery. Feminism serves, for these scholars, as inspiration, as challenge, as focus, as organizing theme. The political commitments of the writers involved, insofar as these are made explicit, range from Marxist to vaguely liberal. I note this to allay any suspicion that one particular brand of feminism is more susceptible than some other to the dogmatics of the circle dance. This is not necessarily so. Liberals as well as radicals and socialists of many stripes have formed the circle and narrowed the boundaries of discourse by eliminating, or seeking to eliminate, undesirable elements.

To happy specifics, then. Thurston writes in a generous, populist spirit. She notes the extraordinary number of adult women reading romances (more than twenty million by her estimate), not so that she can then throw up her hands in horror and condemn their mindlessness but in order to take seriously the literary genre that engages them. And what she finds is fascinating. The new paperback romance novel came to full bloom during the same years that saw the rise of feminist politics and writing. While those who have bought into the notion that the "masses" are "overwhelmingly passive, manipulated, and dominated from above" see in the romances a reaction to feminism, Thurston finds feminist themes running through many of the texts. The heroine is an individual in her own right. She "possesses a passionate drive for self-determination and autonomy." The romance narrative is one of "reciprocal sexual satisfaction." Male heroes shed tears. In three-fourths of the texts in which a rape occurs, the point that it was not the woman's fault is made explicitly by the male hero. And so on.

Rather than being the "opiate of the female masses," these tales that reach millions are reflective of an upsurge in female assertiveness, especially of the erotic sort. The romances, Thurston claims, "constitute the first large and autonomous body of sexual writing by women addressed to feminine experiences," and she worries that feminist antipornographers would drum this literature out of business if they succeed in their efforts. This may, in fact, be an explicit intent of one segment of the antipornography ranks, since the sexuality elaborated in the romances is normatively heterosexual—or so Thurston hints. She writes, "To suggest that heterosexual bonding is in itself inherently conservative and inimical to women, as some feminists have done, is to both deny human needs and turn a blind eye to where grassroots social change has and is taking place."

Similarly, and from a very different vantage point, the German Marxist-feminist project outlined in *Female Sexualization* speaks to the politics of everyday human life as reconstructed from personal memories of the socialization and "sexualization" of the female body: "Frauenformen," the writers call it. Borrowing heavily if critically from the work of Foucault, Haus and the other members of her "collective" aim to "denaturalize the body," to extricate the social and historical body from various "naturalistic and ahistorical conceptions." They are tuned in to a politics of identity that is bodily-based. Countering Epstein's "raw physiology" reductionism, the participants in this project understand that the body is a site in and through which complex formations of identity occur and that human beings do not conform to social norms concerning the body in ways that are uncomplicated. Although I grew a bit weary of the lengthy, detailed reconstructions of memories concerning body hair, legs, postures, tummies, and all the rest, I was impressed by the thoughtfulness brought to bear and the theoretical acumen that facilitated this reflective effort.

The most interesting feature of the book is its coming to grips with the thinking of Karol Wojtyla (Pope John Paul II), specifically his lectures on the "theology of the body" written before he became pope. These socialist feminists describe Wojtyla's procedure as "remarkably modern . . . quite sophisticated." As they sum it up, Wojtyla privileges the dignity of the human person who is never to be treated as a means to another's end, whether in work or love. He rejects utilitarianism and egoism. He refutes the notion that human beings are slaves to the sexual drive and repudiates the view that this drive is evil. "Wojtyla does not consider desire to be morally wrong in itself; what would be wrong would be the subordination of the will to desire." Because, on Wojtyla's view, humans are social and sexual beings, the sex drive must be integrated into morality—into personhood, self-determination, free will, an inner life, and responsibility to others. This is a sexual ethic based, in Wojtyla's words, on pleasure "without treating the person as an object of pleasure," whose ultimate goal is "integrated love, which incorporates all human impulses" and involves "full and deep appreciation of the beauty of the [other] person."

The authors note that Wojtyla, with feminists, conceives of the domain of love and sexuality as a discursive and political battlefield over which each seeks to impose a ethical order. They give Wojtyla credit for having "learnt from Marxism," but finally his position must be struggled against, they conclude, because it is too normatively restrictive in opposing abortion and embracing heterosexual or potentially generative intimate relationships. What is remarkable about all this is just how difficult such a discussion would be within academic feminist circles in the United States because the tradition of social thought shared by this group of German feminists and, in large part, by Wojtyla, is not dominated by the categories and assumptions of liberal discourse.

Anyone interested in culture, politics, history, and literature will profit from reading the remaining four books under review. First, the collection edited by Higgonet, Jensen, Michel, and Weitz, *Behind the Lines: Gender and the Two World Wars,* is a vital entry in the new feminist scholarship on war and warmaking, on the construction of motherhood as a feature of national security, for example, and whether and, if so, how nations traffic in gendered representations in their war/peace politics. The multiple authors of this text refuse to traffic in banalities and overwrought analogies. They teach us much that we might not even want to know. For example, Sandra Gilbert's path-breaking essay, "Soldier's Heart: Literary Men, Literary Women, and the Great War," supplies us with startling examples of the upbeat prowar literature of many women writers and feminist activists in the World War I period. My favorite is Rose Macaulay who, in her poem, "Many Sisters to Many Brothers," expressed envy of the soldier's liberation from the dreariness of the home front in these words: "Oh it's you that have the luck, out there in blood and muck." Concludes Gilbert: "In the words of women propagandists as well as in the deeds of feather-carrying girls, the classical Roman's noble *patria* seemed to have become a sinister, death-dealing *matria.*"

Second, Joan Scott's essays in *Gender and the Politics of History* compel us to recognize that any "unitary concept," including, of course, male, female, power, oppression, equality, "rests on—contains—repressed or negated material and so is unstable, not unified." She offers, among her many insights, a sophisticated discussion of the "difference" question. Scott rejects the idea, following Martha Minow, that equality versus difference constitutes an opposition. "Instead of framing analyses and strategies as if such binary pairs were timeless and true, we need to ask how the dichotomous pairing of equality and difference itself works. Instead of remaining within the terms of existing political discourse, we need to subject those terms to critical examination." Within their very different frameworks and projects, and without heavy theoretical thematizing of the issues at stake, Loraux's *Tragic Ways of Killing a Woman* and Banta's *Imaging American Women* carry out Scott's call to subject existing terms to critical examination.

Third, Loraux's ninety pages are a marvel of condensation. Homing in on one question—how women in the tragedies are done to death—she shows us that Greek tragedy "as a civic institution, delighted in blurring the formal frontier between masculine and feminine and freed women's deaths from the banalities to which they were restricted by private mourning." The suicide of wives and the sacrifices of virgins are, of course, most important. Suicide is the "woman's solution." A man "worthy of the name could die only by the sword or the spear of another, on the field of battle." Importantly, "the woman in tragedy is more entitled to play the man in her death than the man is to assume any aspect of woman's conduct, even in his manner of death." Chillingly and powerfully, there is, for women, "liberty in tragedy—liberty in death." By resisting any temptation to dogmatize, to take the Greeks to task one more time for, in Epstein's words, suppressing "women's rights," a remarkable achievement indeed as there were no "rights" of any sort to suppress, the concept of rights being entirely foreign to the Greeks, Loraux opens a window into the world of Greek tragedy that was, at least for me, and I assume for many others, previously closed.

Finally, Banta's enormous work is wonderfully evocative. She begins with some rather loose definitions of imaging as "the making of visual and verbal representations . . . and responses to these artifacts at every level of society." There is, she notes in line with Scott's theoretical discussion, "no unity, no access to interpretive certainties, no absolutes, no guaranteed rapport between seeing and knowing in a society struggling with conventions that were in the process of creating still newer conventions." If Banta had been in the room as I read these words, I would have kissed her. Without in any way backing off political implications; without in any way diluting awareness of and concern with gender; without in any way muting the feminist energy at work in her text, Banta offers up ideals and images that have simultaneously differentiated and "nationalized," constructed unities and marked separateness.

She discovered that between 1876 and 1918 the images being offered about the American female to the public at large were "not only varied to the point of potential self-contradiction, they were all-pervasive." She finds the Beautiful Charmers, the New England Woman, the Outdoors Girl, even the Feminine Charms of the Woman Militant. Changes in "feminine ideals" were responses to "wider social forces, idealizations and discontents," and themselves helped to deepen or to soften these contradictory forces. For example: promoting visions of the militant as an attractive woman, the New Woman as an affirmative idea, was taken up as one way to gain public approval of social change. At once commercial, personal, political, and aesthetic, one set of images frequently provoked a counter-set. For every Woman Militant there were several Mothers as Angels, and visions of the winged female decorated classrooms, churches, and libraries. Indeed, these restrictive idealizations, for example, "Angels, We Call Them Mothers Down Here," a 1921 pop song, invited satiric and surreal counterpoint. Banta expands upon the contributions of several authors of *Behind the Lines,* when she elaborates the many feminized ways in which America herself is and has been represented—as Columbia, as Iron Amazon, as Sacred Mother, as the Girl He Left Behind. This is a splendid effort.

Toward the end of her remarkable career, Hannah Arendt and her colleague, the political scientist Hans Morgenthau, had the following exchange, reported in Elisabeth Young-Bruehl's biography of Arendt. Morgenthau queried: "What are you? Are you a conservative? Are you a liberal? Where is your position within contemporary possibilities?" And Arendt responded: "I don't know. I really don't know and I've never known. And I suppose I never had any such position. . . . And I must say I couldn't care less. I don't think the real questions of this century will get any kind of illumination by this sort of thing." Arendt was right. Those feminist texts that proclaim, in effect, "shut up and fight" or "shut *them* up in order to better fight" offer illumination into nothing except the workings of dogmatic minds and ideological projects. Contrastingly, those feminist writers and scholars who refuse to join the circle, who retain their independence of mind and thought, in the long run better serve any feminism worth its salt. By that I mean a feminist position open to debate, committed to democracy, prepared to pursue politics as the art of the possible.

Notes

Originally published in *Partisan Review* 57, no. 2 (1990).

1. Publication information for the books mentioned, in order of their discussion, is as follows: Janice Doane and Devon Hodges, *Nostalgia and Sexual Difference* (New York: Methuen, 1987); Catharine MacKinnon, *Feminism Unmodified* (Cambridge: Harvard University Press, 1987); Cynthia Fuchs Epstein, *Deceptive Distinctions* (New Haven: Yale University Press; New York: Russell Sage Foundation, 1988); Claire Duchen, *French Connections* (Amherst, Mass.: University of Massachusetts Press, 1987); Demaris Wehr, *Jung and Feminism* (Boston: Beacon Press, 1987); Donald Meyer, *Sex and Power* (Middletown, Conn.: Wesleyan University Press, 1987); Carol Thurston, *The Romance Revolution* (Urbana: University of Illinois Press, 1987); Frigga Haus, ed., *Female Sexualization* (London: Verso Books, 1987); Margaret Higgonet, Jane Jensen, Sonya Michel, and Margaret Weitz, eds., *Behind the Lines* (New Haven: Yale University Press, 1987); Joan Scott, *Gender and the Politics of History* (New York: Columbia University Press, 1988); Nicole Loraux, *Tragic Ways of Killing a Woman* (Cambridge: Harvard University Press, 1987); Martha Banta, *Imaging American Women* (New York: Columbia University Press, 1987).

9

Sovereignty, Identity, and Sacrifice

> But we are coming to the sacrifice.
>
> *Edmund Blunden, "Vlemertinghe: Passing the Chateau, July 1917," from* Poems of Many Years
>
> Splendid you passed, the Great Surrender made.
> To: All of His Majesty's Forces—Great War—1939–1945.
>
> *A plaque dedicated by Mrs. Iris Gray, Vancouver, in the name of her son, Charles Gray, RCAF, Christ Church Cathedral, Vancouver*
>
> The sacrifice you make will never be forgotten.
>
> *President George Bush, Christmas Eve Message to American Troops, 1990*
>
> Sacrifice ME [a. F, ad. L]
>   1. Primarily, the slaughter of an animal as an offering to God or a deity. Hence the surrender to God or a deity, for the purpose of propitiation or homage, of some object or possession. Also *fig.* the offering of prayer, thanksgiving, penitence, submission, *etc.*
>   2. That which is offered in sacrifice; a victim immolated on the altar; anything offered to God or a deity as an act of propitiation or homage.
>   3. *Theol.* a. The offering by Christ of himself to the Father as a propitiary victim in his voluntary immolation upon the cross. b. Applied to the Eucharistic celebration regarded as a propitiary offering of the body and blood of Christ in perpetual memory of the sacrifice offered by him in his Crucifixion.

126

> 4. a. The destruction or surrender of something valued or desired for the sake of something having a higher or more pressing claim; the loss entailed by devotion to some other interest. b. A victim.
>
> Oxford English Dictionary

When I was at work on my book *Women and War,* a realization slowly but irrevocably grew on me. It was, in some respects, a happy dawning; in other ways, my crystallizing convictions troubled, vexed, and haunted, for one incessant and insistent theme emerged from the several hundred "war stories" I encountered: the theme of sacrifice. The young man goes to war not so much to kill as to die, to forfeit his particular body for that of the larger body, the body politic, a body most often presented and represented as feminine: a mother country bound by citizens speaking the mother tongue. Consider two lines from a rhapsodic evocation of a feminine American republic written by one Virginia Frazer Boyle to memorialize the youthful sacrifice of the patriot Nathan Hale, who was hanged by the British at the age of 21 as a spy during America's revolutionary war. Hale's last words, "I only regret that I have but one life to give for my country," stirred Americans then and now.

> Oh, motherland, these are thy jewels, that blazon the shield of thy breast,
> Oh motherlove these are the truest—the hearts that have loved thee the best.[1]

These and other stirring tales of female involvement in the project of forging and sustaining a sacrificial national identity challenge the many texts, some but not all by feminists, that lay the blame for war, as well as the causal explanation *of* war, on the doorstep of male aggression. This reductive claim came under compelling pressure and grew less and less believable the more I read, pondered, and studied. Some aggressive drive peculiar to the male sex did not surface as the most potent theme that drove men to their deaths in time of war. It was a relief, then, that my own young son was probably not a beast lurking and awaiting the chance to bare his fangs and shed some blood, not his own; but a terrible sadness, too, a foreboding recognition that Plutarch's *Sayings of Spartan Mothers,* repeated by Jean-Jacques Rousseau, might linger yet, just beneath the surface of everyday, conscious recognition, poised, ready to emerge full-force in a full-fledged, popular war. And it must be noted that in the 1991 Gulf War the sacrificial theme resurfaced. For a brief time it was in full flower. One congressman from Pennsylvania, himself a Vietnam veteran, articulated the pervasive view that "the people now truly believed the presence of their sons and daughters is worthwhile. It doesn't make the pain go away [should a son or daughter be killed] but with the country so united, it helps people to deal with the tragedy. Maybe this time the Gold Star mothers won't be wondering 'Why?' "[2]

To appreciate why mothers might not cry "Why?," consider the Rousseau I have in mind: he who honors Spartan mothers, whose sayings Plutarch detailed in volume 3 of his *Moralia,* reproducing tales, anecdotes, and epigrams that constructed the Spartan woman as a mother who reared her sons to be sacrificed on the altar of civic necessity. Such a martial mother was pleased to hear that her son died "in a manner worthy of [her]self, his country, and his ancestors than if he had lived for all time a coward." Sons who failed to measure up were reviled. One woman, whose son was the sole survivor of a disastrous battle, killed him with a tile, the appropriate punishment for his obvious cowardice. Spartan women shook off expressions of sympathy in words that bespeak an unshakeable civic identity. Plutarch recounted a woman, as she buried her son, telling a would-be sympathizer that she had had "good luck," not bad: "I bore him that he might die for Sparta, and this is the very thing that has come to pass for me."[3]

Mother and mother's milk serve as foundations for civic-spiritedness and willingness to die. Just as the adult man who lacks respect for his mother is a wretch, "a monster unworthy of seeing the light of day," so the citizen who does not love and adore his country and every day "feel the eyes of his fellow-countrymen upon him every moment" is no real citizen. The authentic citizen is "so completely dependent upon public esteem as to be unable to do anything, acquire anything, or achieve anything without it."[4] And creating such citizens is the primal and primary female civic task. Rousseau describes the female "citizen" as follows: "A Spartan woman had five sons in the army and was awaiting news of the battle. A Helot arrives; trembling, she asks him for news. 'Your five sons were killed.' 'Base slave, did I ask you that?' 'We won the victory.' The mother runs to the temple and gives thanks to the gods. This is the female citizen."[5]

The potent love of mother country, and willingness to serve and protect her, will shrivel on the civic vine if mothers no longer figure overpoweringly in the affections and upbringings of their children. This was Rousseau's conviction and it is one repeated, deeply inscribed, in the political thought and consciousness of the West, nowhere receiving a more grandiose elaboration than in the philosophy of Hegel and in his theory of the triumphant *Kriegstaat.*[6]

We all know, in broad strokes, the story Hegel tells. Hegel, as a young man, celebrated the national ideal to which the French Revolution gave birth with its *levée en masse,* the first mass mobilization of men, women, and children for all-out war. His vision of the family, civil society, and the state is densely textured and impossible to characterize simply. What follows is radical surgery, but I do not think I have amputated any essential body part.

As a state-identified being, the *self* of the male citizen is fully unfolded and made complete. The state is the arena that calls upon and sustains the individual's commitment to universal ethical life, satisfying expansive yearnings through the opportunity to sacrifice "on behalf of the individuality of the state." For with the state comes not simply the possibility but the inevitability of war. War transcends material values. The individual reaches for a common end. War-constituted solidarity is imminent within the state form. But the state, and hence the nation, comes fully to life only with war. Peace poses the specific danger of sanctioning the view that the atomized world of civil society is absolute. In war, however, the state as a collective being is tested and the citizen comes to recognize the state as the source of all rights.

Just as the individual emerges to self-conscious identity only through a struggle, so each state must struggle to attain recognition. The state's proclamation of its own sovereignty is not enough: that sovereignty must be recognized. War is the means to attain recognition, to pass, in a sense, the definitive test of political manhood. The state is free that can defend itself, gain the recognition of others, and shore up an acknowledged identity. The freedom of individuals and states is not given, as such, but must be achieved through conflict. It is in war that the strength of the state is tested, and only through that test can it be shown whether individuals can overcome selfishness and are prepared to work for the whole and to sacrifice in service to the more inclusive good. The man becomes what he in some sense is meant to be by being absorbed in the larger stream of life: war and the state. To preserve the larger civic body, which must be "as one," particular bodies must be sacrificed.[7]

That is the great and terrible story. For many who yearn for a transformed world, these formulations no doubt sound pretty awful and, they might insist, we have put sure and certain distance between ourselves and the Hegelian state in this matter. I am not so sanguine. To expose the doubts I harbor, I will move backward, to pre-Hegelian moments and traces of sacrificial civic identity, and then forward, to post-Hegelian signs.

The *is* is states and the entanglement of our identities with them, so much so that a *will-to-sacrifice* may be inscribed in and through, indeed be constitutive of, our selfhood, male and female. This is a strong claim. Let me try to back it up. Before Rousseau, before Hegel, before the modern nation-state, the idea and ideal of sacrificial political identity had been forged in the hoplite warfare of the Greek phalanx, where the will to sacrifice was also a triumph of the will—what B. H. Liddell Hart calls the "chief incalculable" in warfare. Victor Hanson writes, "Along with regimental spirit, an even better incentive for hoplites to stand firm was the sight of their own commanding officer, the *strategos,* fighting alongside them in the very front ranks of the army."[8] This preparedness to die was much enhanced by the sight of gray-bearded grandfathers fighting alongside smooth-faced grandsons. The affair was overwhelmingly familial and tribal. The Spartans, the model for later civic republicans and early-modern state builders, honored only two identities with inscriptions on tombstones: men who had died in war and women who had succumbed in childbirth. Both embodied the sacrificial moment of civic identity. In Athens, too, death was anonymous on the funerary *relievi* with the exception of the soldier and the child-bearing woman.

The sacrificial motif is also played out in all the world's major religions. Sacrifice is the way to obtain something, and sacrifice assumes a kind of magical force which can even compel the gods to respond favorably to human pleas. Sacrifice itself is a slippery concept, one that merges and blends notions of the one who sacrifices and the one who receives sacrifice. In Christian theology, for example, Christ is both a high priest (sacrificer) and a victim (the one sacrificed). The notion that the gods need and desire sacrifice was, of course, challenged fundamentally by Christianity, because Christ's sacrifice was to be a forfeit of such measure—God's own Son—that no further sacrificial victims were required. As we all know, things have not quite worked out that way, and much of the force of political theology and doctrine lies in the way religious and metaphysical concepts migrated, so to speak, to the political domain and gave, and give it, a sacrosanct cast of such awesome and compelling fiat that sacrifice can still be seen as meet, right, and (so to speak) proportionate.

Ernst Kantorowicz, in his classic, *The King's Two Bodies,* traces the ideal of *pro patria mori.* He begins by reminding us that the word *patria* referred initially to a hamlet, village, or township. The warrior died for loyalty to his lord rather than some abstract juridical ideal or territory. But around the twelfth to the thirteenth centuries, the concept underwent a transformation and began to refer to kingdoms and nations and to have deep emotional and symbolic content. Kantorowicz writes that "neither from the idea of polity-centered kingship nor from that of the state as *corpus morale, politicum, mysticum* can there easily be separated another notion which came to new life independently of, though simultaneously with, the organological and corporational doctrines: the *regnum* as *patria,* as an object of political devotion and semi-religious emotion."[9]

The community having been endowed with a "mystical" character, the *corpus republicae mysticum,* sacrifice in her name grew more exigent, not only defensible but obligatory. The Christian martyr who had sacrificed for an "invisible polity" becomes the soldier who remained faithful unto death— the model of "civic self-sacrifice." Christian doctrine, then, having transferred the political notion of the *polis* to the city of God and honoring those who died in her name, now transmutes to underwrite (not without tension) the "new territorial concept to *patria*."[10] Kantorowicz speculates that much of the force of this new patriotism derived from "ethical values transferred back from the *patria* in heaven to polities on earth."

The death of the warrior *pro patria* was interpreted as self-sacrifice for others, a 'work of *caritas*.' (Greater love hath no man than this.) The theme of brotherly love was struck again and again. Men who were killed in a campaign (the example is the crusades) died "for the love of God *and his brothers*' and received 'eternal beatitude according to the mercy of God.'"[11] In the thirteenth century, Kantorowicz continues, "the Christian virtue of *caritas* became unmistakably political" and was "activated to sanctify and justify, ethically and morally, the death for the political 'fatherland.'"[12] This love for the wider body is declared by St. Thomas to be founded in "the root of charity which puts, not the private things before those common, but the common things before the private . . . the *amor patriae* deserves a rank of honor above all other virtues." The magnanimity of the soldier's sacrifice is celebrated in verse and song for, to the soldier, his brothers and his "fatherland" are dearer than his life. "Thus it happened that in the thirteenth century the crown of martyrdom began to descend on the war victims of the secular state."[13]

I here make a breathless and rapid leap to the twentieth century and J. Glenn Grey's work, *The Warriors*. Grey examines the impulse to self-sacrifice characteristic of warriors who, from compassion, would rather die than kill. He calls the freedom of wartime a communal freedom as the "I" passes into a "we" and human longings for community with others find a field for realization. Communal ecstasy explains a willingness to sacrifice and gives dying for others a mystical quality, there being, as Grey finds, a similarity between the self-sacrifice of soldiers and the willingness of martyrs to die for their faith. "Such sacrifice seems hard and heroic to those who have never felt communal ecstasy," writes Grey. "In fact, it is not nearly so difficult as many less absolute acts in peacetime and civilian life. . . . It is hardly surprising that few men are capable of dying joyfully as martyrs whereas thousands are capable of self-sacrifice in wartime."[14] Nor are the women exempt from a sacralizing of sacrifice. There are hundreds of hair-raising tales of bellicose mothers, wives, and girlfriends writing to the combat soldier and requesting the death of the enemy as a tribute, or gift, to her.

I am more interested in the construction of the noncombatant female's will to sacrifice her loved ones. Just one example will be taken, from my book *Women and War.* Vera Brittain's voice is lodged securely in the ranks of woman pacifists and antimilitarists, and she has become a heroine to contemporary feminist antiwar activists and thinkers—not, however, without some ambiguity. In *Testament of Youth,* Brittain hankers after her wartime months in Malta (during the Great War) because Malta had come to seem a "shrine, the object of a pilgrimage, a fairy country which I knew I must see again before I die. . . . Come back, magic days! I was sorrowful, anxious, frustrated, lonely—but yet how vividly alive!"[15] But it is Brittain's wartime diaries for 1913–17, published as *Chronicle of Youth,* with which I am here concerned. Brittain believed England must enter the war and could not remain neutral. Not to come to the aid of France would make England guilty of the "grossest treachery." Feeling much of the time as if she were dreaming, Brittain logged entries of how her father raved at her brother not to volunteer, while brother Edward, with a bit of class snobbery, told "Daddy" that "not being a public school man or having any training," he would not possibly understand how impossible it was for others to remain in inglorious inaction.[16]

Brittain understood the action required of war fighters in sacrificial terms. Disdaining her father's lack of courage on behalf of her brother, she noted the "agony of Belgium," remarking bitterly on "the unmanliness of it, especially after we read in *The Times* of a mother who said to her hesitating son, 'My boy, I don't want you to go but if I were you I should.'" Brittain's beloved, Roland, longed to take part in the war, finding in the possibility of sacrifice something "ennobling and very beautiful." After Roland died, Brittain capitalized the personal pronoun—"Him"—transfiguring Roland into a latter-day Christ in her entries about him. He died and became, in "His" sacrifice, a beatific figure for her. "On Sunday night at 11:00—the day of the month and hour of His Death—I knelt before the window in my ward and prayed, not to God but to him. . . . Always at that hour I will turn to Him, just as Mohammedans always turn to Mecca at sunrise."[17] Apotheosized in death, Roland lives on. The life of the individual is a fit and worthy sacrifice so that the body politic may live.

Women have often been keepers of the homeland flame. I saw this in action during a trip to Poland in 1983, two years after the 1981 military coup which outlawed Solidarity. At popular shrines throughout Warsaw, where citizens had constructed large crosses on the ground outside churches out of flowers, twigs, political notes and signs, and other homey material, there were always crowds gathered during the day. The crowds consisted of many young people, but, most significantly, mothers and grandmothers with young children, instructing them in national and Solidarity lore, teaching them songs of patriotic identification and resistance and, it must be said, animosity toward their oppressors. We do not use the term "mother tongue," as I already indicated, for nothing. There is great strength and hope in much of this, including what ought by now to be our recognition that totalitarianism can never utterly efface, mold, or stamp human beings, churning out the deracinated robotized entities the totalitarian mind requires and fantasizes about (and, oddly and importantly, the enemy of totalitarianism also needs to sustain his or her alternative). But there is, also, much cause for concern.

Let us, therefore, ask: whence this identity, this identification of self and nation? A caveat: the identification and the will-to-sacrifice of which I write is not a single phenomenon, but many. There is a contrast between *publica caritas* of the medieval sort and the overheated nationalism or civic bloodlust characteristic of classical civic humanists and twentieth-century dictators alike. As an instance of the former, I have in mind Caluccio Salutati's exclamations that the sweetness of one's love for the *patria* is such that one must not cavil at crushing one's brothers or delivering "from the womb of one's wife the premature child with the sword."[18] Salutati was extreme, but that sort of extremism has, alas, been the norm in many of the great and horrible events of our own century.

A question and a caveat: how did it come about that war for the king, then for country, then for more abstract ideals and demands for the "imagined community," got intermingled and served to frame the horizon within which the will-to-sacrifice was, and is, ongoingly forged? Max Weber writes of the "consecrated meaning" of death for the warrior, the conviction that his death alone provides the needed support for the "autonomous dignity of the polity resting on force."[19] Only a preparedness to forfeit one's own life rounds out, or instantiates in all its fullness, devotion to the political community, and only such devotion affords any dignity to a politics that would otherwise turn on brute force. Although a state cannot survive if it attempts to embody a universalistic ethic of *caritas,* without some such ethic, coercion alone reigns; hence the importance of the "consecrated meaning" of the warrior's death. But many of the deaths, the civic sacrifices, in our own epoch have not been those of warriors, whether just or unjust, but of civilians, the noncombatant sacrifices of total war. Noncombatants are molded from the same civic stuff as war fighters. And it is this shaping to and for a way of life that needs to be tended to if we are to assess the power civic identification retains to construct individual and collective identities.

During the Gulf War, we learned how "Baghdad Schoolchildren Are Made Ready for War." The correspondent for the *New York Times* noted that children were readied for "sacrifice" through "weekly outdoor military drill," during which they chanted, ranted, and play-acted their loyalty to their "father-leader," President Saddam Hussein, and hurled insults at President Bush.[20] This brings to mind a byline: "Tripoli, Libya, March 28, 1986. Colonel Muammar el-Qaddafi claimed victory tonight in his confrontation with the United States over the Gulf of Sidra." Thus began the story from the *New York Times,* a tale of national unity in the face of a powerful external foe. The United States was represented in a victory rally, attended primarily by soldiers, sailors, and boy scouts (the accompanying photo showed an all-male cohort) and by a tethered cow. In a spasm of violent, symbolic identity reaffirmation, aroused young men slit the throat of the hapless animal on whose side President Reagan's name had been painted in both Arabic and English. Before American television crews, the young men kicked and jumped on top of the dying (female) animal, smeared themselves with her blood, reaffirming their identities against an enemy they had devirilized by transforming a collective "Him" into a placid female animal they brutally sacrificed.

In recent years, we read of protests that resulted in upper-class Indian martyrs who immolated themselves to counter what they perceived to be a stark injustice. "Dramatic self-sacrifice," *Time* magazine called it, and quoted the father of a young man who burned himself alive: "My son has done the right thing. Some good will flow out of his sacrifice."[21] President Fidel Castro's political troubles are noted, given his need to appeal incessantly "for sacrifice at precisely the moment when his moral right to rule Cuba is more widely questioned than ever before."[22] One of the slogans of the Mothers of the Disappeared in Argentina read: "Those Who Die for Life Cannot Be Called Dead." These women sought to make sense of the unwilling sacrifice of their sons and daughters to a repressive regime. And a Russian philosopher, Alexei Losev, whose work has been rediscovered as state communism crumbles, tells a tale of self-sacrificing love for Russia. The tale was penned in late 1941, at the height of the war, after a German air raid bombed out his home near Moscow's Arbat Square, killing his family. What is remarkable is not so much the totality of identification and sacrifice he proclaimed and extolled but the fact that young Glasnost-era Soviet writers foregrounded Losev's essay, "Motherland," as an alternative to the depredations of communist rule, speaking, as it did, to wholehearted involvement with community of a sort that need not be coerced. A sample of Losev's chilling yet powerful words:

> The common life is our Motherland. She brings us into this world, and then receives us after our death. . . . Outside a community there is not an individual. . . . There is nothing in a human being that is above his community. He is an embodiment of his community . . . but what does one call this personal life, this life of an individual, when a person is born or he dies, when he grows up or withers away,

when he is healthy or ill, and all this taking place within the sphere of communal life, a correct, normal, and natural state of the world, in which everything separate, isolated, specific, personal, and unique manifests itself only in the context of an integral whole, in the context of communal life, in the context of things necessary, legitimate, normal, harsh, and inevitable, but nevertheless, one's own, dear and precious, in the context of one's Motherland. Such a life is called a sacrifice. Motherland calls for sacrifice. The life of the Motherland is in itself an eternal sacrifice.[23]

Being part of a way of life is no simple process of inculcation into a society's rules and practices. Rather, it is a matter of creating and sustaining the identities of persons and collectivities. Images of being "at home," of a homeland, of being homeward bound, are visions of safety, enclosure, of special and particular ties. "Homelessness," whether that of individuals or whole peoples, is most often constructed as a personal tragedy, a social problem, or a volatile geopolitical dilemma. Individuals carry images of home within them and project those images out into and upon their worlds. Nations are conceived as large and either warring or friendly families. Studies of children indicate that the human young occupy a densely textured *political* world at whose core lies the notion of "homeland." Robert Coles, in his work *The Political Life of Children,* finds that attachment to homeland is personalized by children as motherland or fatherland. "Nationalism works its way into just about every corner of the mind's life," Coles writes, adding that if an observer is attuned to the symbolism and imagery deployed by children, he or she will find "a nation's continuing life . . . enmeshed in the personal lives of its children."[24]

Children seize upon symbols and have ready access to a nation's "name, its flag, its music, its currency, its slogans, its history, its political life." Coles notes that the entrenched notion of a homeland is double-edged, at once inward-looking, a place where one "gets one's bearings," a domicile, a source of spiritual and social nourishment and outward-projecting, protecting us from "them," from foreigners who, all too easily, become enemies. Both aspects of homeland imagery turn up in "the developing conscience of young people" everywhere, concludes Coles after studying the politics of children on five continents.[25]

The upshot of Coles's story is modern nationalism, *sic et non.* It is inevitable, in some form or another, for we must all locate ourselves in a particular place. Is it good or bad? Both. The nationalism in personal identity may encourage social commitment to and for one's homeland and its people, on the one hand, or energize fear and hatred of the homelands of others, on the other. One way or another, we are all marked, deeply and permanently, by the way political life gets embodied in images of motherland and fatherland; so much so that the human body itself is politicized, taking on the markings of one civic realm as compared to another.

Nationalism is the overriding political passion of our time. In the era since World War II, new nationalisms have deployed war or, perhaps better put, colonial wars have created new nationalisms. Between 1945 and 1968, 66 countries became independent. Benedict Anderson notes that every successful revolution since 1945 has been defined in national terms and that the end of nationalism is "not remotely in sight." Nationalism is the most "universally legitimate form" and "universally legitimate value in the political life of our time."[26] This nation is an "imagined political community—and imagined as both inherently limited and sovereign."[27] It is imagined because each member of such a community lives in some image of communion with other members. As well, communities can be distinguished by the style in and through which they are imagined.

Sovereignty enters the picture for obvious reasons. It is a concept constitutive of, as well as derivative from, nation-state formation and identity: a Western historic form that has been, and continues to be, universalized. Sovereignty incorporates both a drive toward freedom from the domination of another and a particular understanding of power. Historically, much of the power of the concept of sovereignty lay precisely in its encoding of the absolute, perpetual, indivisible power of a masculinized deity—a deity whose power was absolute as a penultimate political form. State power, the power of the legitimate ruler and promulgator of laws, tamed and ordered domestic politics even as it set the boundary for autonomous self-sovereignty. The earthly sovereign shared many of the attributes of his divine counterpart. For Bodin, for example, sovereignty was the power of an absolute *dominus* over a vast domestic space.

If there is any force to my musings concerning the metaphysical traces embedded in the full-blown theory of sovereignty, the genealogy of the concept is nested in the powerful and pervasive construction of God's sovereign dominion, force, and will over what would have remained a formless void had He not exercised His omnipotent volition. Sovereignty over time shifts from king to state, and this state cannot alienate its sovereignty. As God's will is singular, so must the sovereign's be—at least once it is formulated as a "general will," and most certainly this singularity must pertain in "foreign affairs."

The constructions of sovereignty allow us to make more sense of the will-to-sacrifice as it shifts from personal liege loyalty to a feudal lord to an abstract, juridical, imagined tie that nevertheless calls forth sacrifice in its/his (the sovereign's) name. But another dimension must be added to this already rich mulch. I noted above that most modern nation-states are construed in feminine terms. The sovereign may bear a masculinized face, but the nation itself is feminized, a mother, a sweetheart, a lover. One can rightly speak, as Anderson does, of "political love," a love that retains the fraternal dimensions of medieval *caritas* but incorporates as well a maternalized loyalty symbolized domestically: the nation is home and home is mother. No more than one chooses one's parents does one choose one's country, and this adds even greater force to the nature of political love. We fall in love early through language, "encountered at mother's knees and parted with only at the grave," and through this language "pasts are restored, fellowships are imagined, and futures dreamed."[28] This is demanding but well nigh irresistible—a *force majeure.* The child's will-to-sacrifice flows from embodied ties to both parents that project outward into a more generalized relationship to a feminized motherland, a masculinized sovereign state. No wonder most of us most of the time "obey."

One of the most poignant and horrible instances of sacrifice and obedience in our time is the terrible blood sacrifice demanded by the sovereign gods of the fascist state who construed their nation not so much in language as in blood. And loyalty reverted to a personal bond, an oath to a godlike leader. We all know of the Final Solution, but few know of the Final Sacrifice (the term is Gerhard Rempel's from his book *Hitler's Children: The Hitler Youth and the SS*). Starving, bewildered Hitler Youth were thrown into the final months of the war when Hitler and "determined SS officers conspired to generate a children's crusade to shore up crumbling defenses and offer thousands of teenagers as a final sacrifice to the god of war."[29] The schemes were brutal; the results horrifying. Thousands of children between the ages of eight and seventeen perished in suicidal sabotage attempts and last-ditch stands. Five thousand young people, male and female, were thrown into the "twilight of the gods" in the last spasm of the agony of Berlin; five hundred survived. What was most astonishing to observers was the determination of these children to "do their duty until they were literally ready to drop. They had been fed on legends of heroism for as long as they could remember. For them the call to 'ultimate sacrifice' was no empty phrase."[30] The grotesqueness of all this signifies, in admittedly extreme form, the macabre dimension of the *will-to-sacrifice* as it has been constituted in the politics of an unusually virulent form of sovereignty.

The nation-state is a phenomenon that cannot be imagined or legislated out of existence. Needing others to define ourselves, we will remain inside a state/nation-centered discourse of war and politics, for better and for worse, as long as states remain the best way we have devised for protecting and sustaining a way of life in common. But we can try to tame and limit the demands of sovereignty. We can, perhaps, move toward what I am tempted to call a post-sovereign politics. I have in mind a politics that shifts the focus of political loyalty and identity from sacrifice (actual or *in situ*) to responsibility. My targets are both images of the sovereign self as an unproblematic, unified, sharply boundaried phenomenon and the sovereign state in its full-blown, untrammeled instantiation.

A politics *sans* sovereignty: is it possible? What would it look like? How would it forge civic identities in such a way that blood sacrifice, that of the self or enemy others (whether internal or external), is not so pervasive a demand and possibility? I cannot develop a vision of such a politics here in any full-blown sense, but I can indicate where we should turn for help: to the rich body of thought penned by Central Europeans over the past several decades. I have in mind Adam Michnik and Václav Havel as the two central figures in creating a theory of civil society, a politics, in opposition to authoritarian, sovereign state apparatuses. Havel writes of politics as "practical morality . . . humanly measured care for our fellow human beings." He never uses the word sovereignty in any of his writings, nor has he, to my knowledge, launched into sovereign discourse since his election as president of Czechoslovakia. But he does write of identity and responsibility, of accountability and deed-doing. What is most astonishing about his letters from prison is the fact that they are utterly devoid of maudlin, self-sacrificial constructions. They are filled, however, with a sense of identity as an ongoing, lifelong process of becoming—no notion of a completed sovereign self here—and of responsibility as that which cannot be cut to the measure of a man's hubris. And sovereign discourse historically has been nothing if not hubristic.

Havel writes of a post-totalitarian system and antipolitical politics in his struggle to get away from the rigidities and excesses of the discourse of war and sovereignty. He urges us into a post-sovereign political discourse, a move from sacrifice to responsibility.

> I feel that this arrogant anthropocentrism of modern man, who is convinced he can know everything and bring everything under his control, is somewhere in the background of the present crisis. It seems to me that if the world is to change for the better it must start with a change in human consciousness, in the very humanness of modern man.[31]

An ethic of responsibility means one is answerable, accountable to another, for something; one is liable to be called to account. One is also a being capable of fulfilling an obligation or trust; reliable; trustworthy. This presumes, indeed requires, a particular construction of what Charles Taylor called "the modern identity," one constituted in and through the notion of self-responsible freedom. Softening the demands of the iron grip, sovereignty-sacrifice, does *not* mean so loosening the bonds of reason that the self flies off in all directions and can find no good reason to prefer *this* to *that* and can hear in such notions as "responsibility" only a dour and crabby moralism.

A few final thoughts can be given as intimations of an alternative, then. As many critics and observers point out, claims to sovereignty and national self-determination cannot, any longer, trump all other claims in instances of conflict. Post-Nuremburg, the issue of crimes against humanity and human rights has been a shaping force in the world arena and will continue to be such. Human rights may be a weak reed against deadly force, but it is often the only weapon besieged peoples have, and it offers a lever (and demands its sacrificial victims, too) others can use to enforce the notion that geo-political and cultural definitions of nationhood must, at this time in history, be open to chastening by universal principles.

Whatever force *human* rights may have in years to come, the plurality of cultures and proliferation of nations are here to stay. As Hélène Carère d'Encausse has argued, attachment to a nation is "an accomplishment of civilized men, not a regression. The nation-state is not a tribal construction. Elements of familialism and tribalism may reverberate and are certain features of any genealogical construction of the modern identity, but they do not dominate." Identification with a national "imagined community" is a complex, many-sided construction with many corners. It taps particularism and universalism. Indeed, one might argue that it *requires* such, being composed of normatively vital aspects of both ethnicity and universal values—organic integration and voluntarism.

The point is that human beings require concrete reference groups in order to attain individuality and identity, but too complete immersion in such groups limits the boundaries of identity and of identification to fixed familial, tribal, or territorial lines. John A. Armstrong, in a piece entitled "Contemporary Ethnicity," worries that extreme voluntarist individualism leads to the loss of a coherent identity.[32] By contrast, universalism, including statist demands, which would extract the "last full measure of devotion" most of us would willingly offer to family and dear friends, denatures such nonvoluntarist obligations and commitments, reconstruing and abstracting them to constitute mandated blood sacrifice in the name of the collective, a sacrifice of "radical severity," in George Kateb's words.

Kateb muses on the question of sacrifice as a mandated obligation. According to Kateb, no one has a moral obligation to die; hence, conscription is illegitimate. One *may* sacrifice oneself for a "child or defenseless loved one," but to construe this possibility in contractual terms is "to cheapen it." Kateb

detects a perhaps unavoidable conundrum in modern constitutional repub-
lics cast as universal: on the one hand, and in the light of individualist
construals, the social group is not idolized; the collective is not sacralized.
This makes possible the free flow of "self-sacrificing love" toward particular
individuals or groups. On the other hand, the "mandated obligation to die"
emerges with greatest force "only in an individualist moral universe" in
which persons have been stripped of ties of great robustness and insistency
to particular others. This way of casting matters is mine, not Kateb's, but his
argument tends in this direction and leaves us suspended in a political and
moral universe in which sacrifice is legally mandated, although the legitimacy of such demands is challenged even as, or even if, one recognizes that
the demand itself is a reaction to a strongly individualist social order.[33]

Feminist moral theorizing, now poised between the poles of the so-called
justice and care perspectives, offers no promise of a resolution in this matter.
Critics of the justice perspective—critical because it posits an autonomous
moral agent capable of applying fundamental rules through the use of abstract reason and in the service of universal values—offer as an alternative
care, the caring, connected self. But the sacrificial political identity I have
traced is very much a relational, embedded, interdependent self. Care—
caritas—sacrifice: these are ancient themes, not new ones; primal constructions, not modern discoveries. What we require is a complex moral universe,
a world of justice *and* mercy, autonomy *and* caring, particular ties *and* universal aspirations. In such a universe, one adumbrated in the work of a Michnik
or a Havel, freedom and responsibility are living possibilities; the self is very
much a modern identity, at once committed and aware of the irony and
limits to all commitments; prepared to sacrifice, but wary of all calls to sacrifice. This identity is in the main antiheroic. The heroic emerges, when it
does, as a modern form of *Hier ich stande. Ich kann nicht anders.* The stress is
on the *Ich,* and the presumption is that none should be commanded to do
the supererogatory; none should be required to give the last full measure of
devotion. But to live in a universe in which no one was thus prepared, in
which no such *Ich* was any longer constructed and nothing was worth sacri-
ficing for, would be to live in a moral universe impoverished beyond our
poor powers of imagination.

The final words shall be Havel's.

> The problem of human identity remains at the center of my thinking about hu-
> man affairs . . . as you must have noticed from my letters, the importance of the
> notion of human responsibility has grown in my meditations. It has begun to
> appear with increasing clarity, as that fundamental point from which all identity
> grows and by which it stands or falls; it is the foundation, the root, the center of

gravity, the constructional principle or axis of identity, something like the "idea" that determines its degree and type. It is the mortar binding it together, and when the mortar dries out, identity too begins irreversibly to crumble and fall apart. (That is why I wrote you that the secret of man is the secret of his responsibility.)[34]

This, remember, is from a man who insists one must never lose one's sense of absurdity.

Notes

An earlier version of this essay was published in *Millennium: Journal of International Studies* 20, no. 3 (1991): 395–406. This version originally published in Marjorie Ringrose and Adam J. Lerner, eds., *Reimagining the Nation* (Buckingham, England: Open University Press, 1993). Reprinted by permission.

1. Cited in Jean Bethke Elshtain, *Women and War* (New York: Basic Books, 1987), 28. Here is a woman, and her number is legion, praising motherland and conflating it to motherlove and each, together, demanding and in a sense "feeding on" the sacrifice of the stalwart son.

2. Cited in David Shribman, "Victory in the Gulf Exorcises the Demons of the Vietnam Years," *Wall Street Journal*, March 1, 1991. A Gold Star mother is one whose son (now, perhaps, daughter) died in a United States war. The Gold Star is a commemorative emblem she receives from a grateful government.

3. Plutarch, *Moralia*, vol. 3, trans. Frank Cole Babbitt (Cambridge, Mass.: Harvard University Press, 1931).

4. Jean-Jacques Rousseau, *The Government of Poland* (Indianapolis: Bobbs-Merrill, 1972), 87.

5. Jean-Jacques Rousseau, *Emile*, trans. Allan Bloom (New York: Basic Books, 1979), 40.

6. I recognize, of course, that Hegel's *Kriegstaat* is also a *Reichtstaat*. This underscores my point that wars in a state system are not random failings, but that they are extraordinarily complex, rule-governed human activities.

7. See the complete discussion in Elshtain, *Women and War*, 73–75.

8. Victor Hanson, *The Western Way of War* (New York: Knopf, 1989), 107.

9. Ernst H. Kantorowicz, *The King's Two Bodies: A Study in Medieval Political Theology* (Princeton: Princeton University Press, 1957), 237.

10. Ibid.

11. Ibid., 241; citing a letter by Pope Urban II.

12. Ibid., 242.

13. Ibid., 244.

14. J. Glenn Grey, *The Warriors* (New York: Harper Colophon, 1970), 47.

15. Vera Brittain, *Testament of Youth* (New York: Wideview Books, 1980), 291.

16. Vera Brittain, *Chronicle of Youth: The War Diary, 1913–1917* (New York: William Morrow, 1982), 89–90.

17. Ibid., 101 and 308.

18. Kantorowicz, *King's Two Bodies*, 245.

19. H. H. Gerth and C. Wright Mills, eds., *From Max Weber: Essays in Sociology* (New York: Oxford University Press, 1946), 335.

20. Elaine Sciolino, "Baghdad Schoolchildren Are Made Ready for War," *New York Times,* January 8, 1991.

21. Edward W. Desmond, "Fatal Fires of Protest," *Time* Magazine, October 15, 1990, 63.

22. Charles Lane, "Low Fidelity," *New Republic,* January 7, 1991, 25–30, and ibid., January 14, 1991, 28.

23. Alexei Losev, "Motherland," *Literary Gazette International,* May 1990, 14–15.

24. Robert Coles, *The Political Life of Children* (Boston: Atlantic Monthly Press, 1986), 60.

25. Ibid., 63.

26. Benedict Anderson, *Imagined Communities* (London: Verso, 1983), 13.

27. Ibid., 15.

28. Ibid., 140.

29. Gerhard Rempel, *Hitler's Children: The Hitler Youth and the SS* (Chapel Hill: University of North Carolina Press, 1989), 233. See also Jay W. Baird, *To Die for Germany* (Bloomington: Indiana University Press, 1990).

30. Rempel, *Hitler's Children,* 241.

31. Václav Havel, *Disturbing the Peace* (New York: Knopf, 1990). A tall order, intimations of the long haul, if not the long march.

32. See Hélène Carére d'Encausse, "Springtime of Nations," *New Republic,* January 21, 1991, 22, and John A. Armstrong, "Contemporary Ethnicity: The Moral Dimension in Comparative Perspective," *Review of Politics* 52, no. 2 (1990): 166.

33. George Kateb, draft manuscript.

34. Václav Havel, *Letters to Olga* (New York: Henry Holt, 1989), 145.

T H R E E

Children, Bodies,

Families,

and Feminism

F our hot potatoes here. The first, "Feminists against the Family" (if memory serves, this was the title given the piece by *The Nation*; I had called it, less provocatively, "Feminists and The Family"), led to such a firestorm of attack and even vituperation that I was altogether taken aback. For I had been of the view that no perspective is above criticism; no theory closed off from debate; no advocacy exempt from contestation. In the words of my critics, I was told that this was wrong—or that *I* was, another matter altogether. I was open to correction and reproof in most things, but not to the notion that what political interest and commitment requires is to "shut up and fight." The piece was published in 1979, when perhaps things were rather too raw. Or so some told me, suggesting that my essay may have been warranted but it was "premature"; a historic corner had yet to be turned, and the like. Unsympathetic as I am to a Marxist metaphysics of immanence (for that is what much of this came down to), I demurred. Having our say is a democratic birthright, and the politics of displacement I took up in this long-ago piece has, if anything, deepened since. The dynamic of such a politics plays a featured role in my 1995 book, *Democracy on Trial,* but for *The Nation* piece I elaborated on the theme as intimated in my first work, *Public Man, Private Woman: Woman in Social and Political Thought* (1981). So I didn't invent the politics of displacement for the purpose of this particular essay, but I think it served me well. With Edith Piaf, "Non, je ne regrette rein." (Well, more or less.) My views on a number of issues have changed since 1979, but my criticism of 1970s feminists *against* the family holds.

The critique of repressive feminism is a second entry from the late 1970s when a certain version of radical feminism exerted a powerful sway and was, at the time, influential in shaping the terms of political debate on women's issues, often to not very salutary ends, in my view. I now recognize that what was beginning to take shape, and what I was grappling with in my criticisms, was that ideology of victimization that came into full flower about a decade later. I here alert us to a politics that busied itself embracing rather than repudiating the terms of women's oppression—and the language of "oppression" was inescapable—rather than challenging these. By inverting matters, the abject woman as victim took center stage as *the* discursive subject of feminism and as a political subject. "Symmetry and Soporifics" and "Against Androgyny" are intelligible read against a backdrop of feminist forays into psychoanalysis. Before "difference" became a battle cry, androgyny or symmetry, a search for sameness and a kind of indistinguishability between men and women, prevailed. It is this blanking out of difference, bespeaking a kind of loathing of female bodies themselves, that is here at issue.

10

Feminists against the Family
(and Subsequent Controversy)

Whatever its sins against generations of mothers and daughters, the family has served the women's movement well: located by feminists as the key to female oppression, it has been offered up as *the* institution to reform, revolutionize, or destroy if feminist aims are to be realized. As a catalyst for rethinking the terms of public and private reality, the family has also provided feminist thinkers with inexhaustible material for dissecting the human condition from the vantage point of this, its central bête noire.

Much that is exciting and fruitful emerged from this ferment. Connections between sexuality, authority, and power were opened up for debate in a provocative way. Women were encouraged to create conceptual and linguistic tools to help them pierce the patterns of social reality. Through consciousness raising, hundreds of women began to view themselves less as passive recipients of revocable privileges and more as active, responsible human beings. But from the start something was terribly wrong with much of the feminist treatment of the family. By "wrong" I don't mean so much careless or unscholarly by traditional canons of historic and social science methodology, though one saw evidence of both. I refer instead to an imperative more deeply rooted and bitter, which erupted from time to time in mean-spirited denunciations of all relations between men and women and in expressions of contempt for the female body, for pregnancy, childbirth, and child rearing.

In my view, the feminist movement has contributed to the discrediting of what Dorothy Dinnerstein, a psychoanalytic feminist thinker, calls the "essential humanizing functions of stable, longstanding, generation-spanning primary groups"; and the "virulent, reckless, reactive quality of much feminist rhetoric against the biological family, against permanent personal commitments of adults to childhood . . . against childbearing itself [has occurred] ironically, when women and men have been in the best position to minimize the oppressive features of human biology." The result has been the creation of what I shall call a *politics of displacement,* which erodes personal life even as it vitiates the emergence of a genuine public life. This feminist politics of displacement, in turn, helps to provoke a troubling mirror image. How has this come about?

The key to feminist politics lies in a phrase that has served simultaneously as an explanatory principle, a motto, and an article of faith: "The Personal Is Political." Note that the claim is not that the personal and the political are interrelated in important and fascinating ways not yet fully explored and previously hidden to us by patriarchal ideology and practice; nor that the personal and the political may be fruitfully examined as analogous to one another along certain touchstones of power and privilege, but that the personal *is* political. What is asserted is an identity: a collapse of the one into the other. Nothing "personal" is exempt, then, from political definition, direction, and manipulation—neither sexual intimacy, love, nor parenting.

By reducing politics to what are seen as "power relations," important thinkers in all wings of the women's movement, but centered in the radical feminist perspective, have proffered as an alternative to the malaise of the present a rather bleak Hobbesianism rejuvenated in feminist guise. For if politics is power and power is everywhere, politics is in fact nowhere and a vision of public life as the touchstone of a revitalized ideal of citizenship is lost. These are serious charges, and I shall document them by turning to the manner in which radical feminist images of the "sex war," centered in the family, are served up as a substitute for social and political struggle.

To have a war one needs enemies, and radical feminism (as distinguished from liberal, Marxist or socialist, and psychoanalytic feminism) has no difficulty finding him. The portrait of man which emerges from radical feminist texts is that of an implacable enemy, an incorrigible and dangerous beast who has as his chief aim in life the oppression and domination of women. Ti-Grace Atkinson attributes this male compulsion to man's a priori need to oppress others, an imperative termed "metaphysical cannibalism" from which women are exempt. Susan Brownmiller's male is tainted with an *animus dominandi* which makes him a "natural predator." Mary Daly's male is less bestial, more ghoulish, a vampire who feeds "on the bodies and minds of women. . . . Like Dracula, the he-male has lived on women's blood." Women, however, escape the curse of original sin, being accorded a separate and divergent ontological status. In their views on male and female nature, radical feminists sadly confuse "natural" and "social" categories (as they accuse apologists for patriarchal privilege of doing by manipulating the terms "nature" and "culture" for their own ideological ends). For if male and female roles in society flow directly from some biological given, there is little or nothing politics can do to alter the situation.

Although women escape the curse of an unblessed birth, they are treated to considerable scorn by radical feminists under the guise of "demystifying" their "biological functions." Pregnancy is characterized as "the temporary deformation of the body for the sake of the species." Shulamith Firestone rubs salt into the wound by relating a story of a group of malicious children who point their fingers at a pregnant woman and taunt mercilessly, "Who's the fat lady?" The fetus is labeled variously a "tenant," a "parasite," and an "uninvited guest." Heterosexual sex is reduced to "using people, conning people, messing over people, conquering people, exploiting people." And love? A "pathological condition," a "mass neurosis" which must be destroyed. Childbirth is painful and hideous. Motherhood is portrayed as a condition of terminal psychological and social decay, total self-abnegation and physical deterioration. The new mother is "barely coherent . . . stutters . . . bumps into stationary objects." What has all this to do with politics? The answer, for radical feminists, is everything, given that the "personal is political."

The only way to stop all this, they go on, is to eliminate the patriarchal nuclear family. The argument runs something like this: because "tyranny" begins in biology or nature, nature itself must be changed. *All else* will follow, for it is biological "tyranny," the sex distinction itself, that oppresses women. Having accepted as a necessary and sufficient condition for social change the total "restructuring" of relations between the sexes, Firestone, for example, fizzles into a combination of trivial self-help ("a revolutionary in every bedroom") and a barbaric cybernetic utopia within which every aspect of life rests in the beneficent hands of a new elite of engineers, cyberneticians animated by the victorious Female Principle. Brownmiller's solution to the sex war lodged in male biology and the "rape culture" that is an automatic outgrowth of man's unfortunate anatomy is a loveless Sparta, a "stalemate" in the sex war in which women have been "fully integrated into the extant power structure—police, national guards, state troopers, local sheriffs' offices, state prosecuting attorneys' offices, armed forces"—in other words, just about any male activity that involves a uniform, a badge, a gun, or a law degree.

These suggested solutions to masculine perfidy and biological "tyranny" exemplify a politics of displacement, for they cannot be specified with any concreteness nor acted upon, remaining utopian and abstract; at other times they envisage a female takeover of the extant "power structure," thus vitiating consideration of the structural dimensions of our current crisis, which lie in the specific practices of production, the nature of life work, and the problems of political accountability and of social stratification along lines of ethnicity, class, and race as well as sex.

Except for its ludicrous caricature of the married person as a family fanatic busily engaged in putting single people down, a more recent and sophisticated treatment of radical feminist themes, Ellen Willis's *Village Voice* article, "The Family: Love It or Leave It," avoids many of the crude oversimplifications I have cited. Willis expresses much of the richness and ambivalence internal to family life and to an honest contemplation of that life. Finally, however, her essay collapses under the weight of several contradictions. She insists, for example, that familial matters include public issues that should be the grounds for political decision making. Yet she provides no basis for genuine political action because her strategy remains steadfastly individualistic. ("If people stopped . . . If enough parents . . . If enough women . . .")

Indeed, it is difficult to determine how and why "people, enough parents, women" could mount an effective assault on the public issues Willis finds embedded in our private lives if one of her other claims, that capitalists "have an obvious stake in encouraging dependence on the family," is as overriding as she says it is. She fails to realize that one could make precisely the opposite case—with strong support from historic case studies, something Willis never sees fit to provide—that capitalists have historically had an interest in breaking up family units and eroding family ties. The capitalist ideal is a society of social atoms, beings not essentially connected to one another, to a time, or to a place, who could be shunted about according to market imperatives alone.

Liberal feminism's indictments of family life and men are less bloodcurdling, although Betty Friedan couldn't resist the alliterative "comfortable concentration camp" as a description of suburban housewifery. Friedan's women vegetated as menfolk went off to the city and "kept on growing." Friedan's presumption that the world of work within capitalist society is infinitely preferable to the world of the home is a linchpin of liberal feminism and serves to highlight the class-bound nature of their reflections. Friedan certainly didn't have eight hours a day on an assembly line in mind when she denigrated familial life and celebrated work life. Elizabeth Janeway, another liberal thinker, insists that a man has it over a woman in contemporary society because he knows where he stands; he receives rewards according to preexisting standards of judgment in the marketplace. Women, however, out of the running for the prizes, are confused as to their "true value" (i.e., market worth). Women can take care of this unfortunate state of affairs as individuals, acting alone and being political simply by being "role breakers," a move that simultaneously puts them into the market arena and "threaten[s] the order of the universe."

Marxist feminists put forth conflicting views of family life, but those operating within an orthodox Marxist-Leninist framework are locked into a narrow econometric model that sees both the family and politics as epiphenomenal, having no autonomous not semiautonomous existence of their own. Within this perspective, politics is displaced onto economic concerns exclusively and, paradoxically, depoliticized as a result. Mothering becomes "the reproduction of the labor force" or "the future commodity labor power." Should a mother take umbrage at this characterization of her alternately joyous and vexing activity, it is taken as evidence of her "false consciousness." (There are, however, feminists working within the Marxist tradition who have a more complex image of familial life, and I discuss their views briefly below.)

Taken all in all, the image that emerges from contemporary feminism's treatment of the family is that of a distortion so systematic that it has become another symptom of the disease it seeks to diagnose. One of the key symptoms of this disease—this "legitimation crisis"—is a widespread draining of society's social institutions, public and private, of their value and significance. In stripping away the old ideological guises that celebrated motherhood and denigrated women, extolled the dignity of private life yet disallowed parents the means with which to live in decency and with dignity, feminists performed a necessary and important service. But unmasking an ideology and constructing a sound theory are not the same activity. Ironically, a new feminist ideology has emerged to replace the old patriarchal one. It, like the old, exerts a silencing effect over free and open debate on a whole range of issues having to do with female sexuality, the conflicting demands of contemporary heterosexuality, pregnancy, childbirth and child rearing, and family life, even as it provides no alternative vision of a revitalized concept of "citizenship."

My concern is with that antifamilial feminist ideology that has become linked up in the popular mind with efforts to erode or destroy the meaning and relations of family life *in the absence of any workable alternative.* I have described the complex process at work as a politics of displacement, a form of pseudopolitics in which the symptoms of social breakdown are construed as the disease itself, allowing the deeper dimensions of the crisis to go unchallenged.

Feminist thinkers, in their quest to identify the breeding ground of patriarchal privilege, found a sitting duck in the family. But this is as much attributable to our confusion and malaise over the family's proper social role as it is to feminist prescience. Since the advent of the Industrial Revolution, Western society has faced a "crisis in the family" with each successive generation. The chain of events set in motion by industrialism eventually stripped the family of most of its previous functions as a productive, vocational, religious, educative and welfare unit. As these functions were absorbed by other social institutions and practices, the family remained the locus of intimate, long-term reproductive relations and child-rearing activities. The strains of these shifts are reflected historically in the works of great novelists, political and social theorists, and the theory and practice of psychoanalysis.

The feminist movement is, then—at least in part—a direct outgrowth of the intensification of contradictory burdens and demands on family members. The family is a product of uneven development, existing as a purposeful and vital unit within *every* extant society, yet resisting, within capitalist society, total domination by relations of exchange and the values of the marketplace. Diverse aspects of social practices collide within the family: little girls, for example, may be inculcated with the American ideology of equality of opportunity, receive an education identical to that of their brothers yet, simultaneously, learn an ideology of womanhood and domesticity incompatible with the other ideological imperatives they also hold. Nevertheless, the family, however shakily and imperfectly, helps to keep alive an alternative to the values which dominate in the marketplace. It serves, in the words of Eli Zaretsky, as a reminder of the hope that "human beings can pass beyond a life dominated by relations of production." This vital role played by the family in modern life is recognized by a minority of feminist thinkers who hold the socialist and psychoanalytic perspectives. Indeed, one of the most lyrical evocations of the importance of holding on to that which is valuable in family life, if social relations are not to become thoroughly brutal, may be found in the words of Sheila Rowbotham, a British Marxist feminist, who writes of the family as a "place of sanctuary for all the haunted, jaded, exhausted sentiments out of place in commodity production. . . . The family is thus in one sense the dummy ideal, the repository of ghostly substitutes, emotional fictions. . . . But this distortion of human relations is the only place where human beings find whatever continuing love, security, and comfort they know."

Each child taught to see himself or herself as unique and unconditionally loved, a being (to draw upon Kant) having "dignity," not merely a "price," represents a challenge to the terms of the market system, just as noninstrumental human intimacy is a similar affront to increasingly sophisticated attempts to merchandise every area of human sexual life. Yet these family ties and relations are fragile, subject to strains and breakdowns and to a coarsening that reflects in miniature the abuses of the world outside. Reported incidents of child abuse, for example, rise dramatically during periods of widespread unemployment and economic despair as outward frustrations, in another variant on the politics of displacement, are displaced privately onto the family's most vulnerable members.

The politics of displacement is nothing new under the political sun. Past examples that spring to mind include the policies of the Romanov czars who, over the years, implicated Russia in some external imbroglio whenever they wished to shift public attention away from their domestic politics. A more sinister instance is the use of German Jews as scapegoats for the widespread social dislocation and hardship that followed the end of World War I, a politics of displacement perfected by fascism. In the history of American capitalist expansion and labor strife, one finds the frequent pitting of poor white and black unemployed against each other in such a way that each group saw the other as the source of its misery and corporate oligarchs escaped serious political challenge. Feminism's politics of displacement reveals its true colors when a feminist thinker assaults a social unit, already vulnerable and weakened by external and internal strains, as both *cause* and *symptom* of female subordination. In so doing, those feminists direct attention away from structural imperatives and constraints and promote a highly personalized sexual politics that is simultaneously depoliticizing, individualistic, and potentially pernicious in its implications.

The implication of a feminist politics of displacement for politics itself is simply this: a displaced pseudopolitics vitiates attempts to articulate an ideal of public life as the deliberate efforts by citizens to, in the words of Sheldon Wolin, "order, direct, and control their collective affairs and activities, to establish ends for their society, and to implement and evaluate these ends." Feminism's politics of displacement renders politics hollow, first, by finding politics everywhere; second, by reducing politics to crude relations of force or domination; and third, by stripping politics of its centrality to a shared social identity. It erodes private life by construing it as a power-riddled battleground, thus encouraging a crudely politicized approach toward coitus, marriage, child rearing, even one's relationship to one's own body. It shares with all spinoffs of classical liberalism the failure to develop a vision of a political community and of citizenship that might serve as the touchstone of a collective identity for males and females alike. As Michael Walzer put it recently: "What made liberalism endurable for all these years was the fact that the individualism it generated was imperfect, tempered by older restraints and loyalties, by stable patterns of local, ethnic, religious or class relationships. An untempered liberalism would be unendurable." Feminist thinkers have yet to confront this sobering realization.

Exchange

In an article in The Nation *last November, Jean Bethke Elshtain criticized the writings of several prominent radical feminists. Among her complaints were: these writers scorned the family as a viable humane institution; by finding all human relationships political they made politics meaningless; they confused symptoms of family breakdown "with the disease"; they were practicing a "politics of displacement." Her article drew an unusual number of provocative responses, which we have held off publishing until we had sufficient space.—The Editors*

"Out of Context"
Newark, N.J.

Jean Elshtain's quotation from *The Mermaid and the Minotaur* in her article "Feminists Against the Family" [*The Nation,* Nov. 17, 1979] is, to begin with, *literally* inaccurate. Between typographic marks that conventionally indicate verbatim excerpts, a blurred condensation of one fragment of my prose is spliced together with somebody's inadequate paraphrasing of another fragment. University professors aren't normally prone to such unscholarly errors. Was this a clerical slip-up of some sort?

What is more disturbing, however, is that the *spirit* in which Elshtain refers to my comments on some recent feminist rhetoric against the family differs profoundly from the spirit—one of unqualified identification with feminism's old and persistent core impulse—in which I made them. They were part of my analysis of the historic situation surrounding the current explosion of that core impulse. This situation has engendered (*a*) female rage of unprecedented depth, the sources of which it is clearly vital to understand, and (*b*) a powerful, constructive surge of female societal concern. Professor Elshtain (*a*) deplores that rage without any reference to its sources, which were very carefully explored in just the passage of *Mermaid* from which she quoted, and (*b*) neither honors nor identifies herself with that constructive societal concern. I want your readers to know how strongly I object to being quoted, out of context and incorrectly, in what could look to them like support of her statement. *Dorothy Dinnerstein*

Elshtain Replies
Amherst, Mass.

First, because Ms. Dinnerstein charges that she has been quoted in a way that is "literally inaccurate," I shall cite in full the two sentences from which I drew large portions. Dinnerstein states (*The Mermaid and the Minotaur,* page 275):

> What the historic impasse we have reached has done, in other words, is discredit the essential humanizing functions of stable longstanding generation-spanning primary groups, functions that are by tradition women's concern. This may account for the virulent, reckless, reactive quality of much new feminist rhetoric against the biological family, against permanent personal commitments of adults

to children ("children's liberation"), indeed against bodily childbearing itself (at just this moment in history, ironically, when the oppressive features of that aspect of our biology have become obsolete, and its pleasures optimally accessible to those who choose them).

Frankly, I cannot understand her complaint. The terms "virulent, reckless, reactive" are hers, not mine. Her contention that the "essential humanizing functions of stable longstanding generation-spanning primary groups"—in other words, family and kin ties—have been discredited and that this puts all of us in a situation of risk as well as possibility is one with which I heartily agree. My point, not hers, is to characterize a politics with ragefulness, as distinct from moral anger, as its motive as a politics of displacement. Dinnerstein may not agree with my political analysis but in that case it is her responsibility to proffer an alternative.

Second, Dinnerstein claims that I neither honor nor identify myself with the "constructive surge of female societal concern." This charge can only arise from a sloppy misreading of my piece. I state unequivocally in the opening paragraphs that much that is "exciting and fruitful" has emerged from feminist ferment concerning the family. I insist that the accomplishments of the movement have occurred on a number of levels and that, as a result of feminist rethinking, "women began to view themselves less as passive recipients of revocable privileges and more as active, responsible human beings." I applaud those feminist analysts who have investigated the contradictory dimensions of contemporary family life in exploratory rather than single-dimensional ways. I condemn a social system that subjects family ties and relations to hideous strains brought on, in great measure, by economic inequality. I urge feminists to confront more fully and completely than they yet have how truly terrible a thoroughgoing system of predatory individualism would be if those "essential humanizing functions" to which Dinnerstein refers were to undergo further erosion. I am saddened that Dinnerstein failed to understand. *Jean Bethke Elshtain*

"Politics of Fragmentation"
Fayson Lakes, N.J.

I would like to reply to Jean Bethke Elshtain. As a feminist, as the woman who created and taught the course "Female Sexuality, Power and Identity" at the New School for Social Research in 1973, as the sociologist who pointed out the need for structural changes in my review of Janet Chafetz's *Masculine-Feminine or Human?* in *Contemporary Sociology* in May 1975, and the need for women to struggle for alternative work hours, child care, and redistribution of income on a panel with Jessie Bernard during the Eighth

World Congress of Sociology in Toronto in 1974, I feel qualified to make this reply.

I wonder whom Elshtain is attacking. Women like Carolyn Downer and Jean and Lolly Hirsch, who—at considerable risk to themselves—taught women new things about their bodies, childbearing, and contraception? The women who put together *Our Bodies, Ourselves?* Or women like Pauline Bart who pinpointed the prejudices in standard medical school texts on gynecology and obstetrics? She accuses feminists of a politics of displacement. Is she trying to substitute a politics of fragmentation for the women's movement? Whom does she assume she serves with that? Radical as well as liberal feminists are attacked with the charge that feminist thinkers have done little but condemn the family, the only "sanctuary" apparently left to people in capitalist or postcapitalist society. Does Elshtain know of those thinkers on the left (some of them men) who believe it is precisely this sanctuary quality, along with the isolation and individualism of the American family setup, that allows a capitalist economic structure to continue unchallenged because it provides an island of peace to the alienated American?

Not all feminists are man haters and family haters. To say so is an attack on the women's movement in general and the many nameless women who identify with it because it speaks up for their needs and rights, who feel grateful for the new strengths it has given them. . . . Women's dissatisfaction with their burdens is indeed a political issue and if something went wrong it is indeed because not enough women got together to carry such political issues into the public arena.

As someone who read all the feminist literature she could find to support a Ph.D. thesis on women, I cannot even remember reading that the family must be destroyed, unless I accept Elshtain's out-of-context quotation from Shulamith Firestone. Elshtain gives little convincing evidence of the systematic distortion with which she claims feminists have treated the family. Feminists have pointed out oppressive aspects of the patriarchal family setup, yes. It was the media that gave us distortions of the goals, activities, and pronouncements of the feminist movement. Elshtain seems to imply that it is the family that provides the most important humanizing influence on people. I wonder if she has read any recent data on wife and child battering, family violence, suicide, and divorce? . . .

Does Elshtain have a workable alternative to the "antifamilial feminist ideology"? There were attempts to create new types of families—in the communes, in groups of women and sometimes women and men who shared residences and tried to bring up children jointly. It is unrealistic to expect alternatives to traditional structures to spring up overnight—they appear as isolated efforts here and there. And how is an "alternative vision of a revitalized concept of 'citizenship'" going to make everything well all of a sudden?

It is not the feminists who are to be faulted for our contemporary social malaise and the absence of political community and a "collective identity for males and females alike." By laying the blame on feminism, Elshtain does precisely what she says the feminists have done: create a politics of displacement. Does Elshtain realize that by attacking feminism she attacks the only social movement left in America that is still working toward meaningful change? If she focused less on extremists and radical theorists and more on women themselves, in all their diversity, strengths, and pains, she might— perhaps—be able to see attempts by women toward control of their "collective affairs." As for establishing ends for our society, we have a long, long way to go. It would be good to see women like Elshtain working with, instead of against, us. *Maria Maxfield*

"Individuals' Discontent"
New York City

In discussing my recent article on the family, Jean Bethke Elshtain asserts that my strategy for change "remains steadfastly individualistic ('If people stopped . . . If enough parents . . . If enough women . . .')." The clear implication of the passage Elshtain refers to is that if people (parents, women) were to reject certain assumptions about the family, they would organize to demand changes in the conditions of work and child rearing, and in the economic system generally. Politics aimed at social reform or revolution is always "individualistic" in this sense; it begins with individuals' discontent with their condition. When "enough" people see a need for change, they start or join a movement.

Elshtain also quotes and criticizes out of context my statement that "capitalists have an obvious stake in encouraging dependence on the family." My argument was that capitalism has undermined the authority of the family and its ability to provide economic security for its members; yet for that very reason, it is in capitalists' interest that people look to the family for what remnants of security it offers—as opposed to demanding more social services or radical economic change. In other words, the contradiction is in the system, not my essay. *Ellen Willis*

Elshtain Replies
Amherst, Mass.

Ms. Maxfield has systematically misread my essay and then gone on to attack her distortions of my arguments. Let me attempt to sort a bit of it out. First, I was quite clear about whom I was criticizing, and why, and that my criticism was lodged on the basis of those theoretical presumptions, found in various modes of feminist analysis, which exude a "politics of displacement." Maxfield begs this question and attempts to deflect attention away from it by citing women and groups responsible for changes in the medical treatment of women, etc., she claims I have slighted. Second, I thought I had made it clear that feminist rethinking of private relations has resulted in much that is stimulating and valuable. Third, I too read "all the feminist literature" I could find in the preparation of a Ph.D. thesis on women and politics. The insistence that the family must be destroyed or smashed (rather than reformed or reconstructed) is a theme running through much radical feminist literature from *No More Fun and Games* to the present, an insistence that can also be found in some polemics that call themselves Marxist feminist.

Finally, Maxfield questions whether I "know of" thinkers on the left, including men, who believe that the "sanctuary" quality of the family allows "a capitalist economic structure to continue unchallenged." She is joined by Willis who puts forth as a foregone conclusion the contestable presumption that if the family were thoroughly eroded, "radical economic change" would be demanded. I know of these arguments and disagree with them; indeed, I find them morally repugnant and politically dangerous. The notion is that if everybody were thoroughly miserable, literally homeless, we would all get together and demand social justice. Nonsense. I suggest Maxfield and Willis take a look at the sorts of regimes built on the twisted souls of persons whose lives, public and private, have crumbled around them. A politics animated by what Nietzsche called *ressentiment* is the most likely response and such a politics goes by the name of fascism, whether of the left or the right.

As to the accusation that I am trying to substitute a "politics of fragmentation for the women's movement"—again, nonsense. What "women's movement"? Feminism is already divided along lines of theoretical demarcation and real, not bogus, considerations of class, race, religion, and ethnicity. To pretend such fragmentation doesn't exist is to live in a fantasy world. As to my focus on "extremists and radical theorists"—Betty Friedan hardly seems to be an "extremist," and Marxist feminists of the sort I criticize disagree with the radicals. My essay focused on the best-known statements of *feminist theory* and the consequences for politics flowing from that theory which I found unfortunate. It was intended as a contribution to the ongoing creation of a more coherent feminist theory, for theoretical advance is made only through critique. But Maxfield insists on categorizing me as the enemy. It is that sort of dogmatism that ill serves feminism. *Jean Bethke Elshtain*

"Haven for Whom?"
New York City

Jean Bethke Elshtain astutely notes the disturbing streak of self-hatred—the contempt for the female body and reproductive cycle—hidden in certain feminist writings. But in praising the family as a haven in a heartless world (to use the famous phrase of Christopher Lasch), she fails to ask the crucial question, Haven for whom? The distrust of many feminists for the family as now constituted is a response to the fact that at present the burden of maintaining family life falls squarely on women: they are the ones balancing two jobs—paid work (let's not forget that most women work out of economic necessity) and housework—a burden that becomes exponentially more taxing if child care is added. If a woman cannot do all this with consummate grace, her predicament is seen as a personal failure, not as an abdication of responsibility on the part of her husband or as the refusal of society at large to support her in her laudable struggle to preserve an oasis of intimacy (through day care, child-support payments such as exist in France, universal maternity benefits, or even a "mother's preference" in job placement and advancement comparable to veteran's preference). If her marriage breaks up, as it stands a nearly 50 percent chance of doing, the low value placed by both her husband and society on her years of nurturing and upholding noncommercial values is made painfully evident: the world of work penalizes her for her years out of the job market, the law will very likely fail to acknowledge the extent of her contribution to the marriage and to her husband's economic position, and in roughly four out of five cases her husband will fail to pay court-awarded child support (so much for the joys and responsibilities of fatherhood!). A woman is entitled to ask herself if it is wise to commit her destiny—and her children's well-being—to an institution she is given the responsibility but not the power to maintain.

Elshtain nowhere addresses the very real problems faced by women today, who find that they must choose between family and work (as men do not) in the absence of support systems for child care and in the absence of a commitment on the part of many men to maintain the haven whose benefits they enjoy. For a recognition of this central dilemma one must turn to the feminists: they are the ones pressing for paternity leave for men, family leaves for both sexes, more flexible work schedules, an end to discrimination against pregnant women and older women . . . and for a general recognition that both sexes ought to share in the day-to-day responsibilities of family life. (As for the middle-class bias she sees in the feminist glorification of paid work, is she really unaware of feminist efforts to organize the "pink-collar" occupations, or of the eager movement of women into blue-collar jobs still jealously guarded as a male preserve?)

If Elshtain really wants the family to be an alternative to the soul-destroying values of the marketplace, she should recognize that it is feminists whose actual program would do most to accomplish that goal, and make the family a haven for *all* its members. *Katha Pollitt*

Elshtain Replies
Amherst, Mass.

I am pleased that Ms. Pollitt concurs with my distress at the "disturbing streak of self-hatred" imbedded in some contemporary feminist thought.

It is interesting to me that my views have been assimilated, by Ms. Pollitt and others, with those of Christopher Lasch. Lasch and I differ in several significant ways. Briefly: Lasch no longer finds the family the important and necessary "haven" and touchstone of human identity it once was. For Lasch, the family is more thoroughly suffused with market imperatives and capitalist social relations than is compatible with my views; moreover, there is in Lasch's notion of haven much more of a sense of "retreat" than I wished to signify. As I stated in my essay, "each child taught to see himself or herself as unique and unconditionally loved, a being (to draw upon Kant) having 'dignity,' not merely a 'price,' represents a challenge to the terms of the market system. . . ." Children, despite all, are still being taught that in thousands of ordinary homes. That this task is made extraordinarily difficult by the exigencies noted by Pollitt is most certainly the case. *Jean Bethke Elshtain*

"Out of Date . . ."
Westbury, N.Y.

Jean Elshtain's lead article on feminism and the family is simply out of date. While an unknowing reader might be pulled along by the logic and prose of the piece, someone familiar with the current feminist movement knows that a major shift on views of the family has been in the works since at least the mid-1970s. Feminists themselves have rethought the extreme antifamilialism of their early positions. And just as this about-face is completed and publicly trumpeted in *The New York Times Magazine* (Betty Friedan, "Feminism Takes a New Turn," Nov. 18, 1979), the *Peoria Journal Star* (Nov. 30, 1979), and numerous papers in between, *The Nation* features an anachronistic attack informed by Shulamith Firestone and various defunct radical feminist organizations.

You need to publish a current analysis of feminism and the family to set the record straight. *Jan Rosenberg*

" . . . and Antifeminist"
Merrick, N.Y.

I read with dismay your recent article "Feminists against the Family." *The Nation* publishes articles on feminist thinking so seldom that it is unfortunate that it has chosen to print an article that is misleading, inaccurate, and, above all, antifeminist. The article extrapolates from the theories of one group, the radical feminists, and projects the tenets of that group onto all feminists.

Feminists, by and large, are not antifamily. While we agree that the patriarchal nuclear family victimizes its members, the thrust of mainstream feminism is to strengthen and reform family structure. Feminists espouse various actions, such as legislative and community efforts, not merely "personal politics."

Further, to suggest that liberal feminists and their goals are middle class is simply untrue. It was women mine workers, not Betty Friedan, who fought for the right of women to work in coal mines. Feminists' struggles for such things as social security reform, day-care centers, equal pay and opportunity benefit all women—working class and middle class, those who work in the home and those who work outside the home. *May Beresin, Ph.D.*

Family Politics
Brooklyn, N.Y.

I read Jean Bethke Elshtain's article with much interest. Recently, I have participated in meetings of the National Women's Health Network and the American Public Health Association. While neither organization is particularly radical, both groups have memberships that include fair numbers of feminists of various political perspectives. I was struck many times over the course of the meetings by how much the feminist perspective on women's health has broadened. Our discussions are focusing on problems of conception as well as contraception and abortion, sterility as well as sterilization, and our concerns include childbearing and rearing, accessible child care, and so many problems that are clearly part of "family life."

At these meetings, some of us had our children with us, and many of us found one another engrossed in defining and working on our own family issues, traditional nuclear or otherwise. Because we have found politics everywhere . . . our personal decisions regarding marriage and relationships, child rearing and bearing, and sexuality have become political.

I think that the rhetoric of the earlier days of the feminist movement reflected a newly articulated fury and frustration; what seems to be happening now is a more sober consideration of our realities. Ms. Elshtain cites Betty Friedan's indictment of family life. In a more recent piece, "Feminism Takes a New Turn," Ms. Friedan observes that the initial agenda of the movement was inadequate, that we need an agenda for the 1980s that will focus on the family. It is also interesting to note that The Boston Women's Health Book Collective followed *Our Bodies, Ourselves* with *Ourselves and Our Children.*

The most politically radical feminists may disagree, but it does seem to me that the feminist movement as a whole has begun the exploration of "Family" and all that that can mean. The issues of control and power, however, are just as inherent in that as they have been for us in the worlds of work and education. *Wendy A. Lebowitz*

"Feminism's Diversity"
Burlington, Vt.
Jean Elshtain's article leaves me cold—probably because I don't understand much of it. It is laced with too many catchwords from the language of political rhetoric that have been used to cover so much ideological territory as to have become meaningless.

However, there is an aspect of the article that I feel needs more emphasis than Ms. Elshtain accords it: the overwhelming fact of feminism's plurality and diversity. It is true that on occasion she speaks of "radical feminists," "liberal feminists," or "Marxist feminism" in order to qualify her definitions, but these instances are exceptions. It would be extremely misleading for other readers to assume that "feminism" is limited to those viewpoints that she has used to illustrate it. As with Christianity, the discussion of a few points of Presbyterian or Methodist doctrine is hardly sufficient to define the subject, or explain it to a Buddhist.

There are, indeed, many "family feminists" around—I coin the phrase since I've not encountered before the necessity to make such a distinction. I meet them every day and I am surprised that Ms. Elshtain has not. *Constance L. Kite*

"A Tiny Minority"
Austin, Tex.
"Feminists against the Family" by Jean Bethke Elshtain presents a very misleading picture of feminism. Among other questionable devices used to develop her thesis, Ms. Elshtain has chosen slanted and unrepresentative data. The women's movement is a vast sprawling body of men and women with various levels of commitment from conservatism through liberalism to radicalism. No one knows the real numbers, but it is quite likely there are millions in that center liberal group, while the far-left radical segment makes

up, perhaps, 2 to 4 percent of the whole. And yet the author takes her proof, in the form of quotations, only from that tiny minority. As to space allowed, she used nine paragraphs attacking the radicals but only one for those millions of moderates. . . .

Data can also be slanted by omitting pertinent facts. This, for example: "The only way to stop all this [scorn] . . . is to eliminate the patriarchal nuclear family." Some radical feminist, somewhere, may have said this, but moderate feminists (of both sexes) recognize fully the value of the family as a primary group and wish to preserve it in *a modified form*. We would eliminate the patriarchal features but not the family itself. The pertinent fact omitted here is that when the second wave of feminism surfaced (in the 1960s), the family already had about an 80 percent record of failure. (Add the divorce rate to the estimated number of marriages that remained intact but were unhappy.) We are not to blame for that failure.

Two other beliefs of the moderates are significant here, too. Contrary to the impression given in the article, feminists are not indifferent to children but would like to see fewer children with far better care than they generally receive today. And most female feminists want an ongoing, committed, intimate relationship with a congenial male. They are not anti-man.

On page 499 the author departs completely from reality: "Ironically, a new feminist ideology has emerged to replace the old patriarchal one." (True enough.) "It, like the old, exerts a silencing effect over free and open debate on a whole range of issues having to do with female sexuality, pregnancy. . . . My concern is with that anti-familial ideology that [aims] to erode or destroy the meaning and relations of family life *in the absence of any workable alternative.*"

We have *not* silenced the debate and we *do* offer an alternative.

Only since the rise of feminism have people spoken freely of battered women, abused children, incest, rape, and displaced homemakers. No one even guessed at the extent of these problems until feminists brought them to light. Now they are discussed in many group programs and in our publications.

As to that "workable alternative," where has Ms. Elshtain lived that she is unaware of the countless dual, egalitarian households in which both adults share child care, house care, and sometimes even the earning? These are easy, comfortable arrangements, free of any power struggle. Contrary to the author's assertion, the personal is *not* always political. Only if a situation involves power does it become political.

Feminists do not want power over men. They wish only to be accepted as persons and to share in the decisions that shape their lives. Ms. Elshtain, who is apparently a privileged person, does her sisters a grave disservice by presenting such a distorted picture of one of the most important movements in history. *Mary Frederick*

Elshtain Finale
Amherst, Mass.

These letters suggest either that my piece is "simply out of date," focuses disproportionately on "the far-left radical segment" of the women's movement, or is "misleading, inaccurate, and, above all, antifeminist."

Ms. Beresin's charge that the piece is antifeminist is scarcely worth responding to, given the fact that I discuss with approval feminist thinkers who represent the psychoanalytic and socialist perspectives and urge the further development of modes of feminist thought that take into account the concerns I raise in the essay. The notion that it is "misleading" derives, in part, from the claim of letter writers that I concentrate on only a few radical feminists to the exclusion of the vast majority who don't espouse the positions I criticize. This is an interesting charge because, on the one hand, the letter writers clearly wish to differentiate themselves from the view of the radical feminists yet, simultaneously, they are angry with me for doing precisely the same thing. If I followed the logic of several of these respondents I could, in turn, accuse them of antifeminism for their own obvious disagreements with the "far-left radical segment."

The notion that the piece is "out of date" derives from a blindness, widely shared among Americans, to *theoretical* concerns and a socially sanctioned inability to think theoretically. Similarly, an essay analyzing a Marxian text would be assaulted because that text dates from 1871 and is undeniably "out of date" if one's standard of reference is 1980. Americans seem to think that thought goes out of style as quickly as each year's fashions. Texts, however, have a life of their own. The feminists' texts I criticize are read, in turn, by successive generations of young women and young men who need to know that there are alternative theoretical perspectives. It would be politically and morally irresponsible for a scholar to turn her back on the task of critique because the text is "out of date"—being some eight or even eighteen years old. If the respondents really think the radical feminist movement is defunct they, not I, are seriously out of touch. I suggest they read Mary Daly's *Gyn/Ecology*, or is it "out of date," having been published in 1979?

Several of the writers signal a "major shift" in thinking on the family with the publication of Betty Friedan's piece, "Feminism Takes a New Turn," which appeared shortly after my own essay. Friedan's piece supposedly makes mine all the more "anachronistic." But have they seriously examined that article? The kind of family arrangement Friedan celebrates as exemplary (flextime, husband and wife sharing fully and equally in child care and career) is possible, at best, for the top 10 to 15 percent of the American population. Her "rethinking" amounts to an overall accommodation with corporate capitalism which can—perhaps—accommodate the interests and needs of some upper-middle-class professionals. (Friedan hopes, by the way, that corporate capitalism will somehow be humanized in the process of such accommodation: a fragment of liberal overoptimism we should long since have laid aside as delusory.) For less-privileged families we get, among other things, the reiteration of the need for more child care—whether government-, union-, or industry-sponsored. This is simply *not good enough*. It is too late in the day to settle for restatement of the need without close specification of what is to count as quality child care and how feminists will promote and protect the needs of the child, not just the needs of women who must or need to work, or the interests of capitalism in having them work, the vast majority at low-paid, unskilled jobs. The situation hasn't changed much for the Norma Raes. Picture what sort of child care her company would provide in order to facilitate labor on the part of women!

Why should liberal feminist always anticipate the most favorable outcomes of social change, including policies they advocate? Feminists should be fighting, not calling for, franchised child care for private profit—a phenomenon that has been called "Kentucky Fried Children." However, in advocating government-sponsored day care, feminists should be aware of the dangers inherent in political control of the socialization process, possibly turning children into raw products for the political system to recruit. It can't happen here? Why not? The smug, self-congratulatory mood of the Friedan essay and that of several of the letters (e.g., Frederick's fulsome, class-blind recounting of "countless dual, egalitarian households" with "easy, comfortable arrangements," on and on) is altogether unwarranted. I suggest these women read Lillian Rubin's *Worlds of Pain: Life in the Working Class Family* as an antidote to their class blindness.

The feminist movement is at a crossroads: either it can move in directions that deepen the real, structurally induced divisions *between classes of women* or *work to identify those issues that, in fact, divide women.* In denying those issues or treating them as a kind of afterthought, feminism suppresses some of its own potential constituency. The belated recognition of some of the issues I call for as central hasn't yet led to the necessary exploratory, self-critical rethinking. The truth of the matter is: there is no functional alternative to the family for 85 to 90 percent of the American population. The truth of the matter is: the old routes to success even for the minority of relatively privileged women (based on family backgrounds of income, status, education) are beginning to close up, and we must think of creative ways to respond. The truth of the matter is: few women as a portion of the population have "made it" or can. Will we see those simply consolidating their gains and falling into a single-dimensional view of the social world? Several of these letters suggest we will.

Two final comments: Ms. Kite was left cold because she didn't understand much of my article, given, she complains, that it was "laced with too many catchwords from the language of political rhetoric." I hope she is not referring to such esoteric notions as "citizenship" or "political community." Ms. Frederick resorts to a gratuitous ad hominem by insisting that I am "apparently a privileged person." I refuse to enter a proletarian sweepstakes with Frederick but if I did I bet I'd have a good chance of winning it. *Jean Bethke Elshtain*

"Feminists against the Family" was originally published in *The Nation,* November 17, 1979; the correspondence in *Exchange* appeared April 5, 1980. © 1979, 1980. Reprinted by permission.

11

Liberal Heresies: Existentialism and Repressive Feminism

> The structure of the mind is being battered from inside. Some terrible new thing is happening. Maybe it'll be marvelous. Who knows? Today it's hard to distinguish between the marvelous and the terrible.
>
> *Doris Lessing*

The contemporary feminist movement has from its inception described itself as a movement for the liberation of women. But the nature and meaning of that liberation has yet to emerge with clarity; indeed, there is much confusion as to whether individual women must be liberated in order to take their rightful place within the social arrangements of contemporary capitalist society, or whether social structures themselves must first be altered in order to create liberated women. My purpose in this essay is not to review all contemporary feminist positions on the question of liberation. Instead, I begin by asking why, thus far, no coherent, powerful, and politically compelling articulation of a theory of liberation that could serve both as concrete historical analysis and as a force for social transformation has emerged from the women's movement. Why, despite all the ferment and fervor, has feminism thus failed? In Norman Birnbaum's words: "We continue to lack a vision of our ends. We have no conception of the dimension and structures of a fulfilled or even a viable political community."[1]

There are various explanations for this failure, but, upon examination, these seem to be mere rationalizations. The comforting notion that the women's movement is young and "needs time" to work through its conceptual problems in order to come up with a clear vision no longer suffices—if indeed it ever did. Feminist theory, as Richard Wollheim observed recently, is not much further along now than it was in 1869 when John Stuart Mill published his classic essay *On the Subjection of Women*.[2] This observation refers to the movement's understanding of the individual, particularly the female individual, *in society* and its appreciation of the connections between individuals and a social whole within a specific historical situation. Yet without such an understanding social theory quickly becomes trivial or pretentious—full of sound and fury, signifying, ultimately, very little indeed.

Another reason proffered for the failure of feminist thought is the notion that all previous theories of politics, because they were written by men, are unsuitable to the purposes of women. Women must "start from scratch"; thus American feminists until recently rejected psychoanalytic theory in toto on the grounds that Freud was a sexist and that his ideas were thereby tainted. The entire history of Western thought is sometimes tossed out the window as the product of males in male-dominant societies.[3] In this way, feminists have absolved themselves of the painstaking process responsible criticism demands, namely, getting inside explanatory theories of politics, determining which issues and conclusions are central to any given theory and which are not, and then criticizing the theory on grounds that come to grips with those factors that sustain it.[4] Under the demand that thought be immediately relevant and applicable to "the struggle" and under the continued tacit sway of presumptions they claim to have rejected, feminist analysts too often have recapitulated a mode of discourse that vitiates critical thought and thus serves neither the liberation of women nor the transformation of society.

This essay is divided into four major sections. I begin with an attenuated but not, I hope, unfair characterization of the classical liberal theory of the individual. Second, I argue that one of the most important responses to liberal theory and modern "mass society," the existentialism of Jean-Paul Sartre, locates in the heart of its critique a particularly crude version of the classical liberal theory of the individual. Third, I examine two leading statements from the radical feminist wing of the women's movement—first, because of their conceptual ties to Sartrism and, second, because, of all theories of women's liberation, radical feminism claims the most but offers the least. By unpacking its major presumptions and conclusions and by examining its purposes and claims, I show why radical feminism correctly deserves to be called *repressive.* I conclude with a first approximation at articulating what a clear and responsible social theory of human liberation must recognize and incorporate within its vision of the future. To this end I turn to psychoanalytic theory for a set of critical concepts that revolve around human complexity and moral agency. I agree with Juliet Mitchell that a rejection of psychoanalytic theory is fatal for feminism[5] and, I would add, for all contemporary social thought. The repression of psychoanalytic insights militates against the emergence of a mode of self-reflection that a *genuine* movement for human liberation requires and must foster if it is not to carry into the future the systems of domination of the past.

The Classical Liberal Theory of the Individual

The liberal tradition is not of a piece. The political theorist must be prepared to trace key points of conceptual demarcation within that tradition carefully in order to avoid a Procrusteanism which equates liberalism in an oversimple and nonproblematic way with the notion of possessive or abstract individuals. In criticizing the liberal theory of the individual, one should ask whether there may not be certain features of that theory that represent important and worthy ideals one may wish to retain and to resituate within an alternative framework of explanation. This latter point is critical to the concluding section of the essay. For the moment, however, my focus is on those aspects of liberal theory that distort our understanding of human beings and their social world.

What kind of being is presupposed by classical liberal thinkers? This is a question on the level of ontology. It is sometimes answered directly by the political theorist; more often, however, one must be sensitive to what kind of being the theory *presupposes* or *requires*. A reading of the classic texts of early liberal thought demonstrates that a fundamental assumption of liberal theorists like Hobbes and Locke is that the individual is related to society in ways that are external and instrumental. By "external" I mean that being a part of society is not seen to change or alter individuals in any fundamental or meaningful way. By "instrumental" I mean that social institutions are seen to exist in order to preserve, protect, and defend the self-interest of individuals and to enable such individuals to make "mutually beneficial bargains."[6] The liberal individual is a social atom, a self-contained monad, whose relationship with others in political society is defined in formal-legal terms and whose liberty consists in minimally regulated acquisition and the maintenance of a private sphere of life into which the public sphere does not intrude.

Even as society exists to serve instrumentalist purposes, the human being is a creature guided by instrumentalist reason. His thought is determined by considerations of marginal utility. His relations with others are regulated by that calculus James Glass calls the "phenomenology of liberal externality" and Hobbes terms "reckoning consequences."[7] Within the strongest version of the liberal perspective, the human mind is construed as asocial if not antisocial. Men are said to be totally free beings who constitute their own "universe of meaning."[8] Hobbes's theory of human nature, for example, depicts an abstracted, ahistorical, atomistic, and aggressive creature.[9] Hobbes's mechanistic epistemology or logic of explanation disallowed the possibility of first envisaging and then exploring a link between the individual and society that might go beyond surface externals.

Although Locke, in his *Two Treatises of Government,* broke from Hobbes's rigorous and uncompromising mechanism, he remained attached to a mode of explanation that presupposed abstract and ahistorical individuals on the level of ontology. Locke treats the human mind as a kind of vessel or repository assigned the passive task of reflecting and copying material given to the senses. External impressions create sensations within the mind from which the individual may, through a process of solipsistic introspection, derive ideas. But Locke's individual cannot go beyond what is given—a social world depicted either as an entity that threatens the individual should it become too powerful or as a powerful conglomerate of means that may be deployed on behalf of his interests.[10] Because liberal theory makes the mistake of presuming that all values are simple private values or compounds of private values, it cannot provide, as Robert Paul Wolff has argued, the grounding for a life in common.[11] The liberal theory of the individual connects with, and serves to justify, theories of liberation as a freeing of an ontologically "free" self from social constraints.[12] Individuals are said to be "free to choose"; their actions are either perceived as private and egoistic or, less frequently, as altruistic acts of supererogation that go beyond the minimal requirements of everyday life. Altruism is the only alternative to self-interestedness within liberal thought, and it remains an individual, not a social, value. Part of the "poverty of liberalism" is its impoverished view of human nature. Liberal theory strips human beings of their location in "time, place, culture, and history" and sees all limitations of human will and the constraints imposed by human morality as inessential and uninteresting facts about the human condition.[13] It leaves out, as Walter Lippmann once remarked, all the "first and the last" things of human life. Wolff comments: "In the classical social contract theories, this systematic setting to one side of the fundamental facts of birth, childhood, parenthood, old age, and death results in an image of the public political world as a timeless or static community of adults, met together to transact their collective business."[14] Yet post-Lockean liberalism also includes the Kantian account of moral agency, the depiction of a being who has obligations and duties to self and others, and Rousseau's vision of the political community as a moral community that transcends the totality of private interests, the depiction of a life in common in which justice replaces instinct in the motivation and conduct of the citizen. I shall return to this aspect of the liberal tradition later. But first I will examine various proposed alternatives to liberalism.

Liberal Theory Recast:
The Existentialism of Jean-Paul Sartre

One might suppose that theorists who claim to have rejected liberalism would incorporate within their thought those features of human life liberalism strips away. But, alas, things are often neither simple nor reasonable. The philosophy of Jean-Paul Sartre is a case in point.[15] To those unfamiliar with the internal history of feminist debates, an examination of Sartrism as a prelude to a critique of radical feminism may seem odd. The point of assessing Sartre's thought is simply this: Sartre's existentialism recasts and, in some instances, goes beyond the liberal theory of abstract individualism. Sartre's categories, in turn, are taken up by his disciple and colleague, Simone de Beauvoir, to form the basis of her classic feminist text, *The Second Sex*. De Beauvoir's presumptions on women and society are scattered throughout contemporary feminist literature, and they are explicitly deployed by radical feminist analysts; thus, through a process of assimilation, Sartrian categories have helped structure, define, and limit radical feminist thought.[16]

I shall examine Sartre's existentialism with reference to the interrelated problems of his theory of human nature, his understanding of human action, his view of the relationship between individuals and groups, and the moral and political implications of his conclusions. This requires probing Sartre's thought on two levels that enrich and inform one another. In order to assess Sartre's logic of inquiry critically, I explore simultaneously those latent meanings that begin to force their way to the surface as one immerses oneself in Sartre's universe. This second level of analysis turns on a recognition that the so-called style of a work bespeaks the character and mind of its author in ways both profound and subtle.

Sartre's profuse elaboration of obtuse terms, his labyrinthian twists and turns, his ultimate capitulation to moral nihilism, and his leaps to sanction the shedding of blood and to celebrate the nobility of violence force the theorist to ponder why a mode of thought that sees human life as "violence . . . on violence"[17] and a system of "violence and terror"[18] should exercise any appeal at all. This question, in turn, leads to a consideration of human aggression and desire to control. It also points to consideration of a theory of "naïve self-love":[19] a theory that declares human beings totally unique and set apart from *all* else; a theory that refuses to consider seriously the problems of either self or social limits; a theory that enables the few to distance themselves from the many by excoriating those who refuse to seize their absolute freedom as existing in "bad faith."[20] This question remains implicit throughout my discussion of Sartre and emerges, explicitly, in my critique of repressive feminism.

I begin with Sartre's theory of human nature. In *Being and Nothingness,* Sartre presents an atomistic conception of the individual: The person is an isolated monad confronting an external social world set off against, and in opposition to, his free project. Sartre's ontology presupposes the natural state of human beings as one of a war of all against all. This violence is held in check by greater violence—by a system of terror known as society. Sartre's adoption of the liberal theory of the individual has been selective, not systematic. For example, he could have incorporated Kantian or Rousseauian notions of substantive reason, moral agency, and the just society. But these important features of post-Lockean liberalism are excluded, and we find instead a bleak reiteration of an a priori and fundamental human asociality.[21]

Sartre's vision of the existentialist actor on the stage of history reads as a kind of distorted parody of self-made man—a being with no ties to bind him to the past nor to hold him in the present. Sartrian man is free-floating—a person passionately engaged with history who has no history. Dependence on others is a loss of freedom. For Sartre, relations between persons are neither natural nor intrinsic; instead, they are instrumental and calculated, although they may be "masked" with such notions as brotherhood. Beneath the "false unity" of such mystifications lurks a constantly re-created world of violence and terror. Reciprocity, Sartre argues, only mystifies the command-obedience structure of the group.

Because the unity of the group comes to it from the outside, Sartre denies the possibility that human beings may be internally linked to one another through such powerful mechanisms as identification and shared purposes. He denies human sociality absolutely. Sociality is simply the oppression of some men by others—it is the violence of emerging alienated freedom, and violence on this violence. Sartre lives in a "world haunted" by his fellowmen. To live in such a world "is not only to be able to encounter the Other at every turn of the road; it is also to find myself engaged in a world in which instrumental-complexes can have a meaning which my free project has not first given to them."[22] Others are what stand in my way. Others are part of the realm of facticity or givens, obstacles to be overcome. Groups form and are held together by terror. Fear of violence and death alone drives individuals to form groups, and this same terror prevents groups from dissolving. "Terror is mortal solitude . . . the guarantee that my neighbor will stay my neighbor; it binds my neighbor to me by the threat of violence it will use against him if he dares to be 'unbrotherly.' "[23] Hobbes put it this way: "The passions that incline men to peace, are fear of death; desire of such things as are necessary to commodious living; and a hope of their industry to obtain them."[24]

Human freedom and liberation are the overcoming of the world of facticity, including one's past, one's social relationships, and finally, one's own death by returning to an original ontological solipsism in which the individual is the total and absolute sovereign of himself.[25] This condition, called freedom, is the annihilation of givens; it has no limits. As Bernstein observes, "this is just as true for a person in a free humanistic society as for a person in a concentration camp."[26] Within Sartrian existentialism, any society is a totalistic abstraction, an instrument of terror; thus, the need to distinguish between more or less faulty and exploitative social forms is eliminated. Problems of class, race, and sex are flattened out to be replaced by a universal human condition in which the prisoner and the prince share an oppressive social world. All ways of life, for Sartre, represent an "endangering morass into which men sink who refuse to assume their full human stature."[27] One assumes one's full stature when the past and other persons, in the most fundamental sense, no longer exist for oneself. My past becomes "that self which I no longer am."[28]

The amelioration of a world of scarcity, the abolition of oppressive and exploitative structures, would not remove the presence of a past nor the existence of human beings who, as Other, constrain me. Because I *am* my projects I must struggle incessantly against those who would disallow me my total freedom to act[29]—whether in an egalitarian or unjust society. Even in a world of plenty, Sartre's individual would remain alone and human activity would take the form of "appropriation." Possession for Sartre is a form of being. A person possesses unceasingly. *All* activities are a mode of appropriation, including knowledge and play. Sartre describes skiing as the possession of a visual field and the conquest of space. The links to abstract individualism in its most virulent form as a theory of possessive individualism are clear.[30] Rather than countering the destructive intrusion of the language of exchange and the market into all spheres of life, Sartre perfects that intrusion. As a result his world is shrunken and impoverished—persons are emptied of inner resources of renewal and richness. That our thoughts and actions may bear multiple meanings for us—for we are diverse—is denied.

The Cartesian distinction between consciousness and matter is central to Sartre's thought.[31] In *Being and Nothingness* Sartre conflates social being and social consciousness. Consciousness is, quite literally, an open book; repression, unconscious mental processes, or a hidden interior life do not exist. Should a person suffer from, say, an incapacity to work or inexplicable attacks of anxiety, that person, in Sartre's view, is in total and full possession on the conscious level of the motivations and meanings of his actions. The "liar already is in complete possession of the truth he is hiding." This individual, the nature of whose consciousness is "of the nothingness of its being," must nevertheless be in total possession of the truth about himself and others at all times—otherwise he is labeled as one in "bad faith," or worse.[32] The split between consciousness and matter is also evident in Sartre's treatment of the human body. He regards it at best as a nuisance—an unacceptable constraint—for it represents those ties to matter that man must transcend. Sartre calls the body "one of the strongest sources of nausea"[33] because it reveals to us the realm of contingent matter.

Sartre's discussion of the relationship between social consciousness and social being and his treatment of society as a unified system composed of reciprocally integrated elements, bears an uncanny resemblance to the functionalism of Talcott Parsons. Sartre shares the functionalist presumption that social structures are ossified objectifications of function.[34] Sartre's society, like that of the functionalists, contains constituted and constituting groups. The functionalist depicts this interrelationship as society's normal state—one of equilibrium—and functionalist theory both describes and justifies maintenance of a society's status quo so long as its various parts are in functional balance with one another.

Sartre has no powerful response to functionalist presumptions because he, too, has eliminated or eviscerated those concepts central to a critical analysis of individuals in society, including repression and alienation. Unlike the functionalists, Sartre is passionately devoted to social change. He has given frequent expression to his disdain for, and utter condemnation of, bourgeois society. But this leaves him with a problem: If the social order is corrupt and degraded by definition, and if individual consciousness reflects that social order on a single conscious plane, where can a source of renewal be found? By collapsing appearance and reality, by according neither complexity nor depth to the human subject, Sartre's existentialism, like functionalism, cannot provide a concrete analysis of human mind and human relationships *in history.* Sartre's way out is a robust voluntarism: The slumbering beast of humanity must, from time to time, engage in a spontaneous outburst, an act of the will, which is likely to be violent and dangerous but which represents his freedom and transcendence.

Pause for a moment to envisage Sartre, at work writing *Being and Nothingness* or *The Critique of Dialectical Reason.* He is thinking about people, human beings. Before him stretches an apparently endless sea of faceless, nameless, anomic entities stuck in the practico-inert, in their series of reciprocal isolation. Group action alone can break through and disrupt this anomic seriality. But Sartre's theory of group action forms no part of a coherent social vision, for Sartre takes action on its own terms: in and for itself. It is *only* at the very moment of action, as seriality is swept away, that men realize their free project. Thus, Sartre's group can never be linked by a Rousseauian general will nor, as Freud urged, by reason and Eros, but only by terror with will as the motor of the deed. It is difficult to determine what distinguishes Sartre's notion that group acts of will cannot be a feature of a set of conscious intentions (because groups know *how* they act but now *why*) from fascist celebrations of the "deed" and the "act" that he would personally despise. Fascism also conceived, in Mussolini's words, "of life as a struggle in which it behooves a man to win for himself a really worthy place. . . . The fascist disdains an 'easy' life."[35] Fascism, too, was "always . . . a doctrine of action."[36] The purpose of mentioning this conceptual connection is to make a serious point: Within the framework of Sartrian existentialism, the possibility for, and necessity of, moral judgment is blunted. That Sartre would condemn fascist doctrines of action does not alter this judgment: Indeed, insofar as Sartre eliminates the question of historic agency tied to individual responsibility and social purpose, his actors are more likely to deceive themselves as to their own motives and purposes.

Sartre grounds individual choices in freedom. But that freedom is nothingness. Although Sartre asserts that men must be totally responsible, that they must, quite literally, assume the burden of the world, he gives no grounds for preferring or following one course of action as against others. Without locating his convictions in his logic of explanation, Sartre's choices are ultimately gratuitous. "There is no reason to value one rather than the other: this is Sartre's own grand conclusion."[37] Sartre's assertion of total responsibility—that the individual is responsible for *every* act of suffering, humiliation, degradation, torture, destruction, and annihilation in the world—disallows any reasonable moral stance; if I am responsible for everything, I am responsible for nothing. "The business of any morality," Sartre concludes, "is to consider human life as a match which can be won or lost, and to teach men how to win."[38] This is surely nihilism in a particularly cold and instrumentalist sense.[39] Moral discourse—as opposed to grandiose calls for totalistic responsibility—rests upon a series of concepts that are tied to reasons of a certain kind. To act morally, I assert, through the use of reason, certain principles. This means I can be called upon to give reasons for why I acted, or did not act, as I did. Action alone can never be its own justification.[40]

Repressive Feminism:
de Beauvoir and the "Radical Feminists"

I have characterized as repressive the major statements of that wing of feminism which terms itself "radical." I use the term advisedly. It is not deployed in a loose and pejorative sense but as a careful depiction and evaluation of a version of liberation that, as it is internalized by individual women, requires that they deny whole dimensions of their lives and experience. These denials are then buttressed and kept in place by incessant and intrusive demands for solidarity and by the constant reiteration of doctrinal truths. Ultimately the denial is itself denied and placed, as a burden, a judgment, and an accusation, upon others with the implicit aim of silencing them. In donning what Abigail Rosenthal calls the "mask" of totalistic protest, a kind of brutality parading as feminism serves repression by burying the problems clustered around "the contradictory desires and refusals of contemporary heterosexuality."[41] In this way, women simply continue to shore up, not challenge, the status quo by making the avoidance of self-knowledge a programmatic requirement.

I do not question the genuine problems and suffering faced by women within this—or any other—society. But I do question the level at which radical feminist arguments are couched: insultingly simpleminded; replete with open contempt for rigorous, systematic thought; insistent upon a naïve and dangerous rejection of the need for tentativeness, deliberation, and criticism in both politics and the arts that cannot be expected to turn on a single set of simple truths. Radical feminism becomes the paradigmatic instance of repressive feminism in the degree of self-repudiation and denial it demands and in the muddled and ultimately numbing incoherence of those analyses it offers.[42]

The major statement of radical feminism, Shulamith Firestone's *The Dialectic of Sex,* is a tract riddled with unsubstantiated assertions, distortions of history, wild leaps from one premise to another without any mediating terms, half-truths parading as the whole, and intense confusion on the level of epistemology; indeed, it is difficult to know where the critic should begin a critique. There is yet another disquieting question: Why has *this* book received the praise and attention it has among feminist writers—even those who do not share Firestone's perspective?[43] What does it say about the contemporary feminist movement? What are the intellectual roots or origins of repressive feminism? To answer that question I must turn for a moment to Sartre's disciple Simone de Beauvoir. I mention the connection with Sartre because it is a critical one de Beauvoir herself acknowledges repeatedly in her work; moreover, Firestone dedicates her book to de Beauvoir to acknowledge her own indebtedness in turn. I shall concentrate upon only two central dimensions of de Beauvoir's analysis: One of these dimensions figures in her work *explicitly;* the other emerges *implicitly* but *powerfully* in her analysis. The explicit dimension lies in her theory of human nature, male and female, and the relation of those natures to civilization. The implicit dimension is de Beauvoir's censorious repudiation of female bodies and sexuality for which her work provides powerful indirect and, at times, open evidence.

De Beauvoir, deploying Sartre's categories of the Being-in-itself and the

Being-for-itself, identifies women, as does Sartre, with nature. Human civilization begins where nature ends. This would appear to leave women stuck outside civilization. Sartre himself is quoted as stating that women's nature is "fixed," that is, "determined by their unfortunate sexual anatomy, which limits them to roles approximating the non-conscious, unalienated Being-in-itself."[44] De Beauvoir would not second the above view without criticism, and in *The Second Sex* she softens Sartre's terms of discourse by writing of the realms of Transcendence and Immanence—her visions of the for-itself and in-itself. Woman, trapped in Immanence, represents, for man, the Other. Man enjoys Transcendence—that world of action or the world in which there is a possibility for action. Woman is defined in her relation to man and by what she *is* (Immanence). What "peculiarly signalizes the situation of woman is that she—a free and autonomous being like all human creatures—nevertheless finds herself living in a world where men compel her to assume the status of the Other."[45] De Beauvoir quotes a writer who declared that the "body of man" had its own integrity and "made sense" apart from that of a woman, whereas the latter "seems wanting in significance by itself."[46]

Human civilization—indeed humanity itself—is for de Beauvoir male; woman is "the incidental, the inessential as opposed to the essential. He is the Subject, he is the Absolute—she is the Other."[47] Woman is trapped in service to the species. De Beauvoir would spring her from this dark and terrifying world of the biologically given (de Beauvoir's discussion of female biology bespeaks a powerful need to distance herself from that biology) in order that she might enter Transcendence as well. The woman, like the Sartrian man, must be free to act, to use her beliefs as a vehicle for the will. De Beauvoir associates all the "loftiest human attitudes"—heroism, revolt, disinterestedness, creativity—with that male world of Transcendence that has been denied to women. Why does de Beauvoir deny other ideals one might consider worthy, including friendship, loyalty, a sense of justice, respect for persons, compassion, devotion, basic decency? Presumably because these ideals and qualities implicate us with others *in* society and thus cannot characterize the abstracted ahistorical individualist acting out his project on the transcendent stage of history—they are the ideals of human beings tied in social relations to others and are thus unworthy and consigned to the mire of the practico-inert.

De Beauvoir wants women to become "great," like those men who have taken the weight of the world on their shoulders. She considers the biographies of famous women paltry, tiresome, and pallid compared with the exploits of great men. But she offers no criterion for assessing greatness save greatness itself. This is the stuff of nihilism. Greatness is no criterion at all: It is an empty term devoid of specific content, a kind of free-floating vapor that conjures up visions of battles between godlike male heroes who bestride world history above the contemptible facticity of everyday life. De Beauvoir offers neither moral nor critical grounds on which to judge the daydreams, delusions, and deeds of historic megalomaniacs who have "taken the weight of the world upon their shoulders" and wreaked havoc in the process. De Beauvoir's celebration of Transcendence and repugnance of Immanence are ultimately contemptuous of the lives of ordinary human beings, male and female, but they involve a *particular* dismissal of women, the majority of whom remain stuck in Immanence.

De Beauvoir accords to women no sense of the integrity that may emerge from being a female human being alive in a female body *in* history—not *above* it. Rather than bucking the long tradition of misogyny that encourages repugnance of the female body, she joins the chorus. Her antiseptic discussion "The Data of Biology," which opens *The Second Sex*, shows how de Beauvoir must hold her material at arm's length and couch it with an almost impenetrable cloud of technicalities. This much finally is clear: (1) de Beauvoir, in viewing woman as "the victim of the species," traces the original oppression of woman to her biology; (2) de Beauvoir portrays the male through various forms of mating patterns as imbued with a sense of virile domination (for example, the life of the male is "transcended" in the sperm, and so on); (3) the female, violated by definition for being born female, suffers what de Beauvoir calls *alienation*. This alienation is grounded, not, as Marx would have it, in oppressive and exploitative social structures and arrangements, but in her *biological capacity* to bear a child. Pregnancy is described in foreboding terms as the alienation of woman from herself; the fetus is characterized as a "tenant" who feeds, parasitically, upon its mother's existence. De Beauvoir's cold language splits this process off from human emotion and social relations.[48] It is the pretense of one who believes she has found the worm in the apple when, in fact, she has lost the apple for the worm.

Menstruation is portrayed as a veritable chamber of horrors. Childbirth, in words lifted almost verbatim by Firestone, is "painful and dangerous."[49] Nursing exhausts the mother—it can never, apparently, be a source of any satisfaction or pleasure or profound emotional importance. One particular statement reveals the depth of de Beauvoir's hatred of the female body. She calls a woman's breasts "mammary glands" that "play no role in women's individual economy: *they can be excised at any time of life*"[50] (emphasis mine). A male physician who expressed such cavalier disregard for the delicate sensibilities of a woman about to undergo mastectomy would, quite correctly, be denounced for his sexism. The wonder is that the criticism has not been applied to de Beauvoir; instead, radical feminists have tended to accept both her major points of theoretical demarcation and the specific evaluations they lead to, including the contempt of the female,[51] without criticism.

The level of denial necessary for a woman not to read such passages as a repudiation of herself is chilling. In this sense, radical feminism serves as a vehicle for repression—it reinforces those unconscious fears and anxieties disproportionately linked, particularly in sexually repressive societies, with the female body. Thus, radical feminists serve the cause of shame, guilt, inhibition, and despair; they harbor an unfocused, self-destructive anger that turns inward upon the self.

What does the repressive feminism disguised as radical feminism presume and demand? I turn to Firestone. Firestone lodges the oppression of woman in *nature* itself, in the human body; indeed, she finds oppression in the "animal kingdom." (She later says that it is from sex dualism that oppression "springs.") By deploying the term to cover the basic division between male and female, Firestone gives up "oppression's" critical bite and its historic meaning. Thus she deprives the theorist of a major conceptual tool in her effort to develop critiques of specific modes of oppression and domination *in history*. By locating oppression *outside* history, Firestone gives up at the start, if she is to be consistent, any possibility for understanding the current oppression of women and its historic roots, as well as the hope that critical thought and action can ultimately help change the course of events. But internal consistency and coherence are not her trademarks, and so she continues undaunted. Human society—all of human history—is one long tale of the domination of the male sex class over the female sex class. Because nature produces, or is the locus of, the fundamental "inequality" (and thus "inequality," too, loses its critical role in political discourse), nature must be changed. Feminist efforts should be directed at an alteration in biology, and all else will follow. Firestone's scenario runs, roughly, as follows: (1) Free women from biological "tyranny"; (2) this "freedom" will undermine the social unity based on *biological* reproduction and the family; (3) all systems of oppression reared on the family will be eroded. The schema is pat, neat, unconvincing, and mechanistic.

Firestone's "solutions," her modes of *praxis*, are individualist and trivial. She calls for "revolutionaries in every bedroom," an event that "can't fail to shake up the status quo."[52] (If one presumed that oppression began in bedrooms, the statement might be true even as it remained trivial.) The analysis is replete with the language of possessive individualism: Women must *seize* control, *own* their own bodies, and become masters of a cybernetic-technocratic society in which all human needs and wants will be supplied in an efficient, painless manner without any further worries about work, life, love, sexuality, marriage, responsibility, respect, or devotion. Firestone's rhetoric swarms over social relationships and human traditions like an invasion of locusts. In her eyes, nothing at all is redeemable. She, like de Beauvoir, degrades women as some sort of prelude to freeing them. Pregnancy is barbaric. Children peer at pregnant women and ask what is "wrong with the fat lady." Their husbands' sexual desires wander. The woman stands in tears before her mirror. Pregnancy is the "temporary deformation of the body of the individual for the sake of the species."[53] It is a gallery of horrors and it is false—as false as all those old paeans to undying love, unproblematic romance, and total motherly self-abnegation. Firestone's logic is deadly because it reinforces in the name of the liberation of women the shameful attitudes toward the female body (including pregnancy, childbirth, and nursing) developed within a society that has yet to face the full meaning and power of sexuality as Freud understood it. (I must, alas, leave the undocumented fantasies Firestone calls "history" to others.)[54]

Ti-Grace Atkinson, a second leading radical feminist indebted to Sartrian existentialism, presents us with a theory of war, not politics. She hardens the battle lines by deploying a militaristic language to describe the "war between the sexes." All men become not merely *opponents* but *enemies*. "Who is the enemy? Where is he located? Is he getting outside support? Where are his forces massed?" and so on.[55] Women are oppressed, and men, the enemy, are doing it. Atkinson calls this a causal class analysis. (It has, of course, nothing whatever to do with Marxist theory.) Adopting the Sartrian notion of a group as a false unity imposed as a function of more powerful grouping individuals, Atkinson terms love (a "psychopathological condition") one of the enemy's weapons. (Women who claim to "love men" are thereby condemned for having identified with the oppressor.)

Atkinson's repressive moralism denies human sexuality as a potentially creative and critical source of social relations by narrowing the view of sexuality to the reproductive function. It is only with puberty, and not until then, that the "genitals" become important—the very genitals that Atkinson puts on a par with "skin color, height, and hair color" *in importance*. By tying sexual awareness to reproduction, thus denying infantile sexuality, Atkinson can repudiate the notion that individuals need be differentiated into two sexes. Either she has never been around children or she is overlooking their sexuality—"no small achievement, by the way," as Freud stated.[56] Anyone who has spent time with children of either or both sexes knows and must insist on the truth of this observation: That the child's body and the integrity of that body as the grounding of a child's reality and mode of expression are the earliest and most resonant dimensions of a child's life.[57]

Finally, Atkinson repeats in her feminist vision the Hobbesian nightmare, as filtered through Sartre, of life as nasty, brutish, and terror ridden.

Men are posited as metaphysically (that is, ontologically), insecure and frustrated, with two a priori needs: (1) substance and (2) the alleviation of frustration through the *oppression* of others. This second principle Atkinson terms "metaphysical cannibalism." The male oppressor has a *natural, given,* ineradicable, ineluctable—the point cannot be overstressed—will to power, an a priori, ahistorical *need* to oppress others. There would appear to be no way out save for women—who apparently enter the world without such a need—to kill or dominate all men if they would end the oppression of women. Atkinson poses an extreme voluntarism grounded in "will" as the source whereby women will reshuffle who is cannibalizing whom in her humorless, asocial, embattled, martial universe. Freud's comment on Alfred Adler, another proponent of an original will to power, is apt. "It might surprise one that such a cheerless view of life should meet with any attention at all; but we must not forget that, weighed down by the burden of its sexual desires, humanity is ready to accept anything when tempted with 'ascendancy over sexuality' as a bait," even a system in which "there is no room . . . for love."[58] Let me speak plainly: Radical feminism as articulated by Firestone and de Beauvoir—with its easy evocation of enemies, its rejection of care in the presentation of ideas, its obliteration of important conceptual and real distinctions, and its absorption of ideas that have allowed for and fostered women's oppression historically—denies women respect as rational moral persons and requires that they, in turn, deny their sensuous, social natures.

Toward a Social Theory of Human Liberation

I shall now turn to a way of seeing that involves an alternative explanation and a theory of human nature and liberation as intrinsically social. I shall articulate what, in my view, an adequate depiction of a social theory of human liberation must include: a vision of the complex human subject, a coherent account of the nature of the relations between individuals and society, and an assessment of those moral determinations any responsible theory of historic agency requires. In order to find additional understanding of the nature of the human subject, critical theorists would do well to turn to Sigmund Freud, who also offers a depth psychology that allows us to distinguish between appearance and reality. That Freud has been a particular target of radical feminism is in itself indicative of the repressive function of that feminism. (It also bespeaks an inability to distinguish between psychiatric practice in the United States, which Freud himself criticized, and psychoanalytic theory.)

I have insisted that a theory of human nature is implicit within every political theory. I have looked at and criticized several features of the classi-

cal liberal theory of the individual as abstracted and individualist. To move
to a *social* theory of liberation, one must posit some compelling and coherent notion of human *sociality* as a constituent feature of human nature.
David Rasmussen has summarized a view he terms "dialectical sociality" as
follows: (1) individuals are beings who do not create the world but discover
liberation and autonomy as possibilities through conscious social *praxis;*
(2) human identity and autonomy are always in relation to others, for individuals are beings dependent upon one another within a situated historic
matrix; (3) liberation cannot come through the putative freeing of an atomistic self.[59] In this view, liberation is both an individual and a social issue.
One looks to social structures, institutions, and arrangements and asks, How
does this given world of meaning deny to individuals within it the realization of a self intrinsically tied to other selves? How, in other words, do social
structures damage, or help to fulfill, the needs of the human subject?[60] How
can individuals come to critical consciousness or awareness of their given
worlds?

Only a concrete analysis based on these and similar questions can serve
as a force for sustained action, for only such an analysis abolishes simplistic notions of individualistic rationality and liberation. Instead, this type
of analysis shows that the meaning of human life is not achieved simply
through a process of taking or seizing power, repudiating what is given or
achieving control, but by coming to terms with those social factors that
define us, that we have internalized, and some of which we can change. A
social theory of human nature presupposes a view of the mind itself as constituted in part by our intrinsic need for, and relationships to, others.

What can Freud offer to these considerations? Freud begins with the
concept of a human being situated in history, one who, for better or worse,
needs others and cannot escape his irreducible sociality. Freud's aim was to
determine how people become the people they are, and his theory points to
the particular intersections of individual lives with a human cultural heritage. In William Gass's somewhat excited prose, "the responses which the
baby's behavior generally receives ensures that from its first squalling, purple
moment forward most of the connections between the child's neurons will
be social, and that social structures will sink into the psyche like stripped
autos into river-silt."[61] Or Russell Jacoby: "psychoanalysis discovers society
in the individual monad. The critical edge of psychoanalysis is rooted in this
dialectic: it pierces the sham of the isolated individual with the secret of its
socio-sexual-biological substratus."[62] Human infants live in dynamic interrelationship with their cultures as mediated through the persons of parents
and, later, through schools, peer groups, work life, and so on. This interrelationship is never of a piece: It is profoundly ambivalent. Society is inter-

nalized along with its inherent and unresolved tensions, binds, and even contradictions. Freud's powerful concept of repression helps us to come to grips with the necessary but ambivalent link between persons and others in our social world.

Freud recognized that there could be no greater indictment of a society than the lifelong inability to act in ways free from debilitating shame and the destructive repetition of the past that society imposes upon its members—in varying degrees depending upon sex, race, and class—from birth. He recognized and articulated a theory that explains and understands the full extent of the deformation of human possibility within faulty social forms, because defects in social arrangements, according to psychoanalytic thought, have psychic consequences. The recognition and exploration of these "psychic consequences" led Freud to condemn a sexual morality he noted as "civilized" in an ironic vein, a morality that bore in a heavy and unconscionable way upon women. Disagreeing that women were "naturally" inferior and passive, Freud wrote, "On the contrary, I think that the undoubted fact of the intellectual inferiority of so many women can be traced to that inhibition of thought necessitated by sexual suppression."[63] A civilization that can satisfy one portion of its participants only through "the suppression of another, and perhaps larger portion" and that suppresses those who make its existence "possible by their work, but in whose wealth they have too small a share" is a civilization that "neither has nor deserves the prospect of a lasting existence."[64]

Freud, then, serves the feminist theorist who would articulate a theory of human liberation that incorporates a *specific* treatment of the repression of women as part of what must and can be changed. Freud enables us to pose certain complex problems from the angle of *both society and the person within society.* That is, we can ask from the perspective of the social whole: What does society demand and exact from individuals who give over their instinctual energy to constitute and to serve it? What social structures and arrangements are central in this process? And, from the vantage point of the individual in society, we ask: How can I determine what of that which is given to me supports and helps to constitute structures of oppression? How can I differentiate those notions from the worthy ideals I would preserve and relocate in a transformed society? How can I distinguish between the irrational projections I place upon, or into, the world and my realistic assessments of that world? How can I turn to social purposes that are genuine rather than replicate destructive patterns that emerge from my own history but that I then attempt to disguise as something else in order to fool myself and others? Freud termed the capacity to distinguish between those times when one must "control one's passions and bow before reality" and those in which one must "take arms against the external world" the "whole essence of worldly wisdom."[65]

I have insisted that a social theory of liberation must incorporate a rigorous version of a complex human subject. One must explore women in relation to men, the proletariat in relation to owners, masters in relation to slaves—each is implicated in a dialectical relationship. Freud enables us to pierce through the sham of certain crude evocations to "passionate antiauthoritarian"[66] women who disavow all hierarchies, all male values, and male-identified women. These women fight unwaveringly to end the oppression of women everywhere in order to usher in that new day in which a "value revolution" based on some vague "female principle" shall rule supreme. This soft but fierce, antihierarchical but authoritarian, open but censorious, new woman is a variant on a creature who should by now be familiar to us all: She is the "old man." Thus, repressive feminists fail to see that the reverse side of the coin that features the ontologically aggressive, dominating male with a given need to oppress others is precisely a passionately antiauthoritarian, feeling, intuitive, cooperative, and caring woman. They are a perfect dialectical match, because if one expunges the male side of the coin the female imprint vanishes as well.

Such idealizations require a rejection of that knowledge of self and others essential to any critical theory of liberation. For genuine self-knowledge demands an unswerving, reflexive consciousness that confronts the possibilities of becoming something other than I am based on an awareness of my ambivalence of what, precisely, it is that I am. Repressive feminism, however, *embraces the terms of female oppression* by projecting onto men all that is evil, ugly, domineering, authoritarian, and destructive in the world and preserving for women (after they have initially taken on "male" traits to defeat men) all that is loving, caring, cooperative, nonauthoritarian, and non-power oriented. In Rosenthal's words, this "mask" silences women and denies them a self-knowledge that must include "knowledge of the consequences of actions, of the social basis of one's psyche, of the historical basis of one's society and of the transformative possibilities of all three."[67] Women, by rejecting self-knowledge for the mask of repressive feminism, sustain and fortify the impoverishment of human subjectivity and the "reassuringly official know-nothingness of civil life."[68]

I shall now turn to further considerations of the links between individuals and society with reference to the third criterion that an adequate social theory of human liberation must include, namely, a way to assess questions of historic agency. How does one go about thinking through the following question: Is or is not a particular group, say radical feminists, a genuine or a bogus social group, that is, one with a *real* or a fraudulent claim to our attention? Let me explain the question and its purposes. Stuart Hampshire indicates correctly that Freud "clearly knew" that the question of group identity could be answered only with a social theory.[69] This is not much help, but something else Freud knew might be: He insisted that the mere holding of interests in common, society as a means to serve instrumentalist purposes, could not tie individuals and the social whole together. No, something else was required, and that "something else" he termed "identification," a nexus with others that provides a powerful and dynamic link, a glue that underlies any "community of feeling" and without which social life becomes impoverished and oppressive.[70] Oversimply, the identification of a society's members with one another requires and is built upon a diffused erotic time—aim-inhibited libido turned to the task of civilization. The dynamic concept of identification, then, affords an understanding of the ties of persons to one another, without which such ties remain a set of formalisms at best, a burden and a terror at worst. Such ties are strengthened and promoted if those ideals associated with such post-Lockean liberal thinkers as Kant and Rousseau—notions of moral agency and civic virtue—are embraced as worthy and resituated within altered social forms rather than repudiated as liberal and thereby automatically tainted.

Hampshire argues that Freud gives us no criteria whereby we can distinguish genuine social groups—those with authentic claims to historic agency and to representing true human needs—from those that are fraudulent. Hampshire overstates the case. Many of Freud's later works lead the critical theorist to the view that the problem of distinguishing authentic from bogus (including repressive) theories of social change must include an assessment of which theories realize the claims of Eros and then strengthen the bonds Eros and reason can *ideally* provide, namely, forms of social expression tied to rationality and shared purpose. Psychoanalytic theory helps us to decide, with some coherence and clarity, which of the groups that make claims on us is inauthentic.

How, for example, do Freudian concepts assist us in assessing the demands and purposes of the two following hypothetical groups, each claiming to represent the wave of the future? Group 1 requires the elimination, repression, and repudiation of the human subject from its political vision by denying unconscious mental processes and claiming that human beings are totally transparent. This is done through the postulation of a set of abstracted claims people are exhorted to believe and to act upon that make no contact whatever with their everyday lives, their sense of integrity, and their need to make meaning of their lives. Freud would deny the mantle of legitimacy to Group 1 or any other group that raised the banner of revolt by eliminating human complexity, moral agency, and ambivalence—by being, to put it bluntly, contemptuous of human beings.

Group 2 requires as central, not tangential, to its theory of social change the incarceration, abuse, maltreatment, and even death of several *categories* of persons. (The *centrality* of this necessity is important to grasp: It means that such deaths or maltreatment do not present themselves as regrettable possibilities but are set forth as theoretical and political *necessities.*) Thus fascism could not, within a psychoanalytic framework, raise the banner of authentic social revolt. Neither could *any* theory that requires that we destroy and slay others in large numbers as a prelude to the just, free, liberated society. Freud's opposition to war applies to all hypothetical Groups 2 that would claim our attention and support. In a discussion of why he exhorted passionately against war, Freud observed that war rends social bonds, that it "brings individual men into humiliating situations, because it compels them against their will to murder other men" and thus exists "in the crassest opposition to the psychical attitude imposed on us by the cultural process."[71] War involves regression. "It rends all bonds of fellowship . . . and threatens to leave such a legacy of embitterment as will make any renewal of such bonds impossible for a long time to come."[72] War "strips us of the later accretions of civilization," it decivilizes.[73]

Several examples may clarify and help to distinguish those groups that fall under the rubric of Group 2 and those that do not. The question, to repeat, is not violence *simpliciter* but the essential and necessary embrace of violence. Thus, a movement for national liberation that begins by attempting to end colonial rule through available nonviolent avenues but is finally driven to revolt by the destructive power and intransigence of colonial rulers would not be condemned under this rubric if the theory of national liberation under which the revolt occurred held violence as a hideous but sometimes unavoidable dimension. Similarly, the struggles for civil rights of the 1960s and the protests against the Vietnam War that, coincidentally, involved injury and even death cannot be denied a claim to historic authenticity *on that account alone,* for, aside from those few members of the radical student movement who were in love with death and destruction, such injuries and suffering were not integral to these movements.

Freud held that states and societies that permitted every misdeed on the highest level and leaders who committed acts of violence, deliberate lying, and deception, yet demanded sacrifice and obedience from the citizens they treated as children, would influence the moral development of individuals in a direction that permitted and encouraged barbarism. Freud's ideal was to move toward modes of social thought in which reason replaces aggression and domination. To this end, movements for social change must strengthen, not eliminate or weaken, reason and provide for the transformation of aggressive impulses into those higher categories within which that energy is transformed for the tasks of social life. A movement—any movement—for liberation that appeals to unreason, that expresses contempt for those it would free, that spits upon our deepest human emotions and feelings as nothing but a charade, that embraces an ugly and loveless vision of reality, that provides us with no clear and reasonable way to get from here to there, is a bogus, not an authentic, movement.

Conclusion

I have attempted several things in this essay. First, I examined several of the core assumptions within classical liberal discourse in order to draw out their implications for theories of human nature and political society. Second, I demonstrated that certain components of liberal thought are smuggled into, and reinforced within, Sartre's existentialist philosophy. Third, I argued that de Beauvoir's version of feminism, indebted as it is to Sartre and thus, implicitly, to the most asocial presumptions of classical liberalism, goes even further to pile on assumptions about women that can be seen to be repressive. Fourth, I made the case that the wing of the contemporary feminist movement that has taken the mantle "radical" unto itself has carried the repudiation of the female even further than did de Beauvoir. Both Firestone and Atkinson evoke a totalistic negativism that strikes at the very core of real or potential female integrity and offers to women symbols of denial in the guise of liberation. Repressive feminists, in theorizing the life out of the world, provide powerful indirect evidence of the devastating results of a repression that has spread to thought itself.[74] Finally, I moved to articulate what a social theory of liberation must include if it is to serve both as concrete historical analysis and as a force for social transformation. I argued that such a theory must incorporate a view of the complex, self-reflexive human subject, an adequate conception of the link between the individual and society, and must enable us to distinguish genuine from bogus movements for social change.

One final word on those feminist analyses I have called repressive: It is important to remember, lest any reader unfamiliar with these analyses thinks I have been unduly harsh, first, that radical feminism *requires as central to the theory* a repudiation of the *female* subject. All ambivalence, doubt, ambiguity, and emotion tied to the social relations of heterosexuality and family life, and a devotion to openness in debate, are expunged to meet the demands of monocausal doctrinal truth. Second, radical feminism, by assimilating sexism to an ahistoric notion of patriarchy (or sexism or male chauvinism) *requires as central to the theory* that men be "put in their place." This putting in place has taken a variety of forms (including mass incarceration and mass extermination, as well as old-fashioned domination), none of which allows a woman to distinguish which persons in positions of power bear greater responsibility for the maintenance of the status quo or to assess which social forms are most responsible for institutionalized sexism. Third, radical feminism *requires as central to the theory* a view of men as ontologically dominated by a will to power, an a priori need to oppress women; thus it results in a stultifying set of moralisms, condemnation rather than explanation. It is a doctrine that would eliminate all social bonds or the possibility for such bonds, and thus it denies both our social natures and our painful and arduous efforts to retain something of value in a world that increasingly devalues persons. Repressive feminism's punitive condemnation of others bespeaks a desire for total domination and control rooted in unmediated, narcissistic rage.

Camus makes the observation that, although each of us carries with us our places of exiles, our crimes, and our ravages, we have a moral responsibility not to inflict them upon the world. Repressive feminism sends forth its places of exiles, its crimes, and ravages, like an army of necromancers. It challenges the darkness with greater darkness; it is a vision of raw destructiveness, a theory, not of politics, but of war. As I began this essay, I took Bob Dylan's warning (which emerges from his own confrontation with the demons of fear and despair) as my watchword: "Let us not speak falsely now/ the hour is getting late." The time has come to call things by their real names. When a radical feminist calls the relationship of mother to child one of "shared oppression" and presumes that this exhausts the meaning of that relationship to those human agents who live it, when she urges women to repudiate their bodies or to join in the "total destruction" of "all vestiges of sex class" (that means, first the elimination of the family and then all else will follow), it is time for persons of conscience, male and female, to speak up. To maintain silence in the face of such egregious and dangerous incoherence is not to fight the plague but to give ourselves over to the cold nihilism of its terror.

Notes

Originally published in Michael J. McGrath, ed., *Liberalism and the Modern Polity* (New York: Dekker, 1978).

1. Norman Birnbaum, "Critical Theory and Psychohistory," in Robert Jay Lifton, ed., *Explorations in Psychohistory* (New York: Simon and Schuster, 1974), 198.

2. Richard Wollheim, "Psychoanalysis and Feminism," *New Left Review,* no. 93 (September–October 1975): 61.

3. Eva Figes, in *Patriarchal Attitudes* (Greenwich, Conn.: Fawcett, 1970), dispatches Rousseau in eighteen pages of blistering, vacuous prose and asks the momentous question, why should a document as "illogical" as *The Social Contract* have exerted such appeal and influence? The entire book is an exercise in condemnation, not explanation.

4. William E. Connolly, "Towards Theoretical Self-Consciousness," *Polity* 6 (fall 1973): 3–35.

5. Juliet Mitchell, *Psychoanalysis and Feminism* (New York: Pantheon Books, 1974). Although I disagree with Mitchell's structuralist epistemology and thus the interpretation of Freud that flows from it, I applaud the book as a genuine and brave attempt to *think* in a systematic, responsible, and coherent fashion.

6. Robert Paul Wolff, "There's Nobody Here but Us Persons," in Carol Gould and Marx Wartofsky, eds., *Women and Philosophy* (New York: Putnam, 1976), 134.

7. James M. Glass, "Schizophrenia and Perception: A Critique of the Liberal Theory of Externality," *Inquiry* 5 (1972): 116.

8. David M. Rasmussen, "Between Autonomy and Sociality," *Cultural Hermeneutics* (1973): 8. Cf. Steven Lukes, *Individualism* (New York: Harper and Row, 1973). Lukes points out that, within the individualist postulation of human nature, certain unchanging features, including psychological features, are given *simpliciter* apart from, and with no necessary reference to, social context. This leads to an abstract or abstracted concept of human beings.

9. Thomas Hobbes, *Leviathan,* ed. Michael Oakeshott (New York: Collier-Macmillan, 1966), 99.

10. John Locke, *Two Treatises of Government,* ed. Peter Laslett (New York: New American Library, Mentor Books, 1965), 395–96. See also Robert Paul Wolff, *The Poverty of Liberalism* (Boston: Beacon Press, 1969), 197. Social values, for Wolff, are not "private values nor compounds of private values, or in any way reducible to private values."

11. James M. Glass, "Epicurus and the Modern Culture of Withdrawal: The Therapy of Survival," *American Politics Quarterly* 3 (1974): 313–40. Cf. G. W. F. Hegel, *The Phenomenology of Mind*, trans. J. B. Baillie (New York: Harper Torchbooks, 1967), on the "unhappy consciousness." Hegel writes: "The essence of this consciousness is to be free, on the throne as well as in fetters, throughout all the dependence that attaches to its individual existence, and to maintain that stolid lifeless unconcern which persistently withdraws from the movement of existence, from effective activity as well as from passive endurance, into the simple essentiality of thought. Stubbornness is that freedom which makes itself secure in a solid singleness, and keeps *within* the sphere of bondage. Stoicism, on the other hand, is the freedom which ever comes directly out of that sphere, and returns back into the pure universality of thought. It is a freedom which can come on the scene as a general form of the world's spirit only in a time of universal fear and bondage, a time, too, when mental cultivation is universal, and has elevated culture to the level of thought. . . . The freedom of self-consciousness is indifferent towards natural existence, and has, therefore, let this latter go and remain free" (244–45).

12. See R. D. Laing, *The Politics of the Family and Other Essays* (New York: Pantheon Books, 1970), for another variant on this view.

13. Wolff, "Nobody Here but Us Persons," 130.

14. Ibid., 133.

15. A brief but important caveat: I shall draw almost exclusively upon *Being and Nothingness*, not because I am unfamiliar with Sartre's later work but because it is the presumptions of his earlier existentialism that have seeped into radical feminist theories of liberation. I also rely on the R. D. Laing–David Cooper translation and précis of *La Critique de la raison dialectique*. Sartre himself blessed it explicitly as a "very clear, very faithful account of my thought" that reflects its translators' "perfect understanding" of that work. (See Sartre's Foreword to R. D. Laing and David Cooper, *Reason and Violence* [New York: Vintage Books, 1961], 6.) To ignore the impact of *Being and Nothingness* on the thought of others because Sartre has subsequently moved toward a version of Marxism is to ignore thought as a social activity that influences others and to accept Sartre's self-proclaimed move from existentialism to Marxism as self-evident. Surely a theorist's self-description must be taken into account in any assessment of his work, but this does not mean it must be accepted without question. It is possible for people to misdescribe their own enterprise—sometimes in major ways. Sartre's later Marxist claims must be evaluated, not accepted or rejected uncritically. I have not undertaken such an evaluation, but my own reading of such works as *Search for a Method* (New York: Vintage Books, 1968) convinces me that Sartre has not succeeded in synthesizing with Marxism an existentialism tied to the phenomenological tradition of Heidegger and Husserl. I, for one, do not believe this can be done unless one is willing to scuttle the historic meaning of Marx's thought and to eviscerate two of Marx's most powerful categories: alienation and a social theory of human nature. One cannot get out of complex theoretical problems, as Robert Paul Wolff notes in another context, by using the word "dialectical" a lot.

16. A second thread that flows from Sartrism and has profoundly influenced radical thought is exemplified in the works of R. D. Laing. Laing's existentialism, too, is tied to abstract individualism and to a loveless vision of a thoroughgoing instrumentalist social world; thus Laing is ultimately incapable of offering a genuine conceptual alternative to unjust and oppressive social orders. Laing's influence on theories of women's liberation has been less profound than de Beauvoir's, but his specific attacks upon the family have been taken up, primarily by radical feminists, as further proof of the unrelenting hideousness of contemporary life unto its innermost parts. Again, as with de Beauvoir, radical feminists have not been moved to ask themselves whether Laing's bleak vision is a necessary emergent from his theory, a purposeful distortion of predominant trends, or a condemnation rather than an explanation tied to a set of unexamined assumptions about human beings. See Laing, *The Politics of Experience* (New York: Ballantine Books, 1970), and his other works.

17. Laing and Cooper, *Reason and Violence*, 165.

18. Ibid., 138.

19. Sigmund Freud, *A General Introduction to Psychoanalysis*, trans. Joan Riviere (New York: Touchstone Books, 1963), 252.

20. See the growing body of literature on narcissism. Christopher Lasch's review essay "The Narcissist Society," *New York Review of Books,* September 30, 1976, 5–13, is a good place to begin for an overview. But the best starting point for a theory of the destructive psychodynamics of narcissism is, of course, Freud in his bold essay, "On Narcissism: An Introduction," written in 1914. The essay appears in Sigmund Freud, *General Psychological Theory,* ed. Philip Rieff (New York: Collier Books, 1963), 56–82.

21. If Sartre is familiar with Rousseau's critique of Hobbes's theory of human nature, namely, that Hobbes presents as "natural," unchanging, and given a vision of human nature that, instead, depicts those human characteristics that have emerged within and characterize a particular type of society, he either finds it unconvincing or irrelevant. (This critique is to be found in Rousseau's *Second Discourse on Inequality.*)

22. Jean-Paul Sartre, *Being and Nothingness,* trans. Hazel Barnes (New York: Philosophical Library, 1956), 485.

23. Cited in Maurice Cranston, *The Quintessence of Sartrism* (New York: Harper and Row, 1969), 41.

24. Hobbes, *Leviathan,* 102.

25. Sartre, *Being and Nothingness,* 457. Cf. Freud's discussion in "Narcissism," 57. Freud writes: "The libido withdrawn from the outer world has been directed on to the ego, giving rise to a state which we may call narcissism." Narcissism involves an omnipotent view of the self, framed with utter disregard of limitations and a boundless ambition. The narcissist tends to see opponents as enemies, for he needs to maintain absolute control. His self-esteem might collapse if it were not maintained, to use Sartre's language, by the existence of those we label as Other or persons in "bad faith." For to be Other (that is, not-me) is by definition already an offense.

26. Richard J. Bernstein, *Praxis and Action* (Philadelphia: University of Pennsylvania Press, 1971), 151.

27. Germain Bree, *Camus and Sartre* (New York: Delta Books, 1972), 91. Sartre denies categorically the existence of an unconscious mind and repudiates all depth psychology. He argues that individuals can be transparent to themselves in a complete and thoroughgoing fashion. Consciousness, for Sartre, is not that rich set of conscious, preconscious, and unconscious qualities or forces described by Freud, but consciousness of the nothingness of one's own being. Sartre reserves the opprobrium of bad faith for those who hide this truth from themselves. His vision of bad faith is a caricature of the human mind—all flat, unidimensional, unambivalent. Think of Sartre's mind as a series of operations ranging over a straight, flat surface that stretches horizontally but not vertically. Thus a person *knows* in his capacity as deceiver the truth hidden from him (but not *truly* hidden) in his capacity as the one deceived. All knowing, for Sartre, is a consciousness of knowing. He attributes to the concept of the unconscious the role of deceiver and the legitimation of this deceit. He asserts incorrectly that Freud's concepts of ego and id cut the psyche in two. He claims that the superego or censor *knows* what it is repressing. This means that the censor always acts in bad faith. Sartre is incapable of dealing with the question of complex human motivation within the framework of his explanatory theory. For Freud's defense of the

unconscious, see his 1915 metapsychological paper "The Unconscious," which appears in Freud, *General Psychological Theory*, 116–50.

28. Sartre, *Being and Nothingness*, 462. Cf. Cranston, *Quintessence of Sartrism*, 28.

29. See Freud, "Narcissism."

30. See C. B. MacPherson, *The Political Theory of Possessive Individualism* (Oxford: Clarendon Press, 1962).

31. But see Sartre's discussion in *Search for a Method*, 32–33, n. 9, in which he moves away from the stark bifurcations of *Being and Nothingness* without, however, rejecting the notion of "bad faith" or "will."

32. See chap. 2, sec. 1, of *Being and Nothingness* for Sartre's discussion of a frigid woman as an instance of bad faith for which Freud "could not account." We are not told the history of the woman's frigidity. Instead, she is judged as one whom "marital infidelity" has made frigid. This woman deploys a pattern of "distraction" in her sexual relations with her husband in order to prove to herself that she is, in fact, frigid. She distracts her "consciousness" (there is, remember, no repressed unconscious for Sartre) from the genuine pleasure she experiences. Her behavior toward her husband is labeled by Sartre a paradigmatic case of bad faith, for the woman consciously becomes—she wills herself to be—frigid, and she knows that she is doing this. The doctrine of "bad faith" requires such cold-bloodedness. People "will" themselves to be sick.

33. Margery Collins and Christine Pierce, "Holes and Slime: Sexism in Sartre's Psychoanalysis," in *Women and Philosophy*, 118. Why the authors call Sartre's theory "psychoanalysis" is thoroughly mystifying, for Sartre has no theoretical links whatever to psychoanalysis.

34. See Laing and Cooper, *Reason and Violence*, 146–47.

35. Benito Mussolini, "The Doctrine of Fascism," in John Somerville and Ronald E. Santoni, eds., *Social and Political Philosophy* (Garden City, N.Y.: Doubleday Anchor, 1963), 425.

36. Ibid., 429.

37. Bernstein, *Praxis and Action*, 150.

38. Sartre, *Being and Nothingness*, 485.

39. Sartre's irresponsibility emerges from an assumption of totalistic moral responsibility according to which the universe must be regarded, in de Beauvoir's words of interpretation, "as one's own." One must "belong to the cast of the privileged: it is for those alone who are in command to justify the universe by changing it." Simone de Beauvoir, *The Second Sex*, trans. H. M. Parshley (New York: Knopf, 1963), 671.

40. By rejecting *any* notion of a nonrelativistic human essence (human "essence" is defined by Sartre in *Search for a Method* as a social predicate alone, "a fixed collection of determinations"), Sartre countenances moral irresponsibility and the manipulation of persons individually or en masse.

41. Abigail Rosenthal, "Feminism without Contradictions," *Monist* 57 (January 1973): 42.

42. Surely one of the important tasks for critical feminist theorists is to reclaim the honorable title "radical" from those who have described themselves, inaccurately as I shall demonstrate, in those terms.

43. A recent survey of contemporary feminism, Gayle Graham Yates, *What Women Want: The Ideas of the Movement* (Cambridge, Mass.: Harvard University Press, 1975), offers an eclectic, noncritical, hotchpotch in the guise of analysis. She describes Firestone's book as "brilliant and discerning" and Firestone as one of the "most profound" among contemporary feminist analysts (84–85). Perhaps one should not make too much of this, coming, as it does, from an author whose grand conclusion is that "In the final analysis what is true is what we believe" (189).

44. Collins and Pierce, "Holes and Slime," 125. An important question, one I must reserve for future consideration, is why Freud has been struck with, and condemned for, this view—one he did not hold—even as Sartre, who explicitly states it, goes scot-free and becomes for many feminists a male hero.

45. De Beauvoir, *The Second Sex*, xxxix.

46. Ibid., xvi.

47. Ibid.

48. Such distancing of oneself from resonant and highly charged matters is a standard feature in feminist literature that defends abortion on the grounds that a woman "owns" her own body. From the language of possessive individualism, it is easy to slide into the view that the developing fetus is a parasite, a "tenant," or that abstraction, the "products of conception." In this way the fetus's potential humanness is expunged from view and the serious moral issues raised by the abortion issue are held at arm's-length or denied altogether.

49. De Beauvoir, *The Second Sex*, 27.

50. Ibid., 24.

51. Thus Sherry B. Ortner, in a piece entitled "Is Female to Male as Nature is to Culture?" in Michelle Z. Rosaldo and Louise Lamphere, eds., *Women, Culture and Society* (Stanford, Calif.: Stanford University Press, 1974), 67–87, follows de Beauvoir by locating women, not in nature, but "closer" to it as a result of their biological functions, "social roles" (how a "social role" can be in or close to nature is not explained), and psychic structures. To buttress her argument, Ortner cites the "hard data" provided by de Beauvoir, including such data as the following: "The breasts are irrelevant to personal health: they may be excised at any time of a woman's life." Not surprisingly, Ortner goes on to depict pregnancy as a sickness, the fetus as a parasite, ad nauseam. Why this reductionistic callousness should lurk in the heart of an essay that purports to be both feminist and radical is the problem I set out to address and have attempted to understand and to explain through the conceptual category "repressive feminism."

52. As my old logic teacher might put it: "If my grandfather had wheels, he'd be a trolley."

53. Shulamith Firestone, *The Dialectic of Sex* (New York: Bantam Books, 1972), 198.

54. One example: Firestone declares that witches "must be seen as women in independent political revolt: within two centuries eight million women were burned at the stake by the Church—for religion was the politics of the period" (*The Dialectic of Sex*, 15). To wade through this single instance of irresponsibility and absurdity tries

one's patience as it takes one's time. Firestone cites no references. She does not tell us *which* two centuries are involved—presumably they occurred during the medieval period, given her reference to "the Church," as that was the only epoch with *a* Church. Firestone assumes without discussion, debate, or citing sources that *all* witches were women (thereby ignoring the many men condemned as witches) and that all these women were in "independent political revolt." I shall not cite the vast and growing literature on the topic save for one of the most recent major studies: Richard Kieckhefer, *European Witch Trials: Their Foundation in Popular and Learned Culture, 1300–1500* (London: Routledge and Kegan Paul, 1976). I have not found a single responsible scholar, either during my six years of medieval studies or subsequently, who has actually worked with the extant sources and lived with the materials, who shares Firestone's presumption—or presumptuousness! Firestone's disregard for the truth of matters—indeed, her casual assassination of the truth—and for the necessity to search for it painstakingly are characteristic of her entire book. For those interested in an overview of women in the Middle Ages by a fine British medievalist, see Eileen Power, *Medieval Women* (Cambridge: Cambridge University Press, 1975).

55. Ti-Grace Atkinson, "Radical Feminism," in Shulamith Firestone, ed., *Notes from the Second Year: Women's Liberation* (New York: P.O. Box AA, Old Chelsea Station), 33.

56. Freud, *A General Introduction to Psychoanalysis,* 274.

57. Cf. Peter Winch, "Understanding a Primitive Society," in Bryan Wilson, ed., *Rationality* (New York: Harper Torchbooks, 1971), 78–111). "The life of a man is a man's life and the life of a woman is a woman's life: the masculinity and femininity are not just *components* in the life, they are its *mode*" (110). I hope I need not add that this insistence on the integrity and importance of human bodies as a mode of lived expression in historic time, this recognition of differences, in no way compromises either a social theory of liberation or a theory of equality that turns on equality of respect and treatment.

58. Sigmund Freud, *The History of the Psychoanalytic Movement,* ed. Philip Rieff (New York: Collier Books, 1972), 90–91.

59. Rasmussen, "Between Autonomy and Sociality."

60. I concur with an observation by Richard Wollheim that a social theory of liberation must be grounded in a notion of human needs, which alone can provide social thought with the beginning of a theory of human nature that abandons conceptual and moral relativism. See Wollheim's review essay "Trouble in Freedonia," *New York Review of Books* 23 (June 24, 1976): 37.

61. William Gass, "The Scientific Psychology of Sigmund Freud," *New York Review of Books,* May 1, 1975, 26.

62. Russell Jacoby, *Social Amnesia* (Boston: Beacon Press, 1975), 29.

63. Sigmund Freud, " 'Civilized' Sexual Morality and Modern Nervousness," in Philip Rieff, ed. *Sexuality and the Psychology of Love* (New York: Collier Books, 1972), 36.

64. Cited in Richard Wollheim, *Freud* (New York: Viking Press, 1971), 262–63.

65. Sigmund Freud, *The Question of Lay Analysis,* trans. James Strachey (New York: Norton, 1969), 27.

66. See the Susan Sontag–Adrienne Rich exchange, "Feminism and Fascism," *New York Review of Books,* March 20, 1975, 31–32.

67. Rosenthal, "Feminism without Contradictions," 38.

68. Ibid., 42.

69. Stuart Hampshire, "Struggles over Theory," in Lifton, *Explorations in Psychohistory,* 235.

70. Sigmund Freud, "Why War?" in Philip Rieff, ed., *Character and Culture* (New York: Collier Books, 1970), 144.

71. Ibid., 145, 147.

72. Sigmund Freud, "Reflections upon War and Death," in *Character and Culture,* 111. Freud notes that the abrogation by nations of their moral ties has a "seducing influence on the morality of individuals" and, in time of war, leads men to "perpetuate deeds of cruelty, fraud, treachery and barbarity" incompatible with civilization—deeds they would themselves have held, at one time, impossible (112–13).

73. Ibid., 132.

74. Sigmund Freud, "Negation," in *General Psychological Theory,* 213–17.

12

Symmetry and Soporifics:
A Critique of Feminist Accounts
of Gender Development

Would you like to live in the "symmetrical" society? If this is a question you've not previously put to yourself, perhaps it's time you did. A symmetrical social world is one the most important feminist theorists of gender development propose to put in place of the "asymmetrical" world we now inhabit, one they condemn as being systematically deranged. This derangement, in their view, flows in a direct line from child-rearing practices, usually called "socialization," to political, economic, and social structures on a broader scale. That is, the thinkers I shall take up assert that their arguments are *politically* compelling because they have demonstrated in theory a tight *causal* nexus between familial arrangements and public outcomes. Why our gender arrangements are so badly botched and how they can be transformed radically to attain a world of gender symmetry is a matter I shall explore with a skeptical eye.

But before I turn explicitly to this new variant on a fairly traditional concern—socialization—a few words on socialization theory itself are in order. The question socialization theory seeks to answer is simply put: How is it that persons and their social contexts may be said to be related to one another? Alas, it is not so simply answered. But socialization theory, which first came into use in mainstream political discourse in the 1950s, proposed to answer it. Most practitioners of political socialization have been rather unabashed celebrants of the status quo. The most systematic, and powerful, version of socialization theory may be found in the functionalist approach to social explanation. For the functionalist all elements in a social system are linked together in a way that promotes, if things are going smoothly, equilibrium: all units neatly tied together in a relationship of interdependence. On this account, the family gets linked "functionally" to the total order, as both family structure and function are largely determined by the "needs" of the "macro-order."

Socialization, then, is the way in which infant "recruits" become full-fledged participants in a tautly structured social system. The theory tends toward a determinist explanation that strips individuals of agency and can treat "failures" in socialization only as instances of "deviance" (not protest)! What feminist accounts feature is a questioning of *why* socialization has gone forward in ways they find oppressive to women. But the problem here, and it is one I shall take up below, is whether one can finally construct an alternative account of the individual/social relation if one occupies much of the same conceptual terrain as the standard socialization-functionalist models. Although classic functionalist doctrine masked the question of power, there was an implicit assumption that in a hierarchical, well-ordered social world an importunate entity—the overall system or society—pulls other institutions along without the rude incursion of outright coercion or the use of force. *If* one were to make the presumptions about power lodged in classical functionalist theory explicit, it would look very much like standard "top-down" presumptions, with those on "top" having more power than those "down" below.

It is important to situate current feminist debates within this—and other—broader intellectual and doctrinal currents, for it helps us to make sense of the project and the aim of "symmetry," which is very much the notion of a reordered social system in a *new,* but good, condition of equilibrium. The ideal symmetrical world is construed as a social universe in which the sexes have identical, or nearly so, commitments to, involvements with, and interest in child rearing, often called reproduction, and careers (often called production). This "symmetry" holds across the board, even into the world of sexual fantasy, at least for the Total Symmetrist. It is my conviction that symmetry emerges as a soporific, one that aims to blur or eliminate gender-based differences but would do little to eradicate gender-based injustice.

I shall lead into my subject by noting an important distinction, one taken for granted as the backdrop to the explanatory frameworks I shall explicate and criticize, between biological sex and social gender. Though one cannot altogether sever biological maleness and femaleness from the social creation and meaning of norms of masculinity and femininity and the distinctive parts men and women play in the human story, the accounts I shall take up propose a very sharp fissure between the two. A brief caveat also seems necessary when one takes up these highly charged matters. Here is mine: I think it is vital and important to develop a social theory that gives us rich and robust pictures of how people live, that moves us closer to understanding the kinds of lives that various social structures and diverse societies support. And I certainly favor both the loosening up of rigid and destructive sex roles that lock people into positions and practices for which they may not be well suited and the elimination of gender-based, structural injustice. The problem, then, with the theories I shall take up is that they fail, in the first instance, to provide the "rich and robust picture" I note as desirable. There are no recognizably *human* lives of either adults or children engaged in complex social relations in these accounts. They fail, as well, to provide a *coherent* notion of how we are to move toward a more sexually egalitarian society.

This essay is divided into four parts. First, I shall make some preliminary comments on psychoanalytic theory and what it offers to social theory construed as an *interpretive* enterprise. Second, I shall submit the three most widely discussed and disseminated feminist accounts of gender to a critique that moves on a number of levels, theoretical and political. Given the daunting problems of methodology and theory articulation posed by *any* appropriation of psychoanalysis for social explanation, and given the explicit political aims of feminist gender theorists, theoretical *and* political arguments are invited and required. Third, I shall propose an alternative in this sense: I shall indicate what an alternative account must account for, or take account of, that seems to me to offer a more coherent theory and a more plausible, and democratic, politics. Finally, I shall conclude by drawing the gender debate into a series of brief reflections on that crisis of contemporary culture Christopher Lasch has called one of narcissism.

I thought of calling this essay "The Case of the Missing Child." Were a search for this missing person conducted in the pages of the most important feminist treatments of gender identity and development, the case would go unsolved. For what is conspicuously absent in these texts is a recognizable human being of *any* sort, including the youthful, the very being whose development each claims to explain. It may seem unreasonably contentious of me to suggest that children are not really present in texts that specifically treat childhood development. I hope my quarrel here becomes clearer as the argument develops. But let me just indicate that there are specific and important features of children that get bleached out of the accounts I take up. To be sure, there are voracious infants (in Dinnerstein) and developing children snarled in a number of asymmetrical, gender-linked, familial knots (in Chodorow), but their respective contributions to the perspectives I shall explore nowhere capture the sense of children as *beings* or the being of the child, in part because children are not treated as agentic, reflective, capable of thinking and acting their ways in and out of complex situations, and so on. Why is this a problem? To answer, one must take up the nature of social explanation itself. For example: for social scientists devoted to positivist analyses and abstract formal models far removed from their subject matter, the missing child poses no particular problem, for *no* human subject has ever intruded

upon the tidy order of their schemata or undone the rigor of their correlations. Nor, for that matter, does the missing child figure centrally within
most Marxist debates, which are couched on the level of modes of production, structures, and the State, and grounded in universal, aggregate abstractions like "class." To be sure, all sorts of people can be theoretically subsumed
within the conceptual space occupied by a term like "class" or "the State,"
but they are, none of them, particular or distinctive, nor can they be: a
systematic theory of the sort Freud criticized as *Weltanschauung,* "an intellectual construction which solves all the problems of our existence uniformly
on the basis of one overriding hypothesis, which, accordingly, leaves no
question unanswered and in which everything that interests us finds its
place,"[1] washes out the particular in favor of making vast claims and a broad
sweep.

I shall be clearer in a moment about how it is I think psychoanalysis can
be appropriated by social theorists without making it the centerpiece in a
tautly drawn and rigid circle of certainty of the sort positivist explanation
and the quest for lawlikeness lead to. My objection is not to "abstract" theory, for every theory, whose coin of the realm is and must be conceptual, is
abstract. Instead I am arguing against *abstracted* theory, against concepts
far removed from what it is they purport to explain. (Those who wish to
pursue this epistemological debate can turn to many important and influential critiques of positivist social science, and these critiques hold whether
the thinker in question comes with the label "radical" or "mainstream" or
"conservative.")[2]

Psychoanalytic theory, as developed over forty years by Freud, is not, and
cannot claim to be, a predictive science. That is, it cannot be reasonably
deployed to construct a set of presumed universalisms, as feminist gender
theories do, along the lines of "If *x*, then ineluctably *y* . . ." Such arguments
are not only culture-bound, they are culture-blind, for the extraordinary
complexities and diversities of human cultures, of intersubjectively shared,
hence public, symbols, meanings and ideas, as well as individual creativity,
variations, and consciousness, get fused together and then overassimilated
to explanatory frameworks that presume to explain everything from one's
basic "something." Why this won't do is what I hope to show.

The case of the missing child, then, *should* pose a dilemma for the thinker
indebted to psychoanalysis, and if it does not there is, I shall argue, slippage
in the version of psychoanalytic theory being taken up. For one might suppose that the theorist who turns to psychoanalysis would be interested in
grinding her analyses fine, in bringing things down to the most concrete and
basic levels, to cultural realms inhabited by human beings, not by statistics.
One can reasonably hold to this hope, for psychoanalytically based accounts

are about how we get to the beings we are, males and females alike. As conceived by Freud, psychoanalysis is preeminently a theory of the psychodynamic self, the discontented citizen of civilization, the night traveler who wakes in wonder or in terror, the rational irrationalist, the romantic hero or heroine, the vulnerable child, the builder, the destroyer, the giver, the taker, the authoritarian, the anarchist, attempting to carve out a livable life, in history, between the intractable pole of necessity and the ephemeral dream of possibility.

My initial objections, my concern with whether the accounts I shall take up proffer a plausible picture of what they purport to explain, speaks to important theoretical debates that are linked, in turn, to political questions. There *are* approaches to social theory that require the analyst to construe her subjects, including children, as importantly self-defining, expressive, and active agents, not as mere social "products." A rich notion of the subject is featured in various interpretive or hermeneutical studies of human life and culture. For the interpretive theorist, and it is an interpretive account with a "critical edge" that I shall propose below, the essential task of theory is to probe meanings, individual and social.

A second, not unreasonable expectation to hold as one plunges into texts that acknowledge Freud as their honorable godfather if not their infallible patriarch, is that the authors would show evidence of knowledge of debates about Freud's method. Freud's remains *the* psychoanalytic theory; all later revisions and recantations have to position themselves with or against, for better or for worse. At this point it is worth recalling that Freud's devotion to a scientific world-view did not blind him to the somewhat rueful recognition that his peculiar science could not be contained within a language which failed to make essential reference to the human being as meaningful. Given this recognition, he could not, and did not, claim that he had promulgated a set of laws with the power to predict. Instead, what one could do with such resonant theoretical concepts and constructs as projection, displacement, regression, repression, identification, the Oedipus complex, and so on, was, on one level, to forge an explanation having the form of a *post-hoc* reconstruction of a particular individual's psychic history, which, if the account was detailed and "thick" enough, might have broader applicability to an understanding and explanation of human psychic life in more general terms. This reconstruction could not be a venture of the positivist-historiographical sort. Freud made no claim that he had got things *wie es eigentlicb gewesen* (as they really were). Instead, the psychoanalytic dialogue, grounded in a powerful theory, aimed at the active *construction* of an explanation that made sense to the analyst—the better interpretation being one that could account for more details than some alternative—and made sense to the subject as offering a rock to stand on, a foundation from which he or she could move into a less tormented future.[3]

Freud's persistently fresh case histories retain their vitality because, in seeking to explain, he never explained away by abstracting his explanation from the intrapsychic world of his subject. Before others, particularly cultural anthropologists and social historians, embraced the notion, Freud had mastered the art of "thick description," the commitment to present human contexts as tangled webs of meaning, both open and hidden. If done well, the theorist's explanation should take the reader or critic "into the heart of that of which it is the interpretation"[4]—in Freud's case the densely populated world of the human mind. Despite Freud's occasionally reductive statements and hopes, his method and his own account of that method locate psychoanalysis firmly as one of the most powerful of the "human sciences," the *Geisteswissenschaften*. For within psychoanalytic theory, language (linguistic expressions), action, and nonlinguistic experiential expressions all become grist for the theoretical mill, but not in isolation from one another *nor* from a powerful dialogue of a certain kind, the psychoanalytic setting. Unlike those who would model human sciences after a mechanistic account of nineteenth-century natural science, psychoanalytic theory, if it is to remain true to its most potent expressions and possibilities, cannot take the form of prediction or postdiction. Instead, the psychoanalytic thinker must rely on the *coherence* of interpretive accounts, on the inner links between minute details and higher level abstractions.[5]

Following through on this interpretive imperative, if what is being understood is the gender development and identity of human beings, a coherent interpretation should help us to "get inside" the worlds in and through which such development and identity emerges—the inner world of children and the social world, first and foremost, of families. We must be able to see that world from the "inside out." It is particularly important for an analyst of radical sensibility to avoid replicating in her account the manner in which many academic psychologists and sociologists devoted to so-called scientific analyses have constituted the human subject, child and adult, as an "object." This object bears only a thin relation to real, active human subjects though it is frequently confused with the "real thing." This guarantees a particular sort of tendentiousness as social explanation and the concrete arrangements and experiences of the social world, including, centrally, human subjects who are born, grow up, work, love, and finally die, pass one another by.

Often these exercises are relatively harmless, fading into that obscurity reserved for those who persist in repeating things that were not worth saying once. But occasionally matters are not so benign. For when world changers, like their status quo counterparts, set about conflating human subjects and social life with their "scientistic" theory or ideology, and then one day discover that the real world is recalcitrant, its human subjects frustratingly intractable, they may wind up embracing a politics that aims to bring reality into conformity with their abstract system. This may require "reconstructing" real persons into the sorts of "objects" their discourse has constituted in the first place, thus inviting a manipulative or coercive political strategy.

The minimal point for now is this: theoretical commitments secrete political imperatives; theoretical frameworks have consequences as to the social arrangements they either call into question or call for, they either move to undermine or aim to sustain.[6] Our understanding of human beings and their social worlds will vary dramatically depending on whether we view those beings and that world through the lens of abstracted categories and formal models which aim to give us the Big Picture, to excavate some underlying causal context of which social participants are said to be unaware, or whether we embrace a mode of theoretical reflection that places human self-understanding and self-definition into the heart of theory construction. To do the latter yields both a different theory *and* a different politics. First, it makes the interpretive theorist's life complex; she cannot set about making vast proclamations about the world and the folks who inhabit it without making a serious effort to explore and to enter empathically into their contexts and meanings. Second, her theoretical commitments exude a certain humility as she confronts the inexhaustible richness of a *single* human life. If she is to be consistent, to ensure coherence as between her approach to social theory and her political stance, she must embrace a strategy of social change which incorporates as essential the assent of human beings to the changes being made. In what such "assent" consists is a controversial and arguable point; I am not calling for a vote, say, as to whether or not to end laws requiring segregation of the races. Rather, what I have in mind is a public debate of a certain sort which must precede, and be a concomitant of, social changes that will affect human beings, their children, and their communities. I am positioning myself against the notion of a social engineering elite or a vanguard *imposing* changes "for the good of" others when those others have had no opportunity to participate in the process of change, even to take up an oppositional stance.

One implication of all this is that a radical agenda that fails to garner the reflective adherence of the people in whose behalf its dream of change is being dreamt is an agenda that either will fail of realization or whose realization must be coerced and manipulated. There is a moral distance separating interpretive thinkers, whose method, as I sketch it, commits them to radically democratic political change, from defenders of an increasingly undemocratic status quo and, as well, from tough-minded revolutionaries who will remake society at whatever human cost and who dismiss opposition to their plans as so much "false consciousness."

Bear in mind, briefly, the claims thus far lodged. I have claimed that the most widely disseminated feminist accounts of gender development fail to give us a recognizable picture of the human child in her social world, in part because these analyses do not construe the child as an importantly self-defining human subject. I shall extend and defend this claim below. Second, I have insisted that theoretical commitments gear political options and pro-posals. What is required next, as I explore specific accounts, is an appraisal that traverses the terrain between theoretical argument—are the arguments coherent or unconvincing and why?—and political ends—does the politics flow logically from the theoretical conclusions (for good or ill) or has the author gerrymandered the discussion in order to focus attention only on the most favorable possible outcomes of her agenda for change? and so on.[7] If feminist gender arguments are to be compelling as theory *and* politics, there must be a concretely specific connection between the particular nature of "private" arrangements and public outcomes, both by way of explanation as to what is wrong and by way of prescription for what must be changed. This is a requirement gender theory forces upon the critic, for gender theorists insist that they have explained where the problem lies; seen what must be done to put things right; and foreseen what the effects of transformation along the lines they demand must be.

There are three central texts involved: Juliet Mitchell, *Psychoanalysis and Feminism;* Dorothy Dinnerstein, *The Mermaid and the Minotaur;* and Nancy Chodorow, *The Reproduction of Mothering.* Each of these texts involves a different appropriation of psychoanalysis for purposes of feminist social thought, though each winds up with basically the same thesis as to what is wrong and what must be done to achieve a gender revolution. For each locates the ultimate, underlying causal context for human malaise in what is called the "universal fact" that it is women who mother. This thesis cannot, finally, bear the explanatory weight placed upon it.

I turn first to Mitchell's account, one which suffers from an excessive abstractedness that is far removed from Freud's own method.[8] Like those structuralist thinkers to whom she is indebted, Mitchell believes that struc-tures, laws, and ideological formations are the agents of history. Persons are construed as vehicles for the ongoing operation and transmission of struc-tures and laws. For one of the points of structuralism is the elimination, or what is called the decentering, of the subject. Questions involving inten-tions, purposes, understandings, meanings, are set aside as irrelevant. Ac-cording to the structuralists, one can seal off social explanation from any fieldwork data or inferences concerning human beings and one can, therefore, engage in what might be called disembodied social theory. Mitchell's persons emerge as objectified entities subject to universal laws. Psychoanalysis, in turn, becomes the way we acquire the laws of human society *within* the unconscious mind and how these laws, which underlie and underwrite patriarchy, function within each of us unawares. Within Mitchell's frame, women are prevented from constituting themselves historically as subjects; her analysis squeezes out any room for subjects to reflect their situations.

Psychoanalysis is set up, by Mitchell, as scientific laws operating in the sphere of reproduction, a sphere construed as an analogue of the sphere of production for which we also have scientific explanatory laws. The human beings who emerge with such complexity in Freud's case studies are stripped by Mitchell to the bare bones, to objects acquiring laws as unaware, passive reactors. Despite Freud's repeated warnings that unconscious mental processes should not be reified and made thinglike or lawlike, Mitchell writes of the Unconscious as the object of psychoanalytic science. When Freud deployed the language of "laws," he referred to probabilities and tendencies to be found in human mental life, for example, the pervasiveness of mental conflict. He denied, as I noted above, that psychoanalysis could be a predictive science. Freud's complex subject gives way to an ahistorical woman inculcated into the human order under the workings of the inexorable laws of patriarchy. Although Mitchell's woman is present at the initiation ceremonies, she is an un-self-aware initiate, and her unreflectiveness continues into adult life. The Law of the Father she carries about is held in the Unconscious, which operates with no regard for the human subject it inhabits; it is more a machine in the ghost than the ghost in the machine.

Culture is treated as an unspecified whole. Beneath all the "apparent" variations in economy, ecology, history, religion, politics, art, and language an adamantine deep structure, universal and formal, operates. But if the Law of the Father can be deployed to explain the life of the Zuni, the life of the female professional, and the life of the queen of England, what, ultimately, has been explained? Mitchell's evidence that women, and all others, fall under the universal edict of patriarchal laws is simply definitional. It goes like this: as members of the human order, women *by definition* must operate under the laws of patriarchy, for patriarchy is *culture itself.* Mitchell states: "This symbolic law of order defines society and determines the fate of every small human animal born into it."[9] Part of this law and order is the dictum that it is women who mother. Freud's stress on psychic bisexuality and the child's identification with both parents (hence two genders) fades into the background.

Mitchell's way out of this structuralist iron cage is a move to Lévi-

Strauss's claim that women have been universal objects of exchange. This, strangely, becomes a ray of hope. It turns out that the law of patriarchy, including the incest taboo, operates to maintain a situation in which women are construed as universal exchange objects in *all* cultures, and it is patriarchy that "describes" this so-called universal culture. Evidence as to diverse ways of life is bypassed or brought into line with a series of purely abstract claims which Eleanor Burke Leacock calls "unwarranted teleology" belied by actual anthropological and historical evidence.[10]

By setting psychoanalysis up as a series of ahistorical, universal categories, Mitchell's only way out is to challenge the Law of the Father. This leads to her most implausible move and claim, namely, that the incest taboo, though essential to precapitalist social formation, is "irrelevant" under capitalist economies which do not turn on woman exchange. The contemporary "ban on incest," in Mitchell's terms, is stressed "so loudly" because we no longer, strategically, require it. Political change demands doing away with the incest taboo, the Oedipus complex, and hence women's gender construction as a process of feminization.

If the incest taboo is but an artifact of the exchange of women capitalist society had made redundant, it seems our best bet lies in undoing the tangled skein of patriarchal law lodged in the taboo itself—in upending our current familial relations. But given Mitchell's previous tie-up of the incest taboo and the Law of the Father with human culture itself, it is difficult to imagine what will supersede it. A primal horde? A self-limiting polymorphously perverse paradise? Or will we choose to behave "as if" such a taboo still exists in order to prevent the sexual exploitation of children by adults on whom they are dependent? These questions go unanswered. Instead, Mitchell speaks vaguely of a cultural revolution to usher new structures into being. "It is," she concludes, "a question of overthrowing patriarchy," but this desideratum, within the frame of her own analysis, has about as much chance of success as overthrowing the law of gravity.[11] I believe there is much more flexibility in our situation. But to demonstrate this requires a more fluid, less rigid appropriation of Freud. I will turn next to an account that sees psychoanalysis, hence gender development, through a different theoretical lens, though the ultimate conclusions are very like Mitchell's. This is, at best, problematic.

Dorothy Dinnerstein's *The Mermaid and the Minotaur* provides a startling alternative to Mitchell's rationalistic, formal account. Her work should be located within the wider project of cultural, left-wing Freudianism of which Norman O. Brown and Herbert Marcuse are the best-known representatives. Dinnerstein begins her discussion with what she calls the "normal psychopathology" of the human race, a starting point that I shall question below. Dinnerstein's descriptive language of our current conditions (which, of course, yields evaluative conclusions) is extreme. Characteristic descriptive terms include "intolerable," "diseased," "malignant," "maiming," "pathological," and "poisoned," and, at one point, motherhood is termed "monstrous, atavistic."[12] Dinnerstein's argument is grounded in the Kleinian concept of "splitting" as a basic process in human mental life, one that, for Dinnerstein, is importantly "getoverable."[13] Dinnerstein places the greatest explanatory weight on the oral stage and the preverbal level of development. It is always difficult to attempt to take theoretical account of what happens before human beings become language users. My quarrel with Dinnerstein is not that she has made this attempt, or even that she has made this the centerpiece of her argument, but that she creates what, in philosophic terms, is called a "privileged" epistemological position, having a foundational imperative that overrides all that follows. For preverbal development, she insists, under terms of female mothering, leads inexorably to a vast array of specific evils that flow from the splitting that such mothering trails in its wake.

Dinnerstein's argument runs along these lines: (1) the "normal" condition of the human species is psychopathological—maladaptive and life threatening; (2) this malaise has its roots in our intolerable gender arrangements; (3) what is intolerable about these arrangements, what makes them maiming and oppressive to everyone, is that they are "asymmetrical," leading to specific paranoid and other defenses around gender; (4) the central marker of this asymmetry is the fact that "for virtually every living person it is a woman" who provides the first and most important "contact with humanity and with nature." All of this leads to the conclusion that female monopoly of child care, given all Dinnerstein packs into it, makes the human race mad. Indeed, she foresees the end of civilization, and soon, if something isn't done to "break the female monopoly over early child care."[14]

I shall linger, for a moment, over two of Dinnerstein's key presumptions. To the extent that these presumptions can be seriously challenged or questioned, her overall analysis and the high-pitched claims that go with it are at least partially eroded. First, the notion of "normal" psychopathology. Every critical social theorist posits some characterization of a transformed human condition as a contrast model of what things might be or become if certain changes were made. For example, Marx's conception of "alienation" comprises both a condemnation of the distortion of humanity that emerges under conditions of exploitation and oppression and the promise of a more complete, even transcendent human possibility once those conditions have been eliminated. The problem with Dinnerstein's argument along these lines is its utopian absolutism. Her language blurs important distinctions. If, for example, we are all "normally" deranged, what are we to make of those unfortunate souls who cannot function at all in the world, victims of persistent and destructive delusions or fixations of one sort or another? Are they simply more "normal" than the rest of us? This easily gets silly. Or, if it is the case that we are all in the grips of a shared, universal psychopathology, how is it possible for anyone to attain the merest intimation of what a normal, nonpsychopathological human condition might be? If we have always been crazy, perhaps that *is* the human condition.

Dinnerstein pulls something of a sleight of hand here. Her premise of "normal" psychopathology is parasitic upon some absolute but tacit standard, one thus far not approached by any known human society anywhere at anytime, of what robust psychic health for the human species would look like. Where does this standard come from if all we have ever known is psychopathological? Marx's vision of the nonalienated future made explicit contact with his assessment of life in noncapitalist historic eras and societies. But Dinnerstein doesn't give a defense of why it is we should find her utopian promise plausible as an alternative to what we have got. Surely these questions are central ones. What a social theorist must be about, if she is not to lapse into abstract evocations, is to attempt to sort out those features of the human condition that cannot be changed, we being the kind of beings we are and none other, and those miseries attributable directly to exploitative social forms. Evading these considerations, Dinnerstein launches her program for world change from a therapeutic perspective which ushers in the dictum that the sick must be made well; this, in turn, requires doctors to prescribe the medicine. What we get, then, is a people-changing enterprise, always a high-risk undertaking, particularly for those said not to know their own minds who are to be changed along lines dictated by those who have figured things out. My criticisms here are not narrowly rationalist ones that yield excessive caution, but flow instead from a recognition best called dialectic. A new world will always be parasitic upon an old one; we can never simply leapfrog into another era by gerrymandering gender arrangements or anything else.

A second presumption Dinnerstein privileges is that splitting, occurring most importantly in the preverbal stage of development, is the key to the psychopathology of our gender arrangements. One dimension of this privileged starting point is the insistence that the oral stage and preverbality set a powerful *causal* context for all that follows. The effect of this portion of her argument is to undermine any account of language as that which makes human beings vitally and irrepressibly self-defining and self-creating. By putting so much weight on the stage when we do not use language, Dinnerstein, ironically, could be thought to reduce the import and use of language by construing meaning as a putative correspondence between words and states of affairs. Dinnerstein, surely, would not share this view; however, by eviscerating the possibility that human beings, through language, can "talk" their way into and out of alternative ways of being by changing their self-descriptions, she joins hands unwittingly with narrow rationalists who also underplay or ignore humans as speaking subjects.

A second dimension Dinnerstein privileges is the notion of splitting itself. I cannot here enter into a full-fledged theoretical debate drawing on the vast, but contradictory, clinical and analytical evidence in this area. But what seems to be going on in *The Mermaid and the Minotaur* is a strong notion of splitting involving not only *mechanism* but *meaning* and *content*, one that has causal consequences for individual subjects and for *all* of human life and history. Given the position splitting occupies in her scheme of things, Dinnerstein would have strengthened her case had she spent a bit more time defending her notion against alternative possibilities. Another and related problem is the fact that Dinnerstein, in an unmediated way, links splitting along gender lines to the totality of arrangements in the social and political world. This tight construal is not persuasive. I shall get to this point below, but, first, a few words on splitting. A first, crude notion of splitting was held by Janet and characterized by Freud, in "An Autobiographical Study." Freud writes: "According to Janet's view a hysterical woman was a wretched creature who, on account of constitutional weakness, was unable to hold her mental acts together, and it was for this reason that she fell victim to a splitting of her mind and to a restriction of the field of her consciousness."[15] Though Freud's views grew richer and more complex with the emergence of the structural theory of mind, the concept was not as central to his theory as to that of later thinkers, including Melanie Klein. The problems, and richness, of the thesis go hand-in-hand, for splitting is used to refer to a host of manifest behaviors or activities "whose nature evokes hypotheses concerning either an underlying rent in the process of awareness or alternatively the simultaneous experience of contradictory, mutually exclusive events within awareness."[16] Some thinkers construe splitting in essentially negative or defensive terms, stressing the vicissitudes of internalization. Others argue that splitting may be a nondefensive dimension of the way in which the infant mind *must* work simply to organize itself and to participate in experience.[17] The upshot of this latter view is that splitting *can* take on defensive purposes, but that the mechanism has limited theoretical cogency within the frame of an analysis of pathological mechanisms of defense.

I cannot sort out these debates here. But it is important to note, once again, that splitting is granted such heavy theoretical weight for Dinnerstein that psychopathology emerges as an *ordinary*, not an extraordinary phenomenon.[18] The relation between "infantile normative" and "adult pathological" splitting is problematic, but for Dinnerstein there is a smooth conduit between the two. She seems unaware of the leap she is making from preverbal development to the entire structure of complex social systems. Another irony: given her dramatic leap, she winds up fusing two incompatible phenomena, a Hobbesian characterization of what *is* with a romantic view of what *is-to-be*. At least Hobbes was consistent. Given his depiction of a dire human condition, he opts for a coherent, if unacceptable, conclusion: absolutist control to prevent the abuses that flow from the human condition itself.[19] But Dinnerstein does not bridge the gap between her despair, even contempt, for how we now are with her utopian picture of what we will or can be if . . .

Let me explain. Dinnerstein observes correctly that "the private and public sides of our sexual arrangement are not separable, and neither one is secondary to the other."[20] She goes on to insist that *every* aspect of these arrangements is traceable to "a single childhood condition." But does this latter claim follow coherently? She states that both our private and public arrangements "will melt away when that condition is abolished," that condition, remember, being the fact that it is women who mother and destructive splitting which follows. To explore this contention, one must take the measure of the malaise Dinnerstein locates in gender-based distinctions in the first place. She presumes a world in which psychological imperatives, instilled from female mothering, flow upward and outward, resulting in women who depend "lopsidedly on love for emotional fulfillment because they are barred from absorbing activity in the public domain" and men who depend "lopsidedly on participation in the public domain because they are stymied by love."[21] This outcome is inexorable, "woven into the pattern of complementarity between male and female personality that emerges from female-dominated early childhood."[22] Male privilege and female oppression (the "universal exploitation of women") are caused by asymmetry. Why? Because female power in the preverbal stage is so overpowering for male and female infants, but with different results for each, that mother-raised humans will never be able to see "female authority as wholly legitimate."[23]

One curious aspect in this account is the way in which Dinnerstein constitutes the infant as a powerfully sensual being with tumultuous feelings but omits the fact that this infant has a complexly functioning mind and becomes, rather early on, a sophisticated language user who, through these aspects of language and mind, is complicatedly self-defining. What follows is a corrective to Dinnerstein's construal of humans as not only *in part* but as *nearly completely* "infantile." Children are inventive language users, despite the fact that adults, bent on making them sensible and rational creatures who think about the world "realistically," aim to shrivel that expressivist spark down to manageable proportions. There is little sense in Dinnerstein that children, or adults for that matter, have minds which can be put to purposes not ultimately or finally or "really" reducible to infantile drives, desires, or wishes. For Dinnerstein we remain infants. In her discourse adults emerge as willful, capricious, frequently devious, hugely voracious, alarmingly untrustworthy, narrowly self-seeking, and clingingly dependent. There is, of course, a partial truth in all this, but it is a truth Dinnerstein takes for the whole. I know a child lurks in each one of us, threatening to erupt, disrupt, or fall apart. But that is not all we are. To reduce male activity to the defensive and destructive historymaking of naughty boys and female activity to the playacting of maternal menials or coy sex kittens (with some possible redeeming social features) is to sink into one-dimensionality.

Let me elaborate. Dinnerstein's characterization of the public world is abstract and denunciatory. She does not distinguish between the many kinds of activities that fall within what we usually consider the public domain; nor does she indicate which of these activities may be properly seen as "political" and which are something else. In other words, she has no *political* sense of the public world. For a political theorist, this is a serious shortcoming. There are other problems. Dinnerstein describes the public world as both historymaking and "nature-assaulting"; indeed for her historymaking is coterminous with assaults against nature, against the female. Women, embodying nature, have been excluded from historymaking but have also refrained from nature killing. Men, in murdering nature, are in the first and last instance also getting back at their mothers. All in all, it seems a rather good thing Dinnerstein's women have been exempted from the thoroughly nasty business of historymaking. (Though, finally, they are complicit.)

Before I continue with my reservations and disagreements, let me note that I accept it as given that much current male and female self-definition is defensive in relation to one another (whether this is best explored through the prism of "splitting" is another issue); that human beings, at least some of the time, *over*-define themselves as "real men" or "true women" defensively, given their internalized images of the opposite sex. To the extent that this is the case, we must aim to enhance our capacities to secure our male-female identities in ways that are less limiting. But this is not Dinnerstein's project. She accepts no limits on human "freedom" once the thorny matter of gender asymmetry is ironed out. Hers are a set of maximal claims that begin by locating men *in* history destructively, and women *in* a rigid dichotomy between nature and culture.

In an important essay, "Natural Facts: A Historical Perspective on Science and Sexuality," L. J. Jordanova traces the antecedents of a presumed nature/culture split to the rationalizing discourse of eighteenth-century science.[24] In documenting the way in which the categories of "nature" and "culture" emerged, Jordanova challenges feminist accounts that assume these categories.

The nature/culture split entered feminist discourse with Simone de Beauvoir's *The Second Sex*. De Beauvoir located men squarely in the realm of Transcendence as Being-for-themselves and women in the bog of Immanence as Beings-in-themselves. De Beauvoir's model offered an unambiguous linkage from nature/culture, woman/man, to oppressed/oppressor. According to Jordanova, it made "women . . . the bearers of ignorance and men of knowledge," rather a baffling notion to set as the basis of feminist discourse.[25] In de Beauvoir's argument, men and men alone are declared the agents and bearers of culture; women, the flip side of the coin, outside civilization, in nature, are inessential to culture though they are a necessary condition for the reproduction of human life, a process de Beauvoir does not find one of the tasks of culture.

Although Dinnerstein's use of the dichotomy is not so severe in its devaluation of women's traditional spheres as de Beauvoir's, she repeats the notion that women are oppressed and victimized because they are located in "nature." This is a serious distortion. Anthropologists and social historians have shown that there are "no simple scales on which men and women can be ranged."[26] Moreover, Dinnerstein's diminishes women, historically and presently, by presuming that they would have given their consent, albeit tacit, to a social situation which was one of unrelenting debasement or infantilization. We know of no human society based on such debasement which has enjoyed a continuing existence. The upshot is: rather than countering the categorical rigidities that have plagued our understanding of past and present social life, Dinnerstein retains several of them. Jordanova makes a telling point against this hardening of the categories when she states that "one of the problems with the current promiscuous use of the nature/culture dichotomy in relation to gender is that it has taken the claims of Western science at face value, and so lapsed into a biologism which it is the responsibility of the social sciences, including history and anthropology, to combat."[27]

Given the fact that she carves up the social universe along the lines of a nature/culture dichotomy, Dinnerstein proposes, as *the* solution to all our ills, a break in the female monopoly of early childcare. Only this will defuse female linkage with nature and female oppression by culture. She calls for men and women to "mother" in identical ways and to participate in the public world in full parity. Were this done, our public and private arrangements would be transformed in one fell swoop. Children would no longer grow up maimed and maladaptive; nature would no longer be assaulted; history would no longer be destructive. To attain this end two sorts of preconditions are required. The first is psychological (just described) and the second, not political but *technological*. This technological condition is characterized as "the practical possibility of making parenthood genuinely optional, the concrete feasibility of adult work life flexible enough so that men and women can take equal part in both domestic and public life"—something, she insists, that is "already available," just as the restructuring of childrearing, if we really want it, is ready-to-hand.

On the road to sex equality, something curious has happened: important considerations involving the structure of our political and economic life are drawn in ad hoc and reduced to "technological" factors. In this way Dinnerstein reflects rather than challenges a dimension of the current public world she deplores—the tendency to reduce vital human issues to technical problems amenable to technological resolution at the hands of social engineers. Surely the public conditions she requires for her solution to asymmetrical disorders are profoundly and inescapably political. But she has no way to handle these issues because she has neither a political analysis of the present nor a political vision of the future.

Because Dinnerstein evades how it is, politically, we shall get to the world of gender symmetry save through willing it (given that the "technological" prerequisites for its implementation currently exist), her prophecy encounters no points of friction. One *political* precondition that stands in her way is the self-identity of women themselves, one still tied for most to primary responsibility for care of the young. This cannot be attributed wholly to the defensive aspects of femininity flowing from centuries of enforced domesticity, not even within Dinnerstein's analysis. I refer back to her insistence that women have certain qualities not given over to nature killing *because* of their roles in the arrangements Dinnerstein wishes to overturn. Women, identifying with Mother (Nature), have no need to plunder and rape her. What Dinnerstein foresees, in her post-gender-revolution society, is a world in which all the present plunder, exploitation, and nature assaulting of men will have melted away, and all the loving, concern, and caring now almost exclusively female traits (in her view) will remain, shared by men and women.

Is this convincing? If the gender revolution will radically alter men, turning them away from destruction and toward nurturance, why will it not also alter women, turning them away from nurturance and toward destructive historymaking? Women, it seems, stay as "sweet as they are" even as they gain full public power. In the process they will not take on the bad male qualities previously denied to them. Human nastiness evaporates on Din-nerstein's road to the future. It doesn't suffice to say Dinnerstein looks for-ward to integrating the now split parts of her goal, rather than simply abol-ishing the unsavory stuff. For what needs to be integrated, but cannot, argues Dinnerstein, given that we are all mother-reared and split, are current gender rigidities.

Finally, what seeps through Dinnerstein's pages is a form of evangelical sexual liberationism that fuses the promise of destroying old repressions, fulfilling immediate desires, and ushering in future happiness. I do not find this palatable medicine in an era of supply-side economics, the rising danger of a nuclear confrontation, and additional confirmation (as if this were re-quired) of the repressive nature of state socialist regimes. These dangers and dilemmas require the concerted political efforts of men and women who share a humane vision *now,* not generations away once the symmetrical world is attained. And it *is* possible for men and women to work together, politically, as citizens rather than to regress, incessantly, as Dinnerstein's men and women do, into an infantile *pas de deux,* mamas and babies waltz-ing into the apocalypse. Her vision is fantastic and has all the appeal of other apocalyptic prophecies, for at base each promises, once and for all, an end to it all since everyone, deep down, knows that the revolution the prophet requires to forestall the end she foresees is impossible to attain in practice.

I shall move, now, to a very different framework, and hence account, of gender development from Dinnerstein's in Nancy Chodorow's book, *The Reproduction of Mothering.* Chodorow owes as much to functionalist sociol-ogy as she does to psychoanalysis. She draws heavily upon a theory or model of the relationship between the family and society developed in the func-tionalist sociology of Talcott Parsons in two essays written in 1942 and 1943.[28] Her implicit acceptance of this model precludes taking up the self-understanding of social participants, or seeing social worlds as webs of meaning. Her model presupposes a stable congruity or "fit" between the modern industrialized economy and the nuclear family, a tie-up challenged by the new family history. Family functions are given. Male and female roles are predetermined and "asymmetrical," a term deployed by Parsons. These roles revolve around the division between what Parsons called the instru-mental, adaptive father and the nurturant, expressive mother. Parsons saw the division as necessary to the ends of maintaining the equilibrium of so-ciety. The family, in his functionalist terms, was one substructural buttress in a pattern of systems maintenance; in other words, the family is construed instrumentally. Functionalists hold to a unilinear theory of history which, in the words of Lawrence Stone, "ignores the ups and downs of social and intellectual change, the lack of uniformity of the direction of the trends, and the failures of the various trends to synchronize in the way they ought if the paradigm is to fit. Above all, by sweeping broadly across the vast spectrum of highly distinctive national cultures, status groups, and classes, these theories reduce the enormous diversity of social experience to a uniformity which has never existed in real life."[29] Chodorow shares these aspects of the functionalist paradigm. Now, this sort of perspective exudes a political stance that stresses stasis; Chodorow, however, beginning from the same premises, wishes to bring about revolution. I shall explore whether this can convincingly be done or not given her own analysis of the situation.

Human subjects are constituted by Chodorow's discourse as objectified role players, turned out as oversocialized beings stuck in a rigid "sex-gender system and sexual asymmetry."[30] Sex itself, Chodorow argues, and sexual desires and fantasies, including the progressive "libidinization" of various zones, as well as final gender identity, are *wholly* "social products." There is little depth psychology in this scheme of things. Instead, there is a sociological construct, a product of social factors, that gets construed as exhausting the "psychological." The human subject as a desiring, fantasizing, self-defining agent is lost. Children are human clay awaiting their molding into "gendered members of society."[31] By stripping human beings of any self-sustaining, autonomous capacities for fantasy, by evacuating them of sexual drives as in any way bodily and given, by ignoring consciousness and language, Chodorow eliminates children and adults as beings who may "dwell in possibility," to use Emily Dickinson's blithe turn of phrase, beings who are sentient and imaginative, capable of reflection, of symbol making, of identifying with beings outside the asymmetrical knots into which she ties up the family and, from there, the broader social world.[32]

Chodorow's account, like Dinnerstein's, involves a few central premises. The lockstep ordering goes like this: (1) the normal pattern of human gender development leads to the construction and reproduction of male dominance; (2) our gender arrangements are blatantly asymmetrical, hence systematically disordered; (3) this derangement generates male dominance and female subordination because psychologists "have demonstrated unequivocally that *the very fact* of being mothered by a woman generates in men conflicts over masculinity, a psychology of male dominance, and a need to be superior to women,"[33] pointing to the conclusion that it is women's mothering which guarantees continuing male dominance and female subordination: the cradle-rocking hand strikes again! Her conclusion suggests a counterfactual, namely, that men not mothered by women exclusively experience no need to be superior to women and are not warped by a psychology of male dominance. Whether this is so or not is a matter for exploration on many levels; but there is compelling anthropological evidence to suggest that *the* male psychology Chodorow finds inevitably caused by female mothering is not as universal as she claims. Indeed, many men in our own societies, mothered by women, have no apparent need to bully women nor to dominate them.

To the riposte that, although such men do not engage in bullying or domineering *action* vis-à-vis women, they may still harbor vestiges of a fantasy world in which subdue women, my response would follow along these lines: it is not the business of feminist politics to expunge fantasy. To hope to create a world in which male fantasies have been sanitized of any content that might contain brutalizing images, however fleetingly, is to embrace a moralistic politics that easily turns repressive. There is a vast difference between a fantasy and a brutal rape. What society can and must do is *punish the action, not move to eradicate the fantasy.* Otherwise we require moralistic thought control.

Back to Chodorow's sex-gender system, then. In her terms, it is set up as "a fundamental determining and constituting element" of society; it is "socially constructed, subject to historical change and development, and organized in such a way that it is systematically reproduced," though there is, in fact, no sense of historic movement or change in her analysis.[34] Given this tautly drawn system, Chodorow cannot take account of human beings as reflective and active; instead, they are reactive, shaped by external forces, primarily by the "object relations" of family life. Most puzzling, in a psychoanalytically oriented account, is the disappearance of embodiment. In her understandable determination to construct a social analysis, Chodorow excises the body-subject. Zones become libidinized only—and this is quite extraordinary, for it turns children into precocious Benthamites—because the child recognizes, calculatingly, that this will help to attain personal contact. If what one is explaining is gender identity, it is a rather serious omission to disconnect the body. Shrinking embodiment down to "variables" termed "biological," Chodorow's arguments constitute human beings in, and through, a series of prefixed social predicates.

Though Chodorow explicitly discounts biology as important in any deep way to her account in her book, she later acknowledged that "biological variables" are something feminists must be open to, for we are, after all, "embodied creatures," and there is "certainly some biological basis, or influence," etc. But biological "variables" are precisely what I am not concerned with, for their incorporation only leads to tedious social sciency notions of "interaction" and "multiple causality." To call the body-subject a "variable" is baffling indeed, for the fact that we are never-not-our-bodies and never in the world save as body-subjects seems a rather more basic and ungetoverable reality than to strip our bodies down to size as but one "variable," among others. Variables don't grow up, grow ill, make love, grow old, and die. This paring the body down to size is not radical at all; it is typical of academic social science and a throwback to plain, old-fashioned dualism.[35]

There is more. Children in *The Reproduction of Mothering* identify not so much with recognizably real, particular mothers or fathers but with role players, again making Chodorow's indebtedness to functionalism clear. Following as she does Parsons's vectors of gender-specific, socially induced identifications is unconvincing, in part because one gets no sense of *families* in social settings, no thick description of the social worlds of intimate human life, nor the complex inner worlds of infant life. Her system appears to squeeze out the central importance of the *quality of mothering and parenting* to the development of the human person. Yet psychoanalytic evidence is clear on this score: what is of vital importance is the *quality* of care the child receives.[36]

Chodorow's system has very little elasticity. Freud, on the other hand, was aware of variations in human possibility, including resolutions to prototypical crises. He recognized that children, like that cunning fellow little Hans, could conjure up fantastic resolutions to important conflicts, not reducible to some standard formula. Chodorow often makes stronger claims for the explanatory power and application of her model than Freud did for his as social explanation. Yet, in the breach, she cannot account for the many human lives that diverge in interesting ways from her static functionalist construction of the sex-gender system.

Here it is worth pondering Chodorow's determination to unravel heterosexual knots and smooth out gender asymmetries. By asymmetry she, and Dinnerstein, mean men and women playing different parts in the social world and having predominant interest in, even effective control over, different activities on the basis of gender identity. This would not seem to be an evil *simpliciter* unless these differences were *invariably* the basis for destructive inequalities or distinctions *always* invidiously drawn to favor one group, to downgrade the other. But by defining "asymmetry" as male dominance, female oppression, Chodorow construes social reality in a way that downgrades women's contributions and magnifies those of men. That is, she winds up sharing the "devaluation of domesticity which is the hallmark of the very sexist society she deplores."[37] Rather than challenging the terms of male-dominant society on the basis of its respective valuation of men's and women's worlds, Chodorow attacks gender differences themselves, seeing them as the root of social evil. It follows that the radically degendered society becomes a prerequisite for social "equality." Indeed, the degendered society becomes by definition, in her frame, one of equality.

Conflating differences with domination, Chodorow has little choice but to embrace the feminist future as a picture of a social world in which human beings are rendered as sexually homogeneous as possible. Denying possibilities for reciprocal interdependency as one plausible outcome of gender differences viewed as complementaries, and as making possible fructifying mutualities at variance with destructive sexual divisions or cleavages, Chodorow embraces the symmetrical future. This leads one critic, Zelda Bronstein, to argue that Chodorow's equation of difference with domination and her call for a nonoppositional social world in which "all good ends are reconcilable" places her squarely within the tradition of mainstream liberal ideology.[38]

In her determination to make things symmetrical, Chodorow does not consider the possibility that her argument might lead to the elimination of differences but would do little to eradicate social injustice. Her call for "more collective child-rearing situations," for example, as demonstrably preferable to what we have in Western societies, is instructive in this regard. She claims, without citing compelling evidence, that more "collective" methods reduce, or eliminate, the fruits of our gender arrangements—"individualism . . . competitiveness." Her terms of description are crucial. Another observer, looking at the same picture as Chodorow, might speak of our concerns with "being an individual," with "moral autonomy," as one aspect of our childrearing arrangements. We would then respond very differently. None of us lauds individualism, which, rightly, has a bad name, but all save those blind to concerns with human freedom and responsibility want children to grow up to be individuals with a sense of moral responsibility, beings who can be held accountable for their deeds. Chodorow points *only* to the possibly good outcomes of collective childrearing, finding no irritants in the image, though there are such, even as she overdraws the bad results of our childrearing. She is insouciant to the potential dangers of flattening out the social world, of erecting a single standard for organizing and evaluating human life.

There is important, and growing, anthropological evidence about male and female power and authority in societies different from our own which calls the symmetry imperative into question. One observer, Peggy Reeves Sanday, analyzing over 150 societies for which detailed ethnographies were available, concludes that the only symmetry of which we know anything— by which she means a rough parity of power between males and females—is grounded in sex differences, not the blurring of those differences. Sanday's study is particularly interesting because she began with the presumption that women were universally subordinated, men dominant.[39] To her initial consternation, Sanday found that the evidence pointed to something very different. Not only was it *not* the case that men were the universal culture creating, dominant sex, women the nature-struck subordinate sex, but there were many societies in which women wielded, or had wielded, great authority and power. In such societies, it was women as bearers of children and nurturers of plant life who occupied central positions in the realm of social authority.

Gender identity leading to the two sexes predominating in different spheres of social life, tied, in turn, to powerful, organizing, symbolic principles, lay at the basis of those societies featuring rough integration between the sexes, as well as those societies that were genuinely separate but equal. In such societies the power to give life—female power—was as highly valued as the power to take it away—male power (yet paradoxically also male weakness, as the male warrior is expendable, making men the expendable sex). Conceptual distinctions demarcating femaleness from maleness, Mary Douglas argues, are universally evident and, moreover, are necessary if human beings are to create cultural forms, are to order their worlds in some coherent way.[40]

Finding peculiar as feminist argumentation though understandable as Western bias the view that male dominance is universal, Sanday says this flows from our tendency to equate dominance with official public leadership. Karen Sacks adds that to view male and female authority in societies like the Iroquois, where women wielded great power, as *unequal* rather than *different* reflects a "state bias in Western anthropological interpretation of prestate politics."[41] When one looks at societies within their own terms, Sanday concludes that female economic and political power or authority flow as a right due the female sex where one finds a "magico-religious association between maternity and fertility of the soil" linking women "with social continuity and social good." In certain West African dual-sex systems, for example, the power and invincibility of womanhood emerges with startling force. "Whether the male chief is big or small," said the woman of a West African solidarity group, "what matters is that he was given birth by a woman."[42] Dozens of societies, it appears, were worlds in which sex differences signaled parity and complementary balance, with neither sex wholly dominant over the other, but with each dominant in particular areas of social life.

Examples of other male-female arrangements unpacked by Sanday feature ways that *formal* male authority is balanced, or undermined, by *actual* female power. This gender balance of power is maintained by culturally sanctioned stratagems, including myths of male dominance though males do not actually dominate. In peasant societies, for example, the appearance of male dominance provides an umbrella beneath which women exercise actual power over key sectors of community life, areas where men are not allowed to interfere. (This was certainly my experience growing up on a farm in rural Colorado, in the American West.) In this world of complex asymmetry, power and authority between the sexes is balanced.

Sanday concludes that arguments calling for sexual symmetry, understood as a world in which males and females have decisions over the same activities and exercise power in identical ways over the same things, makes little sense. No society has ever existed in which the sexes gave equal energy to exactly the same activities and decisions, nor does such a society seem plausible, even desirable. This vision of symmetry conflates equality with sameness and it strikes a responsive chord, Sanday insists, only if "one has no knowledge of the many societies which attach supernatural importance to the creation of life."[43]

The nature/culture split on which the thesis of male dominance/female subordination is based does not stand up to historical and anthropological investigation. There are many societies in which women are the central civilizing influence and men are associated with decivilizing force. Sanday's study suggests that secular male dominance is more likely to occur in societies in which an imbalance has congealed between male- and female-linked activities. The way to combat such destructive cleavage is *not*, it appears, to call for a total fusing of male and female activities and spheres such that no vital distinctions remain—impossible in any case—but to expand the actual and symbolic importance and vitality of female-linked activities and systems of meaning; for, to repeat Sanday's findings, the only symmetry of which we have real evidence has not arisen on the basis of gender blurring but has been grounded in sex differences. This suggests a very different feminist task from that of the symmetrist. The implications are vast, troubling, and complex, and I cannot spell them out here. But I do wish to turn to one piece of powerful contemporary evidence that calls symmetrical presumptions into question.

The work of Diana Grossman Kahn challenges the Chodorow image of parents cloning same-sex children to live in an unchanging world.[44] According to Kahn, Chodorow's argument washes out the complexities of cross-sex identifications. In a series of studies involving over 100 college women, juniors and seniors, with whom she conducted open-ended interviews that went on for many hours, Kahn found that daughters were not "locked into" some automatically second-rate model if their mothers were "traditional wives and mothers." Indeed, such mothers were described, with few exceptions, as strong, active, loving, and supportive. Most important, for feminist considerations, were the roles of fathers as mentors to daughters. The research literature on what are called "achieving women," including feminists, both nineteenth-century and contemporary activists, shows the encouragement of fathers to be particularly important. Kahn found that fathers made their own "unique contribution" to the development of their daughters. Only two of her subjects reported fathers who clearly downgraded their capacities compared with those of their brothers. Kahn concludes, after evaluating the *quality* of actual individual lives and experiences, that mothers and fathers played importantly complementary (not identical or symmetrical) roles. Kahn also challenges the notion that men, by definition, are deficient in their capacities for intimacy. This formulation, she argues, emerges as one-sided and polemical because it makes intimacy, by definition, that of which women are capable—even as it condemns the situation that ostensibly makes the woman superior in intimacy.

Clearly, the ball is now in my court. Given my disagreement with accounts of "sex-gender systems" and calls for symmetry, I must move to articulate some coherent alternative. Perhaps it is worth putting the following questions. What is the point of social explanation? Is it to figure out what is really going on, to probe meaning, to satisfy our curiosity? Is it to determine how to organize the social world in order to help ease its burdens for those men and women who inhabit it and who try, often against daunting odds, to be decent, loving parents toward their children? Or is our end point the implementation of a vision of social change as preordained by a theoretical elite with a blueprint for reordering society? If reform of family life, or gender arrangements, emerges as importantly decent in itself, that is one thing. But if radical change in human intimate life is deemed necessary in order to attain other ends, to remake the world in conformity with some overarching *Weltanschauung,* that is quite another. In this latter instance, theoretical explanation becomes a power play in a cultural struggle and must be eyed, queasily, as such. For those who propose to undo the way we now do things at the most basic level sometimes aim to "reconstruct" the human subject. We are well to be wary, for "reconstruction" (meaning, by definition, that we are now "unreconstructed") all too easily translates into a politics of coercion, buttressed by the notion that the majority of human beings are hapless "products" of social conditioning who do not know their own minds, their "true" interests, or their "real" needs, a sorry state from which the reconstructors have somehow escaped.

In setting down the markers of an alternative, I must be brief. What I shall provide is not a full-blown alternative account, impossible in a short essay, but those imperatives I believe such an account must take account of, or account for. First, a compelling alternative must recognize the singular importance of construing the human subject, child and adult, as self-defining. To the extent that feminist social explanation and ideology eliminates the self-understandings of social participants, and such explanation and ideology gains acceptance and adherence, feminists, paradoxically, promote a set of presumptions that have historically been arrayed against female selfhood. Nobody is well served when human beings are shrunk down to the status of objects or analysis or deprived of consciousness, language, and agency.

A second feature of an alternative account, tied to the first, would be to frame that account, in part, from what might be called the standpoint of the child, featuring the child as a body-subject, seeing his or her world as a complex web of social relations and meanings alive with competing possibilities. Getting inside the child's world means construing child development and the emergence of gender identity as a dynamic discourse, the history of the "I" ("*das Ich*"), framed with reference to what I am not. This dialectic of human development involves complex negations and affirmations. The child is no passive recipient of this process but the active constructor of various possibilities.

The child's inner discourse of the I/not-I is powerfully structured within the ordering dialogue of child and mother. Louise J. Kaplan has traced the child's dialogue of "oneness and separateness," the coming-towards and pushing-aways that are the punctuation points of a process that, in Kaplan's words, "insures our humanity."[45] The evidence of what happens when things go wrong, when children suffer the diseases of nonattachment and neglect, is proof of the child's needs for constancy in the form of specific, adult others. The child does not become a language defining "I" until around thirty months of age, yet well before that she has been interpreting the meanings of space and time, exploring what Kaplan calls the "choreography" of mother and child, carrying on an active dialogue involving mutual excitement, games, and responses. Kaplan demonstrates that the babe in arms is no passive bit of human clay but "an artist," helping "to create the world which holds him,"[46] with a repertoire of "grunts, sighs, coos, postures, droopy-eyed looks, alert looks, finger grabs, head turnings and mouthings, and a set of cries and fretting sounds that give a mother some idea of how she should hold him and interpret the world to him."[47]

The baby is the educator of her own body. She experiments with what it can do. She tests what it cannot. She assays how it all fits together. She locates it in the world.[48] This self-motivation, if all goes well, grows more and more powerful. The child's capacities for translating bodily imperatives into mental activity; her growing emotional complexity; her burgeoning capacity to comprehend and create meaning—all paint a picture of a being with agency, not an indeterminate piece of stuff awaiting molding by the organized forces of society. Another important point, lost in most gender accounts, is the fact that adults-as-parents are not unchanged by the discourse of childhood. Each child, a being unique and like no other, calls forth a variety of responses from her parents. Every child-parent dialogue is distinctive and, in subdued or more dramatic ways, may transform *all* participants.

Just a few other bits of evidence on the child as subject: Rosalind Gould has detailed the ways in which "fantasy activities have a vital place in the child's development, in expanding horizons of thoughts and feelings, and as a potential means of achieving some internal distance from affective dilemmas."[49] Gould shows that the child's "internal well-springs and external world experiences intermingle or oscillate in various ways in fantasy expressions, to the enrichment of both sources of knowledge."[50] Myra Bluebond-Langner, in her account of dying children, documents the two-way nature of a process (socialization) often seen as unilinear, flowing from adult shapers to infant shapees. Not so, argues Bluebond-Langner, for such models fail to grasp "the shifting, unfolding, creative aspects of all human behavior," thereby failing to really *see* children and their world.[51] Her months spent with terminally ill children provide poignant evidence that children are willful, purposeful beings who possess selves, who interpret their own actions, incorporating their self-interpretations and their perceptions of interpretations of others as a way to obtain a view of themselves, others, and objects in the world, who initiate action so as to affect the views others have of them and they have of themselves, who are capable of initiating action to affect the behavior of others toward them, and who attach meaning to themselves, others, and objects, moving from one social world to another and acting appropriately in each.[52]

Finally, in an account at once playful and powerful, Gareth B. Matthews, a philosopher, assays the child as a philosopher. It turns out that "for many young members of the human race, philosophical thinking—including, on occasion, subtle and ingenious reasoning—is as natural as making music and playing games, and quite as much a part of being human."[53] Matthews makes the case for the sophistication of young minds. More provocatively, he argues that adults, in their treatment of "childish" questions, should refuse to play the therapist. Instead, parents and teachers should accept a child's inquiries on the level on which they are couched, rather than scouring every utterance for hints of repressed content. He writes, "Even when one suspects that the comment or question carries considerable emotional freight, addressing the question, rather than treating it *simply* as an emotional symptom, may be part of showing proper respect for the child as a full-fledged human being."[54] His argument here is not that dramatic symptoms should be ignored but that children's expressions of strong views, or children's questions, should not be reductively treated as necessarily symptomatic, thereby abstracting from the child's serious intellectual concerns and development.

A critic might reply at this juncture that he was persuaded by the evidence that children are active agents within a richer social world than the one conveyed in sex-gender system accounts. But, he might then continue, your alternative thus far seems to turn solely on the self-definitional moment of social theory. That is, he might go on, you have made the case for the child as an importantly self-creating subject. But this, in itself, offers no *explanation* of how it is that gender uniformities do emerge, or why it is biological males wind up as men and biological females become women. A child may understand many things, but the stages of her own psychosexual development, in some compelling theoretical form, are not among them. We cannot turn exclusively to the child for this, so how do you propose to *explain* social gender identity?

I would begin like this. We can assert certain things with certainty in advance of any particular, concrete investigation of gender development in specific families and cultural systems. We can, for example, assert that such development will involve the complex emergence of a body-subject within a social matrix. We also know that the human infant comes biologically "prepared" for all sorts of things: there is something like an inner developmental clock that, all other things being equal, will come into play at roughly similar times for human infants. I refer here to nervous system and motor development and the like. We know that babies are self-motivatedly embodied from the start and act in and upon their worlds on the bases of powerful imperatives which (if possible) translate, very quickly, into complex social feelings, emotions, needs, demands, and desires. We know that young children are extraordinarily preoccupied with their own bodies, though what they can or are allowed to do with those bodies varies from culture to culture. We know that it is impossible to rush this age-specific (over a range) developmental picture; a child before a certain age doesn't use language, not because her parents haven't taught her but because she literally *cannot,* given the early structure of mouth and tongue, cognitive capacities, etc. There are biological capacities and limits, then, when one is dealing with human infants and children. That it seems, somehow, "nonprogressive" to note this fact or even to attempt a nonreductive account of human embodiment, is a peculiarity of current discourse which seems to find unacceptable control in every constraint; the heavy hand of oppression in every limitation; exploitation in every necessity.

An alternative account would also begin with another presumption, one supported by extant anthropological theory and evidence, that the division of humanity, on the conceptual and symbolic level, into two distinct sexes is an essential aspect of human identity and cultural life. Males and females, of course, are beings who share in the most basic general characteristics;

yet they differ along recognizable and distinctive lines. To introduce the sex distinction, and to recognize its importance along the whole range of cultural meaning, is not to surreptitiously smuggle in a sex-gender system geared against women. Feminist arguments for gender symmetry are problematic in part because they aim to downplay or render uninteresting one of the most important distinctions of all.

To agree that the sex distinction is ineliminable and important does not mean one must acquiesce in received notions of the "masculine" and the "feminine." Clearly not. To demonstrate that bodily identity is a feature of personal identity, meaning that such identity will also be a sexed identity, one needs a dynamic, developmental account of the human subject. I have traced out such an account elsewhere, one which owes much to Freud's theory of human development as dynamically embodied *and* social, for we are inherently body-subjects.[55] The human body registers itself through a complex inner-outer dialectic in which the human infant makes internal representations to herself of her own body.[56] From her first moments, the infant experiences her body as a source of pleasure and unpleasure that goes beyond the mere registering of sensation. Embodiment implicates her in the active construction of her inner world, in part through the "taking in" of the body's surfaces as part of "external" reality. The human infant does not have the cognitive nor the neurological structure or organization necessary to demarcate tidily inner and outer, internal and external. What the infant does is to incorporate with eyes, ears, mouth, and touch a world complicatedly inner/outer. Slowly, the *I* is built up, in part through complex representations of the child's body, in part through inner representations of the bodies of others (objects) with whom the child is implicated in exquisitely social relations from the start.

Our corporeality bears powerful imperatives for how we come to know and to be. A child can neither negate physically nor transcend conceptually the manner in which his or her body "registers itself" within the successive stages of psychosexual maturation. The body evokes and mediates ways of knowing. Our most original, primitive experiences with the world cannot be understood save as an embodied engagement with the world. At the beginning a child has no sense of belonging to one gender or another, though male and female bodies from the beginning will surely register themselves somewhat differently. But when the child begins her early "sexual researches," certainly by the time the child is five or six, she will have distinguished two central types of embodied beings; though she may remain uncertain as to the full meaning of this distinction, she knows it is important. To live in a sexed social world is not, necessarily, to inhabit one in which differential evaluations, to the detriment of the female, are placed on gender identity.

This much is clear: gender identity is a central feature on the child's formation of a "self." Children locate themselves in their worlds on the basis of gender. This not only makes human sense, it is inescapable. All human beings and cultures differentiate form from nonform and provide the conceptual orderings minimally necessary if that culture is to have any coherent sense of anything whatever. Children live out a deep sense of urgency in and through their bodies: Is mine whole? Is it strong? Will it grow? Am I the "right" kind of what it is I am? Plans to "transcend" or eliminate the importance of gender run directly counter to every culture's world of shared meanings, for gender is precisely what children try to figure out, to work on, and to work through in all cultures, though, of course, the difficulty of the task and the outcomes of such figurings turn dramatically on the social frame within which the child's creation of a gendered self is set.

What would a world in which gender didn't figure centrally, and sex distinctions were downplayed or ignored, look like? It is difficult even to get a handle on such a world, for to be male or female is not just a patina *on* human existence, it is the mode *in* and *through* which life is lived. A degendered world would have to be one in which the repression of infantile sexuality was deep and pervasive in order to forestall moves by children to experiment and play with their own bodies, for only in this way could one prevent the child's inner representations of body surfaces from forming. Children would be barraged with the insistence that sex differences did not matter, were of little interest, were inessential in determining their future identities and existences. This would be a cruel deception. It would also hamper that development of self grounded in the child's emerging linguistic ability to differentiate objects, things, events, and experiences along lines of what is more or less important, what is central or peripheral, and so on. For a child such distinctions will also include "my body"/"other bodies," "male bodies"/"female bodies," "my family"/"other families," etc.

The claim that bodily identity is necessarily a gendered identity, as one feature of personal identity, neither presupposes nor entails social and political inequality between the sexes. The sex-linked distinctions used to justify sexual inequality are not necessarily thus linked. Although sex distinctions in some societies, including our own, have served as justifications for sex inequality, they need not thus serve; moreover, as I argued above, the burden of anthropological evidence suggests that sex distinctions historically have formed the basis for systems of parity of power and authority between men and women. Indeed, the insistence that sexual "symmetry" is the *only* foundation on which to build sex equality *displaces* a political focus upon structures of social, economic, and political equality, lodged importantly in class and race, in favor of advancing rhetorical claims about the transformation of human personalities and gender identities.

A few modest conclusions suggest themselves. The first is that we would all be better off, and come closer to creating a world to our heart's desirings, if we accepted our bodies in better grace and recognized that a sexual *difference* need not be an affront, an outrage, a narcissistic injury, a blow to female self-esteem forced on women by a male-dominant world; that, at present, these voices have found a resonant echo among other reformers and radicals signifies something important. It means, first of all, that there is some important partial truth to this construal, that the world has been set up in such a way that large numbers of females could come to see themselves through such a lens. It means, as well, that many feminist thinkers have implicitly embraced a vision of the human person that flows from, rather than standing in opposition to, cultural definitions of human beings indebted to utilitarian and market images. As those images have shifted from one revolving around the self as a being who must limit present pleasure to guarantee future "goods" (the world of the Protestant ethic and the middle-class producer), to one encouraging a grandiose view of an aggrandizing, consuming self, radicals have often gone along. Committed to modes of analysis based on the notion that what was, and remains, "bad" is overly harsh repression of natural drives in the interest of capital accumulation, radicals continue to speak, and to write, as if the unchained self, free to pursue his or her own ends in untrammeled ways, is a radical notion. In fact, the entire thrust of consumer society is to unleash grandiose ambition and to encourage unlimited self-gratification. The ideal consumer is a being not essentially connected to any other being, nor to a specific sense of place, to rootedness in family, community, or tradition. Such a being is more readily shunted about according to market imperatives. What we are suffering from at present, perhaps most dramatically in American society, is a surfeit of the politics of the grandiose self. Feminist analyses which fail to counter this image may wind up serving, in the warning of Julia Kristeva, as part and parcel of capitalism's needs to rationalize.

Missing, then, and needed is a vision of politics, a theory of the political community, an ideal of the critical citizen as one who shares in the deliberate efforts of human beings to order and direct their collective affairs. But needed as well is some alternative vision of family life that can account for the ways in which it has constrained us as well as the ways in which it is required to make us human. If we continue to locate the family as *the* first and foremost breeding ground of sexist privilege, we will be unable to see the ways in which women, historically, have been empowered by their appropriation of the private sphere as a social identity *in* the world.

Our situation is ambivalent, and we must acknowledge that ambivalence so that we do not make common sense, unwittingly at times, perhaps knowingly at others, with the social engineers and public policy technocrats whose ultimate end is the complete rationalization of all areas of human existence so that "society" as a whole can function more smoothly. It is quite possible for profamily platitudes and technocratic politics to coexist.

We should, instead, strengthen the capacities of human beings to live out long-term ties and commitments to one another. Such relations are based upon, and infused with, values counter to those that prevail on the market or in the instrumentally rationalist world view. Bronstein claims that marriage and the family, or familial-like bonds, are "the last institutional intermediary which still stands as a buffer between increasingly impotent individuals and the organized forces of domination."[57] I would put the matter less starkly, but I agree that we must find some way to engage the problem of the family without, at the same time, impugning the *ideal* of these social relations. With all the problems and abuses that we have become conscious of (child and spouse abuse, most importantly wife battering), we sometimes forget that for the vast majority of individuals the family involves a struggle to hold onto meaning and purpose in a social world in which other public and private institutions have been drained of much of their previous legitimacy and normative force. Perhaps one of our best hopes remains a process of debate and disputation so that we do not follow—in this matter of gender development and relations—previous generations of social thinkers who embraced too readily models that quickly rigidified into conceptual tombs.

Notes

Originally published in Barry Richards, ed., *Capitalism and Infancy* (London: FAB Publishers, 1984). Reprinted by permission.

1. Sigmund Freud, "The Question of a *Weltanschauung*," in *New Introductory Lectures on Psycho-Analysis, Standard Edition*, vol. 22 (London: Hogarth Press, 1953), 5–182.

2. Two of the important critiques include Charles Taylor, "Interpretation and the Sciences of Man," *Review of Metaphysics* 26 (1971): 4–51, and "Neutrality in Political Science," in P. Laslett and W. G. Runciman, eds., *Philosophy, Politics, and Society* (Oxford: Blackwell, 1967).

3. Sigmund Freud, "Construction in Analysis," *Standard Edition,* vol. 23 (London: Hogarth Press, 1953), 235–70.

4. Clifford Geertz, *The Interpretation of Cultures* (New York: Basic Books, 1973), 18.

5. See Marie Jahoda, *Freud and the Dilemmas of Psychology* (London: Hogarth Press, 1977), and Jean Bethke Elshtain, *Public Man, Private Woman: Women in Social and Political Thought* (Princeton: Princeton University Press, 1981).

6. I have drawn on an unpublished essay by Charles Taylor, "Social Theory as Practice."

7. It may be possible that good arguments do not necessarily make for good politics, nor that bad arguments necessarily make for bad politics. Most of the time, however, one's assessment of a thinker's arguments and her politics must be of a piece because the thinker herself has forged such a tight link between the two that they cannot be separated. Even if such a link hasn't been forged, I am persuaded this separation cannot, finally, be made in any tidy way.

8. Juliet Mitchell, *Psychoanalysis and Feminism* (New York: Pantheon Books, 1974). Other structuralist renderings include those of Louis Althusser, Jacques Lacan, and Claude Lévi-Strauss.

9. Ibid., 391.

10. Eleanor Burke Leacock, "The Changing Family and Lévi-Strauss, or Whatever Happened to Fathers," *Social Research* 44 (1977): 235–89.

11. Mitchell, *Psychoanalysis and Feminism*, 416.

12. Dorothy Dinnerstein, *The Mermaid and the Minotaur* (New York: Harper and Row, 1976). Dinnerstein's appropriation of Freud, of psychoanalytic theory in general, is highly selective. For example, Freud's metapsychological papers, case studies, and major theoretical renderings are all ignored. Only *Civilization and Its Discontents* and *The Future of an Illusion* are mentioned.

13. Ibid., 33.

14. Ibid.

15. Sigmund Freud, "An Autobiographical Study," *Standard Edition*, vol. 20 (London: Hogarth Press, 1953), 7–70.

16. Jeffrey Lustman, "On Splitting," *The Psychoanalytic Study of the Child* 32 (1977): 119–45.

17. Ibid., 122.

18. Ibid., 130. "It may be that splitting, by permitting oscillating expression of polar clusters of mental content, provides the requisite psychic 'stimulation,' through which sustained boundary phenomena initially emerge."

19. See the discussion of Hobbes in Elshtain, *Public Man, Private Woman*.

20. Dinnerstein, *Mermaid and the Minotaur*, 159.

21. Ibid., 70.

22. Ibid., 210.

23. Ibid., 179. In this Dinnerstein is importantly wrong, as I argue below.

24. L. J. Jordanova, "Natural Facts: A Historical Perspective on Science and Sexuality," in C. P. MacCormack and M. Strathern, eds., *Nature, Culture, and Gender* (Cambridge: Cambridge University Press, 1980).

25. Ibid., 43.

26. Ibid., 65.

27. Ibid., 67.

28. Talcott Parsons, "Age and Sex in the Social Structure of the United States" (1942) and "The Kinship System of the Contemporary United States" (1943). Both essays are reprinted in Parsons, *Essays in Sociological Theory* (New York: Free Press, 1964).

29. Lawrence Stone, *The Family, Sex and Marriage in England, 1500–1800* (New York: Harper and Row, 1979), 416.

30. Nancy Chodorow, *The Reproduction of Mothering: Psychoanalysis and the Sociology of Gender* (Berkeley: University of California Press, 1978), 9.

31. Ibid., 39.

32. Here, for example, is a bit of first-hand empirical evidence Chodorow's functionalist account would have difficulty with. In a recent conversation with three female graduate students I had taught in a political theory seminar at Yale University, I mentioned that when I was a teenager in the rural American West, I loved movies but could go only occasionally because the nearest theater was twelve miles from our home. But I never got over the impact of certain films, particularly seeing Marlon Brando in "On the Waterfront" when I was around ten years of age. Overwhelmed by Brando's sexual power, gripped by the tantalizing threat he posed, I, in the parlance of that more innocent time, "got a crush" on Marlon. But it was not so simple, for I both desired Brando and longed to be Brando. This was not the first, and would not be the last time that I saw myself as, and in, the male character I admired: I, too, could write like Hemingway; I could be as powerful as Brando. I felt constrained in no way whatever by the fact that these were males, and I was a female, therefore doomed to identify overwhelmingly with "Mommy" and to constrain myself thereby. To my astonishment, my graduate students told me similar tales. They, too, were puzzled at feminist accounts that tidied up the world of identification with "object" by simplistically rigidifying the complexity of cross-sexed identifications.

33. Chodorow, *Reproduction of Mothering*, 291 (emphasis mine).

34. Ibid., 8. Chodorow draws uncritically on Gayle Rubin's essay, "The Traffic in Women: Notes on the 'Political Economy' of Sex," in R. R. Reiter, ed., *Toward an Anthropology of Women* (New York: Monthly Review Press, 1975), borrowing Rubin's claim, one seriously contested by most anthropologists, including feminists, that women's relegation to domesticity makes them "less social, less cultural, as well as less powerful than men." Rubin adopts the notion that women, everywhere, have been "goods" to exchange and that the sex/gender system was set up to facilitate such exchange. Given that we no longer require this exchange, we can do away with sex/gender. Within her functionalist rendering, a conclusion emerges, namely, "eradicating gender hierarchy (or gender itself)"; the dream she finds most compelling is a "genderless (though not sexless) society, in which one's sexual anatomy is *irrelevant to who one is*" (204, emphasis mine).

35. See Judith Lorber, Rose Laub Coser, Alice S. Rossi, and Nancy Chodorow, "On the Reproduction of Mothering: A Methodological Debate," *Signs* 6 (1981): 482–515, and Jean Bethke Elshtain, "Against Androgyny," *Telos* 47 (1981): 5–22.

36. The much-maligned Bowlby remains compelling in his stress on quality of care, though we could, surely, counter the notion that this must be an exclusively

female activity. See John Bowlby, *Child Care and the Growth of Love* (Harmondsworth: Penguin Books, 1965), 13, where Bowlby states that the "quality of parental care is what is of vital importance."

37. Zelda Bronstein, "Psychoanalysis without the Father," *Humanities in Society* 3 (1980): 199–212, 200.

38. Ibid., 207.

39. Peggy Reeves Sanday, *Male Power and Female Dominance* (Cambridge: Cambridge University Press, 1981).

40. See Mary Douglas, *Purity and Danger* (London: Routledge and Kegan Paul, 1966).

41. Sanday, *Male Power and Female Dominance*, 133.

42. Ibid., 155.

43. Ibid., 176.

44. Diana Grossman Kahn, "Fathers as Mentors to Daughters," Radcliffe Institute Working Paper, unpublished. Also her "Daughters Comment on the Lesson of Their Mothers' Lives," Radcliffe Institute Working Paper, unpublished.

45. Louise J. Kaplan, *Oneness and Separateness: From Infant to Individual* (New York: Simon and Schuster, 1978), 27. Another important consideration, omitted by feminist gender theorists, is the thought and practice of mothering, or, better, the ways of thinking and acting tied to, or flowing from, engaging in mothering practices, in which mothers engage. Mothers' concerns for their children, the *meaning* of mothering to mother-subjects themselves, in all its complexity and conflict, must be taken up with cogent empathy and theoretical clarity.

46. Ibid., 51.

47. Ibid., 95.

48. One powerfully compelling feminist complaint has been that female children were restricted in early experimentation with their bodies, in "doing" things physical.

49. Rosalind Gould, *Child Studies through Fantasy: Cognitive-Affective Patterns in Development* (New York: Quadrangle Books, 1972), 273.

50. Ibid., 274.

51. Myra Bluebond-Langner, *The Private Worlds of Dying Children* (Princeton: Princeton University Press, 1978), 5.

52. Ibid., 121.

53. Gareth B. Matthews, *Philosophy and the Young Child* (Cambridge, Mass.: Harvard University Press, 1980), 36.

54. Ibid., 86.

55. See Jean Bethke Elshtain, "Against Androgyny" (reprinted as Chap. 13 in this volume). I would also take account of the work of philosophers Richard Wollheim, Bernard Williams, and Merleau-Ponty on identity.

56. Sigmund Freud, "The Ego and the Id," *Standard Edition*, vol. 19 (London: Hogarth Press, 1953), 12–59. Cf. Richard Wollheim, "The Mind and the Mind's Image of Itself," in Wollheim, *On Art and the Mind* (Cambridge, Mass.: Harvard University Press, 1974), 53.

57. Bronstein, "Psychoanalysis without the Father," 207.

13

Against Androgyny

Although androgyny has become a pervasive feature in contemporary feminist discourse and is widely accepted as a model for a rational reordering of our presently inegalitarian sexual and social arrangements, the notion itself has rarely come in for systematic criticism.[1] It promises a shiny new world where human beings no longer exhibit "negative and distorted personality characteristics," where the "ideal androgynous being . . . could have no internal blocks to attaining self-esteem."[2] Yet, its near irresistibility requires explanation. Why is it that to be against androgyny leads one to be immediately branded as a "naturalist," an "essentialist," or even worse, a "sociobiologist," a "biological reductionist," or the representative of other obnoxious and reactionary viewpoints? The implication is that if one truly understood androgynist claims one would stop thrashing about in the darkness of gendered distortions and join up with the chorus of the future: Androgyny Now! If one refuses to join the chorus and rejects the various ready-made labels androgynists use to ignore their opponents, one must be prepared to make a case for an alternative vision of human psychosexual and social identity as one feature of a potentially emancipatory politics. Repudiating the elide into degendered homogeneity, does not necessarily mean to reproduce our current, unacceptable sexual *division* and our structured sexual inequality.

Androgyny is an old term to which feminist discourse has given new life. In mythology, androgyny was the fusion of male and female, including secondary sexual characteristics, into a single being. This fusion was believed to exert an effeminizing influence, that is, the female characteristics tended to swamp the male. The original androgyne, Hermaphrodite, son of Hermes and Aphrodite, is forced, against his will, into union with a female nymph. The nymph, overcome with desire, snares and literally insinuates herself into the unwilling Hermaphrodite until they are one flesh. According to May, "This vision of female power is one of the persistent threads in the idea of androgyny, at least as seen through male eyes."[3] In the myth's original meaning, the concrete physical intermingling of male and female ushered in a re-union between these formerly separate, sexed beings, and this myth is part of a continuing tradition whose vagaries can be traced through diverse modes of historic representation.

The resurgence of the image of the androgyne throughout history is evocative and suggests that human beings have always been vexed with the existence of two clearly distinct sorts of being within the broader generic frame, human being. For some, this differentness has been an occasion for celebration. For others, it is a concern; and for a few, a calamity. But human beings generally have fantasies, at one time or another, of sexual fusion, of becoming the "other," of wrenching free from the physical constraint or limit of being one sex in one body. The seeds of envy are here, along with the seedbed of narcissistic fantasies of grandiose limitlessness—of attaining what Freud called the "oceanic feeling," if necessary by eradicating the stubborn "other" embodied (quite literally) within the opposite sex. Androgyny, then, is an ancient myth reflecting and refracting those human yearnings, urgent fears and fantasies surrounding human embodiment.

But something happened to androgyny on its way to becoming feminist dogma. Human bodies disappeared—they were dismantled, dismembered, or, at least, dis-remembered. Androgyny was dusted off, stripped of its deeply sensual and sexed roots and its previous mythic meaning. In place of the body, contemporary androgynists put "free will" or "flexible sex roles" or the "union of positively valued traits." Reaching back to androgyny's Greek roots, one feminist philosopher neatly disentangles the term from its mythological foundation and comes up with a tidy etymological derivation, as if the notion originated in a Greek version of Webster's New Abridged Dictionary. "The term 'androgyny,'" she writes, "has Greek roots: *andros* means man and *gyne,* woman. An androgynous person would combine some of each of the characteristic traits, skills, and interests that we now associate with stereotypes of masculinity and femininity."[4] Hermaphrodite and his lusting nymph give way to "the ideal androgynous being," one "who transcends those old categories in such a way as to be able to develop positive human potentialities . . . he or she would have no internal blocks to attaining self-esteem." "It is the flexibility and union of positively valued traits that is critical," writes another feminist literary critic.[5] For some androgynists, androgyny is deployed to knock down what they see as a conceptual prop for systemic sexual inequality in traditionalist presumptions that sexual differences have predetermined social outcomes. For most androgynists, however, androgyny is put forth primarily as a portrait of the ideal human being, one who has, along with the concrete physicality imbedded in the andro-

gyne myth, sloughed off *all* "limiting" sexed definitions, biological and social: "only androgynous people can attain the full human potential possible
given our present level of material and social resources. . . . Androgynous
women would be just as assertive as men about their own needs in a love
relationship. . . . Androgynous men would be more sensitive and aware. . . .
They would be more concerned with the feelings of all people."[6] Human
beings in the here and now can partially succeed in transcending sexual
gender. But the full achievement of an androgynous world is possible only
with the total elimination of sex roles and the "disappearance . . . of any
biological need for sex to be associated with procreation." At that fateful
moment, "there would be no reason why such a society could not transcend
sexual gender."[7]

A vision of pure positivity emerges: an ideal, all-purpose, abstract person
with all nastiness expunged, bodilyness removed, and differences (which
might be points of fruitful tension, debate, or just interest) eliminated. The
androgyne is nonspecific with reference to social location; he or she is "at
home" anywhere, is free-floating with reference to all traditional loci of
human identity. A feminist sociologist, writing on "The Androgynous Life,"
suggests as her ideal person one who "combines characteristics usually attributed to men with characteristics usually attributed to women."[8] The road
to positive androgyny requires the elimination by fiat of any negative irritants in the image. Feminist psychologist Judith M. Bardwick sees the androgyne as the next mental health "ideal." In the feminist future, the "healthy"
individual will be the androgynous man or woman. "We would then expect
both nurturance and competence, openness and objectivity, compassion
and competitiveness from both women and men, as individuals, according
to what they are doing."[9]

A second feminist psychologist, working within a behavior modification
framework, reports that androgyny "does not lie in some far-off feminist
future. Androgyny is here. The research findings tell us so."[10] Androgyny is
already with us, it turns out, because "sex is an easy and obvious independent variable." Abstractly predefining sex as the "*assignment*" an obstetrician
makes at birth "on the basis of genitalia" (as if this were a contingent and
arbitrary matter), the voice of behaviorism finds it clear that sex "is primarily . . . a social fact not a biological fact."[11] We exhibit sex differences, or there
are sex differences, she claims, because people *believe* there are sex differences and act accordingly. Were it not for this stubborn belief, and the sexist
practices it shores up or that rise on the basis of it, "It seems clear that given
the same social situation, the same reinforcement contingencies, the same
expectancies, both sexes will react similarly." Finally, she notes "it is always
satisfying to strike down another sex difference."[12] Having struck them all

down by fiat, she proclaims us to be in the androgynist future, though it is a pity most of us seem unaware of it yet.

Feminist literary scholars seem to find the androgynous myth particularly compelling as the depiction of the ideal artist and the perfect creative mind. As Virginia Woolf writes: "If one is a man, still the woman part of the brain must have effect; and a woman also must have intercourse with the man in her. Coleridge perhaps meant this when he said that a great mind is androgynous. It is when this fusion takes place that the mind is fully fertilized and uses all its faculties."[13] Some critics who celebrate the Bloomsbury group, of which Woolf was a member, as uniquely creative, attribute "this enormous intellectual and artistic productivity" to living the androgynous life.[14]

Androgyny advocates agree that the achievement of a fully androgynous society requires major reconstruction of the human subject. For some, an enlightened androgynous vanguard can move ahead right now to lead androgynous lives. But for society to become truly androgynous, for a world in which one's sexuality is as "innocuous as current reactions to hair color," some sort of social revolution which will bring forth reconstructed androgynous human subjects is required.

A fairly innocuous, simplistic version of the thesis of androgyny as the goal of feminist political ideology is featured in Yates's "androgynous paradigm," which "represents a women- and men-equal-to-each-other view. . . . It holds that tasks, values, and behavior traditionally assigned to one sex or the other should be shared by them both."[15] Yates claims that the "androgynous mode" as "the operating paradigm" is "the most revolutionary of the concepts informing the new wave of feminism. . . . It suggests that men should be equal to women as well as women equal to men. . . . The androgynous position offers a model of cooperation and of rationality."[16] Firestone, on the other hand, offers the extreme androgynous apocalypse as cultural revolution with "the reintegration of the Male (Technological Mode) with the Female (Aesthetic Mode), to create an androgynous culture surpassing the highs of either cultural stream, or even of the sum of their integrations. More than a marriage, rather an abolition of the cultural categories themselves, a mutual cancellation—a matter-antimatter explosion, ending with a poof! culture itself. We shall not miss it. We shall no longer need it."[17] Though not all feminists explicitly adopt visions of an androgynous world, many embrace milder, implicit versions of the androgyny agenda with arguments for the total elimination of all "sex roles" (as if every activity in which a male or female engaged could be pared down to a role, an abstract sociological construct, and thereby readily eliminated by sociopolitical fiat) and the achievement of a society in which all roles are freely exchanged and no one is tied, in any way, to a role that reflects gender identity or definition (if indeed such persists at all).

What androgyny offers—or seems to—to its feminist adherents is, first, an ideal of what human beings can become once they break the bonds of overly restrictive sexed definitions and, second, a vision of an egalitarian future in which all forms of sexual domination and inequality, now buttressed, they argue, by beliefs concerning "natural" sex differences, will have been quite overcome and, finally, a vision of the artist and the creative individual as one who has transcended the muck of matter and attained a purity of thought and expression within the rarified ideal of androgyny. All this—and more—is pegged on a term that falls wholly outside the frame of political discourse as the stock of common, if not wholly agreed-upon, notions available to social participants when they act politically. Androgyny does not arouse political debate and public challenge in the way calls for social justice of equality can, and do. Indeed, part of androgyny's appeal must be the promise it holds forth for a brave new world attained, somehow, through human beings rationally and freely willing to have done with the sexed-old and to embrace the degendered-new, with the androgynous vanguard, through the force of example and a superior lifestyle, leading the way.

Beyond androgynists' explicit commitments there are a number of unacknowledged presumptions imbedded within androgynous discourse which help to account, first, for why this "new" notion of androgyny caught on and remains a standard feature in much feminist thought, and, second, for where the androgynists ought to be located within a wider frame of discursive practices and theoretical traditions. There are two broad features that move implicitly through various androgynists' evocations. Both locate androgynist discourse securely within the boundaries of classical liberal thought. First, *all* androgynists propound as an article of faith, an example of right reason, and an instance of scientific truth that human nature is more or less plastic. Writes an androgynist philosopher, "it seems . . . plausible to assume that human nature is plastic and moldable."[18] More correctly, she should have observed that this "seems plausible" if one operates within a framework of liberal environmentalism. That this is where the androgynists implicitly locate themselves becomes clear when this plasticity is questioned, for the interlocutor is slotted into a fixed, static essentialist posture that reflects perfectly one of the received antinomies of liberal discourse. A picture of the human being as Silly Putty or a Blank Slate goes under the contemporary name "sex-role socialization theory" or, sometimes, "social learning theory." The view is that children acquire their patterns of behavior through a process of external reinforcements. Sex-role behavior is maintained by these same external forces. As these forces change, or reinforcements alter, different "behaviors" will be reinforced and called forth.[19]

Even feminist critics of some versions of the androgynist thesis call upon environmental determinism to buttress the case for their own alternative. For example: a philosopher who questions what she calls "monoandrogynism" (the adoption of a single, uniform androgynist standard for all, though even that is preferable, she says, to what we now have) and opts for an alternative she dubs "polyandrogynism" (in which more options would be open to individuals along masculine-feminine boundaries or markers) reaffirms that human beings are totally products of their external environment. This means the only question for her is: which version of androgynism, given that each alternative androgynous society will socialize people either to make everyone androgynous in one way or to help everyone make themselves androgynous in a number of ways, "is preferable for a hypothetical future society."[20]

The thesis that people are blank slates, totally molded by external pressures, makes the androgynous project sound feasible. One creates the androgynous society and gets the ideal androgynous product. (Of course it is not easy to square the commitment to a prescriptive environmentalism with the robust androgynist voluntarism also embraced by some, an elite who have reconstructed themselves, thus showing others the way.) The presumption is that males and females are, "for all reasonable intents and purposes alike. Differences between them . . . are chiefly due to culture and conditioning."[21] This means that by eliminating the force of present social conditioning what will be liberated is not diverse human potentialities but human homogeneities! Millett declares that "the sexes are inherently in everything alike, *save* reproductive systems, secondary sexual characteristics, orgasmic capacity, and genetic and morphological structure."[22] Her argument that we treat sexual reproduction, male and female sexual responsivity, the entire complex structure of our genetic inheritance together with our morphological characteristics as trivial, uninteresting, and unimportant facts about ourselves is an apt instance of one of the androgynists' opening moves: to cancel out the significance of human sexual differences, in advance of launching any inquiry or making sustained arguments, by treating sexual identity as an arbitrary, external, and contingent phenomenon.

This leads to the second major fulcrum which moves within androgynist thinking, that is, the expressed conviction that the body is a prison, a constraint, an unacceptable limitation from which human beings must be liberated and which they will eventually transcend. If the body is a prison for androgynists, the female body is life imprisonment with torture to boot.

One finds repeated expressions of contempt for the female body.[23] Those who are not contemptuous are often merely dismissive of the body, or they reduce its complex richness as a human standpoint in the world with statements about "biological disadvantages"; for the female, her "role in biological reproduction."[24] Steps must be taken to erase all these biological disadvantages, all the limitations which inhere in sexual identity. The need to hold the body at arm's length and to view embodiment as a trap and a straitjacket is clear.[25]

Androgynists, then, adopt two tacit presuppositions: (1) They treat the human body reductionistically as "nothing but . . ." or "no more than . . ." and *must* see, within the iron cage of their liberal dualism, those who question their rigidity as themselves rigid "essentialists" or "naive naturalists"; thus they evade the possibility that human beings may have a nature of some sort that is not exhausted with reference to the social forces that have impinged upon it. For androgynists, the world revolves around a series of pure opposites: pure freedom vs. total determinism, nature vs. nurture, reason vs. passion, mind vs. body, and so on. (2) They embrace a thoroughgoing environmentalist determinism as the only sure and secure avenue to human reconstruction along androgynist lines. In the androgynist new world, because the right kinds of reinforcers will be present, human beings will exhibit all and only the positive traits of the other. Given their dualist starting point, in which other minds can exist only by inference or analogy, one is presented with the image of an aggregate of androgynes, complete unto themselves and, like *homo economicus* in contract theory, the androgyne is a being fundamentally unchanged by any human relation. For when one reaches the stage of pure androgynous positivity, where no negative intrudes to create friction ("no internal blocks"), and where one lives in a world populated only by other positivities, there can be nothing like a determinate negation anytime, anywhere. At this fateful juncture, social being and social consciousness will have become one. There will be nothing for the dialectic to work on or work through: no rough edges, no unseemly spots, no lines or ruptures, nor points of friction through which doubt, questioning, negation, might erupt.

A case against androgyny can be made in terms of what is required for human beings to locate themselves spatially and temporally within a natural and social world. When we take the human body as a starting point, we locate a corporeal entity of a particular kind within a complex world. From birth this entity is implicated in relations with others. What Freud once called the "momentous and fateful" prolonged dependency of human infants on adult others is assumed embodiment, for children are born as helpless and totally dependent embodied beings. The human body is part of the material reality of nature: we experience that world Schutz calls "paramount reality" (both "inner" and "outer") in and through our bodies. Within the sphere of daily human life, "the individual locates himself as a body, as operating physically in the world, and as meeting the resistance of fellow men as well as of things."[26] The starting point of each and every human being is his or her particular location in space and time; this is, inescapably, the body.

That a social theorist must defend the universally true proposition that human beings can experience the world only in and through their bodies attests to the continued sway of the dualisms inherent in the psychological principles which flow from classical liberal thought.[27] If the androgynists' implicit denials or explicit repudiations of human embodiment were spelled out, the claims would go something like this: (1) personal identity (that which I am) is entirely distinct from my body; (2) the body cannot be said to know, nor can it serve as a vehicle for, or mediator of, knowledge; (3) the only genuine "I" is a rational ego which is analytically distinct from that embodiment to which it enjoys a contingent relation. The implication would be that to specify biological features of human existence, and to draw these into the frame of an overall account of human identity, is to slide, irrevocably, into some sort of universalist, totalist, or ontological trap. In this way, through such evasions, debate on these matters is quashed. Those who argue "my body, myself," and insist upon incorporating biological imperatives into a comprehensive account of the human subject are labeled, within the androgynist frame, as embracing the notion that there are rigid, fixed, innate givens in human nature that appear invariantly and identically in all times and in all places.[28] This is palpable nonsense, but it is understandable and convenient nonsense. It enables androgynists to avoid engaging their strongest opponents, and it reaffirms various antinomies—freedom vs. determinism, innate vs. social, heredity vs. environment, biological explanation vs. social explanation—as mutually exclusive alternatives.

To break down and through the rigidities implicit in androgynism one can begin by asking, simply, what having a relationship which persists over time requires. In order for a relationship to persist for a single day, or even one hour, each party to that relationship must have a continuing identity, must perceive herself as acting and speaking in and through a body which situates her and from which she moves, sees, acts, and can be held accountable for her actions.[29] She must also perceive of the other as a being with similar temporal continuity, one with whom she shares a common humanity, for he, like she, occupies space in the temporal world. The solipsism implicit in classical liberal personality theory cannot account for real relations between persons, for it is not able to recognize others as beings like oneself save by analogy and inference. The recognition of the humanity of the other is not, in itself, sufficient to constitute a persisting relationship. For that to happen, personal identity over time must hold.

There could be no social relations if each person began each day as if it were their first: if individuals lacked memories tied to a sense of self as persisting over time and in space. Memory requires a *particular* history of having lived, as a body, in a social world. Human action turns on such considerations as well. These dimensions of personal identity are part of a human, and thus social, context of which a human, and bodily, subject is the basis. The only way we can know that the same person is in the body, whether our own or some other's, at different times is if we grasp persistence over time.[30] Another essential feature which makes human relationship possible is language. It allows us to differentiate and to classify reality so that we can identify more or less constant subjects and objects of reference. Through language we may single out a particular so-and-so as the same so-and-so, one who may share certain properties in common with some larger, generic grouping; but he is, as well, a unique individual with such-and-such properties.[31]

If bodily identity as one feature of spatiotemporal persistence is an inescapable feature of the human condition, is the division of humanity into two distinct sexes an essential and important, or a contingent and relatively trivial, aspect of this identity? Males and females, of course, are beings who share in the most basic general characteristics; yet they differ along recognizable and distinctive lines. To introduce the sex distinction is not to surreptitiously inject considerations of gender at this point in the argument. To insist that "my body, myself" are temporally and spatially defined, and that this body will either be a male or a female body, says nothing in itself about what we call "masculine" or "feminine" identities or psychologies. In androgynous discourse, remember, the presumption is that the sex distinction *itself* can and must be transcended or eliminated (at least in maximalist statements of androgyny); that human beings can somehow return to a state of nature and to an innocent eye and start to build up language and culture all over again, junking all inherited forms, particularly those grounded in the differentiation between the sexes. This is problematic because important distinctions, like male and female, are not only imbedded in language, they are constitutive of a way of life. To see basic notions as simply or purely arbitrary and contingent is to trash centuries of human concern, fear, desire, denial, passion, rage, joy, longing, hope, and despair in a fit of ahistorical hubris. For human beings do not make distinctions nor draw visions about the most basic things—sexuality, birth, life, death—in wholly capricious ways, but to certain vital ends and purposes. To presume one can simply blur or obliterate even the most fundamental distinction between human beings presumes a great deal.

If one agrees that the sex distinction is ineliminable and important, does this mean one simply acquiesces in received notions of "masculinity" and "femininity"? Clearly not. To determine whether or not the claim that bodily identity is a feature of personal identity implies that a sexed identity, maleness or femaleness, is also necessarily linked with bodily identity, we must turn to a developmental account of the human subject. The human subject is a creation, an emergent from a developmental process over time, in history. Androgynous arguments, notoriously, omit *any* coherent developmental account of the human subject. This is explainable in part by the indebtedness of androgynists to liberal notions of abstract individuals. But there is another reason: androgyny is primarily, in most instances exclusively, focused on adult males and females. Children, save as so much raw material to be molded into future androgynes, are missing from the picture. It is far easier to speak of "mere biology" or "transcending sex roles" if one ignores birth, infancy, and childhood developments.

The developmental account owes much to Freud's theory of human development as a dynamic, ineluctably biological and social process. For Freud the human body "registers itself" through a complex inner-outer dialectic in which the human infant makes internal representations to itself of its own body. This account is a powerful theoretical alternative to dualist, solipsistic, environmentally deterministic, and exclusively ontological notions of the subject.[32] The argument goes roughly like this: from its first moments the infant experiences its own body as a source of pleasure and unpleasure. This goes beyond the registering of sensations of hunger, pain, or pleasure. It implicates the infant as an active, not merely a passive being, in the construction of an inner world through the literal "taking in" of its own body's surface as part of a wider "external" reality. Given this process, the human "I," the self, is always, importantly, an embodied "I." The infant simply does not have the cognitive or neurological structure and organization to make clear distinctions between inner and outer, internal and external. But the infant does take in with eyes, ear, mouth, and touch that external world. Slowly, the "I" is built up in part through complex representations of the child's body, "inner" and "outer," and the bodies of others with whom the child is implicated in exquisitely social relations from the start. The surface of the child's body is from the first "a place from which both external and internal perceptions may spring." It is *seen* like any other object, but to the *touch* it yields two sorts of sensations, one of which may be equivalent to an internal perception. The "I," then, is "first and foremost a *bodily ego:* it is not merely a surface entity, but is itself the projection of a surface."[33]

Our corporeality bears powerful imperatives for how we come to know. The fact that our knowing is essentially tied to our experiences of ourselves as bodies means that the mind and its activities must be conceived in a manner that is "tinged with spatiality." "We are at home in our mind somewhat as in a body," argues Wollheim.[34] The corporeal ego plays a vital role in the child's epistemic constitution of his or her identity. A child can neither physically negate nor conceptually transcend the manner in which his or her body registers itself, and that body must be understood within the terms of each successive stage of psychosexual maturation. The particular meeting of mind-body which emerges from this developmental theory is no chance encounter but involves powerful imperatives. The child evokes the body and its processes as he or she learns. The body involves and mediates ways of knowing. It is neither a substanceless structure, nor a hollow shell, nor inert matter to which no meaning can be imputed or applied. Our most original experiences must be understood with reference to an embodied engagement with the world.

Nothing so far demands that the "I" conceive of itself as belonging to one gender or another from the start; indeed, no such differentiation is possible until the child begins what Freud calls its early "sexual researches."[35] Certainly, by the time the child is five or six, if not before, he or she will have distinguished two types of bodily-sexed beings, though the child often remains uncertain as to the meaning of this distinction and confused on how to make determinations in specific cases. To live in a sexed, social universe is not, necessarily, to inhabit a world in which differential evaluations are placed on "maleness" or "femaleness."[36]

Gender identity, a notion of masculinity and femininity or maleness and femaleness, is one feature in the child's identity formation as he or she enters puberty and young adulthood and, simultaneously, a more complex social world. Children locate themselves in that world on the basis of gender; children seek some measure of security in these matters, for they are of preeminent concern and urgency to them. Rosenthal observes that when Dante wishes to imagine persons in hell, he imagines them as deprived of the security of the knowledge that "one is a man, if one is one, or that one is a woman, if one is one." She continues: "To have outlines and insides that—for oneself and others—*fluctuate dangerously* is to be in hell."[37] For androgynists, the child's concerns are construed as a behavioral response to environmental stimuli exclusively, thus denying the child his or her own integrity as a self-constituting, embodied subject. Androgynists claim that it is possible to achieve *psychological* androgyny or nondifferentiation along markers of maleness and femaleness, as well as "masculinity" and "femininity," without positing bodily identity as a prior condition. This surely begs the issue. For what androgynists must figure out is how to prevent the child from becoming intensely interested in his or her own body and the bodies of others similar to yet different from himself or herself. The child lives out a deep sense of urgency in and through his or her body—is it whole? is it strong? is it attractive? will it grow? am I sick? am I the "right" kind of boy-girl?—and will be unmoved by appeals to transcend or eliminate the importance of gender, for that is precisely what he or she is trying to figure out, work on, and work through.

In the final analysis, however, even the urge to eliminate concerns with gender, to try to institute a human condition in which human beings do not care what "biological sex" they or anybody else may be, in which the distinction between males and females has ceased to be a central and interesting feature of human life, is incoherent and impossible short of the mutation of human beings.

What would a world in which sex distinctions were ignored or denied look like? First, it would be an inchoate muddle, for maleness and femaleness (that is, our corporeal sexed selves) *are* our ways of experiencing the world. In Winch's words, "masculinity or femininity are not just *components* in . . . life, they are its *mode.*"[38] (Winch here refers to male and female as human sexed identity, not to social and cultural notions of the masculine and the feminine.) Second, it would be a hypocritical world of lies and denials. Repression of infantile sexuality would have to go far beyond anything we have known. Children would have to be surveilled night and day in order that any moves to touch, look at, sniff, or play with their bodies could be prohibited and deflected. Only in this way could one forestall the child's inner representations of the surface of its body. Of course, psychic representations of inner drives and states would continue, but the child would be forbidden to see or touch its own or other bodies. Children would be barraged with the insistence that any differences they discovered, despite efforts to preclude childish sexual researches, did not matter, were of no interest, and were inessential aspects of human life. Not only would this be a cruel deception, it would hamper the development of the self, which is grounded in the child's ability to differentiate objects, things, and events along lines of what is important. For a child such distinctions include big-small, family-not family, pleasure-unpleasure, my body-other bodies, male bodies-female bodies.[39] The first great problem which exercises the child concerns his or her body and the bodies of others. Should parents suppress these "burning question(s)," they will damage the child's "genuine instinct of research" and "begin to erode his confidence in his parents."[40]

The rigid suppression of knowledge of sex distinctions or the denial of their importance would undermine the moral order and erode social life.

The category of the serious and the less serious is, as Bernard Williams points out, "itself a moral category, and . . . it is itself a moral criticism to say of somebody that he is regarding a serious issue as trivial or a trivial issue as serious."[41] Those who regard the serious issue of the real, not fantasized, distinctions between the sexes as a trivial issue which the androgynist revolution will eliminate are engaged in a form of abstracted and wishful thinking that posits free-floating pictures as genuine human alternatives. Such pictures ignore social forms and the many-layered complexity of the persons who live in and through them, who *must* live in and through them. History is in some sense both a *physical* and a *psychological* category, for historical accounts by human beings are "about claims to operate with one's body in definite relations."[42] In Showalter's worlds: "The androgynous mind is . . . a utopian projection of the ideal artist: calm, stable, unimpeded by consciousness of sex . . . like other utopian projections, her vision is inhuman. Whatever else one may say of androgyny, it represents an escape from the confrontation with femaleness and maleness."[43]

The androgynist might respond to these charges by insisting that a notion of psychological androgyny need not *ignore* distinctions between the sexes; it simply holds forth the possibility that these distinctions, assimilated to sex roles, a sexual division of labor, and inequality between the sexes, can be muted, disregarded, or become irrelevant insofar as the social world is concerned and insofar as the development of a psychologically androgynous individual is concerned. These are separate and distinct claims. Consider the notion of the "psychologically androgynous" individual. The claim goes like this: without forcing children to ignore their bodies, or the differences between male and female bodies, it is possible through intensive, overt intervention on the part of socializers to downplay sex differences as an *important* distinction between persons. It is, in other words, possible to resist gender identification without deploying the repressive measures previously indicated as needed in order to create children who view sex distinctions as inessential and not terribly interesting characteristics of self and others.

The problem with this claim is that it is grounded in no explanatory account of child development which incorporates both theoretical and empirical dimensions, offers no historic examples, has no base in ordinary language, is buttressed by no clinical evidence: it is a purely abstract claim, repeated rhetorically and pronounced a priori without reference to actual, historically situated human beings. The motive force behind this utopian ideal appears to be a fantasy of the indistinguishability or interchangeability of selves, a wish to return to an undifferentiated state of symbiotic oneness with others or with *an* other. In Secor's terms, the notion of androgyny is that of a person "devoid of context."[44] The process of growing up involves breaking away from such a symbiotic fusion. Only then does the child begin his or her own psychic life. Urges to return to a condition of nonindividuation are the "projection into the future of a totally regressive urge."[45] This makes of androgyny a "limiting and probably reactionary concept."[46] Visions that require that we abandon the distinctions, differences, separations, and divisions essential to any coherent identity and existence are portraits of epistemic confusion and abstract ahistoricity.

Nothing has been claimed thus far—that bodily identity is a necessary feature of personal identity and that personal identity is necessarily a sexual or sexed identity—that either presupposes, entails, or buttresses the continued social and political inequality between the sexes. The sex distinctions of a biological or psychological nature which have been linked historically to inequality between the sexes are not necessarily thus linked. Will inequality always turn on, or require, positing alleged differences between the sexes which then serve both as the reason for and the justification of inegalitarian outcomes? Although sex distinctions have served as a justification for sex inequality in the past, these differences, to the extent that they are not relevant to the distinctions being made, need not serve this function in the future. That is a matter for political struggle. Indeed, the argument that some putative sameness or blending of identities between males and females is the *only* safe and secure foundation for social equality has the precise effect of displacing a political focus upon structures of inequality in favor of advancing abstract rhetorical claims about the personalities of persons.

Androgyny as a social and political ideal is confused. Its proponents offer no coherent account of the androgynous society nor how we are to achieve one. More importantly, when androgyny touches upon or alludes to certain worthy political ideals and principles, these ideals and principles are more coherently and powerfully couched in a political language which is already a feature of political debate and life. Androgyny as a social imperative tends to get conflated with role sharing and with the simplistic notion of each sex exhibiting characteristics stereotypically held of the other. Thus women would compete in the marketplace for the rewards of the society, men would do household tasks, etc. But androgyny as a social category ultimately fails to come to grips with the realities of a world which denies to a majority of its men and women those social goods which characterize the lives of the privileged. Androgyny forces attention back on the blurring or merging of sexual characteristics and diverts attention away from the categories of *class* and *race* as determinants of the social positions of large numbers of male and female participants within American society.[47] Androgyny can neither help to forge, nor even identify, collective movements for social change. Finally, androgynism rests on the proposition that the problem for women lies in the relations which pertain between men and women.

Androgyny, like any term of discourse with a long history, is located in the web of its traditional mythic and symbolic meanings; thus it cannot serve, not now and not in the future, as a politically resonant cry for social change in the way, say, "freedom" or "equality," two powerful terms of *political* discourse imbedded within a net of political meanings, can. No movement for social change will be fought under the banner "androgyny," but many have been and will be waged under the banners "freedom," "equality," "liberty," "peace." The feminist thinker who would articulate a theory of social change that may also serve as concrete historical analysis recognizes that equality, unlike androgyny, is a concept with common, shared social and political meanings. It can serve as a weapon to put pressure upon social practices and institutions in a way that androgyny, lacking this critical purchase, cannot.[48] Arguments for equality of respect and treatment are more securely lodged in the insistence by the political thinker that there are characteristics and qualities all persons *qua* persons share. To state this does not require denying that there are important and vital differences between persons, as groups and individuals, as well. To assert equality as a statement about persons can be deployed as a powerful wedge to press for more egalitarian arrangements. This presumption forces the analyst, if he or she contends that all persons are equal to one another in the most important respects with reference to their shared social universe but finds that inequality in treatment exists, to look to those structures implicated in such differences in treatment. The qualities we all share as sentient creatures who have a capacity to suffer, to feel pain, to experience joy, to possess moral capacities, and so on, override, for purposes of pressing for social equality, those other characteristics not shared by all.[49] There is a dignity, as well as a political resonance to this argument; on both scores, androgynism will forever fall short.

This tour through the inner workings of androgyny and its implications suggests some modest conclusions. The first is that we would all be better off, as well as much closer to creating a world to our heart's desiring, if we accepted our bodies in better grace and recognized that a *sexual difference* is neither an affront, nor an outrage, nor a narcissistic injury. A *sexual division,* on the other hand, one that separates the sexes and locks each into a vector of isolated, alienated activity *is* both a deep wound to the psychosexual identity of the human subject and specific damage to an overly rigidified system of stratification and specialization. In order to fight the destructiveness of the system of sexual division, one must be able to say that the body is good and that a recognition and acceptance of sex differences makes us all richer, not poorer; that these differences enhance rather than constrict our world. The androgynist assault on human sexed identities bespeaks, at base, a contempt for the body, and this contempt will invariably manifest itself in other ways and spheres.

To offer an account of the human being as a subject operating within a body, in a sociohistoric context within which she launches claims, against and toward which she defines herself in determinate relations, is to repudiate abstracted androgynes. Yet the vexing question remains: *Why* androgyny? Why did this notion catch fire? There is yet another, unacknowledged imperative at work within the androgyny debate that may help to explain why the notion is so tenacious. This is an urge located on the level of discourse itself. Androgynism is an instance of what Hegel calls thought which "pacifies itself." Having come face to face with daunting philosophical questions, vexing debates over meaning and purposes, moral dilemmas, and political puzzles, androgynists turned in upon themselves. One way out of their difficulties is to leapfrog over them. This can look like a solution, but it is, in fact, a conceptual copout and a theoretical dead end. Androgyny is sometimes overused in the way "dialectical" is: whenever a thinker bumps up against a stubborn theoretical, analytic, or moral dilemma and seeks a tidy way out that has the additional advantage of being politically correct, he may sprinkle on a "dialectic" here or an "androgyny" there like so many conceptual croutons.

Androgyny, at base, is a very bizarre idea. As featured in feminist discourse, it is a discursive artifact having no essential connection to anything other than itself. It is tied to no real (natural or social) object. Androgynists lodge rhetorical claims involving wholly unreal characterizations of abstract futures rather than struggling to create a set of reflective possibilities for human emancipation within the historic and social world. Androgyny *imposes* a rationalistic external standard upon human subjects and finds them wanting (unenlightened, irrational, living in bad faith, clinging to old superstitions, or wallowing in false consciousness). The androgynous faith is endlessly self-confirming. Not making contact with reality, it need never bump up against opposition, binds, tensions, paradoxes, ironies. A strange purity enters, and the endpoint is silence: the silence of the human subject who cannot, by definition, speak as an *androgynous* subject. In this way androgynism helps to "bury the problems which have gathered behind the contradictory desires and refusals of contemporary heterosexuality."[50] It proffers no ideal toward which people may reasonably aspire. In its dream of the fusion of social being with social consciousness it depoliticizes by eliminating all lines of fault through which critical ruptures might be possible. Androgynists offer up only a politics of displacement which leaves human subjects stuck, once again, in a sexual politics that aims to desexualize the subject. The androgynist impulse is in league, not at odds, with the social world in its primary force. If the androgynist project were activated, it would speed up processes of rationalization; it would further homogenize human subjects. Having first reduced the richness and mystery of the human body as a point of reference, a locus for action, a foundation for identity, and a way of knowing, androgynists point to their one-dimensional creation and go on to confuse real human beings with their impoverished vision. Androgynists are the bland leading the bland.

Notes

Originally published in *Telos* 47 (spring 1981). Reprinted by permission.

1. There have been some doubters and critics, but they have most often concentrated on but *one* feature or dimension of the androgynist argument. See, for example, Cynthia Secor, "Androgyny: An Early Reappraisal," *Women's Studies*, 2, no. 2 (1974): 161–69; Daniel A. Harris, "Androgyny: The Sexist Myth in Disguise," in ibid., 171–84; Elaine Showalter, *A Literature of Their Own: British Women Novelists from the Brontës to Lessing* (Princeton: Princeton University Press, 1977), pp. 263–89; most recently, Robert May, *Sex and Fantasy: Patterns of Male and Female Development* (New York: Norton, 1980). Interestingly, radical feminism's leading theologian, Mary Daly, also rejects androgyny but for this reason: she wants her woman to be altogether free from any taint by the old man. See her essay, "The Qualitative Leap beyond Patriarchal Religion," *Quest* 1, no. 4 (1975): 229ff.

2. Ann Ferguson, "Androgyny as an Ideal for Human Development," in Mary Vetterling-Braggin, Frederick A. Elliston, and Jane English, *Feminism and Philosophy* (Totowa, N.J.: Littlefield, Adam, 1977), 45–69.

3. May, *Sex and Fantasy*, 165.

4. Ferguson, "Androgynous Ideal," 45–46.

5. Carolyn Heilbrun, *Toward a Recognition of Androgyny* (New York: Knopf, 1973).

6. Ferguson, "Androgyny as Ideal," 62–63.

7. Ibid., 65.

8. Caroline Bird, *Born Female* (New York: Pocket Books, 1968), xi.

9. Judith M. Bardwick,"Androgyny and Humanistic Goods, or Goodbye, Cardboard People," in *The American Woman: Who Will She Be?*, ed. Mary Louise McBee and Kathryn N. Blake (Beverly Hills, Calif.: Glencoe Press, 1974), 61. Bardwick's formulation is an open invitation to a new and terrible form of social engineering. There are dangers implicit in any normative ideal of mental health but hers, couched as it is, as the most perfect, most rational, most *healthy* possible, would exert terrible pressure on

real, unrecalcitrant human "material." For a discussion of American feminism's long links with, among others, the social engineering impulse, see William Leach, *True Love and Perfect Union: The Feminist Reform of Sex and Society* (New York: Basic Books, 1980).

10. Kathleen E. Grady, "Androgyny Reconsidered," in Juanita H. Williams, ed., *Psychology of Women: Selected Readings* (New York: Norton, 1979), 172–77.

11. Ibid., 174.

12. Ibid., 176.

13. Quoted in Showalter, *A Literature of Their Own*, 287.

14. Gayle Graham Yates, *What Do Women Want: The Ideas of the Movement* (Cambridge, Mass.: Harvard University Press, 1975), 122. Of course, Woolf, finally, didn't live it, she died it, and Elaine Showalter argues that androgyny was Woolf's way of dealing with feelings that were "too hot to handle"; that, finally, androgyny became a form of repression, "an escape from the confrontation with femaleness and maleness." Showalter, *A Literature of Their Own*, 286, 289.

15. Yates, *What Do Women Want*, 19.

16. Ibid., 117.

17. Shulamith Firestone, *The Dialectic of Sex* (New York: Bantam Books, 1972), 190.

18. Ferguson, "Androgyny as Ideal," 62.

19. See Chapter 6, "Classic Theories of Sex-Role Socialization," in Irene H. Frieze et al., eds., *Women and Sex Roles: A Social-Psychological Perspective* (New York: Norton, 1978), 95–113.

20. Joyce Trebilcot, "Two Forms of Androgynism," in *Feminism and Philosophy*, 74.

21. Elizabeth H. Wolgast, *Equality and the Rights of Women* (Ithaca, N.Y.: Cornell University Press, 1980), 125.

22. Kate Millett, *Sexual Politics* (New York: Doubleday, 1969), 93. Emphasis mine.

23. See, for example, Firestone's "pregnancy is barbaric," with cruel children pointing fingers and sneering, "Who's the fat lady?" Or, alas, even Simone de Beauvoir who, following Sartre, launches volleys against the female body as being "wanting in significance by itself" though the male body has its own integrity and "makes sense." Woman is portrayed as "the victim of the species." Pregnancy is described as "alienation," and, with no apparent awareness of what she is up to, de Beauvoir calls a woman's breasts "mammary glands" that "play no role in woman's individual economy: they can be excised at any time of life." See Simone de Beauvoir, *The Second Sex*, trans. H. M. Parshley (New York: Bantam Books, 1968), xvi, 24.

24. Ferguson, "Androgyny as Ideal," 52.

25. The most straightforward creation of a utopian society based upon contempt for the body and an urge to transcend it remains Plato's *Republic*.

26. Alfred Schutz, *Collected Papers*, vol. 1 (The Hague: Martinus Nijhoff, 1962), xlii.

27. Roberto Mangabeira Unger, *Knowledge and Politics* (New York: Free Press, 1972), 55.

28. May, *Sex and Fantasy*, 80.

29. Stuart Hampshire, *Thought and Action* (New York: Viking Press, 1959), 54–85.

30. Unger, *Knowledge and Politics*, 57.

31. Hampshire, *Thought and Action*, 11–12, 20, 31.

32. See Freud's discussion of the confusion between biological, psychological, and social meanings of "masculinity" and "femininity." From the beginning, Freud adhered to a theory of biological and psychological bisexuality. See Sigmund Freud, "Hysterical Phantasies and Their Relation to Bisexuality" (1980): *Three Essays on the Theory of Sexuality*, particularly the long footnote added in 1915; and the elegant and powerful essay, "A Child Is Being Beaten" (1919), in which Freud demonstrates the internal connection between children's beating fantasies and the "bisexual constitution of human beings."

33. Sigmund Freud, *The Ego and the Id* (New York: Norton, 1970), 16.

34. Richard Wollheim, "The Mind and the Mind's Image of Itself," in Wollheim, *On Art and the Mind* (Cambridge, Mass.: Harvard University Press, 1974), 53.

35. Whether Freud is correct that the distinction between male and female does not become fully entrenched until the genital stage of development or some of his critics are correct that the "certainty" of one's gender occurs earlier is not important in order to make the point that boys and girls experience the surfaces of their bodies as a feature of "external" reality which is taken in and represented intrapsychically in somewhat different ways.

36. Richard Wollheim, "Psychoanalysis and Feminism," *New Left Review*, no. 93 (1974): 64. Wollheim argues that gender identification begins earlier than Freud's account would indicate. But this gender identification still occurs before any full-blown notions of "masculine" and "feminine" develop.

37. Abigail Rosenthal, "Feminism without Contradictions," *Monist* 57, no. 1, 29.

38. Peter Winch, "Understanding a Primitive Society," in Bryan R. Wilson, ed., *Rationality* (New York: Harper Torchbooks, 1970), 110.

39. Sigmund Freud, "Analysis of a Phobia in a Five-Year-Old Boy," *Standard Edition*, vol. 10 (London: Hogarth Press, 1953), 7.

40. Sigmund Freud, "The Sexual Enlightenment of Children," *Standard Edition*, vol. 9, 136.

41. Bryan Magee, ed., *Modern British Philosophy*, "Conversation with Bernard Williams: Philosophy and Morals" (New York: St. Martin's Press, 1971), 154.

42. Rosenthal, "Feminism without Contradictions," 40.

43. Showalter, *A Literature of Their Own*, 289.

44. Secor, "Androgyny," 163.

45. Tony Tanner, "Julie and 'La Maison Paternelle': Another Look at Rousseau's La Nouvelle Heloise," *Daedalus* (winter 1976): 40.

46. Secor, "Androgyny," 163.

47. Barbara Charlesworth Gelpi, "The Politics of Androgyny," *Women's Studies* 2 (1974): 151–60.

48. "Equality" is an intersubjective notion: "androgyny" is not. Intersubjective meanings are ways of experiencing action in society which are expressed in common language; rooted in social institutions, practices, and relations; and serve to constitute those very institutions, practices, and relations.

49. Certain immediate questions arise which, for the most part, political theorists

and moral philosophers have ignored, namely, what about those human beings of whom one cannot assert the full range of what constitutes humans-as-such, provided one adopts the notion? I think of the severely retarded, for example. One could build a case for their having moral claims on others by virtue of the fact that, although they may not be capable of rational thought, dear to the heart of Western philosophers, they certainly can feel pain and experience affection.

50. Rosenthal, "Feminism without Contradictions," 42.

FOUR

Neither Victims

nor Oppressors:

Beyond a Politics

of Resentment

Here addressed in the first four essays is the ideology of victimization in full flower, followed by two essays on women and politics that aim to open up rather than to close down reasonable political possibility. I argue that the most unsavory aspect of victimization politics is that *real* victims often get lost in the shuffle. If *all* women are cast as the universal victims of male oppression, the lives of individual women who live in concrete places and often go through terrible ordeals fade, seem pale by comparison, their troubles puréed in the blender of overheated theories and unsubtle rhetoric. The piece on the battered woman movement takes the side of battered women against a politics that *uses* the horrible fact of battery as a springboard from which to construct a totalistic ideology. Similarly, in "Battered Reason," I question one version of a politics of difference that winds up locating women in an epistemological universe incommensurable with that of men. Drawing this move in jurisprudential theory into a relationship with a troubling criminal case in which a woman who starved her infant to death claimed exculpation because she was abused (although the evidence on that score was ambiguous, to say the least), I urge a return to the notion of extenuating circumstances, well established in our legal tradition, and away from strategies of exculpation. The review essay on the Hill-Thomas debacle, "Trial by Fury," aims to shed light when, it seemed at the time, there was little but heat.

The essay on Las Madres derives from my experiences in Argentina but also from a theoretical recognition of the complexity of women's situations from culture to culture. Together with the question that frames the concluding piece in this section—Is there a feminist tradition on war and peace?—I see myself searching for a politics that helps to gather and to channel essentially peaceful political energies in behalf of democratic possibilities. But such possibilities are opened up *only* if men and women can find ways to work together side by side rather than to bleat at one another across a great divide. Similarly, the circumstances that divide women from one another, and from feminist ideologies, are here displayed in the conviction that complexity is itself a good. By this I mean trying, with our descriptions, concepts, and categories, to come close to the richness of our actual lives and commitments.

14

Women and the Ideology
of Victimization

There are *real* victims in our less than perfect world. The dictionary tells me that a victim is a "living being sacrificed to some deity, or in the performance of a religious rite," or "one injured, destroyed, or sacrificed under any of various conditions." Our word derives from the Latin *victima*. Notice that the victim is gendered as feminine. Should we make much of this etymological fact? There are radical feminists who insist that we must. Their arguments go much beyond cataloging instances, whether historic or current, of female victimization. They hold that the female is the prototypical victim, the victim past, present, and future. This ideology of the victim casts women as *the* victims of male oppression from the inception of humanity; indeed, female victimization takes on foundational status. The story of history is the story of men victimizing women.

Victim ideology diverts attention from concrete and specific instances of female victimization in favor of pushing a relentless world-view structured around such dichotomies as victim/victimizer, guilty/innocent, tainted/pure. The female victim, as I have argued elsewhere, construed as innocent, remains somehow free from sin. An ideology that requires as its original position a picture of woman as Ur-victim is troubling, but it offers its proponents definite ideological advantages. One assumes a stance of purity. To sustain the presumption of purity and the feeling of victimization, however, one must keep upping the rhetorical ante in order to keep rage at a fever pitch. A feminist literary scholar, Patricia Meyer Spacks, warned several years ago, in an essay entitled "The Difference It Makes," that "the discovery of victimization can have disastrous intellectual consequences. It produces . . . one note criticism. Readers newly aware of the injustices perpetrated on one sex find evidence of such injustice everywhere—and, sometimes, *only* evidence of this sort. They discover over and over, in language, structure, and theme, testimony to women's victimization." The upshot, Spacks concludes, is almost invariably a shrill, monotonous rhetoric caught in the self-confirming cycle of its own story.

Feminist Ideology

In the world of feminist victim ideology, women are routinely portrayed as debased, deformed, and mutilated. By construing herself as a victim, the woman, in this scheme of things, seeks to attain power through depictions of her victimization. The presumption, as I have suggested, is that the victim speaks in a voice more reliable than that of any other. (And in this world, remember, there are only two kinds of people—female victims and male oppressors.) The voice of the victim gains not only privilege but hegemony—provided she remains a victim, incapable, helpless, demeaned.

This can be part and parcel of an explicit power play. Or it may serve as one feature of a strategy of exculpation—evasion of responsibility for a situation or outcome. In a recent book called *The Alchemy of Race and Rights,* the author, Patricia Williams, plays the victim card to achieve both ends simultaneously. Acknowledging that the Tawana Brawley accusations in the now-notorious 1988 scandal were part of a hoax, Williams goes on to say that doesn't really matter. For Brawley was a victim of "some unspeakable crime. No matter how she got there. No matter who did it to her—and even if she did it to herself." That is, even if Brawley injured herself, "her condition was clearly the expression of some crime against her, some tremendous violence, some great violation that challenges comprehension." Brawley was the victim of a "meta-rape," and this secures both her victim status and the power plays of those who cynically manipulated the situation. Nagging matters such as evidence and the burden of the proof are dismissed with one ideological maneuver.

A reader unfamiliar with radical feminist discourse should be apprised of how central victimization ideology is to this enterprise. From the early 1970s to the present moment, those radical feminists who begin with a presumption of universal female victimization have portrayed "all men" as violent aggressors and women as Universal Victims. Those men who do not actually rape women use real rapists as "shock troops" to keep women in a state of pervasive fear. One reads a remorseless portrayal of women as exploited and demeaned. At times the world is depicted as a dank nether region in which males appear as vampires and demons feeding "on the bodies and minds of women . . . like Dracula, the he-male has lived on women's blood." Women are all "victimized as the Enemy of patriarchy." Some women escape, but most remain "male defined" and "heterosexist." Hence they are "mutilated, muted, moronized . . . docile tokens mouthing male texts"—this in the language of radical feminist theologian Mary Daly.

Over the past decade, the radical feminist antipornography campaign pushed the victimization theme to harsh extremes. Pornography was likened to Nazi genocide and described as a "holocaust." Hugh Hefner was characterized as "every bit as dangerous as Hitler." The heterosexual bedroom became Dachau as all sexual encounters between men and women, in this pitiless world-view, amount to rape, men being perverted by a "rape ideology." In the interest of preserving male dominance, the law, serving male interests alone, distinguishes rape from intercourse. But, according to Catharine MacKinnon, "for women it is difficult to distinguish the two under conditions of male dominance." Some, whose rhetoric is even more extreme than MacKinnon's, disdain any distinction altogether.

Note that the language of victimization describes women in passive terms. By losing all of the complexities of real victimization, women are recast as helpless prey for male lust. In one of many bizarre twists and turns, women are stripped of choice and construed as helpless dupes: All women are prey; all are assaulted; all are harmed, one way or another. It seems clear that victimization ideology fuels female fear and, paradoxically, disempowers women rather than enabling them to see themselves as citizens with both rights and responsibilities.

Women as Crime Victims

Several years ago I researched the question of women as crime victims. I learned that, on the best available evidence, the assertion that women are the principal victims of violent crime is false. As well, on the best available evidence, violence against women is *not* on a precipitous upsurge as compared with other crimes. Yet popular perception, fueled by victimization doctrine, holds otherwise. For women *think* of themselves as likely crime victims—they have, in fact, assumed a victim ideology that is startlingly out of proportion to the actual threat. The perception of "women as victims" goes beyond a deeply rooted belief that violence against women is skyrocketing: It holds that women are special targets of crime in general and violent crime in particular. Yet the figures on this score have been remarkably consistent over the past decade: Most perpetrators of violent crimes are males; most victims of violent crime are males similar in age and race to the perpetrators. Consistently, the most victimized group is young men.

"Fear of crime" syndrome has a debilitating effect on female behavior, for one internalizes a distorted perception of oneself. For example, habitual television viewers believe they have a fifty-fifty chance each week of being victims of a violent crime—an absurd figure. In 1991, half of the 250 made-for-television movies depicted women undergoing abuse of some kind or another. Often, these shows are given a feminist gloss. In fact, they ill serve women and any feminism worthy of the name by portraying women as in peril in the home, the workplace, the factory, and the street. There is little doubt that victim talk has fueled female fear and taught women to think of themselves as trembling wrecks, doomed to be the victims of individual men, the male system, or both.

I stated at the beginning of this essay that there are real victims. Many of them have been women, and certain crimes—rape, for example—although not confined to women, constitute a terrible story of abuse of some women by some men in all historic times and places. Are there ways to tell the story of actual victimization without falling into a degraded and degrading ideology of victimization? The answer, of course, is yes, and there are thousands of powerful examples. Some are centuries old; others, the fruit of contemporary women's studies scholarship.

Historical Examples

The very beginnings of Western civilization feature stories of female victimization in the first dictionary sense—as a propitiatory sacrifice to the gods. The tales are chilling and evoke real pity and horror because they are rich and precise—because the victims are real characters with names, not abstract ideological constructions. In Aeschylus's *Agamemnon,* for example, Iphigenia struggled "like a goat," and her father committed her to death "like a beast taken from a flock." Euripides for his part twice compares her to a heifer. A less extreme form of sacrifice awaits women in marriage, according to classical scholar Nicole Loraux in her book *Tragic Ways to Kill a Woman:* "Waiting for the domestication of marriage, the young girl is readily compared to an unbroken mare or to a heifer that has not yet felt the yoke. . . . Indeed, if the theme of sacrifice turns on animal metaphor, it is because, like the victim, the girl is a passive, docile creature, to be given and led away." This is not a happy thought, but it has been a pervasive one. It reflected the reality of the woman's "civic death," once her own identity was absorbed and blotted out within marriage.

Augustine turned his attention to female victimization in his great masterwork, *The City of God.* In book I, 19, he defends the violated virtues of women raped in war, insisting that women should not punish themselves. Violation without the will's consent cannot pollute the character. He writes: "We have given clear reason for our assertion that when physical violation has involved no change in the intention of chastity by any consent to the wrong, then the guilt attaches *only to the ravishers, and not at all to the woman forcibly ravished without any consent on her part.* We are defending the chastity not only of the minds but even of the bodies of ravished Christian women. Will our opponents dare to contradict us?" [Emphasis mine.]

This passage is powerful in offering up an argument against the prevailing doctrine of late Roman antiquity that a violated woman must take her own life to preserve her honor if she has been the victim of rape. The woman thus was victimized twice—at the hands of her tormentor and, then, by her own hand in the name of male-defined Roman honor. Augustine aimed to overthrow this double standard, a constraining and oppressive demand that if one's reputation has been "stained," one must do the honorable thing and kill oneself. This is one of many points at which Augustine is remarkably enlightened, not just for his time but ours. Think about how oppressed women have been by the lurid insistencies of "reputation" in many historic epochs. How many times have women been chastised—often by their own mothers—with the harsh query: "What will the neighbors think?"

The Prince, Machiavelli's sixteenth-century handbook of strategic advice on how to attain and hold power, instructs us through indirection on what might be seen as the routine abuse of women. Two dominant views of "the female" are represented. She is either the passive, inert *materia* to be shaped and molded by the active male principle, or *forma,* or she is a dangerously out-of-control bitch who must be whipped into shape. The Prince must do battle with Fortuna, a feminine bitch goddess who aims to control human affairs, and bend her to his will ("master her by force"), just as the wife needs the stick if the man would keep her in line.

Practice Different from Theory

Just how prevalent was routine male abuse of women? We really do not know. Scholars are struggling with such questions, for they recognize that in peasant culture, for example, statements about male authority and female subordination abound, but that such sayings create an image of the couple that is far removed from actual practice. In practice, argues historian Martine Segalen, the "tasks and roles of husband and wife are complementary, interdependent and closely interwoven." As well, doggerel about the cuckolded and "henpecked" male occurs with even greater frequency than braggadocio about male domestic dominance. The new social history—much of it inspired by feminist concerns—suggests that claims to authority and the actual daily practices of men and women in relation to one another often appear at variance. Women's oppression was never so total as some have lamented; male dominance never so complete as some have asserted.

There has been a long alternative to seeing the history of women as an unbroken tale of victimization. Mary Beard, in *Women as Force in History* (1946), distinguished carefully between rationalizations of female subordination and those actual social practices in which women played an important and meaningful role in culture, including what successive epochs understood as "public life." Beard argues that it was with the advent of industrialization and the growth of the middle class that a routinized form of male domination arose in which women, or women of the more privileged classes, became more clearly both the "possession" of a husband and a status symbol of his position in society.

Even a cursory glance at the historical evidence shows us that there always have been women whose thought and action have not meshed with an image of downtrodden victimization. The medieval period, for example, is presumed by many to be an age of machismo par excellence, with knights, Crusades, feudalism, and an antifemale theology. They see an ideology that either damned women as Eve-like temptresses or placed them on pedestals surrounded by troubadours singing moonstruck verse about purity, grace, delicacy, and all the rest. Yet large numbers of women routinely participated in economic life, land ownership, estate management, and even political movements throughout medieval history.

According to medievalist Eileen Power, in her book *Medieval Women,* "women performed almost every kind of agricultural labour" and carried on a variety of trades in the towns. Power notes that most historic evidence for the medieval period is slanted to the upper classes, where the wife began to serve as a symbol of "domestication" and refinement. But this image does not reflect accurately what women, even in that class, actually did. Women could inherit and hold land and offices. Given the frequent absence of men of the noble class on military adventures, women often represented their husbands and ran the fief or manor.

Power concludes that the "dogma of the subjection of women," which became imbedded in the common law and, ironically, in both feminist and antifeminist discourse, has distorted the past even as it plagues the present. The medieval woman "had a full share in the private rights and duties arising out of the possession of land and played a considerable part in industry. . . . The education of the average laywoman compared very favorably with that of her husband. . . . In every class of the community the life of the married woman gave her a great deal of scope, since the home of this period was a very wide sphere."

Ann Douglas, for example, has detailed the manner in which nineteenth-century American women, relegated to a particular sphere, often embraced and politicized it, turning a passive definition into an active vocation.

Actuality or Ideology

The more we know, the less compelling is the *ideology* of victimization and the more powerful are the stories of *actual* victims. For example: One widely accepted tale of the settling of the American West portrayed women as the unhappy companions of men determined to go thousands of miles to gain a fortune or a piece of land. Women wept and did not want to leave their homes, but men forced them into pioneer misery: so one feminist story went. The frontier woman became a "worn and resigned" victim of male hyperactivity, a "forced emigrant" who went through "mortal agony" at leaving behind her previous life.

But recent scholarship tells a more complex tale. Yes, there were many female victims—of famine, of illness, of overwork, of male brutality—but such stories do not predominate. Rather, one learns of women eager for adventure and partners with men in pioneering and carving out a new life. The letters and diaries and fiction written by prairie women tell tales of hardship and perseverance and of women's strength through it all. Carol Fairbanks, in *Pioneer Women,* finds women describing themselves as "tough" and able to "endure and triumph" primarily because of their "mutuality with the earth." And women were survivors: Even in a situation as dire as that of the doomed Donner Party, two-thirds of the women survived even as two-thirds of the men perished.

Perhaps drawing upon one concrete example of female victimization and contrasting it with an ideology of victimization will help to clarify my central theme. In the past several decades, attention has been drawn to the terrible drama of domestic violence. Male battering of women is now a public concern. Hundreds of shelters and grass-roots organizations and a multitude of social and legal reforms have emerged and been secured. The feminist ideology of victimization holds that women are the routinized victims of "patriarchy, capitalism, and male domination" and that this accounts for battering. The number of women abused is estimated as in the many millions, based on the presumption that reported instances are but the tip of the iceberg of abuse. Indeed, the ideologues hold that wife battering is "reinforced" by all the other forms of exploitation to which women are uniquely submitted.

But such abstract claims—a universal condition, an "epidemic," all women are potential victims as all men are potential batterers—belie the evidence. We know that the phenomenon of the battered woman is not a given of social life. In Western industrial societies, social historians have documented cycles, periods of ebb and flow, in domestic violence. Such historic shifts draw our attention to those *concrete* conditions that make battering more likely, and they permit us to ask how we can forestall the emergence of these conditions: social isolation, high unemployment, the breakdown of legally and religiously enforced marital unions, and so on. If battering is a tool of male power used self-consciously by men, in all times and places, to enforce their power, there is little short of a police state with spies in every home that could conceivably stop it. For, remember, to the ideologue, female victimization is a *given* of all known societies everywhere. But a look at concrete and specific victims yields concrete and specific remedies and is far more effective in fighting a situation that ongoingly generates misery.

A strong and supple account of actual victimization should help us to understand the details and complexities of the situation. Thus, we know that as "many as half of the American women battered each year have no blood or legal ties to the men who assault them," according to three of the leading analysts of the phenomenon, researchers Evan Stark, Anne Flitcraft, and William Frazier. This suggests that violence may well be a major symptom of familial breakups at a time of widespread social dislocation rather than a constant feature of secure relationships in stable settings. Moreover, how does one explain evidence that women attack and kill men "almost as frequently as they are attacked and killed"? It is true that women are the prime targets of beatings, but once the situation is "equalized" with guns, the picture changes.

All of this implies that we are not looking at an intrinsic feature of family life but at a likely or possible outcome of family privatization, given the breakdown of social constraints and supports for families. Stripped of ties to neighborhood, place, and a network of kin and friends, the isolated family becomes an emotional cauldron, a privatizing prison. But one cannot even *see* this more complex situation if one begins and ends with the dogmatic sweep of victimization ideology. Carried to extremes, this ideology even dictates a strategy of exculpation for women who are themselves the victimizers.

The Victim as Victimizer

In a recent, terrible case involving a woman who starved her infant son to death, the defense was based on the woman's having been abused by her husband. Turned into a robot, so it was claimed, she was unable to feed her infant even though the husband was away at work all day.

In this story, the ideology of victimization would insist that the woman as a victim of abuse cannot, in turn, victimize others. To indict her and find her guilty, as the jury did, is to victimize her twice. But one looking at victimization as a concrete and specific story would argue that, although it is terrible to be abused, for a twenty-three-year-old woman with a range of options still open to her (she might have given the infant to her mother to care for, as she had done with an older child), to starve an infant to death is more terrible yet. Victimization ideologues portray a woman as less than a fully responsible human being. Feminists who insist we must not strip women of their moral and legal standing as responsible agents argue that one victimized is not automatically excused should she, in turn, victimize. Human dignity demands no less.

Let me, in conclusion, lay all my cards on the table. The most regrettable result of an ideology of victimization is that it plays into the hands of those who are indifferent to concrete victims. It gives the indifferent or the stubbornly sexist all the ammunition they need to dismiss concrete claims by women and to reject specific stories about real victims. The harsh and exaggerated polemicism of the victimization ideology is so one-dimensional and incompatible with real data that it undercuts those who attempt to present a more balanced picture. Given a growing body of evidence, some of which has been extant for many years, demonstrating that women often have been victims of injustice, yes, but they also have played a variety of active roles throughout history and in each and every culture, one must wonder about the politics of resentment that underlies a depiction of women as helpless, demeaned, reduced to victimization.

The issue here joined is one of vital concern, for our beliefs about ourselves and our world help to constitute social practices and individual actions. Told she is the Universal Victim; told that an implacable foe will frustrate her at every turn; told she is an "object"; told she will fail to take her place in the world as it is presently organized unless she becomes a grim ideologue or a "woman-identified woman"; told relations of mutuality between men and women are not only difficult but impossible; she can only wonder whose interests are being served through such distortions, for clearly those of women pummeled with such propaganda are not.

Originally published in *The World and I* (April 1993).

15

Politics and the
Battered Woman

The politics of the battered women's movement brings together a number of vital concerns: the role of the state in intimate relations, feminist analyses of male violence and power, and the ways political activists and professional "social service providers" variously define and intervene in social problems.

Male battering of women is now a public concern. More aptly, it has once again become a public concern. For there are cycles of attention, just as there appears to be a rising and falling in the incidence of battering itself. The value of Susan Schechter's *Women and Male Violence* lies, first, in the fact that it is a detailed and useful, if celebratory, look at the battered women's movement and, second, that it raises questions for political thinking that Schechter, however, fails to develop or treat adequately.[1]

Schechter, who describes herself as a "social worker" turned "activist," wants to get the record down before it is recast by those who may not share her socialist/feminist commitments. She documents efforts on behalf of battered women that, since 1974, have resulted in "over 300 shelters, 48 state coalitions or service providers, a national grass-roots organization, and a multitude of social and legal reforms." She also vows to "topple theories of psychopathology and the intergenerational transmission of family violence, thereby refuting the notion that professionals who subscribe to such theories know more about battered women than feminist activists."

Schechter succeeds in the first of these aims. Of her thirteen chapters, eight burst with a profusion of detail as she traces the origins and growth, the trials, tribulations, and achievements of the movement. This part of her book is zestful political history. But her text falters badly when it comes to general arguments about state intervention in and explanations for wife battering. Schechter tends to round up the usual suspects and trot out the usual categories (patriarchy, capitalism, domination) that obfuscate as much as they illuminate. Even so, her analysis is provocative. The reader who finds

Schechter's explanatory framework thin is invited to think things through in some alternative manner.

Schechter estimates that approximately two million American women are battered annually. Others put the figures even higher—at between three and four million.[2] What do we make of this social fact? Schechter sees but two broad reactions to what she takes as a brute given of social life (or, at least, of "male-dominant, capitalist society"). The first is a prefeminist "socially induced silence" in which the entire system is geared to keeping violent families intact, enveloped in a shroud of privacy. The second is the emergence of a national battered women's movement ("Suddenly . . . desperately . . .").

The key to this shift from denial to eruption, she goes on, lies in the women's movement itself, specifically in the recognition that what happened between men and women "in the privacy of their home was deeply political." A perspectival jolt, a grass-roots feminist response to victimization—and its very success, in turn, prompts professionals (social workers, funding agencies, government bureaucracies) to legitimate the effort, at the same time threatening to strip it of its original *raison d'être*, its participatory élan, and its way of creating political identity. (Schechter highlights tensions within the movement with admirable candor. Areas of disputation and discord grew up around race, sexual identity, children, and ideological cleavage.) This is the narrative that unfolds.

I

Some fascinating questions suggest themselves. How do social "realities" become political "problems"? Who identifies and names "problems" and to what ends? What categories are available to sustain the kinds of impulses to which the battered women's movement is a response? And what implications for democratic politics more generally can be drawn from this instance of single-issue, grass-roots organizing?

One persistent theme running through Schechter's text is the impact of the antiprofessional suspicions of the movement's founders, who marked a vast difference between their participatory politics and the politics of bureaucratic and paternalistic liberalism. Growing out of the heritage of the 1960s New Left, movement activists, initially nearly all middle class and well educated, were suspicious of political models revolving around a policy-making and -implementing elite and a subordinate group of dependent "clients." Movement spokeswomen perceived longstanding "professional arrogance and indifference toward battered women." This initial perception, and the radically participatory ethos of the early phase of the movement, set the stage for later struggles over the hiring of professional staff, assimilation of shelters to extant service networks, and the loss of autonomy that came with government funding.

In this matter of activists vs. professionals, Schechter rejects the provider/client model of social work and welfare—the language of "clients" and "cases." Although she fails to develop her criticism, one might point out how the battered women's movement sees those it serves very differently from descriptions cast in welfare "bureaucratese." A welfare "client" is construed as a consumer of services whose case is "managed" by a professional. But a victim of battering is seen by the movement as a woman who can reconstitute her identity in ways that will socially and politically "empower" her.

By helping the victim to place her individual suffering within a social and political framework, activists hope to set the stage for possible shifts in self-perception. A now-empowered political person, who has overcome her victimization, can move to transform a situation that demeans and threatens her. A welfare client, by contrast, is locked into a static dependency on agencies and experts, leaving little room for transformation. Although this by no means exhausts the complexities of the relationship between movement activists and battered women who use the shelters, it does raise an important question.

I would suggest the following interpretation as a way of understanding the difference, respectively, between the client/case worker and the activist/victim relationships. The feminist volunteer, who may be working up to 16 hours a day in a shelter, is "needed" by women who seek refuge from violence. But she also "needs" them. Their existence as victims points to the reason for her own commitment and simultaneously reinforces a perspective that construes men and families as violent, women as victimized, and so on.

The nuances here call to mind Jane Addams's essay "On the Subjective Necessity for Social Settlements," in which Addams traced the reciprocities linking educated, middle-class female reformers with undereducated, underclass immigrants. Addams understood that the solution to her own problems of self-identity and purpose lay in the creation of a movement that would connect her with others in complex ways. Although the reflective self-consciousness of an Addams is rare, then and now, the activist/victim nexus highlighted by the movement holds open the possibility for mutual self-revelation and change that is absent from the client/provider relation.

Schechter's work would have been richer had she developed an analysis of the tension between creating a sanctuary and constituting a political space; between protecting the vulnerable and binding up their wounds, on the one hand, and politicizing those same individuals in an avowedly feminist direction and sending them forth to challenge the status quo, on the other. Although she nods in the direction of these very demanding concerns, Schechter is frustratingly silent on several further implications of her brief against the professionalization of the movement.

Schechter's text can be read, for example, as an implicit rebuttal of the line of feminist thinking, now apparently in retreat, that derided an unpaid effort, blasting volunteerism as just another instance of female selflessness. *Women and Male Violence* indeed is a celebration of *feminist* volunteerism, highlighting more generally how our social life would be impoverished if such efforts dried up entirely or were totally taken over by public policy and the market.

This analysis also invites a more developed critique of bureaucratic, welfare-state liberalism from a participatory and feminist perspective. Schechter shies away from this task in part because she sees the need for feminists to use the state instrumentally to protect women and punish men. But she regards such reliance as a mixed blessing, and she documents instances of the negative ways in which government agencies move in on movement terrain. She sees, for example, a "nightmare" in the New York City case in which city officials undermined the autonomy of shelter programs by "forcing each battered woman to be verified by a welfare center as eligible for shelter and by giving each shelter resident a two-party welfare check which must be turned over to the shelter to pay for the residents' food and rent. As a result, the shelter becomes like a landlord rather than a trusted friend."

Examples like this one justify movement suspicion of the state. But they ought to do more: they should put pressure on those socialist and feminist visions of a future that project more, and better, than what we've got—a more thoroughgoing welfare system, more and wider-ranging social services, and so on. It is difficult in our political climate to oppose Reaganomics, yet to be critical, simultaneously, of many features of welfare-state liberalism; but that is a posture Schechter's evidence, if not her own analysis, reinforces.

II

Schechter's failure to draw out the implications of her densely packed narrative is not the most serious problem with *Women and Male Violence*. Schechter sets her theoretical sights very high: she wants to explain nothing less than the causes of and the solutions to male violence. But the way she frames the issue—"Why are men violent and what role does violence play in women's oppression?"—dehistoricizes and abstractly universalizes the issue. Schechter falls victim to a tendency to ignore variation between societies, to see in our patterns of gender identity and relation a universal given, and to obscure complex social determinations by construing male dominance as an immutable (or nearly so) feature of the human landscape.

Yet we know that the phenomenon of the battered woman is not a pre-given of social life. In Western industrial societies social historians have located cycles, periods of ebb and flow, in domestic violence. For example: Evan Stark, Anne Flitcraft, and William Frazier document the 1830s and 1840s, the late nineteenth century, and the 1970s as three periods when battering was on the rise and various attempts were made to control it. Earlier social reformers saw the alternative to domestic violence in making women and children wards of the state. Since the 1890s, however, at least until the recent feminist wave, family reconciliation became the byword, coupled with temporary emergency housing outside the home. One way or another, the "permanent dependence of women and children on agency support" was guaranteed, though often without dissolving an ongoing connection to the violent spouse.

Such historic shifts fall through the grid of Schechter's analysis. For her, male domination, or patriarchy, constitutes a theoretical and political *bête noire:* all women vs. all men. Other institutions—economic, social, cultural, political—are reinforced by and in turn reinforce all forms of "exploitation, including class, ethnic, and religious ones." Her presumption of a universal condition with grand causal efficacy lacks subtlety and historical depth.

The story, underscored by her theory, goes like this. Battering is a tool of male power and the self-conscious and purposeful outgrowth of that power. Hence battering is an integral part of women's oppression. Violence against women is rooted in "male domination" and/or "male-dominated capitalist society." Patriarchalism, historically, got intertwined "with the needs of capitalism," thus unambivalently reinforcing male violence. The family, in this scenario, is an arena in which male domination flourishes and violence is deployed *routinely* by the dominant. This is a potent doctrine, but it begs too many questions and obscures too many aspects of the problem of violence in general and violence against women in particular. A strong and supple theory should help to account for detail and complexity; in denying that complexity, Schechter evades a number of problems for political life and thought.

I shall bring forward four concrete questions concerning men, women, and violence in order to show how Schechter's theoretical structure fails as the basis for a provocative or compelling exploration.

1. "As many as half the American women battered each year have no blood or legal ties to the men who assault them," write Stark, Flitcraft, and

Frazier in "Medicine and Patriarchal Violence" (484). This suggests that violence may well be a major symptom of familial breakups at a time of widespread social dislocation rather than a constant feature of secure relationships in stable settings. Perhaps we would come closer to understanding male violence against women if we explored the unraveling of "male authority" in diverse epochs, often linked to brutal vagaries in the political economy.

Schechter consistently speaks of violence against women "under capitalism," but she has no real analysis of how, through what social forces, and in what arenas and institutions capitalism requires or reinforces such violence. This is unfortunate because one might be able to make such a case, demonstrating how capitalism and liberalism historically have undermined the bases of traditional patriarchal authority.

Because Schechter assumes a simple unity between capitalism and patriarchy, she cannot get to first base with this part of the problem. If violence is not so much an expression of secure domination as a signifier of a fear of losing control or a desire to reassert it, the vulnerability of men to a stripping away of their dignity in periods of unemployment, for example, deepens our understanding of the inner tie between violence and economic forces. Hannah Arendt argues that violence appears "where power is in jeopardy"; indeed, she sees power and violence as opposites.[3] Whether one chooses to develop or challenge Arendt's claim, one must reject the simplistic assimilation of power to violence that Schechter offers.

2. Schechter proclaims the family a social and political, not just a preciously private, institution. Few would deny that one cannot insulate the family from its wider social surroundings. But if we were to take this characterization seriously, we would have to underscore the privatizing tendencies of modern life that push toward insularity, atomism, and the breaking of long-term social connections. For battering appears "*only* when persons have been forcibly isolated from potentially supportive kin and peer relations and virtually locked into family situations."[4] This implies that we are not looking at an intrinsic feature of family life but at a likely or possible outcome of family privatization, given the breakdown of social constraints and supports for families. Stripped of ties to neighborhood, place, and a network of kin and friends, the isolated family becomes an emotional cauldron, a privatizing prison.

Schechter recognizes this when she proffers her solution to the problem of male violence (see below), but her theoretical schema affords little space for such awareness conceptually. Exploration of the decreased sociality of families might also help us to understand why the battered woman is three times more likely to be pregnant than the unbattered woman. This reminder ("in the family way") of familial responsibilities and constraints *in the absence of supportive structures* is, it seems, more likely to become one source of dismay, fear, loathing, and subsequent eruption.

3. Why does violence occur in lesbian and gay relationships? Schechter admits that such violence exists, and she calls for more study of the problem. But her insistence that violence is the way men express and shore up their domination over women makes it difficult to understand instances of violence in nonheterosexual unions. This problem is now severe enough that specific shelters to handle it have been set up in several cities. Schechter closes off possible explanatory routes save for evoking "false consciousness," the mimicry by lesbians and gays of the patterns of heterosexual society. But in making this argument she reverts to a social learning theory she has rejected earlier as a possible explanation for male violence against women.

Taking another tack, and seeing violence not as the expression of secure domination but as an attempt to assert or gain control, or as signifying the fear of losing control, we can more readily make something intelligible of homosexual violence. There is a built-in uncertainty, by definition, in homosexual liaisons. The usual role expectations and unconsciously operating checks and balances, the playing off of rights and prerogatives, cannot be so easily wheeled into place. In a chilling way, rage that erupts into violence may aim for clarity on this question.

4. How does one explain evidence that women attack and kill men "almost as frequently as they are attacked and killed" by men?[5] Schechter slides past the problem of female violence by asserting that many women "have no alternative but to kill a spouse" in self-defense. One senses an evasion here. If it is true that women, though the prime target of beatings, display a domestic homicide rate nearly as high as that of men, we confront some curious twists and turns in the tale.

Throughout her book, Schechter rejects the suggestion that there is any "equality" in abuse of the sort hinted at by such formulations as "spouse battering" or "spouse abuse." She is right to do so, given her project. That is, concentrating upon the reality of battering, she correctly detects a pattern of predominantly female victims and male victimizers. Women are not as capable as men of battering with fists and feet: here brute strength remains a major advantage. But women *are* equal when it comes to spouse killing, where weapons compensate for disparities of strength.

To see female violence as wholly reactive, as Schechter does, is to perpetuate our normal cultural expectations in an interesting way. Society as a whole expects men to be more violent than women and anticipates that women will be the more likely victims of aggression. The possibility of male victimization and female aggression defies received presumptions and consequently is not reinforced by police, medical, legal, and mental health structures. Well-established cultural paradigms are brought to bear to construct wife battering as a social problem. This does not hold where the victimized party is male: it is more difficult, given our cultural lens, for us to see this problem, and Schechter's theoretical edifice disallows attending to it at all.

III

Finally, Schechter's proposed solutions to male violence against women are deeply infected by her acceptance of a reified vision of that violence. She proffers a double agenda: one for the "interim," before we have fully reconstructed our society's life, and a second for sustaining that reconstruction. She praises what so far, in her view, has been accomplished by women who worked, for example, to overturn the need for corroborative evidence in rape cases, finding in such efforts a good beginning toward reform of the criminal justice system. To her credit, she alerts us to possible racist use of the rape charge, but she offers no way of instilling that awareness in the law.

Schechter goes on to endorse old laws against wife beating and to urge creation of new ones. We must, as part of the interim strategy, expand the arrest powers of the police and strip the courts of their "sexist blinders," so that they see women as a special legal category requiring special protections. (There is something of a paradox here. At a time when many feminists are challenging the whole concept of protection, Schechter proposes a sweeping reaffirmation of the notion.) Although she observes that expanded "discretionary powers of arrest" may give rise to new abuse of the poor and other vulnerable groups, she is prepared to take that chance even as she sounds the alarm.

Matters get muddled as Schechter describes a potpourri of proposals offered by "other feminists" and "most activists." It is unclear where she stands with reference, say, to advocacy of mandated counseling to condition the behavior of violent men or of "court-mandated, antisexist counseling and education programs" coupled with compulsory punishment for second offenses.

Schechter's frequently offhand notice of possible civil rights concerns in matters of behavior modification is troubling. I agree that "solutions are hard to find," but this difficulty should not justify a refusal to think about the abuses inherent in extending therapeutic powers and responsibilities to the state as part of its policing function.

I cannot enter here upon a full critique of the concept of "reeducation." But let me just mention Arendt's brief attack on those who call upon science to manipulate and control our instincts in the interest of social amity.

Arendt reminds us that violence may sometimes be a remedy to particular, dire situations (her example is Billy Budd), but, and more important, that our capacity for rage and violence is part of a complex repertoire of "*human* emotions, and to cure man of them would mean nothing less than to dehumanize or emasculate him."[6]

While Schechter's interim program relies heavily on a state's policing apparatus she otherwise condemns or suspects, her *solution* to the problem of ending violence against women once and for all requires "a total restructuring of society that is feminist, antiracist, and socialist." It is unclear whether, in her view, such a society would be democratic or whether, indeed, there would be any politics at all. Presumably some sort of state apparatus must be on hand to plan the economy, redistribute resources, and so on (given her commitment to socialism), but this is not spelled out. In Schechter's new society, "family life would be open for community scrutiny because the family would be part of and accountable to the community. Community-based institutions could hear complaints and dispense justice, and community networks could hold individuals accountable for their behavior and offer protection to women. If a false separation did not exist between the family and the community, women might lose their sense of isolation and gain a sense of entitlement to a violence-free life."

Schechter goes no further in specifying how this robust communitarian world—a future perfect *Gemeinschaft*—is to be generated out of a Hobbesian battlefield. Because she assumes that "total restructuring" will produce a moral consensus, she skirts problems of coercion and control otherwise implicit in the plan for hearing complaints and dispensing justice. With every aspect of life opened up for community inspection, she prescribes a world I find singularly unattractive. At least in traditional communities there was room for backsliders, town drunks, loners, dreamers, and harmless eccentrics. In Schechter's society of scrutiny, total accountability and instant justice, the social space for difference, indifference, dissent, and refusal is squeezed out. This is the way matters stand unless or until Schechter, and the many feminists who share her theoretical presumptions, tell us how the future community of scrutiny will preserve any freedom worthy of the name.

I doubt whether Schechter has really considered the implications of her argument. Just 30 pages after her paean to the intrusive communities of the reconstructed future, for example, she states unequivocally that "whom women choose as emotional and sexual partners cannot be open for public scrutiny"—an embrace of the public/private distinction and the possibility for concealment at odds with her image of the new society. There seem to be some loose theoretical threads dangling here.

At long last, however, after theoretical critique and political challenge, it is well to be reminded of the horrible fact with which Schechter begins—that tens of thousands of women are being beaten in this society at this time. Underneath the statistics are human realities that evoke pity and terror. Schechter quotes an account by an activist that portrays the extreme isolation of many rural women and the additional problem this poses in cases of battering and abuse. "Recently in Nebraska," the account relates, "a woman tried to walk to a shelter for battered women that she had heard about. It was 150 miles from her home. She had walked nearly halfway with her small children on back roads when she came to a town that had a volunteer task force on domestic violence, which arranged for her transportation."

A movement that aims to give "women back their lives and dignity" may not warrant the "unequivocal praise" Schechter calls for, but it deserves both praise and recognition from all those concerned with the creation of political space, the development of participatory capacities, and fundamental human decency.

Notes

Originally published in *Dissent* (winter 1985).

1. Susan Schechter, *Women and Male Violence: The Visions and Struggles of the Battered Women's Movement* (Boston: South End Press, 1982).

2. Evan Stark, Anne Flitcraft, and William Frazier set the figures at this higher level in "Medicine and Patriarchal Violence: The Social Construction of a 'Private' Event," *International Journal of Health Services* 9, no. 3 (1979): 461–93.

3. Hannah Arendt, *On Violence* (New York: Harcourt Brace Jovanovich, 1969), 56.

4. Stark, Flitcraft, and Frazier, "Medicine and Patriarchal Violence," 480.

5. Ibid., 479.

6. Arendt, *On Violence,* 64.

16

Battered Reason

Feminism in the West has always been of at least two minds about the nature of male and female identity. Egalitarian feminists hold that there is a single, generic human being. People may, of course, differ in temperament, abilities, and power, but such differences must be assessed by a universal standard. What is excellent in a man, they argue, is excellent in a woman and vice versa. A nefarious deed is nefarious no matter who commits it. The problem for women historically is that men were the paradigmatic exemplars of humanity. Most feminists insisted that women too shared in the excellences wrongly deemed "masculine"; hence women could not fairly be denied access to education, property, the vote, and other civic rights.

This egalitarian or "assimilationist" feminism was always challenged by an argument from women who subscribed to a feminism of "difference." Why accept a single human standard—and a male one at that? Is it not only possible but even desirable that there are many human virtues, and that women may more likely serve as exemplars of some just as men stand for others? Perhaps valor is, in some sense, masculine even as compassion is, in some sense, feminine. The problem for women is that the qualities most linked to women have been devalued overall, that male virtues were rewarded (with medals and high office and official institutional power) while female virtues (succor, temperance, durability) were ranked low in the overall scheme of things. As one feminist puts it, "Men have had more pomp in their circumstances."

The most disquieting developments at the moment come from the "difference" end of the continuum. For, taken to an extreme, difference begins to blot out equality and to lay claim to privilege, or at least to open season on all the cumbersome rules and regulations aimed at achieving fair play. Fairness itself comes to seem a paltry thing in contrast to empowerment, as can be seen increasingly in academic feminist discourse. At one conference I attended, several women vehemently insisted that it would be best to jettison the notion of "equality" altogether. We want "nothing of equality," one participant exclaimed. We want nothing of this "male standard." What she aimed to put in the place of political fights about equality was a "celebration of the female will to power." This seemed a tad murky at best and not a little disquieting, considering how the will to power has worked itself out, politically, in the past. But the specter that is haunting feminism, the specter of difference constructed as a principle designed to trump all other principles, pops up everywhere these days.

One area where the argument from difference has made major inroads is feminist jurisprudence. One finds many, often quite interesting, discussions about whether the "female voice" might not differ—as defendant, witness, and victim—from the male voice and the like. But the debate has escaped the hothouse of the law classroom and academic journals and made its way into the courtroom, often in bizarre and troubling forms that reflect one side of the "will to power" coin. As Nietzsche himself observed, the flip side of an urge to dominate is an urge to submit and then to construe victimization as a claim to privilege.

In the social world of the radical feminist, women are routinely portrayed as debased, victimized, deformed, and mutilated. By construing herself as a victim, the woman, in this scheme of things, seeks to attain power through depictions of her victimization. The presumption is that the victim speaks in a voice more reliable than that of any other. (And in this world, remember, there are only two kinds of people—victims and oppressors.) The voice of the victim gains not only privilege but hegemony—provided she remains a victim, incapable, helpless, demeaned. This can be part and parcel of an explicit power play. Or it may serve as one feature of a strategy of exculpation—evasion of responsibility for a situation or outcome.

Consider an instance in which a woman is cast as both victim and victimizer. How does the difference argument—which seeks to preserve her victim status while simultaneously denying that she could, as well, abuse or "oppress" others—play out? Take a recent, dreadful case in Nashville, Tennessee. The facts are not in dispute. Summoned to an apartment by a man named Michael Bordis whose infant son had "stopped breathing," Metro Police confronted a horrific scene. They found a thirteen-week-old baby boy in the early stages of decomposition. The room occupied by the baby and his half-brother smelled so strongly of feces and urine that it "literally turned your stomach," according to the Metro Police detective who happened first on the scene. The infant's filthy four-year-old half-brother was himself hungry and underweight. It appeared that he fed himself from the refrigerator and had been left alone with the starving infant.

Police arrested Bordis and his wife, Claudette. While in custody and awaiting trial, Claudette Bordis wrote her husband love letters exalting his sexual prowess in graphic terms and describing her favorite sexual activities with him.

Claudette Bordis went to trial first. According to her defense attorneys, the twenty-three-year-old was the *real victim*. They mounted a defense based on the "battered woman syndrome," an exculpatory strategy not available in principle to a male defendant. She could "not be held accountable" for the neglect and death of her child because she was in thrall to her abusive, domineering husband. Although the husband was away at work all day, she claimed to be so bedeviled that it didn't occur to her to care for her child. She never intended to do wrong. To hold her responsible for her deeds was either a "male deal or a prosecution deal or a society deal, but some people just don't get it," the defense attorney insisted.

The defense called a psychologist to the stand who testified that Bordis was "stressed out." This explained the fact that she neglected to feed her son. It also accounted for why she agreed to "dress like a prostitute" and accompany her husband to bars where they picked up men for three-way sexual encounters. Finally, the psychologist testified that the "battered woman syndrome" propelled Bordis to exchange sexually explicit letters with seven male prisoners in other states following her incarceration. The psychologist claimed: "I think our society has conditioned women to accept that they're to serve the men." On this the defense rested. Note that her lawyer did not use the insanity defense; rather, the argument was that Bordis had been robotized by living with a lout. As a victim, her human responsibilities collapsed and she became mere putty in his hands—and this diminished entity could scarcely be held accountable for victimizing another.

The prosecutors weren't having any of it. Tacitly they offered a distinction between extenuating circumstances and exculpatory conditions. They agreed that Bordis was a disturbed woman and had been long before she married her creepy husband. But this didn't inhibit her ability to distinguish right from wrong. They insisted that she was just as accountable as her husband, perhaps even more so, for the knowing torment of her slowly starving child. She had the baby throughout the day and chose not to feed him. The Metro Public Defender's claim that the jurors had a duty to find Bordis "not guilty" because she was a victim of battered woman syndrome amounted to a "trumped-up defense" that itself constituted "an insult to women in the community who are battered." The prosecutor told the jury that Bordis could have put her infant in the hands of others to care for. She could have called her family—her mother had, at one point, cared for the woman's older child. She had choices and she chose, on some level, to destroy her child.

The jury, accepting the prosecutor's argument, found Bordis guilty of first-degree murder. Her husband goes on trial for the same offense soon. The jury decision prompted a letter to the *Tennessean,* one of Nashville's two daily newspapers, from Bordis's mother decrying the verdict and proclaiming, in language more and more familiar in contemporary cultural, legal, and political argument, that Bordis herself was the "victim." She was a "victim" of abuse and now a "victim of society's unwillingness to educate themselves." In fact, the grandmother continued, "I am a victim. I lost a grandson." As a victim she had suffered and her daughter had suffered and, for this reason, the daughter should be let off the hook as she was not responsible for what she did.

What are we to make of all this, and how does it connect to the heated debate over difference? In my own work over the years I have attempted to steer a course between a harsh rejection of difference and a strong plea that men and women seem to inhabit incommensurable moral, cognitive, ethical, and political universes. The stern rejection of any possibility of difference seems mistaken in its desire to forge one generic human standard and its refusal to countenance all distinctions that cannot be traced to some alterable arrangement in social structures; the second seems crazy in its refusal to see how much all creatures we call "human" share and in its repudiation of any possibility of reciprocity and commonality between men and women. Most feminist discourse operates somewhere in this middle range, although the antinomies—denial of difference altogether or making of difference an absolute—pop up more and more these days.

The Bordis case demonstrates how pernicious a difference argument can become when taken to exculpatory extremes. Women are not responsible human agents. They are once again found wanting in what Aristotle called a "deliberative" faculty. The Nashville jury refused to go this route. But other juries have bought a variety of exculpatory strategies, including the so-called PMS (premenstrual stress) defense, which has been used to clear women of charges including driving to endanger, assault, child abuse, even murder. In this matter women cannot indefinitely have it both ways. It is terrible to be abused. But for a twenty-three-year-old woman with a range of options still open to her, despite her entanglement in a wretched relationship, to starve an infant to death is more terrible yet. Moral responsibility doesn't come to us in neat packages, one tied with a blue ribbon, the other in pink. Those who demand full civic standing must be prepared for its responsibilities and its burdens.

Originally published in *The New Republic,* October 5, 1992. Reprinted by permission.

17

Trial by Fury

The Real Anita Hill: The Untold Story, by David Brock

The nadir of commentary on Anita Hill and Clarence Thomas may have appeared recently in a newspaper here in Nashville. The paper reprinted a cartoon featuring two current and one future Supreme Court justices. Seated behind a judicial bench are figures representing "Thomas," "O'Connor," and "Ginsburg." "O'Connor," hand raised to partially cover her mouth, whispers to "Ginsburg": "Watch out when he offers to show you his briefs." The cartoon is entirely predictable in its reinforcement of the rap against Thomas. Its only notable feature is that the figure of "Thomas" is white. His face is as devoid of shading as the faces of "O'Connor" and "Ginsburg."

Clearly the cartoonist flinched. If Thomas were represented as a black man, the cartoonist might be taken for a racist or a panderer to racial stereotypes. Better to bleach Thomas and keep the gender scenario—male predator versus female prey—strict and unimpeded by considerations of race. For the controversy about Anita Hill and Clarence Thomas has become a test of political purism, about gender politics generally, and about sexual harassment specifically, at least as it is defined by those determined to promote a view of men as remorseless victimizers with only one thing on their minds and a view of women as passive victims with nary a sullied thought in their innocent heads.

Do I exaggerate? Consider the unfolding of the melodrama before the Senate Judiciary Committee, which was presented as the primal and prototypical engagement between a powerful male and a "passive" female. "Passive," that is, by Hill's own account. Although Thomas insisted on seeing Hill as a resourceful, energetic, and competent woman, she staked out the ground of her own helplessness, which extended even to her conversations with acquaintances. "I was very passive in the conversation," she reported, referring to a casual discussion with several people about her reaction to the news that Thomas had been nominated to the Court. When Senator Arlen Specter asked, "Excuse me?" she repeated the sorry—but, as it turned out, politically shrewd—refrain: "I was very passive in the conversation."

Hill's representation of herself in such reactive terms struck me at the time as pretty unbelievable. I could not help noting that she was seen by others (not only by Thomas) as a woman quite capable of making her own way through the world and pressing her own case. A female co-worker testified that "when I worked with Anita Hill and I knew her . . . she was not a victim. She was a very tough woman. She stood her ground. She didn't take a lot of anything from anyone, and she made sure you knew it." Clearly Hill was, and is, not only capable, but also ambitious. Which is fine; all achieving people possess such traits, ideally modified by a concern for the decent opinions of others.

Why, then, the retrospective pose of helplessness? Hill gave her reason. "Because I and my reality did not comport with what they accepted as their reality," she said; "I and my reality had to be reconstructed by the Senate committee with assistance from the press and others." Perhaps Hill was not aware that she was endorsing the central and fashionable notion in contemporary feminist theory that (as Ann Scales, a law school professor promoting "feminist jurisprudence," put it) "feminist analysis begins with the principle that objective reality is a myth. . . . Male and female perceptions of value are not shared, and are perhaps not even perceptible to each other."

"I and my reality": these words pithily and a little chillingly capture a controlling idea of our blinkered cultural and academic life. That idea is broadly known as social constructionism. Now, I accept a good deal of the social constructionist approach, and I recognize that the best work in the human sciences is undertaken by those who acknowledge that the world will always be interpreted, and that facts will take on particular meanings in particular frameworks of understanding. Yet there must be limits to this important complication. To go beyond the reality of perspectives to the claim that there are only perspectives, that facts themselves are arbitrary inventions and that there is only "my reality" and "your reality," is to embrace nonsense. And to go still further and argue that the conditions of knowledge change with a change of gender, that men and women inhabit disparate epistemological universes, is to embrace not only nonsense but dangerous nonsense.

Hannah Arendt, in her great essay "Truth and Politics," insisted that politics is kept alive as a human possibility by our need to confront "unwelcome factual truths." If we deny such truths—for example, "the fact that on the night of August 4, 1914, German troops crossed the frontier of Belgium"—we threaten to annihilate that possibility. To be sure, perplexities of interpretation exist, and facts "must first be picked out of a chaos of sheer happenings." Yet these vexations must not "serve as a justification for blurring the dividing lines between fact, opinion and interpretation, or as an excuse for the historian to manipulate facts as he pleases." Thus, granting each generation the right to write its own history does not give license "to touch the factual matter itself." Arendt's words sound terribly old-fashioned today. They even sound innocent—and that impression, too, is a measure of how far we have gone, or how far gone we are, in the belief that any social reality is an arbitrary construction that could just as easily have been any other social reality, and that knowledge is only, or mainly, a form of power, and that power is domination of the kind that pits a simple and unevolving dominator, with his reality, against a simple and unevolving dominatee, with hers.

How immune is the conservative David Brock to this supposedly left-wing epistemological and ideological temptation? Ironically, he is not very immune. His book, of course, is itself now exhibit A or B in this argument or that argument about the Hill-Thomas affair. Some reviewers respected its investigative journalism; but there were less tolerant readings too. Anthony Lewis, for example, found Brock guilty of "character assassination" against Hill and of overall chicanery in refusing to admit that his research expenses were partially defrayed with a $5,000 grant from the John M. Olin Foundation. About the particulars of the case, Lewis had little new or illuminating to say. Brock does acknowledge, incidentally, the Olin Foundation's support; but what Lewis seems to want is a confession that he was bought and paid for, that he "sold out" for a mere $5,000 payment from a "conservative" foundation. *The New Yorker* published a lengthy and interesting rebuttal of Brock, but then it declined to publish Brock's rebuttal of the rebuttal, thereby vitiating the proudly empirical spirit of its own article.

And so it goes: one is compelled to "line up" on one side or the other. Brock is surely right that, "particularly in the university communities and legal circles" that rallied around this controversy, anyone who recognizes complexities in the affair is immediately consigned to pariahdom. It is considered benighted to criticize the mangled way in which the hearings were conducted, or to question whether Thomas's actions, even if he did say nasty things about pubic hair and Long Dong Silver, amounted to sexual harassment in the absence of any evidence that Hill was ever entrapped, threatened, compelled, cajoled, or coerced to do, or not to do, anything. A feminist friend of mine, a respected historian of women, found this out the hard way when she wrote a brief article about the controversy for her campus newspaper in which she fretted that the mounting hysteria might eventually trivialize the seriousness of sexual harassment and, moreover, serve to deepen racial codes about black males. She immediately found herself the object of a sustained campaign of personal vilification.

I do not believe that Brock does a very persuasive job of moving in and through the intricacies of the Hill-Thomas encounter and the subsequent struggle over the event as a litmus test of political purity in the matter of sexual harassment. And yet the greatest shortcoming of Brock's book may not be at all empirical. His most significant limitation is that he shares the very assumption of his opponents: Brock, too, seems to think that facts can be settled with finality by reference to motive.

These are always shaky grounds; but when it comes to sexual harassment, they are the shakiest grounds of all. Billie Wright Dziech, a sexual harassment expert, has emphasized the difficulty posed by the allegation of sexual harassment, and she calls Hill's allegation a "worst possible scenario": "one of those extraordinarily difficult allegations in which there were no witnesses, no compelling evidence, no verifiable pattern of previous harassment by the accused. . . . Most perpetrators have multiple patterns, identifiable patterns and extensive 'track records' of abuse that may continue for years."

This point is important. The charge of sexual harassment poses special methodological obstacles. Almost always it describes a scene of ambiguity, and a scene without witnesses; and so almost always it is essentially obscure. And yet this obscurity must not be exploited. If the controversy about Hill and Thomas has been so susceptible to ideological distortions, and if the dogma that knowledge is power has lent itself so smoothly to the discussion of sexual harassment, it is because knowledge is elusive in this particular instance, not because knowledge is generally impossible.

There *are* such things as the facts, but in the case of sexual harassment the facts are maddeningly difficult to establish. For the charge of sexual harassment describes a situation in which only circumstantial evidence can be confidently adduced. That is why Hill can continue to say, in some of her post-hearing public talks, that "women should be supported regardless of proof." She is hiding a political statement behind an epistemological hardship. For the same reason, her critic Brock may delude himself into thinking that he can get at what "really happened," that journalism can discover the definitive answer. His confidence, too, is misplaced.

To establish that sexual harassment has occurred, it is necessary to rely on more indirect, and therefore more contestable, evidence. On patterns, for example. In observing sexual harassment cases over the past twenty-five years in the university (at a large public institution and a small private institution), it has been my experience that most harassers, as Dziech has written, "have multiple patterns, identifiable patterns and extensive 'track records' of abuse that may continue for years." I know of no single instance in which this has not been true in the cases that were brought to my attention, and to the attention of others in positions of responsibility in the institutions that I have served. But Thomas has never been accused of sexual harassment by any other witness offering testimony under oath in a signed affidavit.

Of course, it is within the realm of possibility that one-time-only harassment might occur. For this reason, Brock's refusal to believe that "Thomas had chosen to harass her [Hill] sexually—and only her—among the dozens of women who had worked for him over the years" is not quite the knockdown argument for which he yearns. But one-time-only harassment, as students of the subject report, is highly implausible. And no one who had direct personal contact with Hill and Thomas in their workplaces came forward to corroborate Hill's account, or to state that there had been any change in her demeanor or in her attitude toward Thomas, at the time that the alleged harassment took place. And that, too, is unusual in these situations.

Consider also the treatment that Senator Robert Packwood, an accomplished harasser, recently enjoyed. Packwood is, by all accounts, a prototypical harasser, with a pattern of abuse stretching over several decades and involving dozens of women; his victims tell stories of his tearing at their clothes, forcing them into sexual encounters, and then working assiduously to discredit them if they reported anything. But the very women's groups that spoke with one voice against Thomas for having allegedly uttered unwelcome and unpleasant words a decade ago were strangely mute about Packwood. Gloria Steinem played the social constructionist card—that is, the political card—by proclaiming that Packwood's actions should be explored and judged "in context." And what context might that be? The answer is simple: the context in which Packwood can be counted on to deliver the votes that various women's groups (NARAL and the Women's Legal Defense Fund, among others) wanted delivered on abortion, affirmative action, and other matters. Politics and politics alone accounted for the reluctance of these national tribunes of the weaker sex to respond to a blatant, egregious, and (finally) admitted string of offenses. Eventually their hands were forced by local outrage and national publicity.

No such patience, however, with Clarence Thomas. He was the wrong sort of fellow from the git-go. I thought he was probably the wrong fellow, too, given his less than stellar accounting of himself during his Senate testimony. Brock forgives all of Thomas's lapses in the matter of constitutional acumen and juridical knowledge by arguing that the Bush handlers didn't serve Thomas well: they persuaded him to stonewall about his philosophy, and he did. It is hard to believe, however, that he was hiding very much light under his tactical bushel. Bush's claim that Thomas was the "most qualified" person for a slot on the Court strains credulity. Still, it was not on constitutional and juridical grounds that Thomas's opponents chose to contest his nomination. "We're going to Bork him," proclaimed a feminist activist quoted by an Associated Press release. "We're going to kill him politically. This little creep, where did he come from?"

Brock does a decent job of showing how the burden of proof shifted to Thomas in a situation in which he, the accused, was deprived of ordinary due process; and he recounts testimony from Thomas's co-workers and employees, many of them women, to the effect that Thomas simply could not have done, and did not do, what he was accused of. This seemed impressive at the time to those of us whose minds were not made up before the hearing started. (Unfortunately, most of the country did not see the panel of interesting and feisty women supporting Thomas; it was aired into the wee hours of the morning on a Sunday night.)

If anything, Thomas comes off in the written affidavits and in the spoken testimony cited by Brock as something of a straight-arrow and a stiff: refusing to meet with staffers in his hotel room during trips on the road because it might smack of impropriety, and firing a female staffer who called a male staffer "a faggot," so Thomas himself testified, because he found this "a slur" and "inappropriate conduct." Even stiffs, of course, put their hands on unwilling women; but we have multiple stories of Thomas's concern with proper decorum, a preoccupation that he deemed especially important for black men, who always operate under a cloud of sexual suspicion.

Brock is not content, however, with indirect and circumstantial evidence. He speculates wildly on certain indisputable facts of the case. Thus, about the documented fact that Hill made phone calls to Thomas well past her years of working with him at one job and then another, and more generally about her wish to stay in contact with him, Brock wonders whether she may have been jealous of his marriage, which was to a white woman. Then Brock begins to offer shabby "facts" of his own. Do we really need to be treated to the accounts by students at the University of Oklahoma that it is Hill, and not Thomas, who is obsessed with pubic hair? Brock quotes a couple of students as stating that they found pubic hair in graded papers returned by Hill. This is as zany as the Coke can story.

And then Brock goes really overboard. Like nearly everybody else who goes near this murky subject, he strays into the shoals of "motive" and besmirches Hill in the way that she and her supporters besmirched Thomas. In Brock's account, Thomas's "motives" are crystal clear: he was defending himself against a smear and an injustice and a conspiracy to "Bork" him.

About Hill's motives, Brock has to work a bit harder. Thus we learn that she is no Reagan Republican, but a "registered Democrat" (horror!) and a liberal, too. We learn that she opposed Thomas's nomination from the beginning. We learn that she had a checkered employment history after Yale Law School and may have resented Thomas because he knew this and therefore helped rescue her by giving her a job at the Equal Employment Opportunity Commission. We learn that she advocated a "hate speech" code at the University of Oklahoma. And so on.

The truth is that none of these facts and none of these speculations establishes any motive with any certainty. Orlando Patterson, in a provocative article in *The New York Times*, was probably right to suggest that both Thomas and Hill were telling the truth as they construed it, that they were both sincere, that they were both recounting their actions as best they understood them. This is skepticism, not social constructivism (though Patterson, too, finally repairs to the grounds of social constructionism). Brock, however, goes further. He believes that if he can provide "probable cause" in the matter of Hill's motivations, which were not made public because her campaign against Thomas was something akin to a conspiracy by Hill and her collaborators, then he, Brock, can nail this whole business down with finality. Again, he deludes himself. Much of the "evidence" that he adduces is hearsay.

More important, this attempt to reward or to punish, to lift up or to cast down, on the basis of alleged motive is misguided. The great motive hunt lends itself only to the kind of innuendo that Hill and Thomas and Brock and almost everybody else who took part in, or commented on, this affair, strongly oppose. Take, for example, the Violence Against Women Act of 1993, pending in the Senate, sponsored primarily by Senator Joseph Biden. The incorporation of "gender motivation" into this dubious piece of legislation accounts for its presumption that rape is a paradigmatic, indeed normative, instance of male domination; and it serves as a rationale for underwriting the reinterpretation of crimes of sexual violence by individual perpetrators against individual victims into civil rights violations by an undifferentiated class of victimizers (male) against an undifferentiated class of victims (female). And this raises the possibility, the specter, that the concrete facts in a concrete case of sexual assault will be much less important in assessing guilt or innocence than the establishment of an "animus based on a victim's gender."

Thus the motive of a crime, and no longer just the committing of a crime, becomes punishable; and the crime is suddenly multiplied as the offender is accused of a sexual battery offense, a civil rights violation, and a hate crime. Which is to say that it will be open season for the hunters who toil in the growing field of sexual assault expertise. This represents the trashing of the truth expressed by Ruth Bader Ginsburg that "generalizations about the way women or men are . . . cannot guide me reliably in making decisions about particular individuals."

How to detect animus? How to make motivation clear? Easy, it seems, for the crafters of the Violence Against Women Act, and for the motive cops that they wish to bring into being. They rely on the platitudes of radical feminist ideology—on a view of the moral and social world that, in the words of Catharine MacKinnon, "stresses the indistinguishability of prostitution, marriage and sexual harassment." In this scheme of things, sex "is normally something men do to women," as MacKinnon says. The actual use of force or violence against a woman becomes less important than whether a woman can ever at any time be said to have "consented" to a sexual encounter or liaison or act, whether in marriage or out. But even "consent" is not really a "meaningful concept" to the ideologues. For the motivation of men is a priori, given in advance. In a society characterized by the "systemic oppression of women," men simply are rapists, actual or in situ.

There is, finally, the dimension of race. It is astonishing how little this matter was discussed in the mainstream media, perhaps because both the accused and the accuser were African Americans. But those who were hoarse in their defense of Hill, and more generally in their pious and politically correct assertions about gender and power and knowledge, might have taken the trouble to observe that they were themselves complicit in the construction of the black male as the paradigmatic sexual suspect.

The tendency to portray black men as sexually rapacious, with a propensity to rape, has long been an unsavory theme in many (white) feminist tracts. In Susan Brownmiller's *Against Our Will*, for example, the "feminist classic" that helped to spur the obsession with rape and the conflation of rape with sex in the minds of radical feminists, it is asserted that the allegations of white women against black men in the Jim Crow South were to be credited, because white women and black women formed a single oppressed category against men. In Brownmiller's words, "The sexual oppression of black women and all women is commonly shared," under slavery and into the present.

It is no wonder, then, that those white political activists, radicals or moderates, who came to the defense of black men accused of rape get transformed, by means of Brownmiller's distorted logic, into "mainstream" defenders of male oppression. Despite ample documentation that many of these accusations of rape were falsehoods, Brownmiller hews to her reasoning, since "we white women did not dangle ourselves," and "disbelief of a woman who said she had been raped" is, after all, a stereotypical feature of "male logic." Please note that the intellectual and moral task for Brown-miller was never to sort out false accounts from true ones. Better to stick with the standard racist account of black male culpability than to disbelieve any white woman at any time! Consider even poor Emmett Till, who whistled at a white woman and paid with his life: Brownmiller regrets his murder but concedes, at the level of motive, his guilt. She knows how to reach back into the hapless Till's mind, and to divine that his whistle, that of a Northern teenager acting out in front of his Southern companions, was no mere "gesture of adolescent bravado," but a "deliberate insult just short of a physical assault, a last reminder to Carolyn Bryant that this black boy, Till, had in mind to possess her."

This is really terrible stuff, but when Brownmiller's book was published in 1975, the praise was pretty much universal. To stand apart and to criticize (as I found out) was to brand oneself as insensitive at best, as complicit with rape at worst. But who can read such an analysis now without squirming at the way in which black males are presented as a unified and dangerous class, as the individual instantiations of a single, collective identity? It seems that a lot of people still don't squirm; this, no doubt, is one reason that the representation of Clarence Thomas as an oversexed black male got such good press.

Nor is that all. If, to this subtext of black male hypersexuality, one adds the fact that, for many blacks, Thomas (in the words of Derrick Bell) "looks black" but "thinks white," you have a volatile mix in which white prejudice paradoxically played into the hands of anti-Thomas forces among blacks who disdained Thomas's politics. Thomas may not have been, as Bush claimed, "the most qualified person" for a seat on the Court, but he was surely right when he remarked, with bitterness, that "in this country when it comes to sexual conduct we still have underlying racial attitudes about black men and their views of sex. And once you pin that one on me, I can't get it off." A poor choice of words, those last few, but he was right about that, too: he can't escape this sort of allegation, and he is prevented from escaping it by many people who fancy themselves to be good and tolerant liberals.

Dusting off hoary stereotypes of male lust and female sexlessness, presenting a world in which sex is what men "do" to women, is one of the more disturbing features of contemporary feminist argumentation; and now, in the wake of the Hill-Thomas affair, it is working its way into our government and our politics. Moderate feminists, equal rights feminists, temperate "difference" feminists, all get shoved to the sidelines in this debate. The radicals who have no use for evidentiary concerns or due process, who prefer abstract victims to concrete inquiries into victimization, now occupy center stage. The bad joke on them, of course, is that they are there not least because it suits men in positions of power in government, law, and the media, especially "liberal" men, to embrace an agenda that enables them to do a good bit of breast-beating about male culpability and female vulnerability. Striking such attitudes is easier and emotionally more satisfying than doing something serious, say, about education and housing and employment. Anyway, who is *for* "violence against women"?

The feminists who are thrilled by the cause of Anita Hill, and by the Violence Against Women Act, seem not to have noticed that such a politics and such a piece of legislation deny women, in the name of women, their full status as citizens, as well as their consideration as responsible moral agents. Given a really massive body of historical evidence, much of it carefully sifted and presented by the scholars in the field of women's studies, that women have played a variety of active roles throughout their history, one must wonder about the *ressentiment* that continues to insist on the depiction of women as passive. Just when it seems that such destructive stereotypes have been put to rest, they resurface like the return of the repressed. So the riposte itself must be ongoingly restated. Instructed that Woman is the Universal Victim, that an implacable foe will frustrate her at every turn, that she is, and may always be, an "object," that she will fail to take her place in the world unless she joins the militant side and enlists the protections of activist lawyers, that her life of intimacy is a life of oppression, that relations of mutuality between men and women are impossible—told all this, most women will surely wonder whose interests and whose desires are served by such twisted pictures, since clearly their own interests and their own desires are not.

Originally published in *The New Republic,* September 6, 1993. Reprinted by permission.

18

The Mothers
of the Disappeared: Passion and
Protest in Maternal Action

All right, my esteemed ladies, the time has come to show you my words were true. Some of you have thought and even said that what this captain wants is for us to give up worrying about this matter so he can gain a little time. That's what you've said and thought. I'm going to prove to you it wasn't so. The Supreme Government has become interested in every one of you, in every single mother of this generous land we have the honor of living in together. And that's because, for the nation's army, there is nothing more sacred than woman and nothing greater than motherhood. It is in defense of that woman and of the values of the home which she seeks to preserve above all else that we have always acted. That women is the sweetheart, the wife, the mother of the fatherland.

Ariel Dorfman, Widows, *1984*

We are what is real, you and I, the mothers. We are so real that the men who may even now be looking down on us and making jokes about the Crazy Ones are afraid. Think of that! They disdain us publicly, have their toadies call us crazy in their papers, but they are afraid of a bunch of women and two men who have the courage to hold signs and walk in the heat of the midday sun.

Lawrence Thornton, Imagining Argentina, *1988*

This is the story of a nightmare. There is no happy ending. The ingredients are the stuff of a tragic political trauma: terror and triumph, despair and hope. I knew little of the nightmare until after the worst had already happened. The bare bones of the story go like this: March 1976, a military coup in Argentina, which, for the first time in Argentine history, creates direct control by the military of all government branches and functions. The coup was justified as a response to the pitiful charade of the government of María Estela (Isabel) Martinez de Perón and to terrorist activity that had by then claimed some eight hundred lives. The leading terrorist groups were the ERP (Marxist-Leninist People's Revolutionary Army) and Montoneros, their far more ferocious Peronist cousins. Government and police officials were the main targets of left-wing terrorism, although civilians also got caught in the crossfire. Right-wing terrorist bands had begun their own assassination campaigns in turn. The terrorist campaign had lost steam around 1975. But people remained apprehensive, yearning for order.

Into this situation, one ripe for such intervention, moved the military. Argentina was to be governed for the next eight years by three successive juntas. This was not a standard Argentine scenario, one in which the military lurked in the background calling the shots. No, the "Process of National Reorganization," the *proceso,* inaugurated by junta leader Jorge Rafael Videla in 1976, gave birth to a period of naked control and state terrorism that claimed an estimated 10,000 lives.[1] The tortured and killed were disproportionately young: 69 percent were between the ages of sixteen and thirty, and 147 were children. No one knows how many babies were born to mothers in captivity. Estimates run to 400–500. No one knows how many of those babies were killed and how many were "adopted" by military families.

It is terrible but true that the deaths of children may enrage mothers and compel them to engage the powerful, in this case, the symbolic fathers in uniform who killed their children. While most, male and female, mothers and fathers, shrunk back, paralyzed with fear, convinced nothing could be done, or tacitly collaborated with the self-anointed bringers of order, a group of intrepid Mothers said: No More. This is their story as I struggled to comprehend, to make their nightmares my own, only to find myself faltering as I tried to tell the tale, flaying myself for my inability to get it right, to do justice to what I had seen and heard. Their story escaped my "poor powers to add or detract."

Intimations of Something Worse Yet to Come

In October 1982, I was in Buenos Aires at the invitation of a center for the study of women in culture and society. The center's work was psychoanalytically driven, and many of the key players in its activities were a group of brilliant, tireless female psychoanalysts. Our sessions were long—one ran for an entire day with a short breather for a quick bite of lunch, a very Protestant schedule, I thought. But there were a few free mornings and one clear, bright, nippy October afternoon opened up. I decided to wander the streets. It was a rather unsettled time politically. The reigning junta spearheaded by General Leopoldo Fortunato Galtieri had been thoroughly discredited by the debacle in the Malvinas/Falklands War; pressure from human rights groups, including "some Mothers," had gained international attention; the economy was in tatters; and Argentines were restless for a change.

My meandering took me past glittering shops stocked with attractive goods, especially chic women's attire. I happened on the Calle Florida, the heart of the city's European-style definition of itself—confiterias, more posh shops, wine bars, respectable old structures culminating with a duck's row of banks and government buildings designating this place, the heart of the city, the Plaza de Mayo, a great public square. There, walking in a silent circle around a monument in the heart of the Plaza, were hundreds of women wearing white scarves, some well dressed and middle class, others in rougher, more rustic attire, their faces a bold contrast to the whiteness of their covered heads. I noticed embroidered names and dates on the backs of the scarves, visible around the necks of these women were photographs of young men or women, some couples, some children. Beneath the photos were printed names and dates. They wore necklaces of despair and grief as others might wear pearls or brooches.

I hurried across the street into the Plaza and joined a small crowd of onlookers. Some passersby clustered for a moment and moved on. Others stood, arms folded, watching. A few mothers whispered into the ears of their stroller-bound children and pointed in the direction of the eerily hushed processional. Some men and women took the sun on nearby benches, munching on empanadas and churros, uninterested in, or unaware of, the slowly moving display of human grief and courage and rage taking place just a few feet away. A tumble of young women, giggling, animated, hair tossing in the breeze, snaked through the tangle of humanity. They were followed by a group of energetic young men, handsome, decked out in the stylish uniform of an elite school, or so I surmised.

"Who are these women?" I asked my hosts. They were Mothers, a sorority bound by loss, the most terrible imaginable. Their children had been "disappeared," the noun turned into a verb. To be disappeared, to be sucked off the street, grabbed in one's apartment or from one's school, often never to be seen again. One sucked up into this nether world of violence joined the involuntary ranks of the disappeared, acquiring a new identity as a *desaparecido*. But I also detected great reticence to speak of the matter. Voices grew softer and suddenly hesitant. Heads shook and lowered. One psychoanalyst, a powerful professional woman, very much immersed in feminist questions having to do with the Symbolic Father and how the female is culturally constructed and how and in what ways all this should be defused or transformed, told me that she and many other professional women felt "ambivalent" about these Mothers of the Disappeared. She claimed they strategically used the Symbolic Mother as *mater dolorosa* and, in this process, wound up deepening and legitimating the mourning mother as the ideal-typical female identity. This "negative critique," to use the fancy but ubiquitous currency of social criticism, went something like that.

Besides, another woman told me, something had to be done about the *terrorista*, the *subversivo*. Certainly no one expected the *proceso* and the excesses of *la guerra sucia*, the "dirty war," but I must keep in mind the context. Now all anybody wanted was an end to fanatical politics of any brand, left or right. And the Mothers, I sensed, had become a bit of an embarrassment with their incessant demand for the disappeared to reappear alive, *aparición con vida*. Shortly before I left the city, the *Buenos Aires Herald,* an English-language paper that has been published continually for over one hundred years, printed an item headlined "Mothers visit unmarked graves." It read, in part:

> Members of the Mothers of the Plaza de Mayo prayed yesterday over unmarked graves at the cemetery where they believe 400 persons thought to have disappeared may be buried.
>
> The Mothers, who for six years have been unsuccessful in their efforts to obtain information on what happened to thousands of people who disappeared during the military's so-called "dirty war" on terrorism, rushed to the municipal cemetery a day after learning that one of the missing was buried there.
>
> The Permanent Assembly for Human Rights (APDH) said on Friday that as many as 400 of the estimated 6,000 to 20,000 who disappeared between 1976 and the present may be buried in 88 unmarked graves in the Grand Bourg cemetery in San Miguel, 25 kilometers west of Buenos Aires.
>
> Cemetery officials and neighbors have said that security officers driving Army trucks brought "six or seven" bodies to bury in the cemetery about once a week while the anti-terrorism campaign was going on. (Sunday, October 24, 1982, p. 13)

I was to learn later that the disappeared, tortured, and murdered went into the ground (if they were buried at all rather than being dumped out of military transport planes into the Rio de la Plata) as N.N., "No Name." The Mothers bore the particular, irreplaceable, concrete names of their children around their necks, framed with the accusatory question: *Donde está . . .?* (Where is . . .?). No Name. It was insupportable.

Has Anything Been Written?

A standard text on Argentine history told me that "the interested observer of Argentine affairs can predict that the armed forces will continue for several years and perhaps for several decades to exert the predominant political role in Argentina and to act as an authority above civilian government."[2] But the text trailed off before the terrible events that gave birth to Las Madres. Amnesty International's 1981 workbook on "disappearances" documented in stark detail the cold mechanics of this ever-more-popular political phenomenon, one not exclusive to Argentina. But the Mothers remained in the shadows, haunting and haunted images, their scarves blurred afterimages, the photos round their necks fading stigmata. At times I wanted to forget I had ever seen them; at others I wanted to return, to march with them, to understand why and how—how they managed to go on when all I could conjure up as I thought of the torture-murder of a child was a life prostrate with grief and corroded with rage.

I discovered a book by anthropologist J. M. Taylor, *Eva Perón: The Myths of a Woman,* which helped me to put one piece of the vast Argentine political puzzle into place.[3] My curiosity had been piqued by the phenomenon of the many impressive, powerful career women—nearly all of them mothers—I had met during my stint in Buenos Aires. (Having live-in Paraguayan maids certainly helped these women to work flat-out and full-time but did not explain the imperatives that drove them into the professions in the first place.) This didn't seem to fit with North American chatter about the horrors of machismo. Nor, for that matter, did the image of the Mothers defying arrest, imprisonment, torture, even death, to march in the Plaza de Mayo.

I learned from Taylor's work that Argentina has long harbored powerful women in its gallery of great ones. Focusing on the strange and many-sided myth of Eva Perón, Taylor showed the political and class dimensions of constructions of Perón, variously, as the Lady of Hope, the Woman of the Black Myth, and Eva the Revolutionary giving birth to revolutionary sons and daughters who proclaimed that whenever they were discouraged, Eva gave them strength. They fought because of her and for her. The vitality of the myths of Evita were such that decades after her death she continued to spark political longing and loathing. Even as revolutionaries still fought under her banner, defenders of the status quo claimed her sanction for their activities in behalf of traditional authority. Various brands of Peronism vied with and against one another even as they pitted themselves against those for whom Evita embodied the worst of womanhood, the bad woman, a whore, who seduced and controlled her husband, Juan. Those who celebrated Eva as the saintly mother had no trouble reconciling her own childlessness with their sanctimonious embrace. No, "she was the mother of the nation as a whole, particularly to the common people and the poor and needy of Argentina" (75). She was the "Spiritual Mother of All Argentinean

Children" by popular acclamation and political fiat. Eva, concludes Taylor, was a woman who used "culturally defined, characteristically female attributes as a basis for power in a role accessible to both males and females," and she was able to do this because Argentine culture, in common with many others, links "images of feminine nature with certain types of mystical power," even "with revolutionary roles" (144–45).

Do not expect a tidy picture. What one finds consistently linked in the many and even antipodal Eva images is a vision of femininity, of "mystical or spiritual power, and revolutionary leadership," and all these elements put "a person or a group at the margins of established society and at the limits of institutionalized authority" (147). The most powerful woman in Argentine history, a spellbinding rhetorician who cried out to rapt assemblies of tens of thousands, held no office. Beyond or outside of institutional arrangements, she was paradoxically free to inhabit many roles, to play many parts, and to be imagined by others in fantastically at-odd ways. This freedom, of course, had built-in limits: she always claimed she was but the poor mouthpiece of Perón: "I do not have in these moments more than one ambition, a single and great personal ambition: that of me it shall be said . . . that there was at the side of Perón a woman who dedicated herself to carrying the hopes of the people to the President, and that people affectionately called this woman 'Evita.' That is what I want to be" (144–45).

She later added that her "permanent vow" was to place herself "entirely at the service of the *descamisados,* who are the humble and the workers" (144–45). The humble and the workers gave her great latitude and cherished her memory even as others excoriated her base influence, her evil seductions, her cruel treatment of any who stood in her way. She was the intermediary between the people and her powerful husband, who claimed that she was "an instrument of my creation." Her work was extraordinary, he added. God himself operated through her; hers were tasks assigned by Providence. Evita did not object (55).

Taylor speculates that the personalized and familial style of leadership wildly successful in the case of the Peróns was knowingly crafted by them to appeal to points of stability (family authority) in an otherwise often disordered political environment. This cultural context gave rise not to images of submissive females but to problematic and very powerful public women. The "gender ideology" of Latin America in general, Argentina in particular, was perhaps more flexible than similar ideology in North America. After all, one encounters large numbers of important women outside the domestic realm and a rich variety of mythic images to portray such women. Argentina regularly sent forth more women into the professions as lawyers and doctors than did the United States. Machismo, it seemed, wasn't nearly so clear-cut a case of dominant fathers versus doleful mothers as culturally parochial, North American polemicizing repeatedly claimed.

This helped a bit, for it reminded me of the continuing force of familial imagery in Argentina in contrast to the United States. Strangely, Taylor spilled few words on Catholicism in her treatment of Evita. Surely, I mused, a religion that includes a Holy Mother as an object of veneration, devotion, prayer, and yearning offers a much more potent symbolism as part of its repertoire than do religions that have been stripped systematically of any such imagery. Had not Martin Luther chastised the "papists" for putting "that noble child Mary right into the place of Christ"? They would have us rely more on "Mary the Mother of Jesus and the Saints," Luther insisted, than on *the* Incarnate Word.[4] With a lively company of female saints, plus the Madonna, the symbolic and spiritual force of Catholic motherhood seemed assured (whatever the political fallout and however one evaluated it) by comparison to symbolically beggared Protestantism, especially in its evermore watery North American varieties. There had been a distinctly, indeed overwhelmingly, ritualistic cast to the silent march of Las Madres that October day in the Plaza, an eerie and unsettling fusion of the living and the dead.

In April 1982, six months before my initial foray into Argentine life, my essay "Antigone's Daughters" had appeared in what turned out to be a short-lived publication called *democracy,* a journal aimed at the independent, democratic left. In that essay I advanced a "note of caution," arguing that "feminists should approach the modern bureaucratic state from a standpoint of skepticism that keeps alive critical distance between feminism and statism, between female self-identity and a social identity tied to a public-political world revolving around the structures, institutions, values, and ends of the state." I took on those brands of feminism that "presumed the superiority of a particular sort of public identity over a private one," a public identity that "would require . . . the final suppression of traditional female social roles." In other words, I argued against the new woman as a variant on the old man.

Drawing upon *The Antigone* as a prototypical tale pitting a woman representing the unwritten imperatives of familial obligation and traditional duty against a king urging that *raison d'état* must override all other obligations, I elaborated a modest morality play for consideration by contemporary feminists. At the essay's conclusion, I drew on Sara Ruddick's construction of maternal thinking as a way of seeing and acting that places the preservation of fragile human life above the instrumentalities of technocratic power.[5] I concluded with these words, "Maternal thinking, like Antigone's protest, is a rejection of amoral statecraft and an affirmation of the dignity of the human person."[6] And I lodged a query: how can one hold on to a social location for contemporary daughters of Antigone without insisting that women accept traditional terms of political quiescence? After all, Antigone fuses tradition *and* radical challenge in her agnostic clash with Creon, who frets insistently that he will not be bested by a mere woman.[7]

Had not mere women in Argentina shown not so much that the emperor had no clothes but that the junta had bloody hands? Does the continual force and fury of the Antigone story help us to sort this out, to come to grips with the phenomenon of Mothers acting *out* in the public sphere, in the open, and claiming full responsibility for their words and deed-doing? It seemed so to me, and the Mothers took on the classical grandeur of Antigone in my mind. Was not George Steiner right that "men and women re-enact, more or less consciously, the major gestures, the exemplary symbolic motions, set before them by antique imaginings and formulations"?[8] Did not important novelists—Ariel Dorfman and Carlos Martinez Morena, among others—knowingly and powerfully play off the Antigone story in portraying women pitted against dictatorial power? Dorfman notes that the missing are deprived of more than their homes, even their lives. "They are also deprived of their graves"; they are N.N.[9] And women are the symbolic, at times politicized, keepers of those graves. In his novel, *El Infierno,* Carlos Martinez Morena depicts the bloody business of the Tupamaro guerrillas in Uruguay and the even more bloody state terror that repressed them and took a huge human toll. He offers the terrible image of a hooded prisoner being pitched from the top of a stadium and, in the aftermath, "his wife battling like Antigone for his body."[10]

Return to Buenos Aires: The Voices This Time

This matter is of no concern to us. These women are mad.

Spokesman for the junta, June 1977

In 1986 I returned to Argentina, having been invited by two friends to lecture. I was officially an academic specialist and I was due in Argentina August 3 for a ten-day stint.

I put in a request: Could interviews please be arranged for me with members of Las Madres? And perhaps, with Adolfo Pérez Esquivel, the 1980 Nobel laureate and an apostle of militant nonviolence, who worked out of his center, Servicio Paz y Justicia en América Latina in the Calle México?

As my airplane, having taxied away from its gate, sat on the tarmac at JFK for half an hour, then an hour, then nearly two, waiting out a terrible thunderstorm in the early August New York mugginess, I read the only book in English I could find with the Mothers in the title. It was a disappointment, featuring the Mothers in but one chapter—this despite the title *The Disappeared and the Mothers of the Plaza,* by two journalists, John Simpson and Jana

Bennett. But I did learn some facts, gained a bit of additional background, and became familiar with a few names. I was reminded of what I already knew: three juntas; ten thousand to thirty thousand disappeared. It was April 13, 1977, a Saturday, when the Founding Mothers, fourteen intrepid women, arrived at the Plaza de Mayo and entered it tentatively, in full view of the presidential palace (Casa Rosada) and wandered ("nervously," said the book) for a few minutes. This group of fourteen encouraged others to join them. Their leader was Mrs. Azucena DeVicenti, who was herself disappeared along with two French nuns in December 1977 and never heard from again. The Mothers were dubbed *Las Locas de la Plaza,* "The Mad Women of the Plaza," by the authorities in an attempt to discredit them.

I read of betrayals, the worst being the story of one charming young man who joined the Mothers claiming his brother had been disappeared; he turned out to be one Captain Alfredo Astiz, implicated in several disappearances, later charged but released and pardoned. The Mothers believe he is responsible for the disappearance of Founding Mother Mrs. DeVicenti as well as the nuns. The Mothers "always resisted any temptation to become a secret society, everything they did was open, including the meetings at which they discussed their strategy."[11] Their numbers grew. Through harassment and arrests, the Mothers succeeded with only occasional lapses in keeping up their weekly vigil in the Plaza. At one point the violence was so great they gathered in churches. But they recouped, gained international attention, and on every Thursday at 3:30 in the afternoon, they continue to this day to gather in the Plaza. They say they will stay until all the disappeared are accounted for and their tormentors brought to justice.

In the most dramatic way possible, the Mothers entered the Plaza de Mayo and made it their own. Interviewing several of the key players in Las Madres, Simpson and Bennett found similar stories, shared concerns, even obsessions. The Mothers succeeded in placing an ad listing the names of 237 desaparecidos in the newspaper *La Prensa* on October 5, 1977. This was a public gesture and was followed by the delivery of petitions with over 24,000 signatures to Congress, calling for an accounting of the disappearances. But little changed. Two hundred of the Mothers delivering petitions had been arrested but were released within a few hours. Many of their fellow citizens refused to see the full extent of the horror and clung to the soothing belief that those who were disappeared *must* have done something to warrant arrest and torture: *Debe ser por algo,* "it must be for something."

Now, as I returned to Buenos Aires, three years had passed since the restoration of civilian rule. The state of siege was suspended officially on October 29, 1983, and President Raúl Alfonsín took office December 10, 1983. The disappearances had stopped and a presidential commission, appointed by President Alfonsín, had produced copious documentation of Argentina's nightmare. Published in Argentina in late 1984, *Nunca Más* immediately became a best-seller—300,000 copies were scooped up in a few months.[12] The commission's report, calling to mind Nuremberg war trial testimony, is a descent into hell. Ernesto Sabato, one of Argentina's most respected novelists, introducing the gruesome testimony, trying to account for the why and how of the proceso, spoke of Argentine history, the scourge of terrorism, right and left, and the peculiar ethos that dominated the Argentine military—its grand, salvific view of itself as the only thing that stood between communistic chaos and decay, on one hand, and protection of authentic Argentinean identity, *argentinidad,* on the other. In their hermetically sealed world of enemies, plots, conspiracies, and subversion, it was not enough to cut the branches off tainted trees; no, the tree of subversion must be uprooted utterly and all its offshoots, from revolutionary armed organizations to progressive Catholicism to Mason to Zionists, had to be destroyed, literally uprooted. Against such a vast conspiracy, the Ford Falcons with unmarked license plates roaming the streets and preying on the young were a necessary defense, a prophylactic against a spreading disease. Absolute brutality, utter caprice; this was the dirty war and the voices of the victims were heard at last. Thousands of detailed stories, each a tragedy rippling out and joining the ripples of other stories, each heartbreaking, each unbelievable. My airplane sleep was even more disturbed than usual.

Telling the Story

They knew I was pregnant. It hadn't occurred to me that they would torture me while we were traveling. They did it during the whole trip: the electric prod on my abdomen because they knew about the pregnancy. . . . One, two, three, four. . . . Each shock brought that terrible fear of miscarriage . . . and that pain, my pain, my baby's pain.

A new cry makes its way through the shadows fighting above the trailer. Graciela has just given birth. A prisoner child has been born. While the killers' hands welcome into the world, the shadow of life leaves the scene, half a winner, half a loser: on her shoulders she wears a poncho of injustice. Who knows how many children are born every day at the Little School?

Partnoy, The Little School, *1986*

I fretted that "merely" communicating the Mothers' despair would cheapen their grief and their political presence, would somehow falsify their voices by situating them in too straitened a framework, too academic a genre. Just as certain *features* of institutionalized Holocaust studies had become problematic to many because of a pervasive encoding of the bathos of mass victimization, I hoped to avoid seeing the Mothers through a prism that reified their loss, freezing them in a posture of permanent grief and requiring, in order that they might continue to serve *my* purposes or the purposes of others, that they remain forever a fixed tableau of maters dolorosa.

In talking to others about the Mothers, I surrounded their words, those voices that told of terror and hope, with as little conceptual and theoretical material as possible. It seemed important not to categorize nor to capture what they had gone through, what they had done, and what the aftermath of it all might be, too quickly. Following our participation on a panel on women, war, and violence, I shared my interview transcripts with my friend, Sara Ruddick, who made good use of the words of one Mother in a chapter in her book, *Maternal Thinking*. But whenever I decided the time had come to "tell the story," I shied away with a tightening in my chest and an experience of rising anxiety. The words of Czeslaw Milosz haunted me. His poetry, he writes, "has always been a means of checking on myself. Through it I could ascertain the limit beyond which falseness of style testifies to the falseness of the artist's position; and I have tried not to cross this line. The war years taught that a man could not take a pen in his hands merely to communicate to others his own despair and defeat. This is too cheap a commodity; it takes too little effort to produce it for a man to pride himself on having done so."[13]

Perhaps my fear about getting it right was its own form of pridefulness at the presumption that I might be able to do justice to such terrible and moving events as torture, loss, grief, and public courage. That, surely, was beyond anyone's powers. As well, matters had grown more complicated because I was by now close to several of the Mothers. One, to whom I gave a copy of "Antigone's Daughters," was a friend and correspondent. That unavoidably dramatized the situation: I needed to do right by Renée, who had lost all three of her children to the tortures—she was a face, a voice, an ongoing presence. Her children—Luis, Claudio, Lila—were real victims with real names. Unable to write about the Mothers myself, I turned to the experts. What did political science have to offer?

Normal or mainstream social science misses the mark, especially accounts that excise "the political" from "the ethical," a real trick indeed when what one is dealing with is torture, murder, and disappearances. The richest social science account is one that finds a way to characterize the politics of terror *institutionally* and politically, unpacking the inner workings of bureaucratic, authoritarian states. Although not concerned explicitly with Las Madres, Argentine political scientist Guillermo O'Donnell, reflecting on the

Argentine experience, looks at the converging forces that made authoritarianism not only possible but well-nigh irresistible: economic crisis, waves of mass popular mobilization (the Perón era), widespread top-down politicization of all arenas of human life, and the turn toward violence as a political means and end. In a climate of "pervasive fear and uncertainty," most voices are silenced, although in some cases the "vertical voice," the ability to address the rulers, usually as supplicant, remains as a limited option.[14] But another type of voice—essential to any political life—is wiped out, a voice O'Donnell calls "the horizontal voice." By that he means the "right to address others, without fear of sanctions, on the basis of the belief that those others are 'like me' in some dimension that at least I consider relevant." Only the operation of this horizontal voice makes possible the creation of "we"—a group political identity. Indeed, horizontal voice is a necessary condition of group formation.

Hoping to find a sharp "opposition to the regime that we supposed many concealed behind a very privatized life," O'Donnell and his wife, Cecilia Galli, investigated the fears Argentines had of falling victim to the junta. In the midst of "pervasive and chaotic violence," what they found was a few occasionally addressing the rulers but rarely, if ever, daring to "use horizontal voice." One had to avoid "the dangerous world of public affairs" (7). The logic of *divide et impera* worked, as any and all "attempts to extend mutual recognition as opponents to the regime" faded and nearly disappeared (15). Indeed, the "obliteration of horizontal voice means that those social sectors whose mode of voicing cannot but be collective are condemned to silence" (14). That is, the vast majority were not those who usually address or have access to vertical channels. People took refuge in private life and then later denied the refuge they had taken. For in responding after the restoration of constitutional government to a new set of interviews (O'Donnell and his wife said the first interview data had been lost), their respondents *claimed* a political identity that had, in fact, been obliterated earlier. They recalled their own thoughts and deeds in a much more favorable light.

Remarkably, the Mothers defied each of O'Donnell's conclusions. They deployed the vertical voice, loudly and incessantly, and that having failed, they did what he argues is nearly impossible—they created a "we," they forged a group political identity on the basis of their shared experience. Condemned to silence, they repudiated the sentence of the regime, took to the Plaza, and voiced their grief and their outrage. They rejected what it meant to be a "good Argentine." They embraced the forbidden—"the dialogical structure entailed by horizontal voice" (13). Having lived an atomized life of grief, they found strength and political identity by deprivatizing their mourning. In light of the overwhelming evidence O'Donnell amassed on privatization, silence, depoliticization, fear, the story of the Mothers becomes, if anything, *more* difficult to understand. Why didn't they succumb? Why did they defy all the social science expectations and conclusions on individual and group behavior in a chaotic, terror-ridden, and punitive surround?

The explanation from a human rights standpoint offers a partial understanding of the Mothers' talk and action, that astonishing dialogue the public appearance of the Mothers generated. Human rights entered into and became constitutive of the political group identity of Las Madres. Political theorist James Tully claims that human rights is "the only bulwark, however fragile, against the brutalization of everyday life in many parts of the world." The notion of human rights, one of the great achievements of Western political culture, is one "part of the normative culture of every country and is advanced by international institutions"; it follows that "the resistance to oppression will tend to take the form of a struggle for the establishment of liberty in its rights form."[15] Tully goes on to argue that dissident groups must practice what they preach inside their own organizations *if* the discourse of human rights is to be politically authentic rather than merely fashionable or cagily strategic.

At least some of the Mothers understood, and understand, rights-talk in its fullest amplification as setting boundaries to their own politics even as it served as a weapon against their tormentors. Countering the cult of death with the language of life and maternal suffering came naturally, so to speak, being deeply encoded in the maternal symbolism and identity of the West, especially in Catholic societies. But human rights language, with its juridical features and its privileging of legal limits to what can or should be done to anyone for any reason, political or not, is scarcely so ancient as a maternal language of mourning and loss. Women came late, relatively speaking, to the juridical identity of official rights-bearing subjects in the West. Many women today, especially mothers in rights-rampant societies such as the United States, are wary of excessive chatter about personal freedom to the exclusion of social responsibility. But that was not the case for the Argentine Mothers. Human rights was, for them, a way to express the timeless *immunities* of persons from the depredations of their governments rather than a vehicle for entitlements. It was a way to say "Stop!" not "Gimme." Rights gave political form and shape to their disobedience, linking them to an international network of associations and watchdog societies, particularly Amnesty International and Americas Watch. Thus the rights discourse of the Mothers never descended into the narrowly individualistic or numbingly legalistic.[16] Armed with grief and rights, the Mothers took to the streets and created a space for antirepressive politics.

In this matter no vast interpretive armature is needed, for the rights-based self-understanding of the Mothers comes through loud and clear in interviews and in their written documents. In a way, rights talk afforded the Mothers a framework within which to canalize their grief, to make it do political work. And those mothers who seemed to me to be coping best were those who had been able to somewhat transcend the vortex of personal devastation in order to make common cause through human rights efforts both within Argentina and internationally. Thus María Adela Antokoletz:

> On the first day there were only fourteen Mothers, in 1977. Since then we have been going to the Plaza uninterruptedly and after a time we started to travel to Europe, to go anywhere we could, to speak to many people, to the media, to spread the word about what was happening. Our struggle has always had a very clear moral purpose; we have always been non-violent; and we have carried out our struggle with dignity. Despite this the costs have been very high. We have been humiliated and offended and mistreated and threatened and blood has been shed. Three Mothers were disappeared as were two French nuns. One of the three mothers was the one who founded the group. I, myself, have never been arrested, though my sister was but she was later released. We never had a narrow political agenda. Ours was a moral protest about political abuse, about how and why people disappeared.

At this point Renée Epelbaum, the mother of three desaparecidos whom I alluded to earlier, in response to my question about what the punishment should be for those who tortured people, kidnapped people, murdered people, said:

> I was asked the same question at the end of a film about Las Madres. My answer was: it's a very painful subject for me. My daughter was thrown into the sea. The man or people who did it are as criminal as those who gave the orders. Both must be punished. We don't believe in such a thing as "due obedience." Human beings are not robots. Human beings are responsible for what they do. They destroyed the rights, the lives, of other human beings. People ought to realize they were committing crimes; they were murdering helpless people. Sometimes I give an example. A man makes a robbery. There is someone who plans the whole thing. Maybe he stays at home. And then some go into the bank and do it. Maybe one kills. He is guilty but I ask you, you must involve all of them. We do not believe in the death penalty. We do not want to torture the torturers. We want justice, not vengeance.

María Adela added, "When justice is not fulfilled, when rights are not cherished, those who killed and tortured will do it again because they got away with it. The military has such a hatred. They cannot believe the judgments against them. They wanted to eliminate an entire generation and then make everyone forget what happened." Renée, sadly and musingly, continued, "You know, we understand that not everyone responsible can be punished—that's utopian. But we must do more than judge the high-ranking ones. This leaves all the rest and they will get restless, those men who were so brave to kidnap people who couldn't defend themselves and are afraid to face judgment."

Moving to a sore point—it was clear nobody much wanted to talk about a split that had by then occurred in the Mothers that cold, damp August of 1986—I asked: "What's the difference between your group and other Mothers?"[17] Renée's answer was a classic recognition that human rights discourse imposes responsibilities on its advocates for how they conduct their own affairs as well as for how they apprehend the wider world of political life. Her words, in full, went like this:

Renée: You know, when we began our struggle, we demanded to know the fate of our children. I lost three; María lost a son; Lydia a son; Marta a daughter and a son-in-law and perhaps a baby because she thinks her daughter was pregnant. We didn't ask the mothers if their children were politically committed. We didn't ask about political beliefs or religious beliefs or social class. It was a pluralist movement. We only demanded truth and justice. We are afraid that some of the leaders of the other group are turning the movement into a class movement. We took a different course, not because of social class but because we want to support all demands towards human rights—including the right to free speech, to have a home, to be educated. We support the Declaration of Human Rights. We don't want the Mothers movement changed into a class movement. Also, there is a question of style. We criticize the policy adopted by the Alfonsín government as too timid. We demand justice strongly. But we know that the current government is not a continuation of the junta. This is just not true. It is not the Alfonsín government which kidnapped, tortured, and killed our children. They are not doing all they should to investigate, to bring justice. But it is not the same thing. We call our line the "foundation line." It is very hard to explain all of this to you. It is a very hard thing. In our group we are all equal. We have differences; we discuss. But Hebe Bonafini, if you didn't think the same as her, accused others of treason.[18] She was bringing the organization to authoritarian ways—giving orders and commands. We had a meeting of the board and we decided in a democratic way what we were going to do. That didn't please her. For a while we went along because we didn't want to show divisions. But now we are living in a democracy and we should not run our own affairs in ways that are against democracy.

María Adela: We have good reasons for going our own way. It has to do with an enormous difference over internal democracy. If we keep quiet and accept a bad situation we become accomplices. And that is not good for the movement. In my opinion, to have several trends is not necessarily bad; it might give us more strength because you get other options and consult and exchange ideas.

Renée: They don't want to discuss the problem. They want to give orders. That is hopeless. It is very sad.

María Adela: Some people have come to us and say we should be unified once again but we have different positions. I emphasize that we believe in moral protest, in democracy.

JBE: Do you expect to go on indefinitely?

María Adela: What we want and think is that the Mothers of the Plaza de Mayo must endure forever, much more than in our own lifetimes. It has to do with having a guardian position on society in order to watch so this will not happen again—not here or not anywhere else in the world.

Renée: To watch and to denounce. Perhaps it won't be necessary to go to the Plaza if here we have transformation and the guilty are punished. But we want to associate, to witness, to denounce every violation. Because you know at the beginning we only wanted our children. But, as time passed, we got a different comprehension of what was going on in the world. Today I was listening to the radio and there was somebody who sings very well who was singing about babies starving. This is also a violation of human rights. Perhaps there is not much that we can do. I repeat something that Lord Acton said, he knew a lot, he said that people for human rights and humanity must realize justice where they can. They must have a sense of hope *and* reality. I explain so many times that when people are interested in our fight, in human rights, that we find friends and supporters everywhere. And we say to everyone; be very alert. We never imagined such a thing could happen here. We were the Europeans of Latin America, a civilized country, not a banana republic. But, you see . . . there are always very dangerous things.

Renée's words are reflected in the January 1989 "Project Proposal of Madres de La Plaza de Mayo—Linea Fundadora," a statement of purpose and a search for international support. "We are certain that our actions contribute to the strengthening of democracy. . . . We are also certain that history has given us the role of being the Memory, so that NEVER AGAIN will there be repression in our country, and the children of our nation could grow and mature in freedom." Specific demands included, among others, continued investigations into the fate of each and every disappeared person plus trials of those accused of disappearances; abolition of Law 23.492 of "full stop" (*punto finale,* or statute of limitations), which ended trials against human rights violators; and abolition of Law 23.521 ("due obedience"), which freed accused violators of criminal charges, declaring their crimes null and void.

But, most important, these Mothers encoded democracy in its specifically liberal understandings—grounded in human rights construed as immunities and duties—into their political self-definition. Through their actions and deeds, the ethical force of an argument from human rights helped to animate quiescent sectors of a moribund and demoralized civil society. Whatever Argentina's future fate, these Mothers would say, human rights can never again be trampled upon with such impunity. That is their wager—one to which they have devoted their lives in the name of the lost lives of their children.

Christmas Day, 1988. An early telephone call. I thought it was probably my mother but it was Renée, calling to wish me a Merry Christmas, and asking after my husband and children, and my parents, too. She especially wanted to know of rites of passage—any graduations, engagements, marriages—all those special moments in the life cycle torn from her, denied observance in her own life, with her own children. I assured her that I had not put the story of the Mothers out of my mind, that I cited her and María Adela in the paper "The Power and Powerlessness of Women" delivered at the University of Leiden, September 1987, tying their politics to that of Václav Havel, then jailed dissident, now, remarkably, president of a democratic Czech Republic.

And I was writing yet another essay, drawing upon something she had said about being a daughter of Antigone. She thanked me and called me her friend. Truth to tell, I was having a lot more difficulty "incorporating material" from my Argentine experience and the politics of Las Madres than I let on to Renée. But I've already done enough hand wringing on this issue. One does what one can. The story isn't over. Not by any means. But this much can be said. The Mothers remained faithful to the dominant image of the mother of their society. Yet they politicized this tradition against a repressive state, both as a form of protection—the state should fulfill its rhetorical claims to defend motherhood—and as a newfound identity—mothers looking for their children, mothers for human rights. By confronting a repressive state and forcing this issue into the streets and the Plaza de Mayo, the iconography of Motherhood in Argentine society was forever altered: from weeping woman to defiant witness. Determined as they are not to have their individual tragedies dismissed as private dramas, the Mothers held and hold to the conviction that if a society censors its memory and denies the past to its children and its grandchildren, hope for a more just social order must always be tinged with desperation, perpetually forlorn.

These are bits of a collage in an unstill life, a world taking shape, struggling to be born, open to the stubborn reality of the everyday and to the "miracle," as Hannah Arendt put it, of new beginnings. A politics of corpses or a politics of "hope and reality"? The jury is out.

We *are* your daughters of Antigone. I did not get to bury my children, as Antigone buried her brother. But I have risked my life to make public their suffering. Now, somehow, I must find the strength to go on living. I can do this because if I do not my children will have died twice, once at the hands of their tormentors and a second time from my silence. Thrown into the sea, tossed like garbage into mass graves, where are my children? I cannot bring flowers, nor pray, nor visit their final resting places. Like the Mothers, the Disappeared are everywhere, wherever a single person is abducted, tortured, killed unjustly. Like Antigone, we will endure beyond our lifetimes. This is what we recognize. This is our hope.[19]

Notes

Originally published in Donna Bassin, Margaret Honey, and Maryle Mohrer Kaplan, eds., *Representations of Motherhood.* © 1994. (New Haven: Yale University Press). Reprinted by permission.

1. E. F. Mignone, "The Military: What Is to Be Done?" *Report on the Americas* 21, no. 4 (1987).

2. J. R. Scobie, *Argentina* (New York: Oxford University Press, 1971).

3. J. M. Taylor, *Eva Perón: The Myths of a Woman* (Chicago: University of Chicago Press, 1979). Page citations in the next two paragraphs are to this source.

4. J. M. Todd, *Luther: A Life* (New York: Crossroad, 1982), 142, 162.

5. S. Ruddick, *Maternal Thinking* (Boston: Beacon Press, 1989).

6. J. B. Elshtain, "Antigone's Daughters," *democracy* 2, no. 2 (1982): 46–59.

7. I will not delve into the firestorm of protest this essay elicited upon publication, as this would offer only a footnote to what seems to me now the perfervid politics of feminism at one stage in its recent history.

8. G. Steiner, *Antigones* (New York: Oxford University Press, 1984).

9. A. Dorfman, *Widows* (New York: Aventura, 1984), v.

10. C. Martínez Morena, *El Infierno* (London: Readers International, 1988), 262.

11. J. Simpson and J. Bennett, *The Disappeared and the Mothers of the Plaza* (New York: St. Martin's, 1985), 161.

12. *Nunca Más: The Report of the Argentine National Commission of the Disappeared* (New York: Farrar, Straus and Giroux, 1986).

13. C. Milosz, *The Captive Mind* (New York: Random House, 1990), 216.

14. O'Donnell's argument is based on the concepts of Albert O. Hirschman in his book *Exit, Voice, and Loyalty* and appears in the first essay in G. O'Donnell, "On the Fruitful Convergences of Hirschman's *Exit, Voice, and Loyalty* and *Shifting Involvements: Reflections from the Recent Argentine Experience.*" University of Notre Dame, Kellogg Institute, Working Paper no. 58. Page citations in the next two paragraphs are to this source.

15. J. H. Tully, ed., *John Locke: A Letter concerning Toleration* (Indianapolis: Hackett, 1983), 15.

16. J. G. Schirmer, " 'Those Who Die for Life Cannot Be Called Dead': Women and

Human Rights Protest in Latin America," *Harvard Human Rights Yearbook* 1 (1988): 41–76.

17. Although there is a difference between the two Mothers groups that emerged after the schism, the Linea Fundadora is more solidly grounded in human rights discourse, in both its political orientation and its internal structure. The Bonafini-dominated Mothers downplayed human rights by comparison to a more conspiratorial and accusatory language of militance, as I note further on.

18. Hebe Bonafini is the powerful, initially self-appointed president of Las Madres from whom the Linea Fundadora group of the original Mothers separated in early 1986.

19. J. B. Elshtain, "Antigone's Daughters Reconsidered," in S. K. White, ed., *Life-World and Politics: Between Modernity and Postmodernity* (Notre Dame: University of Notre Dame Press, 1989), 235.

19

Is There a Feminist Tradition
on War and Peace?

> And this teaching by example is, indeed, the only form of
> "persuasion" that philosophical truth is capable of without
> perversion or distortion; by the same token, philosophical
> truth can become "practical" and inspire action without
> violating the rule of the political realm only when it
> manages to become manifest in the guise of an example.
>
> *Hannah Arendt*

There is no separate feminist tradition on war and peace. A recent work, *Traditions of International Ethics,*[1] includes no chapter on a "feminist tradition." For good reason: each articulated feminist position represents either an evolution within, or a breakout from, a previous historic discourse. Thus one finds feminist Hobbesians and pacifists; liberal internationalists and nationalistic isolationists. What feminist position a particular thinker or advocate endorses will depend upon the tradition in which her feminism is lodged or out of which it emerges. Although feminist antiwar pacifism (variously grounded) is perhaps the best known and most prevalent of feminist positions, it does not stand alone. What I will do in the pages to follow is to offer a sense of the landscape of feminist discourse, historically and currently, on matters of war and peace. To say that it is difficult to assess a "feminist tradition" in matters of war and peace is to understate. Do not expect a tidy picture. Despite the often doleful pleas of feminists for women to unite, women and feminism remain divided on every important war and peace question. There is no clear-cut "feminist way" to discuss how war and peace have been understood. There is, however, a rather rough-and-ready feminist tradition or backdrop to current controversies, and I will begin there.

Feminism emerged in the West as one feature of liberalism, indebted to Enlightenment presuppositions and the doctrine of the "rights of man." I refer, of course, to feminism as a self-conscious enterprise with the publication of Mary Wollstonecraft's *A Vindication of the Rights of Woman* in 1792. Wollstonecraft sought to extend the French Revolution's proclamation of the rights of man to women. She insists that women must be active citizens if they are to pass civic virtue on to their young. She effaces the distinction between men and women where "bodily strength" is concerned by calling for identical educations for boys and girls. What will emerge from educational symmetry, she hopes, is a decisive strike against what she takes to be Jean-Jacques Rousseau's misidentification of virtue—his embrace of what I have called "armed civic virtue." For Wollstonecraft, there is no honor in the soldier, past or present, as the vast majority of soldiers are a mass swept along by coercion and command. Thus a "standing army" is "incompatible with freedom." She condemns Rousseau for exalting "to demi-gods [those] who were scarcely human—the brutal Spartans, who, in defiance of justice and gratitude, sacrificed, in cold blood, the slaves who had shewn themselves heroes to rescue their oppressors."[2] Yet, in general, she endorses many of the ends and aims of civic republicanism—civic virtue and autonomy first and foremost, shorn of their martial dimensions. But she nowhere addresses what the grounds, if any, for war might be. Nor does she spend any time exploring wartime conduct.

Wollstonecraft simply assumes a national identity, paying no attention to the violent manner in which the French Revolutionaries molded that identity by yanking young men out of their local identities, disciplining their bodies to armed purposes, and scraping off the insignia of their particularity by the visible sign of putting diverse human elements into identical uniforms. A supporter of the French Revolution, Wollstonecraft does not engage the presiding revolutionary images. These included paintings of the militant Spartan Mother and Liberty as represented by Marianne, a young female militant with both breasts bared.[3] The civic republican world, for all its female icons, was strongly male-dominant. Wollstonecraft endorses this tradition but hopes that somehow, if men and women receive the same education, a softening will follow as a matter of course. This tension—endorsing "the same" but expecting "the different"—is by no means limited to Wollstonecraft; indeed, if there is a "tradition" of feminism on war and peace, one feature of it is an ongoing repetition or reencoding of a fundamental ambivalence: should women "fight" the men or join the men in fighting? As well, there is also a near-silence on many of the most salient issues of war and peace as they emerged in the writings of Western theorists, moralists, and war fighters: What is a justified war? What should or should not be done in fighting a war? What are the grounds for resistance to political authority, and what is permissible by way of resistance? What is most strikingly displayed as one surveys the history and the literature is the continuing manifestation of an abiding, one is almost tempted to say, ur-ambivalence.

Let me fill in, briefly, other pieces to this puzzle in order to bolster and clarify my assessment. Mary Wollstonecraft inherited a tradition in which women were tied to diverse conceptions of war and peace. One, the historically grounded, legendary, and prototypical Spartan Mother, offers up the woman as a civic militant who bears children that "they might die for Sparta and this is what has come to pass for me." She is one of the prefeminist exemplars who helps to frame later feminisms. For the Spartan Mother, war is the consequence of the existence of an external "other" who poses a threat to one's city, civic republic, or polity. Her identity is entangled with war's honor and the valor of husbands and sons. War is justified for patriotic reasons of state. Later civic republicans, like Rousseau, recalling the glories of Sparta, insisted that the potent love of the mother country, the willingness to serve and protect her, would shrivel on the civic vine if mothers no longer figured overpoweringly in the affections and civic upbringing of their children. There are so many continuing evocations of the Spartan Mother tradition that it would take volumes to catalogue all of them. This much, however, should be noted: for the Spartan Mother, any serious threat to civic freedom is a justified *causus belli*. I know of no systematic discussion in the Spartan Mother tradition, past or present, on the conduct of war. Presumably, war is hell, a sometimes necessary hell. Here Spartan Mothers would vary depending upon the traditions of their own society. I daresay, the mother of historic Sparta and the mother of the United States during World War II would take rather different tacks on this matter, although even here I am not so sure. Eighty to eighty-five percent of Americans endorsed dropping the atomic bombs on Hiroshima and Nagasaki, with no significant gender difference. Women were by no means exempt from a perfervid nigh-exterminationist rhetoric where the Japanese were concerned.

For the Spartan Mother exemplar, both prefeminist and in its feminist variations, there is no presumption against war save on the level of a hope that her country's freedom will never be threatened, from within or without. Grounds for war, or for a crushing of oppositional forces which appear to threaten the polity from within, are primarily those of security—for her family and her nation. For contemporary feminists of the sort whose worldview begins with an inexorable cleavage between men and women, masculinism and feminism, the Spartan Mother can only represent a retrograde "male-dominated" perspective and force, their own advocacy of the destruction or containment of the male enemy to the contrary notwithstanding. Ironically, hard-line "realist" feminists, who believe men and women are ontologically akin to different species and are, as well, in a state of perpetual war, are often far more unrelenting in their views of the necessity for a "sex war" than Spartan Mothers have ever been in their defense of their country's wars. Yet such feminists see in the Spartan Mother's loyalty to her polity and her willingness to see young men die in its defense a loathsome "false consciousness" they disdain to admit into the category "feminist." But to make this sort of dismissive move requires jettisoning much of the feminist tradition, a tradition that historically often moves uneasily between Spartan Mother and Beautiful Soul poles.

To the second main female/feminist exemplar, then, the Beautiful Soul. She enters history—or, perhaps better put, she is secured within the history of the West—with the triumph of Christianity, hence with a presumption against violence and a dream of a peaceable kingdom. For there is what I am tempted to call a "feminization" of ethics associated with Christianity. Finding in the "paths of peace" the most natural as well as the most desirable way of being, Christian pioneers exalted a pacific ontology. Violence must justify itself before the court of nonviolence. Over time, within this broad tradition, men were constituted as just Christian warriors, fighters, and defenders of righteous causes whose violence required (at least in principle) rather elaborate justification. Women, unevenly and variously depending upon social location, got solidified into a culturally sanctioned vision of virtuous, nonviolent womanhood I call the Beautiful Soul. It is important to note here that, although the pacifist and just-war streams in Christianity parted historic company, they remain genealogically related. Both put violence on trial, placing the burden of proof on those who take up arms.

For the Beautiful Soul, this presumption plays out as a nigh absolute interdiction on female violence coupled with a mingling of regret and resoluteness should her society embark on a course of war. If there is one dominant feminist tradition before the twentieth century, it lies in a politicized version of the Beautiful Soul (of which more below). Once again, the tale is by no means simple but, by the late nineteenth century, "absolute distinctions between men and women in regard to violence" had come to prevail.[4] The female Beautiful Soul is pictured as frugal, self-sacrificing, and, at times, delicate. Although many women empowered themselves to think and to act on the basis of this ideal of female virtue, the symbol easily slides into sentimentalism. To "preserve the purity of its heart," writes Hegel, the Beautiful Soul must flee from "contact with the actual world."[5] In matters of war and peace, the female Beautiful Soul cannot put a stop to suffering, cannot effectively fight the mortal wounding of sons, brothers, husbands, fathers. She continues the long tradition of women as keepers of the flame of nonwarlike values even as, in the nonpacifist versions of Beautiful Souldom, it is the woman on the home front who makes the war effort itself sustainable over time. It is important to note that, in time of war, the Beautiful Soul exemplar often elides to the Spartan Mother as women are identified, and identify themselves as, heroines of the home front and upholders of a more or less total *levée en masse* associated with French Revolutionary civic republicanism.

Let's put a bit more historic flesh on the bones of this trope by looking at nineteenth-century suffragist appropriations of Spartan Motherhood and Beautiful Souldom. Votes for women were justified on the grounds of ontological equality between the sexes, on the one hand, *and* female difference, on the other. Some suffragist supporters trafficked in such sentiments as: "For the Safety of the Nation to the Women Give the Vote / For the Hand That Rocks the Cradle Will Never Rock the Boat!" Here an argument for votes for women on the grounds of utility ("for the safety of the nation") and stability ("will never rock the boat") prevails. Presumably, women, once they have the vote, will not rock the boat of national security and male determination of war and peace matters. During America's Civil War, the leading suffragists supported the war effort even as they condemned war. They chided men for having brought the country into war, yet praised the fervent and spontaneous patriotism war engenders: a reaction repeated again and again, most recently in the United States in the Persian Gulf War of 1991. (I offer reflections on the Gulf War and this prototypical feminist ambivalence below.) They decried war's terrible cost, yet celebrated and legitimated the many campaigns fought by women in sanitary commissions, as suppliers, nurses, buriers of the dead. Elizabeth Cady Stanton extolled the "multitude of delicate, refined women, unused to care and toil, thrown suddenly on their own resources" during the war, and she used this story of wartime loyalty and sacrifice as further ammunition on behalf of the suffrage effort once the war was concluded.[6] Stanton supported the Civil War, but she also thundered against "male wars" in other contexts, proclaiming that a "new evangel of womanhood" would put a decisive end to chaos and destructiveness. Here are her words:

> The male element is a destructive force, stern, selfish, aggrandizing, loving war, violence, conquest, acquisition, breeding in the material and moral world alike discord, disorder, disease and death. See what a record of blood and cruelty the pages of history reveal! Through what slavery and slaughter, and sacrifice, through what inquisitions and imprisonments, pains and persecutions, black codes and gloomy creeds, the soul of humanity has struggled for the centuries, while mercy has veiled her face and all hearts have been dead alike to love and hope! The male element has held high carnival thus far, it has fairly run riot from the beginning, overpowering the feminine element everywhere, crushing out the diviner quali-

ties in human nature until we know but little of true manhood and womanhood, of the latter comparatively nothing, for it has scarce been recognized as a power until within the last century. . . . The need of this hour is not territory, gold mines, railroads, or specie payments, but a new evangel of womanhood, to exalt purity, virtue, morality, true religion, to lift man up into the higher realms of thought and action.[7]

This is a pretty tall order. It rather reminds me of the frequently voiced sentiment written by one's friends in one's Senior Yearbook (if you graduated high school in the late 1950s in the United States, as I did): "Stay as Sweet as You Are!" an expression often coupled to admonitions to be successful in life. How the suffragists intended to pull this one off remains a bit murky, but there is little doubt they did intend it. All the problems of war and peace would somehow melt away once the epiphany of the new society was attained. In the meantime: condemn war, either absolutely or strategically; condemn men, either in principle or provisionally; extol women, both for their wartime loyalty and contribution as Spartan Mothers and for their general outlook and principled opposition to violence as Beautiful Souls.

A similar fusion of disparate imperatives and identities emerged in the World War I era with solid Spartan Mothers such as Britain's famous or infamous "Little Mother," who trashed all mewling pacifists, male and female. The "Little Mother" wrote a letter, published in the London *Morning Post,* in 1916, denouncing pacifists and whiners and declaring that she herself was delighted to send her son off to war—the "sacred trust of motherhood" demands no less, for "Women are created for the purpose of giving life, and men to take it."[8] Less violently, one Mrs. F. S. Hallowes in her 1918 book, *Mothers of Men and Militarism,* noted women's equally "passionate love of mother-country. . . . Though we loathe slaughter we find that after men have done their best to kill and wound, women are ever ready to mend the broken bodies, soothe the dying, and weep over nameless graves!"[9] The Connecticut Congress of Mothers issued a "Ten Commandments of Womanhood" which called for Mothers to "Hearten Thy Men and Weep Not" and to "Keep Though the Faith of Thy Mothers, for in the years of thy country's sacrifice for Independence and Union they served valiantly and quailed not."

In this same era, thousands of politicized women who were suffragists agitated for their country's entrance into the war and proclaimed themselves ready to serve. Women of the Triple Entente powers often justified the war on liberal internationalist grounds: the world will be safe only when democracy defeats autocracy. (A bit tricky to square with Romanov Russia's alliance with the British and French democracies, but expressive nonetheless of the liberal internationalist view that only then will the breeding ground for war be vanquished.) In line with such patriotic identification and in the wider interest of destroying the breeding ground of evil (autocracy, militarism), when the Women's Emergency Corps was created in Britain, women queued up in long lines waiting for the doors to open so they could sign up. For such women, the war took on many of the features of a crusade. At the same time, in this era, thousands of other politicized women who were suffragists agitated against the war and for peace and proclaimed themselves in opposition to the war on the grounds of a new internationalism and humanism that would one day trump particularistic national loyalties as well as "militarism," a generic term for the evil of arms, armies, and war.

The World War I era feminist antiwar stance is perhaps best summed up in the notion that there is an "eternal opposition," in Jane Addams's words, between feminism and militarism. It should be noted that women have been linked to peace campaigns at least since the Middle Ages, to antiwar sentiment since the Greek tragedies (by contrast to much of the Spartan Mother tradition): I have in mind *The Trojan Women,* for example, although even here things are tricky. It is well to recall that the maternal Hecuba, mourning the death of Andromache and Hector's son, her grandson, Astyanax, decries his "wretched death" (he has been thrown from the top of the city wall of Troy by its conquerors): "You might have fallen fighting for your city," anticipating, with this line, an honorable Spartan Mother resolution.[10]

The cleavage between peace women and war women made sharply visible a prewar cleavage between militant suffragists (more prevalent in Britain than in the United States) who were prepared to use violent methods ("the argument of the thrown stone") to achieve their ends and the far more numerous group who were opposed to all forms of violence, including violence against property. With the war, the militant suffragists tended toward Spartan Motherhood of the most jingoistic sort. The antiviolence suffragists, in their most visible and dominant incarnation, surfaced as that uneasy amalgam of Spartan Motherhood and Beautiful Souldom noted above. But there was a third alternative—opposition to the war as a logical continuance of the suffrage campaign which, to such enthusiasts, itself meant the humanizing of governments by extending the suffrage to women. Women peace activists embracing this latter idea saw the causes of war in the maladjustment of industrial relations and the failure to pacify states by extending the suffrage. For many, women's nonviolence was a logical extension of maternalism. For others, particularly those associated with a socialist vision, peace was that day when the causes of war (capitalism, imperialism) had been eliminated. Men as well as women could embrace this cause.

My aim here is not to recall a well-documented history but to make explicit the markers of social identity and structures of discourse deployed by antiwar feminists in the World War I era. A Women's Peace Party was formed. At its height in the United States there were 165 group memberships totaling some 40,000 women. The American party was one section of the Women's International Committee for Permanent Peace—the Kantian echoes are apt—which had branches in fifteen countries. Antiwar feminists, in line with what Michael Howard calls "the liberal conscience," pushed for continuous arbitration, for a negotiated peace short of total victory, and for a peace settlement shorn of vindictiveness. In this and other ways, feminists in this period located themselves within the larger frame of pacifist/just war discourse. Women peace campaigners promulgated internationalism, as a worldwide concatenation of peace-loving peoples, especially women, to bring into being the conditions for permanent peace. After the war, women were influential in pressing for the Kellogg-Briand Pact of 1928 declaring war illegal and were on the National Committee on the Cause and Cure of War, which collected ten million signatures on a disarmament petition in 1932. Contemporary feminist and women's peace efforts look back to these and other instances of female activism, much but not all of it under a feminist imprimatur, as historic warrant for their own efforts. Beautiful Soul presumptions against violence are dominant in these and similar efforts: violence is always terrible; women are the special keepers of nonwarlike values; war is a breakdown in a preternatural condition of harmony and equilibrium, realizable and restorable yet again once the various "enemies" of this humane condition and vision are bested.

This version of feminism emerged, as I have already indicated, primarily as a variant of liberal internationalism. But the hope still remains that if women ran things, the things they ran would look much different and be much better (more peaceful) than at present. At this end of the pole, feminism elides into pacifism—a pacifism not grounded in a Christian nonviolent ethic so much as in an often essentialist, even biological argument for women's inherent peacefulness. It is worth noting that all the questions having to do with war and peace historically—what are the grounds for war? what grounds are justifiable and what are not? are there limits to fighting a war, even a "good war"?—melt away if one assumes that once women take over war itself will disappear. This is a very old idea, ongoingly refurbished as feminist ideology. For example, one of the first discursive moments in the history of feminism (retrospectively constructed, for the author in question was not self-consciously feminist) is Christine de Pizan's *A Book of the City of Ladies*. Three goddesses—Rectitude, Reason, and Justice—found her city. Noteworthy in this "mirror of Princes" utopia is the falling away of any nastiness, any dilemma that might implicate the Wise Princess in the perennial dilemma of having "dirty hands." Wars are dramatic by their absence in the City of Ladies. Christine repeats the story of the Amazons, noting "delight in the vocation of arms," and their merciless policy of vengeance, in an exchange with Reason aimed at remembering women whose skills demonstrated that they were "fit for all tasks."[11] Accepting Amazonian escapades as historic truth, Christine nonetheless denies this narrative of female ferocity and martial vigor any contemporary clout. Her own vision of the "lady" and the Wise Princess bars such appropriations.

Christine thus anticipates later humanists, liberals, and rationalists who shared her fondness for Rectitude, Reason, and Justice and found war irrational, stupid, wasteful, and atavistic. This, at least, is a principled version of feminist antiwar activity and antimilitarism and it is one variant on liberal internationalism. The major difference, perhaps, is that fewer feminists would find justification for military intervention on humanitarian grounds than would most historic internationalists, finding in the means a collision with preferred ends. This tendency toward "purism" also constitutes an escape hatch from the problem of "dirty hands." Women scholars and activists prepared to talk about the latter problem fall between the stools of contemporary feminist discourse on war and peace.

This brings me to the turbulations of the present in feminist thinking on war and peace. In order to draw together many of this essay's themes, I will concentrate on feminism's uncertain trumpet—and I say this not to condemn but to reinforce the picture of many competing feminist viewpoints and to issue a reminder of the often clashing endorsements within various modes of feminism. For from its inception, feminism has not quite known whether to fight men or to join them; whether to lament sex differences and deny their importance or to acknowledge and even celebrate such differences; whether to condemn all wars outright or to extol women's contributions to war efforts. At times feminists have done all of these things, with scant regard for consistency.[12] Thus one finds "right to fight" feminists who are endorsed by integrationist feminism incarnated in the United States by the National Organization for Women; revolutionary Marxist feminism prepared to approve "third world revolutionary struggles" as well as to sanction a teleology of violence (if necessary) as part of their own struggle against the bourgeois order; pacifist feminism, sanctified by a plethora of old and new efforts. At the antiwar end of the pole, military women become explicable only as "clones of the male model." At the "right to fight" end, pacifist women are construed as "wimps" and regarded as antifeminist because they find women less capable of soldiering than are men.

It is impossible to survey the whole of contemporary feminist discourse in a few pages; however, it is possible to situate feminist arguments on questions of war and peace inside one of several frames. Interestingly, feminism reproduces many assumptions that structure the historic discourses of realism and just war, respectively, re-creating prototypical characters and arguments. Thus, contemporary feminism has both its "Machiavellian moment" as well as its Beautiful Soul reiterations of a just war and pacifist sort. One characteristic of much of this argumentation is its totalizing nature: women must wage a total war against every aspect of patriarchal society, or women must struggle for world peace and total disarmament and the like. That is, for radical feminist realists who presume men and women are, and have been, in a perpetual state of war, "anything goes" to achieve the overthrow of patriarchy. For feminist pacifists, means must be limited and constrained— not just "anything goes"—but anything is possible, including perpetual peace, once the conditions for war are utterly eliminated.

Let me explore these matters further. This is the way feminist realism of a separatist variety works. They declare every condition of humankind one of total war (undeclared) between men and women. They endorse a Hobbesian social ontology and construe politics as a continuation of war. They advise women to "fight dirty" and make generous use of military metaphors. (Who is the Enemy? Where is he located? How can you best defeat him?) Politics becomes a "paradigm case of Oppressor and Oppressed" and there is a lot of tough talk about sex-war and the need for women to take over the extant power structure (including wearing uniforms and carrying guns) as the only way to end their "colonization."[13] Others in this modality turn to the language of pathology and disease. Men are the carriers of a taint. They have a need to oppress women. The pathology must be destroyed, whether by eliminating or by taming men. This is a version of revolutionary violence toward the end of a society in which, at best, an uneasy truce in the sex-war prevails—unless the Enemy has actually been eliminated, whether through unconditional surrender or a policy of actual reduction of the number of men in the human race. ("The proportion of men must be reduced to and maintained at approximately 10% of the human race."[14]) Women who are not "pawns of men" must be in charge of all changes. The following is a pretty standard summary of a hard-core feminist realism where the present situation is concerned—all-out war, an ontology of violence governing relations between all men and all women everywhere, coupled with an apocalyptic utopian insistence that women, naturally pacifistic, will one day rule in peace.

> Why weren't we prepared for this?—the imminence of nuclear holocaust; the final silencing of life; the brutal extinction of the planet. . . . We have lived with violence so long. We have lived under the rule of the fathers so long. Violence and patriarchy: mirror images. An ethic of destruction as normative. Diminished love

of life, a numbing to real events as the final consequence. We are not even prepared. . . . Wars are nothing short of rituals of organized killing presided over by
men deemed "the best." The fact is—they are. They have absorbed in the most
complete way the violent character of their own ethos. . . . Women know and feel
the lies that maintain nuclear technology because we have been lied to before. We
are the victims of patriotical lies. . . . To end the state of war, to halt the momen-
tum toward death, passion for life must flourish. Women are the bearers of life-
loving energy. Ours is the task of deepening that passion for life and separating
from all that threatens life, all that diminishes life; becoming who we are as
women.[15]

Oddly enough, the triumph of the Beautiful Soul is anticipated in these
often remorseless narratives. The rhetoric of total war dominates; but, ultimately, the victims will vanquish their oppressors. Modified and more
plausible versions of feminist realism and Beautiful Soul variations include,
first, the stance of the National Organization for Women and, by extension,
all rights-absolutist–based versions of feminism.[16] NOW has argued (in an
amicus brief in a case involving the constitutionality of the all-male draft)
that military service is central to the concept of citizenship. It follows that if
women are to gain first-class citizenship, they, too, must have the right to
fight. In some instances this gets coupled with the hope that women will
"humanize" the armed services. Equal-opportunity feminism, then, walks
an uneasy line between presumptions against war fused to insistencies that
women fight wars.

The grounds for war are not discussed in any systematic way save for a
tendency to favor wars for "liberation" and oppose American intervention
for almost any purpose anywhere at any time. This latter predisposition was
strained during the Gulf War, with some 6 percent of the deployed U.S. force
being female personnel. Replaying a familiar hand, a number of prominent
feminist politicians and activists condemned the war as an overreaction (at
best), yet used the war as an occasion to push for total abrogation of the few
remaining statutory limits to women in combat for the American All Volunteer Force. Unsurprisingly, many military women—especially reservists—
told feminist activists to mind their own business: they did not want to fight.
But others, primarily officers and often from military families themselves,
were delighted at the opportunity to test their mettle. My own favorite testimony along these lines is Major Rhonda Cornum's postwar ("as told to")
memoir. Cornum, who was taken prisoner by the Iraqis when the helicopter
in which she was flying crashed, writes of the fact that she didn't want "to go
home without seeing action," for she was prepared to "go to war. . . . Fly and
fight. I loved it."[17] She had chosen to go to a military medical school rather

than a civilian one (she is a flight surgeon), and she and her husband "feel the same way about the big things: duty, honor, country, loyalty. . . . [her daughter] would have thought that I was a wimp if I stayed home."[18] She, for one, wasn't afraid of dying—much worse would be to dishonor her uniform and her country. This is a stance feminist pacifists, whether Christian or those of the strategic sort whose pacifism comes and goes depending upon the occasion, find well-nigh inexplicable. Cornum, needless to say, sees herself as a women's rights egalitarian.

For, remember, emerging from the historic discourse surveyed above is a version of the Beautiful Soul grounded in a pacific, not a violent, ontology. Men may be oppressors, but the condition of society is not "war," it is injustice to be fought by nonviolent means. Analysts in this mode insist that women do have insights to bring to bear on the public world. Women are located as moral educators and political actors. This discourse struggles to forge links between what Sara Ruddick has called "maternal thinking" and nonviolent theories of conflict without assuming that it is possible to translate easily maternal imperatives into a public good.[19] This view differs from celebrations of a peaceful matriarchy. Its proponents recognize that people must grow up to become citizens; and a civic being is not guaranteed nurture but is sure instead to find disagreement and conflict short of war, in the maternal thinking universe, save for truly extreme instances (Nazism, genocide). The pitfalls of this feminism are linked to its intrinsic strengths. By insisting that women are in and of the social world, its framers draw explicit attention to the context within which their subjects act. But this wider surround is one that continues to bombard women and mothers with the formulation that "doing good" means "being nice." Thus, even as stereotypic maternalisms exert pressure to sentimentalize, competing feminisms are sharply repudiating, finding in any evocation of "maternal thinking" a trap and a delusion.

Lynne Segal, in her book, *Is the Future Female?* finds much to praise and to challenge in contemporary evocations of "maternal thinking" tied to a wider set of hopes for peaceful arbitration of disputes. Those who evoke this hope (she includes Ruddick and Elshtain in this company) reject the biological reductionism of many ecofeminists and feminist pacifists (like the late Petra Kelly or Dr. Helen Caldicott, for example, who make much of wombs, harmony, inner peace, and so on). But the view itself is compatible, argues Segal, with many other positions—both radical and conservative, she claims. Unsurprisingly, she finds, real flesh-and-blood women (the majority!) more often than not express both patriotism and "humanitarian revulsion from war." Her case in point is drawn from a series of interviews with British women who wire up weapons for the big arms industry. (Notice the Spartan

Mother imagery lurking in the following statement.) "Our attitude [notes one such woman] was that although it was unfortunate we were involved [in the Falklands War, in this case], once it was upon us we had to get on and do everything to back our boys. People were very willing to work overtime and do whatever was necessary, whether you've got a son involved or not, when it's the English, it's your boys, isn't it? I mean it could be your boy next time."[20]

I am somewhat loath to conclude on such an uncertain note. But this aptly reflects the vagaries of the multiple "feminist" traditions in the matter of war and peace. Perhaps one story will help the reader to better appreciate my frustration. When I was putting together a collection on just war theory, I searched high and low for articles by feminists—indeed, by female scholars—lodged securely within the just war tradition and exploring either feminism or war and peace more generally inside that framework. I turned up almost nothing. Perhaps because women have not been history's war fighters, it has been easier for them—and feminists, too—to treat the matter in one of two often extreme ways: either everything is war and ordinary life is construed as a state of "supreme emergency" with men trying, quite literally, to kill and coerce women, or the concrete realities and limits of the world in which we live are overcome discursively by working toward and arguing on behalf of some Kantian (or more feminized) version of perpetual peace. (I refer, of course, to feminists who are not specifically Christian or ethical pacifists. To the extent they are, their feminism seems less dominant than their pacifism.)

The direction I would tend at this point is toward a version of Christian realism in the Niebuhrian tradition. Here's why: I cling to no shibboleth that women, if drafted in large numbers, would somehow transform the military and the fighting of wars. We are not well served by the abstract language of civic obligation and rights here. One example would be the ways in which theories of justice modeled on macroeconomics, if given a feminist turn and applied internationally, often lead to the imposition of a vision of justice and a norm of gender relations distinctly Western, even North American, on other societies. I recall the unsettling experience of hearing a feminist scholar, herself indebted to such models of justice, justifying the Soviet invasion of Afghanistan because the Afghanis were a patriarchal, sexist society—somehow the Soviets would bring them up to speed! As well, abstracted justice models suggest that we will have the "just society" or a "just international order" only when messy human life and lives conform to a more or less formal model, by definition a static snapshot rather than a theory supple enough to come to grips with the ebb and flow of human affairs and with differences, sexual, political, cultural. If anything, the post–cold war world should disabuse us of the idea that peoples, including women, will, when the crunch comes, be more devoted to an abstract ideal of some future perfect society than to the defense and territorial integrity of their own very specific cultures and "places." This belief is often coupled to a rough-and-ready notion of "human rights" as a minimal standard, a set of restrictions on what governments or opponents or enemies should do to their own or other people.

The realism toward which I gesture has more in common with just war thinking than it does Hobbesianism or Machiavellianism. I call my prototypical civic character a "chastened patriot," one who modulates the rhetoric of high patriotic purpose (hence repudiates the Spartan Mother as a dominant identity), keeping alive the distancing voice of ironic remembrance and recognition of the way patriotism can shade into the excesses of nationalism; recognition of the fact that patriotism in the form of armed civic virtue is a dangerous chimera. The chastened patriot is committed and detached: enough apart so that he or she can be reflective about civic ties and loyalties, cherishing many loyalties rather than celebrating one alone. This version of civic identity is not only compatible with but helps to sustain a "minimalist universalism" without falling into the abstract, juridical naiveté of much liberal internationalism. How such a character—and she might or might not be a feminist, although a feminist variant would be apt—sorts out conceptions of war and peace would be complex, drawing upon the many traditions and currents which have shaped and continue to shape Western life and thought. This seems as good a place as any to stop.

Notes

Originally published in Terry Nardin, ed., *The Ethics of War and Peace* (Princeton: Princeton University Press, 1996), 214–27. Reprinted by permission.

1. Terry Nardin and David R. Mapel, *Traditions of International Ethics* (Cambridge: Cambridge University Press, 1992).

2. Mary Wollstonecraft, *A Vindication of the Rights of Woman* (New York: Norton, 1967), 75.

3. In my book *Women and War*, I introduce several prototypical exemplars as embodiments of particular traditions. The Spartan Mother, the woman who locates the civic above the private and is prepared (even eager) to sacrifice her sons on the altar of civic necessity, is one. The Just Warrior and the Beautiful Soul are the other dominant collective representations in the Western story of war and peace. *Women and War* was published by Basic Books in 1987.

4. Natalie Zemon Davis, "Men, Women, and Violence: Some Reflections on Equality," *Smith Alumnae Quarterly* (April 1975), 15.

5. G. W. F. Hegel, *The Phenomenology of Spirit*, trans. A. V. Miller (Oxford: Clarendon Press, 1977), 399–400.

6. Elizabeth Cady Stanton, Susan B. Anthony, and Matilda Joslyn Gage, eds., *History of Woman Suffrage,* vol. 2 (Rochester, N.Y.: Charles Mann, 1887), 1–2.

7. Ibid., 785.

8. For a full discussion, see *Women and War,* 192–93.

9. Mrs. F. S. Hallowes, *Mothers of Men and Militarism* (London: Headley Bros., Bishopsgate, 1918), 24–25.

10. David Grene and Richard Lattimore, eds., *Greek Tragedies,* vol. 2 (Chicago: University of Chicago Press, 1960), 272, 288 (from *The Trojan Women*).

11. Christine de Pizan, *A Book of the City of Ladies,* trans. Earl Jeffrey Richards (New York: Persea Books, 1982), 40–42.

12. In the discussion of contemporary feminism, I draw freely on *Women and War.*

13. These quotes are from "early" (1970s) feminist texts, but the presumptions are widely shared, as I note, to the present moment. Sources are Ti-Grace Atkinson, "Theories of Radical Feminism," in *Notes from the Second Year: Women's Liberation,* ed. Shulamith Firestone (New York: n.p., 1970), 37, and Susan Brownmiller, *Against Our Will: Men, Women, and Rape* (New York: Simon and Schuster, 1975), 388.

14. Sally Miller Gearhart, "The Future—If There Is One—Is Female," in Pam McAllister, ed., *Reweaving the Web of Life* (Philadelphia: New Society Publishers, 1982), 266–84.

15. Barbara Zanotti, "Patriarchy: A State of War," in *Reweaving,* 16–19.

16. Well, almost. Male rights take a beating in sexual harassment definitions so broad they include "ogling" or "winking" or "suggestive noises." But I cannot get into this matter here.

17. Rhonda Cornum (as told to Peter Copeland), *She Went to War* (Novato, Calif.: Presidio Press, 1992), 4.

18. Ibid., 21.

19. See Ruddick's essays, "Maternal Thinking" and "Preservative Love and Military Destruction," in Joyce Trebilcot, ed., *Mothering: Essays in Feminist Theory* (Totowa, N.J.: Rowman and Allanheld, 1983), 213–30 and 231–62 respectively. See also "The Rationality of Care," in Jean Bethke Elshtain and Sheila Tobias, eds., *Women, Militarism, and War* (Totowa, N.J.: Rowman and Littlefield, 1990), 229–54.

20. Lynne Segal, *Is the Future Female?* (London: Virago Press, 1987), 198.

FIVE

The Search

for the via media

This rough beast of a book has slouched its way to a concluding section, winding down with essays advocating a form of political reason that enables us to avoid equally unacceptable extremes. These essays do not simply advocate, but, if I wrote them the way I intended, model what I call for, display this *via media* in practice in political discourse. Beginning with a sustained argument with Richard Rorty and his particular brand of "ironic" liberalism—for it is too lighthearted, insufficiently weighty—I next turn to American small towns and the ways in which so many of our important writers have found them altogether too weighty by far, bearing down on the human soul and constricting and distorting it. As a small-town girl (Timnath, Colorado, population 185—not really a town but a village), I appreciate the attacks on the small-mindedness of small places, but I am determined to lift up that which is good about small towns. For these were, and are, places where people are compelled to engage and cannot easily repudiate and spurn and ignore their neighbors. That ordinary people in our culture continue to pine for the idea of the small town means they are searching for a landscape that is not necessarily always warm and friendly, but, rather, one that is recognizably human—that has discernible form and scale and invites us to inhabit and to engage it.

The essay on education ("Democracy's Middle Way") is explicitly an engagement with T. S. Eliot's writings on education. On another level it is an *homage* to my father, Paul G. Bethke, who died in September of the year this piece was published but whose end was even then haunting me. My father was a public school educator in Colorado who gave a half century to Colorado schools. And whatever equanimity of temperament I possess is my inheritance from him, just as the feistiness displayed in the engagements in Parts 3 and 4 (in particular) derive from my mother, Helen Lind Bethke's, determination to make war, to fight when fighting seemed necessary. I didn't always agree with her choice of battle sites and weapons, but her fierce determination and her willingness to go to the mat loom very large indeed. But, at the end, it is an image of peace that I hope to offer with my own few, inadequate words on our final words from Albert Camus, in his posthumously published novel, *The First Man*. Although not as poor as Camus's, and rural rather than urban, my own childhood was one without privilege but one of love and struggle and an irrevocable change wrought by school. With Camus, I oppose "logical deliriums" and share his "cry of joy and gratitude for this wonderful life." That, too, should come through in our thinking and writing as a kind of silent prayer.

20

Don't Be Cruel: Reflections on Rortyian Liberalism

> There is only the fight to recover what has been lost
> And found and lost again and again; and now, under
>   conditions
> That seem unpropitious. But perhaps neither gain nor loss
> For us, there is only the trying. The rest is not our business.
>
> Home is where one starts from. As we grow older
> The world becomes stranger, the pattern more complicated
>
> Of dead and living.
>
> *T. S. Eliot, "East Coker," 1914*

We are living in remarkable times. Even as nations and peoples formerly under the domination of the Soviet Empire proclaim their political ideals in language that inspired and secured our own political founding; even as Russia herself flails toward democracy, our own democracy is faltering, not flourishing. People confront one another as aggrieved groups rather than free citizens. And our political philosophers all too often merrily whistle a pick-me-up sort of tune as animosities old and new grow and the storm clouds gather.

One current enthusiasm is an up-to-date version of American pragmatism that reassures us things are pretty much moving along as they were meant to. I refer to the pervasive presence and influence of the philosopher Richard Rorty. Rorty is an intelligent and canny thinker and, at times, a powerful writer. But he undercuts whatever *gravitas* might inhere in his own position with moves in a direction that signals the unbearable lightness of liberalism, or at least one dominant modern version of it. If we are considering the future in light of the unraveling of Marxism, Rortyian liberalism is a good place to start.

By George, I think I get it. Then I seem to lose it. That is characteristic of my Rorty experience. I find his arguments slippery, hard to engage. But I don't think engagement is what Rorty is about. I think he means to embrace us, each and every one, or at least all we who feel comfortable being part of "we liberal ironists," "we liberal reformers," "we pragmatists," "we anti-essentialists," we who "don't do things this way," we . . . we . . . we. In his *Contingency, Irony, and Solidarity,* Rorty uses the we-word nine times in one short paragraph.[1] This is a veritable love fest. As the Beatles sang long ago and far away, "I don't want to spoil the party, so I'll go." What follows may be read as the complaints of a party pooper. (Although, let me just add, I'm happy to be invited to attend.)

I will begin with a primer of assorted discontents that evolve into deeper engagements, a fleshed-out counterpoint to Rorty's positions where Freud, cruelty and self-creation, and redescription, among others, are concerned. I use as my point of departure *Contingency, Irony, and Solidarity* as well as Rorty's recently published philosophical papers.[2]

Reading Rorty, I find myself mumbling, "He remains too much the analytic philosopher." That is a vacant complaint as mumbled, so what is at stake in this lament? It has to do with the nature of argument and the menu of options Rorty presents as alternatives. Rorty has a tendency to argue along these lines: Either you are part of "we liberal ironists" or you are an essentialist or foundationalist. He effectively debunks the pretensions of foundationalism, but he fails in his attempt to chart an alternative because that alternative is cast as a thin version of self-creation, wholly contingent, wholly constructed, utterly historicist, nominalist "through and through," or "all the way down," as Rorty might put it.

Further, Rorty insists that we either seek or require "proof" the old-fashioned way, by *refusing* to earn it, relying instead on analytic philosophical or metaphysical reassurances and closures, or we join the ranks of his army of the contingent "we." Surely the universe of argument is far richer than this formula allows. Surely one can reject the correspondence theory of truth or strong convictions concerning the "intrinsic nature of reality" without opting for the view that truth is solely a property of "linguistic entities," the latter being a position he uses to lump together all sorts of folks he likes of the idealist, revolutionary, and romantic sort. Rorty links his commitment to contingency to a rough-and-ready progressivist teleology (even though he cannot permit himself teleological arguments, he relies tacitly on Whiggish history) when he claims, as but one example: "Europe gradually lost the habit of using certain words and gradually acquired the habit of using others."[3] Aside from the peculiarity of granting agency to a continent, what is at work here appears to be a conviction that although there is nothing intrinsic or essential about anything that has happened or that led to the construction of "we liberal ironists," we are still in pretty good shape if we endorse a loose liberal utopia in which things pretty much continue to move along the way they have been moving because, it must be said, the contingencies seem to be on "our side." At least that is the only way I can interpret a statement such as, "A liberal society is one which is content to call 'true' whatever the upshot of such encounters turns out to be."[4] The encounters in question here are basic bad guys versus good guys stuff in which, over time, the good guys appear to be winning, more or less.

The good guys combine commitment with contingency. The bad guys are all commitment—rigid and unyielding. The good guys reject any notion of intrinsic or essentialist anything and insist that so long as everybody has a "chance at self creation," life is pretty good. The good guy—actually, this character of the ideal sort gets to be a "she" throughout Rorty's discussion—accepts that "all is metaphor," and that neither God nor nature designed anything to some preordained purpose, or at least any human anything. I thought of Rorty's "all is metaphor" during a recent van ride in a driving rain down Route 91 headed from Amherst, Massachusetts, to Bradley Airport in Windsor Locks, Connecticut. My ponytailed, perpetually grinning van driver decided to strike up a postmetaphysical (I think) conversation. "For me, life is one big metaphor," he said. And then he spelled out his general philosophy of life. It was a brief story. My only concern was whether or not the rain-slicked pavement, the low visibility, and the presence of other vehicles was to be construed metaphorically as well. I thought this might be the case because he insisted on turning to me—I was seated opposite in the passenger seat up front—as he celebrated the basic unreality of existence.

Now, what connected my reading of Rorty to this metaphorical ride to the airport? (By the way, I was rather relieved to be back in Nashville, Tennessee, where cabbies are unlikely to describe life as one big metaphor as they drive you home.) I think it is the insistence that life is either to be taken straight up, as grounded and certain, or it is altogether contingent, up for grabs. As I said earlier, surely there are other options. That will be the burden of the case I intend to make.

I am also struck by the fact that Rortyian antiphilosophy is not terribly helpful to the political theorist who rejects Platonism and Kantianism (as do I) but wants, at the same time, to avoid the error of underlaboring, of offering far too thin an account of the body politic. When, for example, I read Rorty's characterization of the ideal liberal society, toward which he believes we are heading, I learn that it is one in which the "intellectuals would still be ironists, although the nonintellectuals would not."[5] What spares this from being a bit of what in the old days would have been called a piece of class snobbery is Rorty's conviction that the latter—the vast majority, one must presume—would "be commonsensically nominalist and historicist. That is, they, too, would see themselves as contingent through and through, without feeling any particular doubts about the contingencies they happened to be." So they are in on the heady project of self-creation, although not so aware of its ironic dimension as the true cognoscenti, "we intellectuals." Somehow I don't think historicist nominalism is going to fly with Joe Six-Pack. And I don't mean fly as an argument—I mean as "story" about reality, about his, or their (the nonintellectuals), reality, despite the fact that this thoroughgoing contingency is the thing Rorty calls "moral progress," one small step for men, one big leap for humankind in the direction of "greater human solidarity."

On Rorty's account, we become more solid the thinner we get because we recognize as contingent all the things that constitute who we are. This means jettisoning as core to our identity that which traditionally constituted it (tribe, religion, race, custom), recognizing them as inessential. All that matters is a brotherhood and sisterhood of pain and humiliation. This smuggles universalism back in, of course, but that isn't the most important point. The most important point is that even in our would-be liberal utopia, people don't and, I would argue, cannot think of themselves as "thoroughly" contingent because when they think of themselves they see concrete fears, pains, hopes, and joys embodied in concrete others—say a grandchild—and it is impossible for them to construe that grandchild, or to tell the story of the coming into being of that grandchild, in the way Rorty says we must.

Minimally, all those nonintellectuals out there would be unable to practice the incessant self-scrutiny required in order to purge "any particular doubts about the contingencies they happened to be." Leaving aside recent evidence on just how deep and wide are the religious commitments of Americans, including belief in God and personal immortality, a noncontingent fragment that appears to infect over 85 percent of the American people, the nonintellectuals I presume. Rorty's evidence for the capacity of nonironists to be wholly historicist and nominalist is pretty thin; indeed such evidence isn't proffered.[6] Rorty holds up the claim, eschewing coming to grips with the evidence. That is a further reason for the difficulties I have when I try to engage his arguments: They are cast at such a level of generality and diffuseness it is hard to know what one is endorsing, if one goes along, or what it might mean to oppose what is being said. At this point, Rorty owes us some stories—some postmodern, liberal-ironical, antifoundational, historicist, nominalist stories. "We" party poopers remain ironical about his ironical liberalism. We need exemplars. We need narratives that do not require the bogeyman of foundationalism and essentialism to frighten us into an under-specified alternative.

Sharing his view that in a liberal-democratic society overly precise and highly programmatic demands and policies are neither required nor desired, we nevertheless ponder, What is his alternative? And when we do that, the images that come to mind are of a world in which nothing is ever distinct or ever stands out in stark relief and in which I am not called upon to make tough decisions of the sort that might require that I reject one version of multiculturalism in favor of a more authentic version of diversity—a choice Rorty would be loath to make because he would want to associate all the things that come down the pike with a vaguely progressivist air or flair as vaguely progressivist, hence worthy of endorsement or at least not worth opposing. I imagine the liberal ironist at a rollerskating rink—watch me whiz by, catch me if you can, I know I'm going in circles but at least I'm moving in the right direction. What does it mean to "acknowledge contingency"? How can I avoid using any "inherited language game"? What can it mean to use a "new language" in a world in which language is always already before me, in me, through me? What counts as a record of failure or success in the Rortyian world of self-creation? Is there an example of a group of persons, a movement, an ethico-politics that has successfully transcended transcendence of the bad universalist sort in order to achieve an authentic universalism of the contingent sort?

A genuinely ironic history and account should puncture our illusions. The Rortyian ironist, remember, is *first* a historicist and nominalist. The ironic part is the bonus, the door prize, in the ideal liberal utopia. The possibility of such a utopia is aided and abetted by a decline of religious faith (I have already called this into question as an empirical matter); the rise of literary criticism that, although it widens the gap between intellectuals and nonintellectuals, all in all seems a good thing; the consensus, or growth toward a consensus, that everybody should have a chance at "self-creation"; and the hope that "with luck"—Lady Luck is a pretty important figure in Rorty's world—modern liberal society can keep telling optimistic tales about itself and how things are getting better. He, for one, sees "no insuperable obstacles in this story's coming true."[7] This is the basis of hope.

By contrast to this rather blithe account, would not the genuine ironist, one with a well-developed tragic sensibility, insist that "we" come to recognize the illusions—the political illusions—imbedded in the progressivist story as Rorty retells it? His ironist—once again a "she"—fulfills three conditions. Each of these conditions is presented as an intramural debate—a matter of "final vocabulary," of "present vocabulary," and the repudiation of some "real" vocabulary, real in the sense of being closer "to reality" or closer to some outside "power" (usually called God, though Rorty might also have Nature in mind). Ironists are folks who do battle over vocabularies and who recognize that "anything can be made to look good or bad by being re-described." Given this recognition, they renounce any attempt "to formulate criteria of choice between final vocabularies."[8] This puts the Rortyian ironist in a "metastable" position.

Surely Rorty's "meta" is a bit too stable, hence not nearly ironic enough. Rorty's ironist is insular and self-enclosed, fighting a fight of words, words, words. Far easier to stabilize this world in the name of destabilization than to confront the thicker reality of lived life, the densities and intractabilities of a world I did not create and do not control. Rorty also encases his ironic self in a cocoon of private self-creation; yet he clearly means to endorse and to serve liberal democratic society as "we liberal ironists" construct the ironic identity as a form of loose community. There is a lot of seepage of private to public and public to private within Rorty's argument. That being the case, it is fair play to take him to task on whether his ironism stabilizes or destabilizes and makes problematic that which the nonironist would cast in the mold of dogmatic certitude. Return with me, then, to the those not-so-golden days of yesteryear Rorty describes thus: "The French Revolution had shown that the whole vocabulary of social relations, the whole spectrum of social institutions, could be displaced almost overnight. This precedent made utopian politics the rule rather than the exception among intellectuals. Utopian politics set aside questions about both the will of God and the nature of man and dreams of creating a hitherto unknown form of society."[9]

Presumably Rorty would say this is "we anti-essentialists' " description of the French Revolution, descriptions being inventions that serve certain purposes. His description aims to show how contingent, even arbitrary, our political characterizations are, and this, in turn, serves to deepen the ironic stance. But that isn't the cause his description of the French Revolution serves: Rather, his bland depiction wipes the blood off the pages. Utopian politics becomes the stuff of intellectual politics. The French Revolution takes on a quasi-foundational status as the mother of all political redescriptions. The modern liberal utopian ironist moves away from the guillotine, to be sure, under the "don't be cruel" rule, but the French Revolution continues to edify, to lie at the heart of the project of political hope.

Rorty describes events in a way that misses the terrible tragedy, hence the deep irony, of the Revolution. In the name of the Rights of Man, or under that banner, tens of thousands were imprisoned and at least seventeen thousand guillotined between 1792 and 1794 alone. One avid executioner bragged that the revolution would "turn France into a cemetery rather than fail in her regeneration."[10] This statement is horrifically funny: the sort of thing that makes the blood run cold. The genuine ironist would describe in a way that foregrounds the Terror and the horror, that holds it up for all would-be Utopians to see. Rorty does the opposite. Why, I wonder? Surely we need continually to be reminded of the mounds of bodies on which nationalistic and revolutionary politics rests. Surely the liberal, above all, must proffer such reminders. Contrast the thinness of Rorty's characterization of the French Revolution in terms of vocabulary change with Camus's story of the Republic of the Guillotine.

> Saint-Just exclaims: "Either the virtues or the Terror." Freedom must be guaranteed, and the draft constitution presented to the Convention already mentions the death penalty. Absolute virtue is impossible, and the republic of forgiveness leads, with implacable logic, to the republic of the guillotine. . . . But at the heart of this logical delirium, at the logical conclusion of this morality of virtue, the scaffold represents freedom. . . . Marat, making his final calculations, claimed two hundred and seventy three thousand heads. But he compromised the therapeutic aspect of the operation by screaming during the massacre: "Brand them with hot irons, cut off their thumbs, tear out their tongues."[11]

The strong ironist would be certain that her description of Revolutionary virtue included a (be)headed count. For her task would be one of making as clear as possible, in as dramatic a way as possible short of some blunt laying down of the law, that virtue all too easily translates into vice; that the tragic and the ironic keep very close company; that self-deception is most visible when illusions are greatest; that any and all claims to purity must be punctured. Rorty does none of these in his few words on the French Revolution. This omission of any mention of the bloodiness of one of history's most grandiose movements of redescription permits, in turn and in tandem with Rorty's overall rhetoric and narrative strategy, far too smooth sailing over tranquilized waters to the present moment as one in which there are no "insuperable obstacles" to the liberal progressivist story.

Writes Richard Reinitz in his volume *Irony and Consciousness:* "Belief in the inevitable growth of human knowledge and progress, and in America as an exemplar of that progress, is one of those pretensions. [The pretensions he here discusses are those depicted by Reinhold Niebuhr as characteristic of American society.] Like all modern liberal cultures, America's culture has for the most part rejected the doctrine of original sin in favor of the irony-inducing pretense to 'objectivity,' the belief that we can keep selfish interests from affecting our understanding."[12]

Don't get me wrong: Rorty would never endorse the cruelty of the Terror. But by holding it at arm's length, by not allowing it into the picture, he more easily preserves intact his own endorsements and future projections and promises. Thus his claim that anything can be made to look good or bad by being redescribed *is* genuinely troubling—ethically and politically. Take the following story, one Camus offered in a speech at Columbia University in 1946 as a way to characterize "a crisis of world-dimensions, a crisis in human consciousness":

> In Greece, after an action by the underground forces, a German officer is preparing to shoot three brothers he has taken as hostages. The old mother of the three begs for mercy and he consents to spare one of her sons, but on the condition that she herself designate which one. When she is unable to decide, the soldiers get ready to fire. At last she chooses the eldest, because he has a family dependent on him, but by the same token she condemns the two other sons, as the German officer intends.[13]

How might this story be redescribed in order to make it "look good"? Rorty, remember, insists on this possibility. I will put the point in stronger terms: He *requires* this possibility in order to sustain his larger argument about the utter contingency and arbitrariness of our characterizations. So it is something that "just happened" that Europe acquired a habit of using other words, words that promote "don't be cruel." Camus describes a moment of genuine terror. He means to evoke our horror and revulsion. He means to do this to alert us to how dangerous the world is and how necessary it is to sustain an ethical-political stance that limits the damage.

Were I to suggest that Camus's story is but one way of describing something that could be as easily described in an alternative way designed to make it look good, I would make myself loathsome; I would become a ravager. Rorty surely agrees with this because he, too, hopes to lower the body count; thus I think it is fair to ask of him whether Camus's story puts pressure on his rather carefree advocacy of the infinite possibilities of redescription. This is a point I will return to in my discussion of just what sorts of stories—political stories—"we liberal ironists" might tell. Camus is an ironist and many call him liberal, but he locates us in the heart of darkness, a place we must visit from time to time, not as one textual experience among many possible textual experiences but as a historic reality and ever-present possibility that cannot be contained by being transported behind a private *cordon sanitaire*. If, as Rorty claims, solidarity is created "by increasing our sensitivity to the particular details of the pain and humiliation of other, unfamiliar sorts of people,"[14] it is puzzling indeed that he steps back from the opportunity to deepen the pool of sensitivity by telling the story of all those unfamiliar sorts of people—peasants in the Vendée as well as aristocratic families and intellectuals (of the wrong sort) in Paris—who lost their heads to revolutionary virtue.

Rorty's Freud is as puzzling in this regard as his French Revolution. Freud is a pivotal thinker for Rorty, serving as one of the masters of redescription and decentering of the self central to the rise and future hope of "we liberal ironists." But I have a rather hard time recognizing his Freud. Freud becomes either too mechanistic (in Rorty's discussion in volume 2 of his philosophical papers) or too much the flower child, an odd combination of scientism and expressivism. Briefly, the story Rorty tells about Freud depicts his project as a knowing demolition of many received understandings—fair enough— and offering, as a consequence, simply "one more vocabulary," his own chosen metaphoric. Pressing just "one more description" is an extraordinary taming of a project whose father characterized himself as Hannibal, Moses, a conquistador. Conquistadors usually aim a bit higher than "one more description." They seek to impress themselves on a territory and a people—to conquer. Freud saw his project in similar dramatic terms, and, as well, he claimed the imprimatur of science and truth. His demolition of his opponents is scarcely the work of a man tossing out "one more vocabulary" for our consideration!

As well, Freud's awareness not simply of life's contingencies but its tragedies, his insistence that psychoanalysis is not primarily a cure-all but the basis for a very "grave philosophy," disappears in Rorty's story. Instead, Freud is assimilated to a too-simple version of socialization theory, not unlike that favored by functionalists and structuralists. Here as elsewhere, in exposing the too-grandiose presumptions of traditional metaphysics and strong Aristotelian teleology, Rorty falls into an overreliance on the categories of analytic philosophy. That is, the absence of an "intrinsic" human nature or of moral obligations that are preprogrammed leads Rorty into a world that is at one and the same time too open and plastic ("any and every dream") or too constricted ("blind impress"). These too-restricted alternatives are strikingly in evidence when he takes up Freud. For Freud's aims went much beyond showing how we are determined and might be free for self-creation nonetheless. *Contra* Rorty, Freud did not give up "Plato's attempt to bring together the public and the private, the parts of the state and the parts of the soul, the search for social justice and the search for individual perfection."[15] Freud's discussions of ego and superego, of war and the self, of the trajectory of individual development—all turn on the connections Rorty claims Freud severed.

A long exposé or unpacking is not possible. I will serve up just a couple of points to put pressure on Rorty's redescription of Freud's project, beginning with "blind impress," which I take to be Rorty's way of insisting that instinct as a form of preprogramming may not be "unworthy of programming our lives or our poems," although this is not terribly clear.[16] "Private obsessions" is another way Rorty talks about what he calls "blind impresses" unique "to an individual or common to members of some historically conditioned community."[17] One way or the other, Rorty is depicting conditioning—conditioning that he doesn't sort out into the biological and the historical, although "blind impress" suggests both.

Either way this rather misses the Freudian boat. Freud could never agree that "socialization . . . goes all the way down—that there is nothing 'beneath' socialization or prior to history which is definatory of the human."[18] To be sure, this is a slippery Rortyian formulation. Perhaps Rorty here means to incorporate bioevolutionary dimensions within the historical. But it needs to be stressed that, for Freud, the human being is a complex physiological entity, driven in ways not at all historically contingent. We are critters of a particular kind. There is a biology, a morphology, a neurophysiology definatory of "the human" and prior to our historic construction in a particular family, time, and place.

For an individual to be forged out of the human, certain things are required, first and foremost human love, for we are "exquisitely social." Freud's understanding of the very possibility for human freedom turns on there being something to us humans that is not thoroughly and exhaustively defined and captured by history. There would be nothing to be discontented about were we as totally historicized as Rorty suggests. Where Freud is powerful—in offering a developmental account, teleologically driven, of what is required in order that a distinctive individual might emerge from the human—Rorty falters. Rorty does insist that one cannot, from the day of a child's birth, rear a child to be tentative and "dubious" about his or her society and culture. But that is pretty much it. Freud goes much further. He does lay down the law (again, the Moses analogy Freud used to understand himself is not unimportant in this regard) and sketches out a clear and mordant theory of development. Conscience—necessary to the don't-be-cruel rule—is not, Freud insists, simply "there," is not given. But it can and must emerge if aggression—the greatest problem in civilization—is to be tamed, curbed, and muted, if not eliminated.

Rorty offers us no developmental account. We cannot, therefore, understand where noncruelty comes from. Freud is insistent on this score. He reverses conventional accounts of the rise of moral ideals. For persons capable of a moral point of view (that is, capable of occupying the position of the other: capable of empathy and identification with those different from themselves) to emerge, what is required is: (1) Specific powerful others (usually called parents) who are libidinally cathected, the objects of both love and hate. This demands constancy in early object-identification. (2) In order for reality testing, essential to mature development and the emergence of genuine individuality, to occur, those others cannot be absent or remote, nor will "objective" structures and institutions do the job; they must be real human beings to whom the child is erotically attached. This and this alone lays the groundwork for the child to become a social being.

The superego has a specific history; it bears a double burden of aggression, a combination of the child's own aggressivity and the child's introjection of parental authority. In order that this aggressivity be bound, the child must engage in a series of complex experiments of thought and action within an environment of loving discipline. Ethical and erotic are necessarily intertwined in moral life. This intertwining escapes the confines of particular families and feeds into, even as it is fueled by, the wider culture.[19] The development of the individual is, of course, contingent in many ways: No one selects his or her parents, place or culture of birth, and so on, but it is not arbitrary. Development has a teleological thrust; it bears within it the seeds of possibility. That possibility is best understood as an attempt to work out what it means to be free and to be responsible in light of predeterminations of an embodied sort and determinations of a cultural sort.

Freud never shirked from specifying the sorts of environments and worlds that gave rise, or had a fighting chance of giving rise, to individuals and those that did not. As well, there would be no point at all in therapy if an ideal of the structural unity of the self were not held up. This is tied, in turn, to the possibility of truth. Hysterics and neurotics suffer from reminiscences, from the telling of inappropriate, false, or obsessive stories. The truth *does* set one free, but it cannot be any old construction—it must "take"; it must be a construction that leads to a recollection that invites a "yes," a liberating "yes," from the analysand.

Now, none of this makes any sense at all if it is severed from a strong developmental account that enables us to sift and winnow some ways of rearing children from others; that enables us to say this is rotten and awful, this is better, this is better yet. Writes Jonathan Lear: "From all we know of cruelty, it is not lovingly instilled. It is cruelty that breeds cruelty: and thus the possibility of a harmonious cruel soul, relatively free from inner conflict and sufficiently differentiated from the cruel environment, begins to look like science fiction." Lear goes on in a footnote to write unabashedly, as did Freud, of the formation of the soul as being "dependent on a certain type of responsiveness. Sanity is a constitutive condition of a fully formed soul. Clinical experience suggests that the closest example of a happy torturer is a torturer who is happier than he normally is when he is torturing. Such people are not stably happy or well-integrated humans. On the whole, it is a tough life to be a torturer."[20]

The upshot of all this is that Freud does *not* deuniversalize the moral sense, as Rorty claims; he reuniversalizes it. Rorty claims that Freud made the moral sense as "idiosyncratic as the poet's inventions."[21] Freud would not recognize this description of his project. It is precisely bad and destructive idiosyncrasy that he aims to reveal and to alter in order that the too-idiosyncratic obsessive, as one example, may take his or her place in the human community, more or less following those rules that make social life possible and dangerous aggressivity against self or others less likely. It is important to bear in mind that Freud is displacing Kantian-Christian teaching about universal moral claims and dispositions, but not in order to eradicate such claims altogether. If Rorty were right about Freud, private life would become impossible—a world of self-creating idiosyncratics continually searching for new descriptions—and public life uninteresting, severed as it is from all that private creativity. But Freud insists that there is truth to be found; that a metapsychological account relocates our understanding of the self by offering a strong story of development, including the emergence of conscience in a way that puts pressure on older projects; that central to this project is love—the work of Eros—which he links specifically to Plato's *Symposium.*

On one account, it is cruel to chide a woman wearing a fur coat: It hurts her feelings. On the other hand, more than the fox's feelings have been hurt in creating that sign of vanity and conspicuous consumption. A careless putdown is cruel, but systematic torture is far more cruel and reprehensible. But leave this aside. I want instead to home in on just where the don't-be-cruel rule comes from. I have already suggested that Freud offers, and would require, a developmental account of restraint from cruelty. In order not to be cruel we must learn that cruelty hurts and harms, and we learn this because the ethico-politics of eroticized moral learning have worked out: We can identify with the other. Freud always bows in the direction of those universal moral norms and rules he challenges, especially Christianity and the Sermon on the Mount, by saying such rules are impossible to live out fully but they may, nonetheless, serve a vital purpose in stemming the tide of aggression.

Our century has been very cruel, probably the most cruel on a public-political scale. Rorty doesn't really offer an account of public cruelty of the fascist-Stalinist sort either, though he clearly stands in opposition to it. But how robust is his stance? With the don't-be-cruel rule in mind, he poses alternatives that, I fear, make us dumber than we have any right to be at this late stage. It "just happened" that liberal societies condemn torture because liberals want to be reasonable and they want this because the contingencies fell out this way. But it didn't just happen. Liberal society and democratic possibility are the heirs of a very strong account—a Hebrew-Christian story—of why cruelty is sinful and must be stopped, beginning with the Roman games and the exposing of children. These were the first cruelties Christianity forbade. You don't torture people because that is a violation and it is a violation because we are all children of God.

If one jettisons the metaphysical underpinning of the don't-be-cruel rule, one must offer an alternative. That alternative is usually cast these days in the form of "universal human rights." Amnesty International doesn't talk about reasonableness; it talks about violation of fundamental human dignity taken as an ontological given, not a historic contingency. It might be an interesting exercise for Rorty to rewrite the declaration of human rights so that it retains its power to condemn, separate, and define yet abandons the basis on which it now does so. Celebrating the decline of religious faith, which served initially to underscore natural law and natural right, Rorty wants to maintain and sustain the injunctions imbedded in such earlier formulations. Here I will take up just one instance where I think Rorty misses the boat on cruelty.

Specifically, I have in mind the stories of rescuers—those who put their own lives at risk to stop the torture and destruction of fellow human beings. Having said "fellow human beings" I have already distanced myself from Rorty's account, for he insists that rescuers who saved Jewish neighbors (his examples, very underspecified, are Danes and Italians) did so not because Jews were "fellow human beings" but by using "more parochial terms," for example that a particular Jew was a "fellow Milanese, or a fellow Jutlander, or a fellow member of the same union or profession, or a fellow bocce player, or a fellow parent of small children."[22] I have read many accounts of rescue and I have never once encountered "fellow bocce player" as a reason proffered by a life-risker for why he came to put his life and that of his family at risk. Ironical reasonableness didn't have a lot to do with life-risking. Indeed, rescuers during the Nazi years talk the sort of talk Rorty aims to supplant. Here are brief examples drawn from five accounts of anti-Nazi activism and rescue:

1. Students from the White Rose society, an anti-Nazi student group from Munich, who were caught, tried, and executed, left behind Five Leaflets designed to animate anti-Nazi sentiment.

> Therefore every individual, conscious of his responsibility as a member of Christian and Western civilization, must defend himself as best he can at this late hour, he must work against the scourges of mankind, against fascism and any similar

system of totalitarianism. . . . For according to God's will, man is intended to pursue his natural goal, his earthly happiness, in self-reliance and self-chosen activity, freely and independently within the community of life and work of the nation. . . . It is not possible through solitary withdrawal, in the manner of embittered hermits, to prepare the ground for the overturn of this "government" or bring about the revolution at the earliest possible moment.[23]

The White Rose students cite Aristotle, St. Augustine, Kant. To be sure, many who endorsed this final vocabulary remained quiescent during the Nazi era; others, to their shame, offered support. But that isn't what's at stake here; what's at stake is the basis for resistance.

2. Rescue in Italy. The Italians spared 85 percent of their Jewish population. The definitive work on this story offers the following by way of insight:

> In many cases after the war, non-Jewish Italians who had saved Jews, when asked about their motivations, were annoyed and even angered by the very question: "How can you ask me such a question?" one man inquired. "Do you mean to say that you do not understand why a devout Catholic like myself had to behave as I did in order to save human beings whose lives were in danger?" Other rescuers insisted, simply, "I did my duty."[24]

3. Samuel and Pearl Oliner interviewed authenticated rescuers identified by Yad Vashem, Israel's memorial to victims of the Holocaust. These rescuers came from Poland, Germany, France, Holland, Italy, Denmark, Belgium, and Norway. Probing the circumstances and the reasons for rescue, they learned that rescuers were "ordinary" people—farmers and teachers, entrepreneurs and factory workers, rich and poor, Protestants and Catholics, distinguished by "their connections with others in relationships of commitment and care." The point the Oliners make runs opposite to Rorty's about immediate identification serving as the basis for rescue—"fellow Jutlander" and the like. Rather, rescuers moved from strong grounding in family, community, church—all were rooted in this way—to "broad universal principles that relate to justice and care in matters of public concern." They rescued because they could generalize beyond their immediate attachments rather than merely enact them.[25] Religious affiliation—overwhelming for both rescuers and nonrescuers—did not per se propel individuals into danger, but the way religious obligation was interpreted by rescuers and nonrescuers did mark a sharp distinction between the two groups.

4. Nechama Tec, a rescued Polish Jew, also relies on Yad Vashem identification of bona fide rescuers. Tec is fascinated and horrified that some Polish peasants "were executed for their selfless help, while others were busy rounding up Jews and delivering them to the authorities." Within Poland, to

help Jews was to risk one's life. This extended to one's family. Among res-cuers there were many religious anti-Semites, but there was something in their religious upbringing that led them to the conclusion that "cruel, glar-ingly murderous behavior towards the Jews was a sin." What religion offered was no certain guarantee of rescue but the possibility of such in light of religious values and teachings. Religion was, then, a necessary but not com-plete explanation for rescue, according to Tec, and it is unclear that anything other than a fundamental, first language of sin and justice could have pro-pelled "ordinary" people (those Rorty would have us construe as thoroughly historic, nominalist, and contingent through and through) into the danger zone.[26]

5. Finally, the best known of rescue books—Philip Hallie's account of the village of Le Chambon, a Protestant commune that, to the man, woman, and child, committed itself to rescue. The entire village was put at risk of massacre. Public duty took precedence. The Chambonnais opened their homes to those unlike themselves—Jewish refugees—at great risk to them-selves. They spoke of an ethic of responsibility; of not wanting to increase the harm in the world; of following the example of Jesus. None talked of an immediate identification with those they risked their lives to save—these were strangers, aliens in our midst, but Christian responsibility is cast uni-versally and meant to be applied concretely so we did what we had to do. Led by their pastor, André Trocmé, the villagers prayed and acted. By attacking evil, they cherished "the preciousness of human life. Our obligation to di-minish the evil in the world must begin at home; we must not do evil, must not ourselves do harm."[27] Trocmé's sermons offered no blueprint, but they did animate a spirit of resistance that required, in order that it be enacted, precisely the identification Rorty denatures. The Chambonnais did not res-cue "neighbors." They rescued strangers. And their determination not to be cruel rested for them on imperatives that were obligatory, not contingent; necessary, not incidental. They could not have acted otherwise, they said.

Now I am acutely aware, as I wind down, of how easy it is to be taken for a moral scold, if not a scourge. (I hope I haven't been that heavy-handed.) These are the days of lightness and froth as well as political correctness, an odd combination of "anything goes" and micromanagement of every word I say and thought I think. Ah well, tribulations of the spirit come and go. And my final point goes like this: What would a Rortyian redescription of rescue that omitted the first vocabularies and noncontingent (to their eyes) actions of the rescuers look like? Have we "progressed" beyond the need for any such "justification"? It seems not, if I may judge from what I was told by the Mothers of the Disappeared in Argentina who speak of universal human rights, of obligations and immunities, of human beings who must not by definition be violated, a strong ontoethical political claim. What would a liberal ironist account of ethical heroism be? I understand what a tragic-ironic account is; one can turn to Camus, among others, for that. But an account that insists on its own incessant displacement is trickier by far.

I am struck by the fact that Václav Havel, former dissident, current president, always playwright, published his collection of essays under the title *Living in Truth*. Havel is insistent that there is an absolute horizon of being; that the world is possible only because we are grounded; that there is such a thing as a "metaphysical offense," an assault on the mystery of the absolute. Here he has in mind the violation of forests, rivers, streams, living creatures. This is the don't-be-cruel rule, but with teeth. As a performer of political thought—my way to describe him—Havel is working with a very rich script that requires the language of totalitarianism, truth, lies, violation, being, nature, the "very notion of identity itself." Truth and lies are contextual but not *merely* contextual. There are false and true vocabularies, and one can distinguish between and judge them and dissent from or assent to them. There may not be a human nature, but there is a *human condition,* described by Hannah Arendt thus: "the conditions of human existence—life itself, natality and mortality, worldliness, plurality, and the earth—can never 'explain' what we are or answer the question of who we are for the simple reason that they never condition us absolutely."[28] It is recognition of this condition as the horizon of thought and action that makes possible freedom and responsibility. This recognition escapes the Rortyian net, comprised as it is of either preordained natures, identities, being, and reality or a thoroughgoing contingency with no "left-over," no "surplus," nothing that is not arbitrary in the first and last instance. Havel's and Arendt's positions elude Rorty's alternatives.

The final words shall be Havel's. I conclude in this way because I want to suggest that without the possibility of creating a Havelian sort of "I," a modern identity at once committed yet aware of the irony and limits of all commitments; prepared to suffer but wary of all calls to sacrifice, we would live in a moral universe impoverished beyond our poor powers of imagination. This Havelian "I" is a thicker being by far than "we liberal ironists."

> The problem of human identity remains at the center of my thinking about human affairs . . . as you must have noticed from my letters, the importance of the notion of human responsibility has grown in my meditations. It has begun to appear with increasing clarity, as that fundamental point from which all identity grows and by which it stands or falls; it is the foundation, the root, the center of gravity, and constructional principle or axis of identity, something like the "idea"

that determines its degree and type. It is the mortar binding it together, and when the mortar dries out, identity too begins irreversibly to crumble and fall apart. (That is why I wrote you that the secret of man is the secret of his responsibility.)[29]

My mission, Havel insists, is to "speak the truth about the world I live in, to bear witness to its terrors and miseries, in other words, to warn rather than hand out prescriptions for change."[30] My hunch is that Rorty wouldn't characterize his mission all that differently, although he would probably want to drop "mission" as too religious sounding. "Truth" would also have to go in order that it be absolutely clear that truth is a characteristic assigned to linguistic properties rather than a strong contrast to lie and a claim that truth and lies are linked to definable realities, as Havel intends. "The world" might also be a bit tricky, as it has too solid and universalistic a ring to it as Havel deploys it. "Bear witness" derives from Christian witness, so it should probably be jettisoned. This leaves warning. But would "to warn" retain its force were all else redescribed or excised? I don't think so.

Notes

Originally published in Daniel W. Conway and John E. Seery, eds., *The Politics of Irony: Essays in Self-Betrayal.* © Conway and Seery. (New York: St. Martin's Press, 1992). Reprinted by permission of St. Martin's Press.

1. Richard Rorty, *Contingency, Irony, and Solidarity* (Cambridge: Cambridge University Press, 1989), 79–80.

2. Richard Rorty, *Objectivity, Relativism, and Truth,* vol. 1, and *Essays on Heidegger and Others,* vol. 2 of *Philosophical Papers* (Cambridge: Cambridge University Press, 1991).

3. Rorty, *Contingency, Irony, and Solidarity,* 6.

4. Ibid., 52.

5. Ibid., 87.

6. Rorty recognizes that most "nonintellectuals are still committed either to some form of religious faith or to some form of Enlightenment rationalism," but he quickly forgets this recognition as a limiting condition to his own argument in the body of his text, perhaps because he construes as contingent commitments what for those thus committed are anything but. *Contingency, Irony, and Solidarity,* xv.

7. Ibid., 86.

8. Ibid., 73.

9. Ibid., 3.

10. Quoted in Eugene Weber, "A New Order of Loss and Profit," *Times Literary Supplement,* January 15–21, 1988, 51–52. See also Richard John Neuhaus's biting "Joshing Mr. Rorty," *First Things,* no. 8 (December 1990): 14–24.

11. Albert Camus, *The Rebel* (New York: Vintage Books, 1956), 124–26.

12. Richard Reinitz, *Irony and Consciousness* (Lewisburg, Pa.: Bucknell University Press, 1980), 65.

13. Camus, "The Human Crisis," *Twice a Year* 1 (1946–47): 21. Lecture delivered in America, spring 1946.

14. Rorty, *Contingency, Irony, and Solidarity,* xvi.

15. Ibid., 303–34.

16. Ibid., 35.

17. Ibid., 37–38.

18. Ibid., xiii.

19. On this, see Freud's complex discussions of the interpenetration of state aggressivity (war) and the moral enactments of individuals in "Thoughts for the Times on War and Death," *Standard Edition,* vol. 14 (London: Hogarth Press, 1953), 273–330; and "Why War?" *Standard Edition,* vol. 22, 196–215.

20. Jonathan Lear, *Love and Its Place in Nature: A Philosophical Interpretation of Freudian Psychoanalysis* (New York: Farrar, Straus and Giroux, 1990), 189.

21. Rorty, *Contingency, Irony, and Solidarity,* 30.

22. Ibid., 190.

23. Inge Scholl, ed., *The White Rose: Munich, 1942–1943* (Middletown, Conn.: Wesleyan University Press, 1983), 74, 82.

24. Susan Zuccotti, *The Italians and the Holocaust* (New York: Basic Books, 1987), 281–82.

25. Samuel P. Oliner and Pearl M. Oliner, *The Altruistic Personality: Rescuers of Jews in Nazi Europe* (New York: Free Press, 1988), 259–60.

26. Nechama Tec, *When Light Pierced the Darkness: Christian Rescue of Jews in Nazi-occupied Poland* (New York: Oxford University Press, 1986), 117, 104.

27. Philip Hallie, *Lest Innocent Blood Be Shed* (New York: Harper Colophon, 1979), 85.

28. Hannah Arendt, *The Human Condition* (Chicago: University of Chicago Press, 1958), 11.

29. Václav Havel, *Letters to Olga* (New York: Henry Holt, 1989), 145.

30. Václav Havel, *Disturbing the Peace* (New York: Knopf, 1990), 8.

21

Our Town Reconsidered:
Reflections on the Small Town
in American Literature

> This then is where I am, and as I settle to work I find I have to
> resolve, step by slow step, experiences and questions that
> once moved like light. The life of country and city is moving
> and present: moving in time, through the history of a family
> and a people; moving in feeling and ideas, through a
> network of relationships and decisions.
>
> *Raymond Williams,* The Country and the City

"Moving and present," writes Williams of his discursive target—country and city—a target similar to my own—town and city.[1] The small town, especially the quintessential *American* small town, exists in narrative, whether "history" or "fiction," always "in contrast to"—at least until the very recent past. The contrast is the city, real and imagined, or the real as imagined, the imagined as real. This essay, then, is about that contrast as a shifting yet stubbornly constant marker of our collective and individual experience. As Americans we have been shaped by small-town life whether that is or is not the life we have lived.

Two items culled from the recent past as constructed for us by the *New York Times:*

December 4, 1984. Jonathan F. Fanton, president of the New School for Social Research, attended a recent benefit dinner where the subject of small towns came up, as it sometimes does (particularly in connection with country weekending), and he was quick to comment: "I find a progressive decline in my tolerance for them," he said. The *Times's* Charlotte Curtis, whiffing at least a breath of scandal, pursued Fanton, asking for clarification of his controversial off-handed remark. She, in turn, tells us that "What troubles him, he said a few days later in his book-lined office, is that some sections of Middle America seem to have become refuges for a new know-nothing-ism." Fanton declares the small town inhabitant a "conscious" know-nothing for, with media penetration of every hamlet everywhere, there is no excuse for being "provincial" and those who are have made a "conscious choice."

March 24, 1985. Although most Americans live in or near cities, nearly half of them would move to places with 10,000 people or fewer if they had the chance, according to a recent Gallup Poll. Presented with seven choices ranging from a large city with a population of a million or more to rural areas, a total of 48% preferred to live in a small town with a population ranging from 2,500 to 10,000, a rural area on a farm or in a rural area but not on a farm. The Census Bureau says 153 million Americans, nearly two-thirds of the nation's population, live in or near urban areas of 10,000 people or more.

These items are evidence of a sort. But of what? Williams is surely right that one faces a crisis of perspective once one moves to delineate terms that conjure up a whole cluster of prototypical ideals and notions. For example: many of us may find prejudice at work in the *New York Times* snippets. But for some, it is the urban professor's snobbish prejudice against a way of life he scarcely knows but chooses to disdain. Others, however, may detect prejudice simmering beneath the surface of the Gallup Poll findings and jump to the conclusion that those who indicate a preference for the small town express racial fears identified with white flight from inner city blacks and Hispanics. A few may go on to note appreciation of the verities of community life and association, a Tocquevillian residue, at work in the poll; others will see little more than nostalgia (deployed as an epithet), a yearning for a world that never existed save in fanciful and illicit rememberings.

Home for the heart or hotbed of hypocrisy, egalitarian foundation of American democracy or breeding ground of petty privilege, a world of strong and authoritative or frustrated and ground-down women, men who exemplify familial and political virtues or petty tyrants who lord it over anybody they can find? These are the contrasts consistently thrown up in literature on the small town. My purpose is not to adjudicate between these contrasting images, nor to declare at one grand point which is "the truth." There are moments of truth in the condemnations and commendations alike, requiring of the analyst an attunement to ambiguity. Sinclair Lewis spoke some truth, vitriolically and exaggeratedly, but so does Helen Hooven Santmyer, at exasperating length, in a tone and through a texture wholly at odds with Lewis's cartoon-caricature definitiveness.

Scholarly Musings on the Small Town

At the outset, let me frame my treatment of works of popular fiction with three scholarly treatments of the town, two historical and one sociological.

The towns of Michael Zuckerman's *Peaceable Kingdoms: New England Towns in the Eighteenth Century* (1970) are very different from Robert and Helen Lynd's *Middletown* (1929), a midwestern town (Muncie, Indiana) with a population between 25,000 and 50,000 in the 1920s, a town the Lynds called a city. Robert Lingeman's *Small Town America: A Narrative History, 1620 to the Present* (1980), traces chronologically and regionally the history of the town in a way that encompasses village and flourishing "small city" alike.

Despite the differences in scholarly approach and target, a few striking and shared themes emerge. Zuckerman sees in the New England town a "broadly diffused desire for consensual communalism as the operative premise of group life in America." Peace was the central preoccupation of these created towns, and peace required "inner acceptance of the canons of concord by the villagers," as there was "no external agency powerful enough to compel compliance. There was, for all practical purposes, only the constable."[2] Law and order had to come from within. The individual, constituted as a communal being, was the only true guarantor of civil peace. Those who threatened "congregational solidarity" were either not let in or were cast out through the practice of "warning out"—a way for the town to spit out "undesirables."

Now what is interesting about this communalism is the fact that it served at one and the same time as a normalizing microtyranny and a seedbed of democracy. The homogeneity of inhabitants led to a wide dispersal of authority encapsulated in that institution elevated to the status of myth, the New England town meeting. Within the town meeting, compromises were often necessary to get consensus, and compromises were possible because of the bedrock homogeneity upon which differences emerged. This was tidy, not messy, democracy.

Lingeman makes similar points in his trek through small-town history. He sees rough egalitarianism and local tyrannies. On the frontier a premium was placed on avoiding "putting on airs," and an aggressive egalitarianism— with the Colt 45 serving as the "great equalizer"—prevailed. But after the passing of the pioneer period, says Lingeman, "economic differentiation, rising fortunes, industrialism" began to impose a class structure on towns, and Frederick Jackson Turner's "liberty and equality" flourished no longer.[3]

The Lynds' *Middletown* is a classic of that sociological genre, the participant-observer study. The Lynds and their associates penetrated Middletown, interviewing at length and classifying exhaustively. Their study does raise a question, is it a *problem?* What did the Lynds unearth and why does it seem worth recalling? First, they found at work in a robust form the yearning for communal consensus Zuckerman notes for the eighteenth century. In the chapter "Things Making and Unmaking Group Solidarity," the Lynds argue that Middletown is a flourishing matrix for a multitude of shifting associations—welfare, trade, commercial, charitable, men's, women's, young people's, and so on. But all these associations strive for a collective sharing that is more than Fourth of July rhetoric, a sharing that is constitutive of a way of life—hence, the rift the Lynds found between "the Protestants" and the dangerous Other, who threatened the internal consensus, the Catholics. An active Ku Klux Klan chapter fanned the flames of doctrinal prejudice with several apoplectic orators warning of the Catholic menace and calling for "convents and nunneries" to be exposed as dens of iniquity. "Fed on . . . threatening rumors, Klan enrollment boomed," write the Lynds, with one woman who was interviewed by one of their staffers hoping to recruit the neophyte sociologist to her point of view by proclaiming that "the Pope is trying to get control of this country."[4]

Here, then, was a town in the throes of the tensions of a traditional consensus threatened (perhaps) by newcomers. It boiled down to this: Do the Catholics belong? Do we let them in, or not? Anti-Klan citizens, including those in the Chamber of Commerce, figured each person's dollar was as good as the next's and "we're all living here together," so we have to figure out some way to get along. The shedding of blood by Catholic boys in World War I seems to have helped, as Middletowners drew a tight connection between civic pride and national identity. In a slogan Lewis might have invented, Middletowners proclaimed: "United we stick, divided we're stuck / United we boost, divided we bust" (487).

One other issue the Lynds hit on that recurs throughout the fiction of the small town is the gender gap. The markers of sexual differentiation are very strong, with women serving as prime keepers of the flame of Womanhood. Women's clubs of many sorts were rife and powerful. Women of both the working and business classes devotedly read Dorothy Dix's column. Mothers and daughters discussed her advice at Ladies Aid meetings (106). Dix promulgated a view of the woman as a thrifty, efficient housekeeper, no mere drudge. Not at all Virginia Woolf's "angel in the house," Dix's homemaker is a managerial expert, a keeper of the flame of familial values, a cultural arbiter to the community at large and a custodian of her husband's career—a formidable figure. Her role is both empowering and constraining. (We see mostly the constraints from our vantage point.)

Middletown men reinforced the view of women as "creatures purer and morally better than men," though the women, according to the men, were also given to petty prejudice and were too easily hurt. Women characterized the men as potentially out-of-control waywards who needed a firm if invisible hand. Middletown women were devoted to their own valorization. For example, the Lynds reproduce portions from a tribute to "woman" read "with general approval at the close of a meeting . . . of the local women's federated clubs in 1924: 'Her words are like enchanted echoes in a beautiful dell and her laughter like the sweetness of bursting magnolia and her beauty like the smiling violet and the laughing morning glory . . . her presence like an altar of holiness and benediction. That spirit has taught me to revere heaven's divinest gift to the world—womanhood" (118). Whew.

Small wonder the Lynds also found that in "general, a high degree of companionship is not regarded as essential for marriage" (118). Men and women led different lives, had different clubs, and gravitated into separate groups "to talk men's talk and women's talk, or the men do most of the talking and the women largely listen" (118). Men controlled commerce and local politics; women controlled education, community charities, and religion through sheer dint of numbers, commitment, and the force of community consensus. To see in this a situation of women's oppression impure and simple is to see too much. To see no problem at all is to see too little.

On this note, I move directly to writers of those fictional narratives. Given the gender gap noted above, I divide the discussion into male and female fictions in order to meditate on whether men and women experienced the same small town.

Men Imagine the Small Town

As a literary genre, small-town fiction is a creation of male writers just as domestic fiction was the early and continuing domain of women. And men were mostly in rebellion against the town, a rebellion designated the "revolt from the village." Among the revolted were Edgar Howe, a pioneer precursor, Edgar Lee Masters, Sherwood Anderson, and, of course, Sinclair Lewis, whose works span the decades from the mid-1880s (Howe) to 1922 (Lewis's *Babbitt*). Men had not finished complaining by 1922, of course, and I shall look at several works from the 1930s (O'Hara and Wilder), the 1940s (Runyon and Faulkner), and the 1980s (DeLillo).

Howe, Masters, and Anderson form a triad of the disenchanted. Their disaffections are also, in part, Sinclair Lewis's. But his is a different sort of representation, not so much depressive as aggressively debunking, or so I argue below.

The mood of Howe's *Story of a Country Town* (1884), Masters's *Spoon River Anthology* (1915), and Anderson's *Winesburg, Ohio* (1919) is somber, a painting gray on gray. Once in a while, the gloom parts as Howe's protagonist-narrator, Ned Westlock, describes "the sweet and patient face of Agnes," who, with "more fortunate surroundings . . . would have been a remarkable woman." As it was, she was "simply . . . mistress of all our hearts." Or: as Masters's Lois Spears proclaims herself in epitaph, "the happiest of women," caring for loved ones, creating order and beauty in home and garden, exalting "Glory to God in the Highest." Or: as Anderson's George Willard, to whom all Winesburg's estranged ones talk, plots his own escape.[5]

For the most part, however, estrangement, isolation, crushed hopes, a horizon of despair are the main elements of Fairview or Spoon River or Winesburg. Reduced to a slogan, it would be, Get out while you can. Howe's Ned Westlock is impressed at an early age "with the fact that our people seemed to be miserable and discontented, [the] men surly and rough, and the women pale and fretful." He cannot understand why they don't "load their effects on wagons" and move on; surely no place could be worse, and some might be better (47). Men and women, including Ned's parents, are strangers to one another, isolated, pent up in their shells, not knowing how to break through the barrier of the other. Life is hard work, the seasons are remorseless, and death comes before reconciliation. In a pre-Freudian era, Howe portrays no world of innocence; indeed, it is a world later writers were to see through Freudian eyes as repressive, desolate, and even mad.

Masters's classic has about it the claustrophobic sensibility of a Freudian case study, an "Anna O." or a "Dora." Appearance and reality fail to jibe. Only symptoms or posthumously spoken self-portraits point to the truth. Symptoms must be interpreted. The first-person reports of the analysand may obscure as much as they reveal. But Masters's often-bitter dead speak truth that requires no subtle interpretation, truth to counter surface lies, unearthing the bitterness beneath the soothing, normal appearances of things. Amanda Barker tells of a husband believed "in the village where I lived" to have "loved me with a husband's love." Not so, he got her with child "knowing that I could not bring forth life / Without losing my own." She proclaims "from the dust / That he slew me to gratify his hatred" (9).

Reflecting the feminist currents alive in his time, Masters tells the story of Minerva Jones, "the village poetess / Hooted at, jeered at by the Yahoos of the street." She is raped and dies prematurely, and "I thirsted so for love! I hungered so for life!" (22). Dorcas Gustine is hated because "I spoke my mind" (44). Margaret Fuller Stack "would have been as great as George Eliot / But for an untoward fate." Wooed and won by a druggist, who promised her "leisure for my novel," she winds up giving birth to eight children, has no time to write, and dies of lockjaw after she has run a needle into her hand "while washing the baby's things." Her lesson to an unheeding posterity is, "Sex is the curse of life!" (48).

Nellie Clark is deserted when village gossip drives away her older widower husband by agreeing that "I was not really a virgin" (62). Elsa Wertman gives birth to an illegitimate child, fathered by the husband of her employer who raises the child as her own. He grows up to be famous, and Elsa cannot cry aloud, "That's my son! That's my son!" (114). Mrs. Merrit goes to jail for thirty years, dying there, because her nineteen-year-old lover killed her husband (196). Only the contented Lois Spears and Mrs. George Reece, whose husband was sent to prison leaving her with children to feed, clothe, and school—tasks she accomplishes with determination and honor—escape the corrosive and deadly taint of Spoon River (55 and 92, respectively).

Women are not uniquely cursed for Masters. His men are haunted, too, and die not knowing why—including Knowlt Hoheimer, the veteran who lies under a granite pedestal "bearing the words, 'Pro Patria.' What do they mean, anyway?" (27). At times, the grotesquerie approaches Kafka at his most wickedly funny (for example, in Kafka's *Penal Colony*). Masters is no surrealist, but his epitaphs are deliberately distorted.

The culmination of Freudian-haunted village, expatriate literature is Anderson's *Winesburg, Ohio*. Reacting against a presumed contrast between town/city as signifying social universes of innocence/guilt, warmth/coldness, belonging/alienation, Anderson writes a counterpastoral; he takes a walk on the seamy side. The book is labored, weighed down by Anderson's absorption of the repression hypothesis. Repressed, the Winesburgians are desperate, limited, unsatisfied, batty. He describes "Louise Bentley, who became Mrs. John Hardy [as] from childhood a neurotic, one of the race of over-sensitive women that in later days industrialism was to bring in such great numbers into the world" (64). Attached to his description is a note of straightforward didacticism: "Before such women as Louise can be understood and their lives made livable, much will have to be done. Thoughtful books will have to be written and thoughtful lives lived by people about them" (64).

As a social agenda, this is vague, but as a literary admonition, it warns us that a treatment nearly clinical in its focus on abnormal psychology is about to unfold. And because it is abnormal psychology, we are not surprised that Louise rejects her male baby on the grounds that "it is a man child and will get what it wants anyway" (73). A note of feminist revolt takes shape but horribly, as cruelty to an infant.

Sex is fraught with dangers—too little, too much. It ensnares. It overagitates. It invites misunderstanding and excess. Most lives wind up at best being humdrum. Many slide into eccentricity bordering on madness. Men and women are, as in Spoon River and Fairview, noncommunicating atoms, longing for and fearing the other. In his crisp, critical treatment of Anderson, Irving Howe makes several revealing points about *Winesburg, Ohio* in particular and the revolt from the village in general. First, *Winesburg* cannot be read as social fiction striving for verisimilitude to social forms. To read the text in that way makes *Winesburg* absurd, "for no such town could possibly exist."[6] By this, Howe means that no ongoing social life on any scale would be possible if individuals were as estranged from daily life and one another as Anderson's gallery of extreme characters.

Second, Howe argues that writers who streamed to Chicago or to Greenwich Village, creating their bohemias and celebrating Freedom, invariably moved to re-create the town or some idealized image of one—as a community of the elect or the select—intending thereby to "recover the intimacy of the town while hoping to realize the freedom they had expected to find in the city." The condition of living in three worlds—past, present, and present/past—made possible the release of the writers' pent-up views on the life they had left behind (though, on another level, were attempting to reproduce). The ugly stuff rose quickly to the surface—not surprisingly, for Anderson (among others) was not just writing "about" but writing his way "out of." Finally, the life of bohemia itself came under scrutiny as many "began to realize how narrow and paltry had been their conception of freedom."[7] As time went by, champions of the revolt from the village often began to remember villages more generously and to see that an abstract freedom that defines itself against *all* constraints is as ultimately unsatisfying as a world in which one finds little but constraint.

Sinclair Lewis's *Main Street* (1920) is the revolt from the village at its culminating point and a work of at least surface feminist urgings. His female protagonist, Carol Kennicott, represents rationalism, enlightenment, daring. The stupefied citizens of Gopher Prairie, smug in their collective belief that they embody civilization at its apogee, in fact signify its nadir. But Lewis's representation of his heroine grates. She is the voice of progress; they the minions of ignorance. But such intolerant self-certainty gives way, if one is open to life's sobering experiences, to a recognition of ambiguity and paradox, to the fact that no individual or cause is unadulterated.

Lewis's style is, on the one hand, social realism—hence, all the detailed descriptions of shops and clothing and wares and human quirks. But on the other hand, he passes judgments in which irony gives way to crude sarcasm: "Main Street is the climax of civilization. That this Ford car might stand in front of the Bon Ton store, Hannibal invaded Rome and Erasmus wrote in Oxford cloisters."[8] One peculiarity of American life is that Americans love to be taken to task by taskmasters like "Red" Lewis. They adore those who assault them and beg for more. Lewis's career (and not his alone) was built upon the fact that denizens of Sauk Centre, Minnesota, honored him as their greatest native son even as the reading public took him to heart for telling them they were ignorant and parochial.

For this reason, among others, Carol Kennicott's perfervid condemnations add up to glancing blows, and no more, for in her own way, she endorses at a deeper level the American way of life she berates. When she condemns Main Streeters as "peasants" and cries, "Isn't there any way of waking them up? What would happen if they understood scientific agriculture?" she is not, as Lewis apparently believed, being a critic. She is, in fact, being a booster. She hates planlessness. She wants experimentation in the education system. Hers is the voice of progress, our most important product (26).

Another reason Carol fails to live up to the heroic form in which she is at least initially cast is her palpable inability to follow through. She jumps from enthusiasm to enthusiasm, lacking patience for the long haul—again, what could be more American? She muses movingly at one point about "the darkness of women," asking, "What do we want?" (197). But her own search leads her to go the route of prototypical male representations: she heads off to the exciting world of the big city (Washington, D.C.), where she is fortunate enough to solve the servant problem straight off ("She had, though it absorbed most of her salary, an excellent nurse for Hugh. She herself put him to bed and played with him on holidays" [411]). A political awakening follows when she decides that institutions, not individuals, are the enemies—Family, Church, Party, Country—and that the best weapon against them is "unembittered laughter," though she never comes off as unembittered herself.

Returning to Gopher Prairie, she learns to her apparent surprise—though this surprise is surprising given her relentless assessments of the small town throughout most of the book—that the whole world is not changing, despite all that city talk about "European revolution, guild socialism, free verse" (426). Her only hope is that all the babies, including her newborn daughter, will finally bring into being the stillborn dreams of their frustrated mothers.

As an imagined female protagonist, Carol is thin. Her motivations are too often petty and her protestations of innocence strained. She emerges as someone quick to judge others but not given to much critical self-appraisal. As a believable female rebel against the small town, she fails. Given Lewis's commitment to realism, this is a serious flaw. The characters are vaporous, save for Will Kennicott. (Perhaps because he is modeled in part on a real small-town doctor—Lewis's father.) The politics is muted, reduced to slogans—"there is a ruling class, despite all our professions of democracy" (98). One is left with types, caricatures, and a heroine whose trumpet blows uncertain.

Babbitt (1922), published two years after *Main Street,* is a Main Street relocated—from rural village to the flourishing minimetropolis of Zenith.[9] George Babbitt, businessman and booster, has a pebble in his shoe, though he has no name for it. Everything should be as "hunky-dory" as he pro-

claims. His wife, portrayed unflatteringly by Lewis as having grown "as sexless as an anemic nun," no longer interests him. Lewis paints Babbitt in
broad strokes, a man worshipping the God of Progress because He gave man
B. V. D.s instead of those wretched old-fashioned undergarments.

Babbitt talks like an automaton programmed for banality, his speech
peppered with colloquialisms: "for the love o' Pete," "by golly," "doggone,"
"first rate," "gosh darn." His politics, save for a lapse from which he recovers,
are probusiness, antiradical, proefficiency, antiwaste, proconfidence, anti-
pessimism. Babbitt is a man submerged in, well, babbittry, who surfaces
briefly, gets glimpses of alternatives, and softens the harshness of his rigid
and stale middle-class ethic, only to sink once again. But with this caveat:
there is hope for the children. Youth emerges (in the person of Babbitt's son,
who has gone against his parents' will by marrying beneath them) as possible harbingers of a marginally different, a slightly less well satisfied, a modestly more daring way of life. By endorsing his son at the book's conclusion,
Babbitt signifies that he welcomes what the next generation may make of
itself—within bounds, of course.

Ironies abound in the revolt-from-the-village literature. Its central and
most famous articulator, Lewis, winds up endorsing the drivenness of the
culture he criticizes. Masters and Anderson (less so Howe) flee the village
only to attempt to re-create it in another setting in an idealized form. Each
professes love for the town he has evoked as a graveyard of human hopes.

As one turns to the 1930s and John O'Hara's *Appointment in Samarra*
(1934), a less intensely claustrophobic, more class-driven, achievement-
oriented culture comes into view. Thematic similarities to the revolt-from-
the-village literature remain: the gender gap, male squirming under female
domestic control, unacknowledged power games, fear of the other. But
Julian English, O'Hara's doomed protagonist, is a very different creature
from the Spoon River depressives, the Main Street parochials, the Zenith
boosters. He is a young man going nowhere fast. His father is a doctor, but he
sells cars. He despises many of those whose favor he must curry or those
whom he must not, minimally, antagonize. Staring danger in the face, he
commits a social indiscretion in full view of the respectable members of the
country club and is placed on the path to ruin.

Most interesting for this essay is the unraveling of the relationship between Julian and his wife, Caroline, a relationship cemented by genuine
sexual attraction and bonding. But deep down, Caroline is "contemptuous
of the men she had known," and Julian is engaged in a self-destructive, inarticulate revolt against not so much Caroline as Marriage and Respectability
and the whole ball of wax, as it were. Caroline's mother expresses the prevailing female view of men precisely: "Men are weak, darling. In the hands of

a woman the strongest man in the world is weak, so don't think any less of Julian or your father or any other man if he has a momentary weakness."[10]

Strikingly, and in contrast to the writers already considered, O'Hara homes in on emerging class differences in which an established upper class is constantly pressed by an aggressive middle-class yearning to go higher. The poor and marginal are left to fight among themselves for the leavings. Gibbsville, having grown from borough to "third class city," is a social order that is at one and the same time congealed and fluid. A social pecking order is established, but within it some go higher, some fall out. Catholics are in, or at least not out. They join the country club. But Jews and Negroes are outcasts. Growth in population, bustling commerce, hustling entrepreneurship—none of these eliminates the apparent need to marginalize whole categories of others. The theme of the outsider, of prejudice against groups, comes to the fore and stays there in the fiction of the thirties and the forties. Men and women may be strangers to one another much of the time, but they form a united front against the real or imagined outsider.

The device used by Thornton Wilder in his enormously popular play, *Our Town* (1938), to portray a world of communal consensus—some tension, yes, but goodwill outs throughout—is to return to a small face-to-face New England village untroubled by threats from "foreigners." In a revolt from the revolt-against-the-village, Wilder offers a paean to "greater understanding," not "judgment." His dead are wholly unlike Masters's. They live in a world of almost unbearable poignancy, having attained a wonderment and generalized love that enables them to break from the living without bitterness or regret. The parries between men and women are good-natured and decent, with the Stage Manager filling in all we ever wanted to know about Grover's Corners.

Emily and George, soon to be wed, embody male understandings of women, female of men, in ways that reinforce rather than challenge those understandings. Emily, for example, is described parenthetically by Wilder as speaking lines "(All innocence, yet firm)," buttressing the notion that women's strength and willfulness emerge in muted forms, through the fluttering of white-gloved, delicate hands.[11] George tells Emily that "men aren't naturally good, but girls *are*." Emily cautions but does not chastise—I'm not "perfect," she tells George, but it is clear that she is very, very good. And so it goes as Grover's Corners fades away in rosy hues.

There is a truth to the story Wilder tells, but it is a partial truth, just as Anderson and Masters tell partial truths. Each of these truths is exaggerated—Wilder's, in part, with reference to the earlier, gloomy distortions embodied in revolt-from-the-village fiction. Nor is anything like balance visible in Damon Runyon's 1946 *In Our Town*, a hilarious, friendly, biting commentary on small-town life consisting of vignettes of a gallery of notable characters. Runyon means to amuse and he does. He writes for an audience grown more hip, more attuned to the wisecrack. His is not a story of the town but of human lives the town makes possible. Much of the time, what Runyon finds when he peers behind the closed curtains of Main Street is the macabre.

Samuel Graze, a six-foot-three-inch, 250-pound bully, beats his wife, who "weighed about ninety-two pounds with her hat on."[12] One day, diminutive Magda warns Samuel she will kill him the next time he beats her. He laughs. But she gets the last laugh. When he collapses in a drunken stupor, she ties him up and beats him to death. The reaction of the town is a collective accolade for Magda. "Everybody in Our Town said it was a wonderful feat for a woman no bigger than Magda Graze to swing a club that big, long enough to kill a man the size of Samuel." She is let off with a reprimand, although a few thought it was "setting a bad example to the other women in Our Town" (11).

A disillusioned Pete Hankins wonders bitterly whether honesty is really the best policy after a series of rebuffs to his honest overtures; Doc Mindler exposes hypocrisy by declaring a quarantine in the seedy section of Our Town, where some of the town's finest indulge their nighttime appetites even as they condemn others in the light of day for possibly scandalous behavior; Boswell Van Dusen, the local editor, confronted with a failing newspaper, begins to berate the citizens rather than praise them and finds his circulation soaring—the more scandal the better; Mrs. Bogane, worn out by serving her husband hand and foot, uses her inheritance to hire servants to wait on her hand and foot; the town's "great American Patriot," Hank Smith, is mocked by Runyon for having received his battle wounds in bars and boudoirs rather than in the battlefield; and the Happiness Joneses, a truly happy family, grow even happier when they win a fortune and share it equitably, much to the chagrin of their disbelieving and jealous neighbors. This is Our Town.

What distinguishes Runyon's portraits from Masters's is their good-natured affection for their characters and their world. Masters cries, Flee, this place will kill you. Runyon says, cracker-barrel philosopher-style, Yup, we've got some real characters, our share of low-life and decent folks, but it's pretty much the same everywhere, isn't it? Runyon's sense is that Our Town is Everywhere, that any collection of human beings of any size will contain its prototypical characters and stories. Masters's dead are more tautly linked to this town, this place, raising the possibility that other places might offer hope.

American writers at mid-twentieth century were people of and in the world. They had been through war. They had seen Paris, and nothing could

keep them down on the farm. But some stayed on the farm, or its imaginative analogue, in their fictions. The greatest creator of a very particular, imagined world is William Faulkner, whose *The Town* (1957) is not about a town
at all but a created space that allows him to tell darkly humorous tales about
the Snopeses. To be sure, he describes the town, Jefferson, as "like all the
other little Southern towns: nothing had happened in it since the last carpet-
bagger had given up and gone home or been assimilated into another unre-
generate Mississippian."[13] The town has the "usual mayor and board of al-
dermen." Politics is inbred and parochial, almost wholly predictable, and
nobody bothers with it overmuch. Of course, there is plenty of chicanery,
but that is to be expected.

Faulkner's world and characters change (to the extent they do at all)
despite themselves. Thus, Uncle Gavin goes to the mat to defend the honor
of Mrs. Snopes. Mother tries to explain about women, morals, and gossip to
Uncle Gavin and Father: "The trouble with both of you is, you know nothing
about women. Women are not interested in morals. They aren't even interested in unmorals. The ladies of Jefferson don't care what she does. What
they will never forgive is the way she looks. No: the way the Jefferson gentlemen look at her" (48). Father denies looking at Mrs. Snopes that way, and
Mother says so much "the worse for me . . . with a mole for a husband. No:
moles have warm blood; a Mammoth Cave fish—" (48). Mother likes her
men warm-blooded, and she strips women of their capacity as guardians of
morals. Women are as likely to be catty as virtuous, she suggests.

The debunking of the myth of woman as proprietor of the moral good,
the reinforcement of the story of women as petty tormentors of other
women through gossip, doesn't end with this exchange. For Uncle Gavin's
dogged defense of the virtue of an unvirtuous woman is comic. He is a knight
misplaced, and Faulkner's narrator-protagonist describes him in wonderfully ironic terms: "What he [Uncle Gavin] was doing was simply defending
forever with his blood the principle that chastity and virtue in women shall
be defended whether they exist or not" (76). Uncle Gavin must hold onto
the image, must keep it alive through his actions, even though the women in
his surround are toughly in tune with reality, including their own vampings.
Faulkner suggests that women are off the pedestal, and only latter-day Don
Quixotes need to keep them there. Written at a time when the wider culture
was rife with the postwar feminine mystique, and a veritable orgy of good
housekeeping, Faulkner taps an underground vein soon to explode into
explicitness in the literature, music, and films of the 1960s.

Now, in the mid-1980s, the nation has passed through a sexual revolution, a technological and media explosion, a war and a war against the war,
civil rights upheavals, and feminist challenges. From playground to Pen-

tagon; blacks have challenged whites; women have identified as Other those they claim overlong thus identified them, and so on. Many determined people spent much time vigorously shaking out all those rugs under which so much had been swept for so long. But this is also a moment when half the American population would prefer to live in a small town. The small town still occupies a strong hold on the American imagination, on our sense of self and place and possibility.

A recent, stunning novel, Don DeLillo's *White Noise* (1985), suggests that what half of us look for when we look to small towns may be lost forever. The town is Blacksmith. The point of interest is College-on-the-Hill. The protagonist, Jack Gladney, is chairman of the Department of Hitler Studies, his own academic invention. Gladney describes the town lovingly: "There are houses in town with turrets and two-story porches where people sit in the shade of ancient maples. There are Greek revival and Gothic churches. There is an insane asylum with an elongated portico, ornamented dormers and a steeply pitched roof topped by a pineapple finial. Babette and I and our children by previous marriages live at the end of a quiet street in what was once a wooded area with deep ravines."[14]

Murray, a recent émigré from the Big City who wants to do for Elvis Presley what Jack has done for Hitler (put him on the academic map in a big way), says: "I like it here. . . . A small town setting. I want to be free of cities and sexual entanglements. Heat. This is what the cities mean to me. . . . I can't help being happy in a town called Blacksmith. . . . I'm here to avoid situations. Cities are fully of situations, sexually cunning people" (10–11). Through Murray, a character affectionately parodied, DeLillo retaps that deep vein in our culture that sees the city as full of situations, temptations, too many, too much—an excess. The town brings things down to size, curbs our appetites, makes more human our desires. Thus, most of the teaching staff at College-on-the-Hill, at least in contemporary culture, are New York émigrés, seeking "the natural language" of American culture through trivia, media, small-town signifiers.

But rather like one of those 1950s science-fiction horror stories in which an apparently placid small town turns out to be the site for hideous and stealthy takeovers by malicious aliens, Blacksmith cannot protect anyone from anything. Murray may be less sexually entangled. But everyone is enmeshed in the world of "white noise," a world penetrated by incessantly operating television sets, humming appliances, a nearby chemical dump site, air currents carrying industrial waste, the never-ending hum of traffic on the nearby freeway. People are afraid. They revel in disasters on the nightly news—how horrible, how wonderful, it isn't us, please give us more, "something bigger, grander, more sweeping."

His academic life partly hustle, partly genuine obsession with Hitler, Gladney is a preeminently contemporary man as family man, loving husband, perplexed but devoted father. The gender gap shrinks in this novel. Jack and Babette are devoted and caring as they minister to and maneuver in and through a complex familial din of many children from many failed marriages. Unlike the Lynds' Middletowners, they are devoted to the "companionate marriage." They tell each other everything, or so Jack believes until he finds out Babette has been withholding from him the most fearful knowledge of all—the story of her fear of death, a fear that pitches her into trading her body for access to an experimental drug that promises to eliminate fear of death. But this lapse in communication and her infidelity do not then make them strangers but more dedicated, if saddened, lovers.

Fear is the preeminent motif of *White Noise*. For a time, Gladney comforts himself, when an airborne toxic incident threatens to turn the family and home that embodies partial surcease, if not escape, into an endangered landscape, by suggesting that "society is set up in such a way that it's the poor and the uneducated who suffer the main impact of natural and man-made disasters. People in low-lying areas get the floods, people in shanties get hurricanes and tornados. I'm a college professor. Did you ever see a college professor rowing a boat down his own street in one of those TV floods?" (114).

But they do. The family is forced to evacuate, and Gladney himself is exposed to a toxic dose of the airborne poison. He begins to grow a tumor that will kill him. And he offers, from his fear, a recognition that we no longer have the Other to fear, not if we are honest with ourselves. DeLillo deftly deconstructs the binary: town/city, us/them:

> There was no large city with a vaster torment we might use to see our own dilemma in some soothing perspective. No large city to blame for our sense of victimization. No city to hate and fear. No panting megacenter to absorb our woe, to distract us from our unremitting sense of time—time as the agent of our particular ruin, our chromosome breaks, hysterically multiplying tissue. . . . Although we are for a small town remarkably free of resentment, the absence of a polestar metropolis leaves us feeling in our private moments a little lonely. (176–77)

DeLillo suggests that we grow up in this sense: that we understand that the cities' torments and our own (if we are small towners) are more like than unlike; that we are all threatened by invisible toxins and noises; that much of our frenetic obsession with the body is a desperate attempt to mask our collective fears. Gladney and Babette are not Man and Woman; they are particular individuals. The family's children are not American Kids, they each differ strikingly from one another. DeLillo's is a world of individualities, not commonalities, a world bounded by family, domestic possessions as the markers and signifiers of life of our times, reconfigured groupings, generalized and scarcely submerged fears. He has no whipping boy or girl; he is neither in revolt from the village nor in revolt from that revolt. He suggests that the genre in its prototypical form is all used up.

I do not find, in fiction by women that focuses primarily on town rather than male/female or domesticity (a vast and rather different topic), this sort of deconstructive moment, but I do find tales of another sort.

Women Writers Represent the Small Town

Novels of "manners," detailed ethnographies of family and domestic life, dissections hilarious or mordant of male-female relations—these, more than small-town fiction, have been the province of women writers. Although many such fictions are set in small towns, the town itself is not a central "character" in the unfolding of the tale. Towns are backdrop, necessary but not central.

To characterize women's fictional representations of town life in the twentieth century, I shall focus on five narratives, beginning with Edith Wharton's *Ethan Frome* (1911), a stark, foreboding story cast as a classic village yarn. The novel's narrator-protagonist describes the New England town of Starkfield as an atmosphere that produces no change in human emotions save, with its "sluggish pulse," to retard them further. Ethan Frome faces the negation of life: "Guess he's been in Starkfield too many winters. Most of the smart ones get away."[15] Exploring why Ethan didn't get away is Wharton's task.

Ethan's turns out to be a doomed fate, not unlike that of a trapped Spoon River resident, or a warped Winesburgian. He has become "part of the mute melancholy landscape, an incarnation of its frozen woe" (14). Playing out his allotted part to the end, for the most part in a haunted silence, Ethan's story is at once tragic and grotesque. He is more victim than agent of his own destiny, and his attempt at transforming the course of things—through the suicides, failed, of himself and his beloved Mattie—only pitch the two of them more completely into the clutches of the complaining, manipulative Zeena, his wife. Bitterness blooms like robust weeds.

A very different story, one in which there is love aplenty amid the unfolding of events, is Carson McCullers's *Member of the Wedding* (1946), set in a small Southern town and dominated by Frankie, a feisty tomboy in revolt against her gender and the constraints of life as an adolescent. She wants adventure. She will move away. She may just change her name. Foiled in a scheme to go away with her adored older brother and his new bride on their honeymoon trip, she determines to leave anyway. "I can't stand this existence—this kitchen—this town—any longer! I will hop a train and go to New York. Or hitch rides to Hollywood, and get a job there. . . . Or I could dress up like a boy and join the Merchant Marines and run away to sea. Somehow, anyhow, I'm running away."[16]

McCullers plays out a dominant motif of male small-town fiction—get out when and if you can—and plants big-city dreams in the head of her determined heroine. The dreams are vague, and they are quintessentially American, including the lure of Hollywood. For many more young women than men, Hollywood represented glamour, fame, escape, a way to turn one's feminine beauty into riches and romance; a way, perhaps, to escape humdrum domesticity. That this dream soured more often than not did little, for several decades, to tarnish its luster. The dream when I was growing up was of looking into the mirror one day and seeing Elizabeth Taylor, who embodied beauty and worldliness.

One of the great scandals created by a book in the fifties was the publication of Grace Metalious's pulpy steamer, *Peyton Place* (1956). Not a serious work of fiction, *Peyton Place* nonetheless had its finger on the American pulse. In an era when Ike was in the White House and all was presumably well, Metalious told a tale of chicanery, rape, incest, narrow-minded bigotry, illicit abortion, illegitimacy, destructive gossip, and fear of destructive gossip.

Her characters are one-line drawings, types like Dr. Matthew Swain, a salt-of-the-earth fellow (who should have been played by Spencer Tracy in the film). Others include Miss Thorton, the spinster schoolteacher, a Smith graduate who returns to "her native New England to teach" out of love of the youngsters; Constance MacKenzie, the beautiful "widow" (really never married), who wants a man but recoils for fear he will learn the horrid truth of her past; Tomas Makris, the "foreign" outsider who comes to town to become public school principal; Lucas Cross, the drunken and violent woodsman "of a now-and-then variety common to northern New England," and so on. Metalious is especially vicious in her characterization of Cross and many others of the poor or marginal class. She shares with Lewis great faith in science, rationalism, and progress, advocating taking lumbering away from a drunk such as Lucas and putting it in the hands of serious young men with B.S. degrees from an agricultural college.

Her incessant obsession, however, is with sex and gossip. For example: Constance MacKenzie's recurrent nightmare is one in which she hears Peyton Place voices describing her as a whore and her child as a "dirty little bastard."[17] Her fears for her daughter, the book's heroine, Allison—who winds up going to New York to become a writer—are that "she'll get in trouble [or] worst of all: SHE'LL GET HERSELF TALKED ABOUT!" (50). Selena Cross the victimized daughter of Lucas, impregnated by her stepfather, feels every eye is on her, "A girl in trouble . . . [a] girl in Dutch" (140). The mother of Norman Page—who received a psychiatric discharge from the army—hoping to persuade him to go along with a scheme to pretend he was physically wounded, hence a hero, conjures up town gossip as the most powerful weapon in her arsenal: "Do you want everyone . . . to think of you as a coward who ran under fire? Do you want to disgrace the both of us so we can never hold up our heads again?" (308).

The obsession of Metalious's characters, especially the women, with gossip, primarily the gossip of women, reflects a genuine social reality—one marker of modes of male and female authority. Gossip in small towns and traditional communities was a powerful method of social control. In his *Letter to M. D'Alembert on the Theatre,* Jean-Jacques Rousseau described the speech of women's societies, noting that much of their conversation revolved around the behavior of other women. Rousseau approved of all this, arguing that such gossip gives women a censoring role. By assuring that the "deviant" will be talked about, sometimes mercilessly, or even ostracized, women use their speech to prevent scandal and to promote civic virtue. As arbiters of the local morality, women are in a power position to keep others, particularly other women, in line.

The suspicion, They're talking about me, or the fear-riddled, pleading question, What will the neighbors think? frequently suffices to check "deviance." Why this is so is a complex question for ethnographers and ethicists, but illicit female sexuality traditionally occupied an honored place at the top of the list of activities to be curbed by being gossiped about and condemned. The aim, most often, was to bring the deviant back into the fold. Should that fail, the person could be driven out, either literally or symbolically, through social isolation. Gossip was both an integrative and a disintegrative force.

Metalious sketches gossip as wholly destructive, with malicious tongues bent on ruining as many lives as possible. In this as in other matters, she distorts—the seamy side is all, or nearly all. The instances of kindness, sharing, and friendship are all too few. Bigotry abounds, and escape is the only solution available to one with ambition and gumption. Unquestioning in its acceptance of a pop-Freudian thesis that sexuality is a normal, healthy urge to be satisfied from the age of sixteen or even a bit earlier, Metalious's is an angry soap opera, an exposé that rips the hypocritical veil from the face of Peyton Place. Hers is a late entry in the revolt from the village, a perfect complement to the emergence in American popular culture of the scandal sheet, a yellow press that specializes in detailing the tawdry. There is always just enough truth in the tawdry to entice us. But it is a cheap entertainment.

An interesting sign of the present moment is the emergence of a woman's literature that sketches the small town in warm but not treacly hues, that traces its filiations and burnishes its surfaces as a world that is a complexly human creation, an important female construction. Susan Allen Toth in her memoir, *Blooming: A Small Town Girlhood* (1984), tells the story of growing up female in Ames, Iowa, and finds it fine.

Ames in her youth had its Other in the Catholic Church. Communal consensus was shored up with warnings about the Catholic menace, the Church's iron hand and idolatry and "most of all the way it could snatch our very children from us and bring them up in the manacles of a strange faith."[18] But Catholic fears played a marginal role, for the most part surfacing only when a Protestant intended to marry a Catholic, which produced a "major social upheaval" in Ames. Toth's homey tales, not sentimental but filled with loving emotion, unearth memories of the world of teenage girls, a world of talk and more talk—talk of "boys, teachers, clothes, gossip. All that talking built up a steady confidence that the trivia of our lives were worth discussion" (70). Women's lives could and should be "attended to." This is the positive face of women's talk.

The world of Ames was democratic on the level of manners, with such events as a box social rigged to "avoid hurt feelings." Most important, being from Ames "meant you were from *somewhere,* from a place that, if your listeners only knew about it, would explain a great deal about you. It is a sense of place my daughter, who has lived for varying times in California, London, and different parts of the Twin Cities, will probably not share. I have not yet decided whether she has suffered a loss or an enlargement" (205). Toth may not have decided, but her book helps us to decide: the answer is both. Her daughter's life has a more diverse horizon, but it is thinned out, lacking the density that being "from someplace" provides. Toth partially redeems the small town as a locus for identity, a place one may leave (as she does, a smart scholarship girl off to Smith) but that one need not "flee from."

And, finally, to that monumental *bildungsroman*—the challenge of Helen Hooven Santmyer's *And Ladies of the Club* (1982), a work much of a lifetime in its creation, which means it takes nearly as long to read—all 1,176 pages of it! The scope of Santmyer's book astonishes. Her project is history as fiction, fiction as history. She strives for verisimilitude and achieves it almost too well. At times, one sinks into the detail of, say, cordage production, or the species crisis, or the unfolding of the disputed Tilden-Hayes election of 1876. One lives out the lives of the core characters, the original members of the Waynesboro Woman's Club, formed in the early summer of 1868. Conceived by Santmyer—obviously many decades ago—as an answer to Sinclair Lewis, whose *Main Street,* says Theresa, a young woman writer near the book's end, "had made her so angry that after a decade she still seethed when she thought of it," *And Ladies of the Club* is must reading as a sociohistorical event, a dense ethnography.

Theresa—Santmyer's alter ego—"set out planning the new book with stubborn concentration. She hoped the times would be better when she had finished, or no publishers would look at it, nor anyone have the patience to read it."[19] The book to be written by Theresa is described as "a long one, covering several generations of life in a small midwestern city: the sort of thing that had been popular a few years back, like *Jean-Christophe* and *Remembrance of Things Past* and *The Forsyte Saga.* She laughed at herself ruefully: she was no Galsworthy. Much less a Rolland or Proust. But she would like to write an answer to Sinclair Lewis" (1169). She did that.

The lushness of *And Ladies of the Club* cannot be captured in a few paragraphs. Santmyer's is not great literature, but it is a monumental narrative of American life. One finds neither pure villains nor virgin saints. There are weaknesses and strengths aplenty, triumphs and tragedies, micropolitical dramas such as the local temperance union's assault on the saloons of German immigrants, and macropolitical upheavals, including the aftermath of the Civil War, booms and busts, and the roller coaster ride of incessant politicking from main street to national convention: it is all there in panoramic and finely honed detail.

What distinguishes Santmyer is that hers is an exhaustive treatment of the nexus between personal and political. She unearths a close linkage between personal and social identity, between the sweep of world events and the shape of individual lives. There is a waxing and waning in involvement in, and obsession with, public events. The men are the major players in politics, to be sure, but all the women listen in, and some (for example, Anne Gordon's best friend, Sally Raush) take an active part within the constraints of the social mores of the day. Ludwig, Sally's husband, says, "Liebe, if you are going into politics with me, there are some things you must learn from men. That you can be personal friends with your political enemies. That you can catch more lies with sugar than vinegar" (134). Mrs. Ballard, a suffragist, cavils, rejecting such counsel: "Politicians! Forgiving for expediency's sake dubious activities of some very dubious gentlemen" (464). It is a great strength of Santmyer's narrative that she does not adjudicate knowingly between these two positions, finding in each a moment of truth.

So politics drives a few men and engages the energy of fewer women. But the results of politics haunt everyone, especially the men who have seen the worst of it. John Gordon, Anne's husband, never recovers from his experiences as a Civil War doctor. On his deathbed, he raves about the war. His son, Johnny, comments: "It should be the happy years that come back in mind, but in delirium, it's the horrors. The war! He hated it so, and now, burning up with fever, it is all he remembers" (863). Women are haunted by their husbands' hauntings and driven by their ambitions. But for the most part, although the women spend plenty of time talking politics among themselves, they are "always more concerned with what seemed to them fundamental matters: births, marriages, deaths, the current scandals" (750). The birth of a child, the illness of a friend—these drive grand-scale politics from the women's foremost thoughts. When everyday life is on a even keel, they become more preoccupied with events "outside."

Darker hauntings come through: Kate, John Gordon's sister, hangs herself, tormented by her attractions to other women, which find no appropriate forum for expression; the local minister's wife dies from neglect and too many pregnancies; Kitty Edwards is driven by a fanatical zeal for perfect housekeeping. But the Waynesboro people are people one learns to care about, especially Santmyer's women. Easily mocked, their endeavors gain elevation in our eyes. The women's club itself is a literary endeavor (of the sort lampooned by Lewis) that does in fact promote an interest in culture. Though some of its members prefer the safe, sentimental, domestic novel, others, including the widely read and well-educated Anne Gordon, urge Zola's *Nana* and Maupassant's *Une Vie* upon club members. The club furnishes the core for the creation of a Waynesboro Lending Library, with the daughters putting their mothers' project on a firm footing a generation later as a tax-funded, civil enterprise, not simply a women's volunteer effort.

Impressively, even Anne's discovery of her husband's infidelity takes eventual shape as a triumph for her. That victory is not of a vindictive sort that exposes the other to anger and ridicule. Indeed, Anne never lets John know she knows. She understands despite her hurt his need to escape the burden of self, of being Dr. John Gordon, from time to time—a man pledged to save lives who oversees far too many deaths. Although her first reaction on learning of his infidelity is that such things happen only in bad novels, she confronts reality, assesses who she is and what she wants, and determines to see it through. No sorrowing *mater dolorosa*, empowered, she becomes the person she pretends to be, as the acting self reshapes the inner self.

There is great subtlety at work here and a challenge to our own therapeutic presumptions about the relation between inner and outer worlds. As Anne Gordon's life—a life filled with tragedy that includes the deaths of her husband and both her children—draws to its close, I wept. Hers is a life well lived, thickly detailed, rich in purpose and friendship, interwoven with the textures of the sights, sounds, smells of a dailiness that, in Santmyer's hands, acquires a clear-sighted sanctity. Hers is truly *the* woman's treatment of the small town—a book that recalls an entire generation, evoking a time and place we recognize dimly, for our lives are much changed from those lived out by Anne and Sally and all the ladies of the club. What, then, is the horizon of the present?

My Hometown . . . A Sense of Loss

In fiction and popular music, the loss of the traditional hometown and a yearning to re-create its strengths form an ironic, plangent commentary on our collective discontents. Home is left or lost but not reviled in such songs as Bruce Springsteen's unsparing, clear-eyed valediction "My Hometown." Springsteen's characters, like DeLillo's, live lives of desperation sprinkled with hope and sometimes honor. Both suggest, as does Santmyer's *magnum opus* (in its detailing so exhaustively a world now lost), that we are all vulnerable beings. The overriding question, then, is not the working out of male-female struggles but an even more troubling fixation: is it possible for the modern human being to be at home anywhere?

Framed in this way, we return to "the small town" as a spatial metaphor, a place within which real characters might emerge and exist in relation to one another and through relations of love, hate, conflict, care, spite, support. Perhaps our ongoing preoccupation with the small town that exists in our cultural and individual myth as a more desirable place to be than the one most of us happen to be in suggests that human life is best thought, and lived, horizontally as well as vertically. By that I mean that insofar as the contemporary landscape is one littered with individuals making their way (male and female alike), and with disintegrated remnants of families and communities, we project ourselves upward and outward in plans of individual success, meaning domination by a metaphor of vertical rise. By definition, as we climb, others fall; they must. Other people are those beneath us rather than beings, real characters whom we must, whether we want to or not, confront on Main Street, in the parlor, on the playing field, in the church choir. Perhaps now having a place we come from, an identifiable landscape, a real space as well as a metaphorical construct, speaks to yearnings that cannot be named other than as a yearning for the small town. Small-town fiction complicates those yearnings, at once warning us off and drawing us in.

Notes

Originally published in Ernest J. Yanarella and Lee Sigelman, eds., *Political Mythology and Popular Fiction* (New York: Westport, 1988).

1. Raymond Williams, *The Country and the City* (New York: Oxford University Press, 1973), 7–8.

2. Michael Zuckerman, *Peaceable Kingdoms: New England Towns in the Eighteenth Century* (New York: Knopf, 1970), 4, 108.

3. Lingeman, Richard, *Small Town America: A Narrative History, 1620 to the Present* (New York: Putnam, 1980), 78–79.

4. Robert S. Lynd and Helen Merrill Lynd, *Middletown: A Study in Contemporary American Culture* (New York: Harcourt, Brace, 1929), 482. Page citations in the next four paragraphs are to this source.

5. Edgar W. Howe, *The Story of a Country Town* (Boston: James R. Osgood, 1884), 47; Edgar Lee Masters, *Spoon River Anthology* (New York: Macmillan, 1923), 52; Sherwood Anderson, *Winesburg, Ohio* (New York: Milestone Editions, 1960). Page citations to their works and to the works of the other authors discussed appear in parentheses in the text.

6. Irving Howe, *Sherwood Anderson* (New York: William Sloane, 1951), 97.

7. Ibid., 61–62, 72.

8. Sinclair Lewis, *Main Street* (New York: New American Library, 1961), 6.

9. Sinclair Lewis, *Babbitt* (New York: Harcourt, Brace, 1922).

10. John O'Hara, *Appointment in Samarra* (New York: Penguin Books, 1945), 208–9.

11. Thornton Wilder, *Our Town: A Play in Three Acts* (New York: Howard McCann, 1939), 52.

12. Damon Runyon, *In Our Town* (New York: Creative Age Press, 1946), 9.

13. William Faulkner, *The Town* (New York: Random House, 1957), 10–11.

14. Don DeLillo, *White Noise* (New York: Viking Press, 1985), 9.

15. Edith Wharton, *Ethan Frome* (New York: Scribner, 1911), 8.

16. Carson McCullers, *The Member of the Wedding* [the play] (New York: New Directions, 1952), 103.

17. Grace Metalious, *Peyton Place* (New York: Julian Messner, 1956), 16.

18. Susan Allen Toth, *Blooming: A Small Town Girlhood* (New York: Ballantine Books, 1984), 15.

19. Helen Hooven Santmyer, *. . . And Ladies of the Club* (New York: Putnam, 1984), 1169.

22

Democracy's Middle Way

"Education is a subject on which we all feel that we have something to say," writes T. S. Eliot, and here one is reminded of Flannery O'Connor's pithy reposte to a query from an earnest young student following a lecture she had given on the state of American fiction. The student fretted that education, the dead hand of the past, must surely stifle many a budding genius. Did not O'Connor find this to be the case? Her typically sardonic response was that, on the contrary, education didn't "stifle enough of them." She would surely join hands with Eliot in holding that everyone has something to say but not everything said is worthy of sustained attention. How to sort the wheat from the chaff, especially on a subject on which all feel they have something to say?

This quickly takes us to the heart of whether or not education can be definitely defined, so to speak. Here we find Eliot steering a course between those who, deploring the "wobbliness of words," opt for a strong stipulative definition that brooks no dissent and those who wobble all over the place, careening wildly in their definitions depending upon the passing enthusiasms of a given moment. The latter temptation is particularly great for educators and the definition of education in a democratic society. We all agree that a good society is democratic. But this is just the beginning of inquiry, for democracy is, in Eliot's argument, not simply a set of procedures, a constitution, if you will, but "a common ethos, a common way of responding emotionally, even common standards of conduct in private life."

Not being simple, democracy does not afford us a straightforward definition of what education in, and for, democracy might be. If we move too quickly to the notion of education for relevance ("to play their part in a democracy"), we may stress watery adaptation above authentic excellence. If we concentrate exclusively on the few, assuming that the many are less vital in the overall scheme of things, the democratic culture necessary to sustain democracy over the long haul will either wither on the vine or not bear fruit in the first place. We are on the horns of more than one dilemma. But Eliot, almost jauntily, is neither discouraged nor deterred, for ours is a vibrant, living language and culture. "We do not want our language to become a dead language," he notes, and only a language and a tradition behind glass, an *immobile tableau*, would yield up a final word on what education means. And even that would not tell us what we, from our living vantage point, want to know. For one culture's definition of education or democracy will not and cannot be identical to that of another. We arrive at democracy and our understanding of education in our own way, framed within a horizon of limited, not limitless, possibility dictated by our historic time and place.

We must, of course, try to fix meanings, for to abandon that attempt altogether would be to live in an amorphous and pointless world in which nobody cared very much about anything. Because a democratic culture is one in which responsibility and freedom go hand in hand, human beings, limited though they may be, can and must sort out the important from the less important; the vital from the trivial; the worthy from the unworthy; the excellent from the mediocre. Democracy is a culture of, and for, the stout-hearted, persons who, in their effort to define and to realize the good life, can live with the certainty that such will always elude them, finally. This the great democratic theorists have always understood.

Robust Democracy

From Jefferson's bold throwing down of the gauntlet to the British Empire, not knowing whether the upshot would be "hanging together or hanged separately," to Lincoln's "nation thus conceived and thus educated," to Martin Luther King's dream of an essentially pacific democratic people who judge their fellow citizens by the content of their character not the color of their skins, democratic culture has been a *wager*, not a frozen accomplishment. Democratic education might not guarantee the robust spiritedness that democratic culture, if it is to be a living thing, requires, but it, too, must be cast in the form of anticipation and stirring expectancy. Democracy alone offers the elusive but nonetheless genuine possibility that "moral equivalents to war," in William James's famous phrase, might be made manifest. "For us there is only the trying," Eliot wrote, and his salutary awareness of the complexity of any and all attempts to define education reflects his keen sense that one can't just draw a bead and begin straight-shooting at a stationary target.

Education, then, cannot mean "exactly the same thing to everybody." Were this so, "the world would be a very dead place indeed." This suggests that any and all attempts to define education locate us in a complex relationship to tradition. That is to say, how we acknowledge and view the past forms a frame of reference for our understanding of the perils and possibilities of the present. We are entangled with and against tradition, and tradition is no more of a piece than education. Indeed, human life itself, in any complex modern culture, is an ongoing contestation over the meaning of tradition and the ways in which we would affirm or challenge that which is given to us in our particular time and place.

One might put it this way. Our own democratic culture is neither an à la carte menu nor a fixed dinner. No one among us could participate in all the multiple possibilities contemporary life spreads before each human subject. Neither is it really workable to be so totally immersed in one mode that no alternative to this conception, this belief, this way of doing things ever presents itself. Eliot reminds us that education is about being in and of one's society, yes, but it also means being able to stand back, take a hard look, and criticize the way of life of which one is a part.

If this criticism runs wild, it may invite the giddy belief that one can reject the entire cultural menu; one can eschew all previous definitions. But this is no genuine alternative either. Indeed, to take the example of heated debates over the "canon," one discerns immediately that the anticanonical camp requires the *idea* of a canon as the basis for its own deconstructive revolt and its presentation of an alternative. The canon functions as a kind of masterthought that governs their anticanonical revolt. This is the sort of thing we simply cannot get out of even if we try. And Eliot thinks it best for us to recognize the ways in which we are entangled in a culture and a way of life, including previous evaluations of literary and philosophical works.

Perhaps one way to characterize our situation—and Eliot is attuned to these matters in a way earnest revolutionaries and grim canonists are not—is its deep and abiding irony. The great modernists are, to the man and woman, ironists. By this I mean that they understand the dilemmas of those in the present who, standing restlessly on the shoulders of giants, teeter and grumble and would leap off and run forward on their own but do not for they recognize that to make *that* leap is not to be "free" so much as terribly diminished. The authoritative traditions to which we are heir bind us, yes, but they help us to see further and to move more surefootedly than we could on our own. The mesmerized worshiper of authority denies himself the critical freedom that is rightly his, a freedom those he idealizes seized and put their own individual stamp on; the agitated negator of all that has gone before preaches a freedom she denies herself, for each and every move she makes is governed by the tradition she casts off and can see only as all-pervasive and menacing.

A genuinely critical education helps us to bring these and other matters to the surface, to engage in a debate with interlocutors long dead or protagonists who never lived save on the page, and, through that engagement, to elaborate alternative conceptions through which to apprehend our world and the way that world represents itself. That, at least, is one way to understand a living language and culture and the education ongoingly defined and imperfectly realized within it. It is the way of the ironical modernist.

"Perhaps," writes Michael Oakeshott,

> we may think of the components of a culture as voices, each the expression of a distinct condition and understanding of the world and a distant idiom of human self-understanding, and of the culture itself as these voices joined, as such voices could only be joined, in a conversation—an endless unrehearsed intellectual adventure in which, in imagination, we enter into a variety of modes of understanding the world and ourselves and are not disconcerted by the differences or dismayed by the inconclusiveness of it all. And perhaps we may recognize liberal learning as, above all else, an education in imagination, an initiation into the art of this conversation in which we learn to recognize the voices; to distinguish their different modes of utterance, to acquire the intellectual and moral habits appropriate to this conversational relationship and thus to make our debut *dans la vie humaine*.

Education and Diversity

Eliot would rather like Oakeshott's attempt at a definition, I believe, given his own conviction that education is to and for a way of life construed *sub specie aeternitatis*.

At the present in our own culture, education is increasingly defined with reference to diversity or, as it is usually put, multiculturalism. But Eliot would ask us to worry about whether or not much of this effort is but a variant on the quest for relevance or adaptation. For we are asked to become "sensitive" not so much to a wondrous variety of idioms and voices as to group exclusivities and grievances. In other words, our definition of education may have become, or is in peril of becoming, inappropriately politicized. In a world of overheated political demands, education is required to serve all sorts of masters and loses its excellence and its integrity in the process.

This claim is easily misconstrued as the illusory ranting of a naïf, so let me spell things out just a bit. Education is never *outside* a world of which politics—how human beings govern and order a way of life in common—is a necessary feature. Education is *always* cast as the means whereby some, or all, citizens of a particular society get their bearings and learn to live with and among one another. Education *always* reflects a society's view of what is excellent, worthy, necessary, but this reflection "wobbles," in Eliot's term, and is ongoingly refracted and reshaped as definitions, meanings, and purposes change through violent or peaceful contestation. In this sense education is political. But this is different from being directly and blatantly politicized.

Consider the following examples. A class takes up the Declaration of Independence and the great pronouncement that "All men are created equal." But women (and many men) were disenfranchised. Slaves were not counted as fully men. How could this be? What meaning of equality did the Founders embrace? How did they square this shared meaning with what we perceive to be manifest inequalities? What was debated and what was not? What political and moral exigencies of that historic moment compelled what sorts of compromises? Might things have gone differently? And so on. This I take to be an instance of reflective political education in and for American democracy—our own version of the perennial dilemma of "the one and the many."

But let me put a second example. A teacher declares that nothing good ever came from the hand of "dead white European males." Their words and deeds are nefarious. They were nothing but racists and patriarchalists, blatant oppressors, who hid behind fine-sounding words. All they created is tainted and hypocritical. Here the matter simply ends. There is no more "wobbliness." All is defined. All is foreclosed. All has been exposed. The world closes in. Debate ends or is discouraged. To express a different point of view is to betray one's own false consciousness or patriarchal privilege. This I take to be an instance of unreflective, dogmatic politicization. It evades the dilemma of the one and the many rather than offering us points of critical reflection on that dilemma. This sort of education fails in its very particular and important task of preparing us for a world of ambiguity and variety. It equips us only for ressentiment.

Education is neither the family nor the state. It is, therefore, neither the primary locus of childrearing nor an arm of governance, and if it becomes such it will fall under the weight of a politically dictated definition. Again, Oakeshott:

> School and university are places apart where a declared learner is emancipated from the limitations of his local circumstances and from the wants he may happen to have acquired, and is moved by intimations of what he has never yet dreamed. He finds himself invited to pursue satisfactions he has never yet imagined or wished for. They are, then, sheltered places where excellences may be heard because the din of local partialities is no more than a distant rumble.

This, no doubt, is an idealized version of education as a nigh-autonomous realm of a democratic culture. We Americans, no doubt, believe that education can never be, nor should it be, wholly safeguarded from outside forces, defined apart from all else. We believe this because we understand, however tacit this understanding may be, that education in and for a democratic *culture* is a porous affair, open to the world of which it is a part yet not so open that it becomes the mere plaything of passing enthusiasms.

The danger in going too far down our present path is that our definition of education itself is imperiled precisely because we have done too little to protect education from the heavy-handed intrusion of those who would have it serve this political master or that ideological purpose. Thus, we increasingly give over to education all sorts of tasks it is ill equipped to handle and which ought not to be ceded to education in the first place: the primary moral education of the child, for example. At the same time, we seem intent on stripping education of what in fact it ought to be about: an invitation to particular "adventures in human self-understanding," in Oakeshott's terms.

Education and Ideology

The implication for a *definition* of education is simply this, and Eliot has put his finger on it: Our democratic country is dependent on responsibility and self-limiting freedom. The danger in any ideological definition of education is that it undermines, even negates, this essential human dimension. We cede responsibility to a Weltanschauung. Because democracy is the political form that permits and requires human freedom as responsibility, any definition or system that sanctions evasion of responsibility imperils democracy. Whether in the name of change or to forestall all change, an ideological system of education is the worst possible way for human beings to order their collective affairs. For once a world of personal responsibility with its characteristic virtues and marks of decency (justice, honor, friendship, fidelity) is ruptured or emptied, what rushes in to take its place is politics as a "technology of power," in Václav Havel's phrase. Responsibility, according to Havel—and he is as surefooted a guide as any currently available—flows from the aims of life "in its essence" that are plurality and independent self-constitution as opposed to the conformity, uniformity, and stultifying dogmas of left- and right-wing ideologues who abandon reality and assault life with their rigid, abstract chimeras.

Eliot, remember, insists that a living language means that words constantly acquire "new associations and lose some of the old ones." But there is a limit to this process of redefinition. Words may, over time, be denuded of meaning rather than enhanced by definitional contestation without end. Part of our own culture's desperate floundering stems from the fact that we have lost any solidity to our understanding of the most basic things. Words have become rootless, homeless.

This has come about for some good reasons—recognition of the "slipperiness" of definitions—and, more and more, for some very bad reasons: cynicism bordering on vulgar antinomianism about the need for at least provisional (and no doubt imperfect) sharing of certain key words (freedom, democracy, truth, fairness, law). If the bad reasons prevail, and we preach and teach nothing but contempt for those norms necessary in order that democratic debate and dialogue are ongoingly reaffirmed, our democratic culture will go into free-fall.

It follows that education is cut adrift, subject to ideologically inflamed demands and enthusiasms or, even more commonly, the victim of capitulation by overworked parents to the reductive ministrations and definitions of various educational "experts" and lobbyists. Whether one or the other, education is surrendered to so-called socialization, and much of the richness and variety and excellence of its meaning is lost. We have grown uncertain, muddled, about the worth of our own traditions and what we can and ought to transmit to our children. This uncertainty stems, not from a robust skepticism, but from a failure of nerve.

This wants explaining. I rely upon Hannah Arendt's essay "The Crisis in Education," in which Arendt ties diminution in authentic education to abdication by adults of responsibility for the world. She writes:

> Insofar as the child is not yet acquainted with the world, he must be gradually introduced to it; insofar as he is new, care must be taken that this new thing comes to fruition in relation to the world as it is. In any case, however, the educators here stand in relation to the young as representatives of a world for which they must assume responsibility. . . . This responsibility is not arbitrarily imposed upon educators; it is implicit in the fact that the young are introduced by adults into a continuously changing world. . . . In education this responsibility for the world takes the form of authority.

Here one is reminded of Eliot's insistence on a *necessary,* not a contingent, link between freedom and responsibility.

Freedom and Responsibility

Let me return to Havel to deepen our understanding of Eliot's claim. A fusion of freedom and responsibility yields a distinct but definite *political* conclusion: Democracy is the political form that permits and requires human freedom, not as an act of self-overcoming, nor pure reason, but in service to others in one's own time and place. To live "within the truth" is to give voice to a self that has embraced responsibility for the here and now. "That means that responsibility is ours, that we must accept it and grasp it *here, now,* in this place in time and space where the Lord has set us down, and that we cannot lie our way out of it by moving somewhere else, whether it be to an Indian ashram or to a parallel *polis*," writes Havel.

Havel believes we are all living in the midst of a general crisis of human consciousness of which Eliot offered powerful intimations. That crisis manifests itself in the spheres of human freedom, responsibility, and identity itself. Acceptance of the risks of free action—an affirmation education in and for democracy makes possible though it does not guarantee—makes one a person and forms the basis of one's identity. Any mode of thought or program of education that reduces human responsibility narrows the horizon of human possibility. To assume "full responsibility" is not to lapse into dour moralism, not to universalize a giddy and boundless compassion, but to take up the specific, concrete burdens of one's own culture. Education that undermines even the possibility that at least some among us may be called upon to "bear witness" is an exercise in speciousness. This is tough stuff. But, then, democracy is not for sissies.

Our malaise over how education is to be defined within our democracy at present stems in part from a culturally sanctioned abdication by adults of their responsible authority as parents and as educators. What on earth is going on when parents complain that their fourth-graders are being taught the intricacies of condom use but cannot read or cipher with any sophistication? What definition of education here reigns? Who has abdicated responsibility for what? Or, alternatively, what agencies, groups, and enthusiasts seek to make education the vanguard or home base of their own essentially extraeducational or polemical efforts?

These are the questions we must face straight-on. In answering, let the chips fall where they may, with this caveat: The crisis in education has not come about because a few self-interested groups have successfully hijacked the system. Indeed, it seems far more plausible that education in America is in its present straits because of a general collapse of authoritative meanings and institutions, an abdication by responsible persons (parents, teachers, intellectuals, politicians) of their necessary vocations. Being free means being able to shirk one's responsibilities, Eliot notes, but being responsible means one does not thus abdicate. The massive abdication of authority by those most responsible for its democratic exercise is a complex story, one ripe for the telling. For now, we must simply note that we are in danger of forfeiting our cultural heritage—indeed, our cultural home—because we have convinced ourselves it represents only the detritus of power and chicanery rather than the way imperfect human beings, only a few of whom were villains, have offered us the fruits of their strengths and their weaknesses, their moments of honor and their hours of despair.

The Living Classics

Let us circle back on Eliot's definitional imperatives and the light touch with which they are proffered. Willa Cather's protagonist Neil Herbert comes to mind. In her novel *A Lost Lady,* the classics provide a "way out" of Sweetwater, Nebraska, to young Herbert by offering to him the "way in" to a new world. Herbert begins reading books in his lawyer uncle's library. All sorts of books. But primarily novels. Cather describes Herbert's discovery:

> There were philosophical works in the collection, but he did no more than open and glance at them. He had no curiosity about what men had thought; but about what they had felt and lived, he had a great deal. If anyone had told him that these were classics and represented the wisdom of the ages, he would doubtless have let them alone. . . . He did not think of these books as something invented to beguile the idle hour, but as living creatures, caught in the very behavior of living— surprised behind their misleading severity of form and phrase. He was eavesdropping upon the past, being let into the great world that had plunged and littered and sumptuously sinned long before little Western towns were dreamed of. Those rapt evenings beside the lamp gave him a long perspective, including his conception of the people about him, made him know just what he wished his own relations with these people to be.

In reading novels, then, Herbert effects a deep, vital, vertical link to the past. He becomes part of a living, breathing tradition. The dead not only come to life in and through these texts, they forge "the conception of the people about him" for Herbert, and, I daresay, for Cather herself and for so many others, men and women, who have, over the years, made that bittersweet journey from a particular bounded place and its tones, textures, and tempo, its ties that bind, to venture forth into the drama and dislocation promised by, indeed made possible through, education.

Young Neil Herbert moves not from a small-town tradition into the dazzling atmosphere of a world that spurns the whole notion of tradition; rather, through his reading of great books, he is guided from one bounded frame of reference to a more expansive set of conceptual possibilities. Recall the passage. Those "rapt evenings" gave Herbert a "perspective," including a strong conception of the people "about him," and helped him to know what he wanted his relations with them to be. If education fails to incorporate within its living definition *strong* stories and conceptions, it cannot launch us into a wider world with the strength of character and firmness and flexibility of purpose democratic thinkers have always presumed as both the cause and consequence of democracy itself.

"Home is where one starts from. As we grow older / The world becomes stranger, the pattern more complicated of dead and living"—these words from Eliot's poem "East Coker" haunt us as we approach the next millennium. Education, he suggests, should help us to appreciate and cherish that complexity, to love this strange world in which we are nonetheless required to be at home. If it fails in this task, more is at stake than "adaptation" or "preparation for citizenship"—our humanity itself is imperiled.

I am thinking about home and education and humanity as I close this modest essay. As it happens, I am in Prague. I have listened to those, including President Havel, who assumed responsibility for their time and place. They could do so—could thus call upon themselves—because they accepted the paradox of modernity. With all its ambiguities and ironies and uncertainties, there remain things worth struggling for, even being called upon to suffer for; it is no doubt a mystery that this should be the case. But it is *not* an accident. The *via media* of which Eliot writes and which Havel exemplifies is no tepid compromise; rather, it is the rare but now and then attainable fruit of the democratic imagination, an imagination nurtured by what can only be called a cultivated religious sensibility.

Originally published in *The World & I* (January 1993).

23

Albert Camus's *First Man*

This work is a marvel, a chalice filling slowly with life's liquidity drop by drop until, overflowing, it trickles over the edge and seeps into the ground, helping to make it fecund. Some have hailed it—this last, unfinished work by Albert Camus—as a departure, a fall into lyricism by this most lucid and spare of writers. It seems not so to me. Rather, what Camus offers us, in this auto-biographical work of fiction, is the world of Jacques Cormery's childhood, of a poor young boy from Algiers who grows up, goes away, but never abandons the working-class neighborhood, the mute, silent, beautiful mother, the tough grandmother matriarch, the limited but lovable uncle, the dense, rich odors and textures of lives lived on the thin edge of desperation. Jacques experiences his world in a harsh and beautiful land as one "without boundaries, [his] head lost in the unremitting light and the immense space of the sky." He was the "richest of children."

This sort of insight can tumble over into sentimentality and cliché. But Camus's ironic intelligence does not permit nostalgia; it shines through this handwritten manuscript transcribed by his daughter, a work found in his briefcase at the site of his fatal accident in 1960, a work withheld by his children until just now because, given "the mood of 1960" (this from his daughter, Catherine), the fear was that publication would only do harm to Camus's reputation in the inflamed, partisan atmosphere of French intellectual life. Camus had "antagonized both the right and the left. At the time of his death he was very much isolated and subject to attacks from all sides designed to destroy the man and the artist so that his ideas would have no impact." What a pity. Camus himself, of course, would have understood his wife's reticence about publishing at the time of his death and would have been touched by his children's decision to publish "in a spirit of brotherhood" now and to explain why publication had been withheld for so long.

Dedicated to "you who will never be able to read this book," his mother,

The First Man begins with the journey of two destitute immigrants, Henri Cormery and his nearly deaf wife, into the Algerian night. A dense night of rain; a birth; the man must begin work the next day. A recurrent theme in this text is the relentless necessity for and the dignity of work, admiration for a hard job well done. The second chapter finds that baby, now the forty-year-old Jacques, making a pilgrimage to the gravesite of his long-dead father, one of thousands of poor Algerians sent to France to die in the "cosmic fire" of 1914. Jacques is struck by the fact that the man "buried under that slab, who had been his father, was younger than he." And he feels? Pity, tenderness, the "overwhelming compassion that a grown man feels for an unjustly murdered child." He came from a family where there were few words exchanged, "where no one read or wrote," and no one had informed him "about this young and pitiable father." It was long ago, lost in the thickets of befogged, inarticulate time and space. After Jacques's brief reunion with his beloved teacher, who has retired to France, the book moves to its center, its heart and soul, Jacques's Algerian childhood.

The grown man "could come back to the childhood from which he had never recovered, to the secret of the light, of the warm poverty that had enabled him to survive and to overcome everything." Small wonder that "each time he returned to Paris . . . his heart would sink." Camus evokes Cormery's childhood world wonderfully. There were games played with apricot pits and old cigars, games with complex rules and rituals, including which boy got the biggest crumb of a highly prized but scarce fried delicacy. Jacques and his chums are "triumphant in their kingdom of poverty." They swim, court parental (in Jacques's case, grandmotherly) ire by swimming a bit too far out; running up the stairs and into their cramped flats a bit too late. The tough-minded maintenance of the poor is not shirked—the white shirts and pressed pants, requiring a constant "work of upkeep," work commented on in a heartbreaking letter to Camus by his teacher, Louis Germain, appended to the text and Germain's response, in which Germain acknowledges that he had no idea about the family's actual situation because young Albert, like his brother, was always "nicely dressed. I don't think I can find a greater compliment to your mother."

For the poor must be proud and it is a labor, this ongoing nurturance of pride. It takes long hours and a reticence that doesn't call attention to itself. Camus writes of Jacques's mother's exhaustion and her muffled feelings for which she could find no words, of the blows of life she sustained without complaint for "her children," including "hard days of working in the service of others, washing floors on her knees, living without a man and without solace in the midst of the greasy leavings and dirty linen of other people's lives." Yet he never heard her "speak ill of anyone" other than to call a few distant relatives "stuck up." Poverty, Camus writes, is not a choice one makes, "but a poor person can protect himself."

A heart worn out "with sorrow and labor" need not be a bitter heart. And young Jacques was a resourceful child, small for his age but gaining the "upper hand, and on the playground, where soccer was his kingdom." This added a torment to his existence, too, because, to stretch out the life of his shoes, his grandmother would "have the soles studded with enormous cone-shaped nails, which were doubly useful: you had to wear out the studs before wearing out the sole, and they enabled her to detect infractions of the ban on playing soccer." Jacques devised various strategies, most of them useless, to outwit his grandmother. Soccer won; he took the blows.

School is his salvation, one for which he pays the price of exile from his beloved boyhood kingdom and his native land. Camus speaks for every child who loved school, who yearned for the coming of autumn, the crispness in the air, the smell of new textbooks, the accolades of teachers, the wonder of new words, by evoking "the powerful poetry of school." One of the reasons Jacques and his best friend, Pierre, "so passionately loved" school was "that they were not at home, where want and ignorance made life harder and more bleak." Jacques discovers a hunger "more basic even to the child than to the man, and that is the hunger for discovery." In M. Bernard's (M. Germain's) class, the children are "judged worthy to discover the world." What a wonderful way to evoke the teacher's vocation; the child's apprenticeship. The teacher's responsibility is great. He or she uproots children in order that they may go further, dig deeper. Some take to this uprooting; for such children it is a bittersweet victory, "this success," for it takes the child out of his or her world, and that which is familiar now becomes a bit alien, as if seen for the first time from a great distance. "At the *lycée* . . . there was no one he could talk to about his mother and his family. In his family no one he could talk to about the *lycée*. No friend, no teacher ever came to his home during all the years before he received his baccalaureate. And as for his mother and grandmother, they never came to the *lycée,* except once a year, when awards were given, at the beginning of July."

There is no glamour here; no radical chic of the sort Camus detested with all his being. He knew Jacques's father (his own) had "died in an incomprehensible tragedy far from his native land, after a life without a single free choice—from the orphanage to the hospital, the inevitable marriage along the way, a life that grew around him, in spite of him; until the war killed and buried him." There is a mystery to poverty, for it creates beings who make the world but are returned to it unknown and unsung. It is a "dreadful and exalted history." Jacques leaves, his scholarship a way out of one world into another, but he never forgets, he never escapes, nor does he try to. As a man, Jacques "had not the slightest desire to have a different family or station in life, and his mother as she remained what he loved most in the world, even if that love was hopeless." His is a world without envy, free from resentment. Small wonder the adult Camus found loathsome the hollow embittering of the poor by their world-be champions on the hard left, those "intellectuals who theorize about the proletariat" but cannot imagine the world of the working poor.

So Jacques, as a man, is a mystery to himself. He is what he has left behind. But he cannot go back. He returns, but he remains in exile; he returns to that place where the sky is "so vast that the child felt tears coming to his eyes along with a great cry of joy and gratitude for this wonderful life." I thank Camus, lost to us nearly forty years ago, for the life he here evokes. A reappreciation of Camus's greatness is long overdue. Perhaps this small gem will trigger renewed gratitude that he lived the life he lived; wrote the works he wrote; fought the good fight and now, at last, may, perhaps, be allowed to rest in honored peace. Now that the clamor of the ideologically inflamed, caught up in their "logical deliriums," is no more, perhaps Camus's commitment to lucidity and his recognition of our brokenhearted yearning for a kind or bracing word, an open face, the saving presence of our fellow human beings, will be greeted with honor and with tears.

Library of Congress Cataloging-in-Publication Data

Elshtain, Jean Bethke, 1941–
    Real politics : at the center of everyday life / Jean Bethke
Elshtain.
        p.   cm.
    ISBN 0-8018-5599-3 (alk. paper)
    1. Feminist theory.   2. Feminism.   3. Women in politics.
4. Language and languages—Political aspects.   5. Political
science.   I. Title.
HQ1190.E43   1997
305.42'01—dc21   97-2054
                                                                CIP